Living on the Western Front

Living on the Western Front

ANNALS AND STORIES, 1914–1919

CHRIS WARD

B L O O M S B U R Y
LONDON • NEW DELHI • NEW YORK • SYDNEY

Bloomsbury Academic
An imprint of Bloomsbury Publishing Plc

50 Bedford Square	175 Fifth Avenue
London	New York
WC1B 3DP	NY 10010
UK	USA

www.bloomsbury.com

First published 2013

British Library Cataloguing-in-Publication Data
A catalogue record for this book is available from the British Library.

ISBN: HB: 978-1-4411-2502-6
PB: 978-1-4411-0930-9
ePDF: 978-1-4411-8270-8
ePub: 978-1-4411-7318-8

Library of Congress Cataloging-in-Publication Data
A catalog record for this title is available from the Library of Congress.

Typeset by Deanta Global Publishing Services, Chennai, India
Printed and bound in Great Britain

CONTENTS

ACKNOWLEDGEMENTS

I am indebted to the staff of the Documents and Sound Section, Imperial War Museum, Lambeth, and of the Rare Books Room in Cambridge University Library. They were always helpful in responding to my requests for materials.

Research for the book was supported by the University of Cambridge's Newton Trust Small Research Grant Scheme. My thanks are due to the Trust's administrators for their generosity, and to Ms Eleanor Dalgleish, the research assistant appointed under the auspices of the Trust, for her careful work in the archives.

The following friends and colleagues commented on various parts of the text: Dr Rory Finnin, Professor Simon Franklin, Dr Jana Howlett, Dr Susan Larsen, Dr Rachel Polonsky, Professor Stephen Smith, Dr Emma Widdis and Professor Emma Wilson. I am grateful to each for their helpful advice and criticism. Additional thanks must go to Ms Emily Drewe, Ms Frances Taylor and Mr Rhodri Mogford at Bloomsbury Academic, and to the reviewers appointed by the publisher who commented on the entire manuscript. My greatest debt is to my wife, for her unfailing support and encouragement. The mistakes and misunderstandings are mine alone.

Introduction

In some ways this is a difficult book to approach. It makes unusual demands of the reader. It has no real beginning or end, no conclusion, no chapters and no index, and the text is spattered with coinages and common words used uncommonly. The oddest of these – 'Befland' – might seem unduly mannered, but Europeans are used to short-lived quasi-states or provinces born of war (Protectorate of Bohemia, Far Eastern Republic, Wartheland), and a convenient term had to be found to define the areas of northern France and western Belgium settled by the British between 1914 and the early 1920s. To add to the reader's disconcertions, quotations and précis govern the text, making it more like a cento than a monograph, and following a story involves flicking from one page to another. But these devices were not adopted out of a desire to pursue novelty for novelty's sake. The former is designed to startle readers into the eager observation of experience; the latter is a response to one aspect of the complex tangle of epistemological problems surrounding the nature of history and its relationship to the past.

In the late 1980s Hayden White pointed out that the narrative structures commonly deployed by modern practitioners are only one way of representing the past. Earlier forms – annals and chronicles – disclose the past differently. Chronicles typically arrange facts and events in a timeline, often with a preamble summarizing the history of the world since the Creation. Annals are concise forms of chronicles, divided by year and attached to columned time lists. Like chroniclers, annalists made little or no attempt to assign causation or significance, at least in secular terms, and essayed no beginnings or ends, again at least in secular terms. Instead of linear stories interwoven with explanations, divided into chapters and bookended with introductions and conclusions, readers of annals are presented with vertical orderings of events that simply start somewhere and break off somewhere else. Things happen, not stories, and then stop happening. Comparing annals and chronicles with narratives therefore raises the question of whether or not the stories articulated by narrators are found in the past or created in the act of narrating.[1]

The point here is not that history selects. The possibilities of history are boundless and the myriad facets of a single moment could detain us indefinitely, if only we could see them. Like Ralph Pendrel, the tyro historian in Henry James' *The Sense of the Past*, we might yearn for unattainable consummations – 'the stillness, from the street . . . the light of afternoons that had been . . . the unimaginable accidents, the little notes of truth'[2] – but the real problem is not that the fullness of the past is irrecoverable or that evidence is always lacking; it is that narrative is the most dangerously seductive of the three forms of history production because it is the most persuasive. We can never know for sure if stories are found or created, but the smooth run of carefully interlocking sentences emblematic of narrative histories, the arguments underpinning the text and the prudent exclusion of material not germane to the thesis create reality effects akin to those found in realist novels. And we know that the realist novel is an illusion, 'a disproportioning of realities', as one master commented, 'a series of seemings' set in a 'part real, part dream landscape'.[3]

What I wanted to do was to disrupt narrative structures and upset realist expectations by imitating an early-medieval annalist – ('Battle of Badon . . . and the Britons were victors'. Blank year blank year blank year. 'The strife of Camlann in which Arthur and Modred perished. And there was plague in Britain and Ireland'[4]) – but it proved impossible. In the first place because every sentence is a kind of narrative, and a kind of explanation, the distinction drawn between annals, chronicles and narratives is more apparent than real. We can never escape from narrative. Secondly, Western historians at least no longer operate in sacerdotal time, or anything remotely like it. We cannot recapture the honesty, freshness and attractive ambiguity of a mind and hand engaged elsewhere and elsewhen, scribing *pari passu* in the margins of an Easter Table whatever secular fragments came to notice and seemed worth recording. We are too knowing for that, too subtle and too demanding and perhaps too fraudulent. We want certainties about uncertainties and a certain degree of explanation. The form of this book is therefore a hybrid of annal and narrative, but the intention remains: to foreground other ways of reading the past, thereby divulging some of history's inherent ambiguities and dilemmas.

How to read the book

The book comprises 107 numbered and dated narremes organized chronologically. The sequence structure was adapted from Sven Lindqvist's *A History of Bombing* and the term 'narreme', used to denote blocks of text that are narratives in themselves and also fragments of longer stories, from

Eugene Dorfman's study of the medieval romance epic.[5] The book may be read as:

1 a quasi-annal – here one simply starts at the beginning and goes on to the end;

2 an anthology of stories – to read a particular story one follows the narreme numbers listed on page 11;

3 a collection of essays – readers may open the book at random and read any narreme as a stand-alone text.

Square-bracketed numbers within narremes cross reference to that narreme number.

I assembled the book by grouping research notes under twenty or thirty headings, rearranging the headings into twelve stories and then disaggregating the stories into narremes. Chronological sequencing of narremes happened only when the writing was finished. At that stage my computer programme, by sorting the entire manuscript into annals, threw up unexplored affinities and disassociations. The consequence is that to some extent the meaning of the content was shaped by technology, not just by the author. This was intended, and readers may find that the annals disclose stories other than those I chose to tell. A certain unevenness of tone may also be detected, and on re-reading the text I find that one or two technical and theoretical problems are of perennial concern. This too was intentional. Like an annal – like any sustained text – this book was assembled over time. It seemed honest to let traces of changes in style and emphasis remain and to allow the same or similar questions about the nature of history to reappear in various guises in assorted stories and narremes.

Two final points. Within narremes only the headings and associated lead sentences are sequential. In most cases the contents range widely over Befland's chronoscape – *Living on the Western Front* is, after all, only a *quasi*-annal. Secondly, just as medieval annals have 'missing' or 'empty' years so this book has missing or empty days. In 1916, for example, only thirty-four appear as narreme headings, though as indicated most narremes do go on to reference other days. If all or some of these 'buried' days, 600 or 700 in total, were disinterred and reconstituted as new narreme headings then new stories would appear. To that extent at least stories are indeed created rather than found.

Sources and themes

Little use is made of scholarly secondary works. Each of the stories and many of the narremes could have referenced any number of economic, social, political, cultural and military histories. It should not be supposed, however, that because I have chosen to ignore them I am altogether unaware of at least some of them, but the intention was not to survey the field. In any case it would have been an impossible task. So vast is the literature that no one could read it all. Instead material was drawn almost exclusively from two groups of sources. The first, published fitfully during the interwar years, is the multi-volume 'official history' series and the associated semi-official histories covering various specialist aspects of the War. Most were written by high-ranking serving or retired officers and most are hard going. One novel from experience and a range of letters, diaries and memoirs comprise the second group. A few of the latter have been published, the rest are archived in Lambeth's Imperial War Museum (IWM). These make for lively, though not easy, reading. Occasionally they have been typed up. More often they remain just as they were written and are succumbing to the attrition of time; faded ink on yellowing letters addressed to family, friends and fiancées, faint pencil scribblings in frayed army notebooks, torn and crumbling bits of paper.

What's surprising here is a generalized graphomania. The IWM alone holds thousands of files comprising diaries, letters, observations and reminiscences of men and women who went to Befland. Some contain no more than a few scraps; many run to hundreds of pages. But perhaps we should not be too surprised. Forster's and Mundella's Education Acts (1870, 1880) and the Argyll, Clarendon and Taunton Commissions (1864–68) revolutionized the British educational system in the interests of the Victorian bourgeoisie and the imperial project. Cleaning up the public schools, founding and reforming universities, introducing science and technology into a curriculum in the main dominated by Divinity and the Classics and, most importantly, enforcing compulsory primary education would, it was hoped, allow British capitalists to overcome their foreign competitors, discipline and indoctrinate the newly enfranchised proletariat and provide a steady supply of trained administrators for the ruling classes' vast and still expanding empire. But this wasn't just a matter of superstructure responding mechanically to base. Change had unintended consequences. One was the democratization of recorded sentiment. For the first time millions had the chance to write down what they saw, thought, felt and remembered about life. The 1890s generation – Befland's cohort – experienced the full force of this educational revolution and the flowering of the 'writing age'.[6]

And experience, not events, is *leit-motif* of this book. There is little on the military, political or economic aspects of the War except as sites of being or frames of experience. There is comparatively little too on the 'trench experience' in all its various aspects – fighting, trauma, dying and killing, etc. These have been covered in scores of monographs. Moreover, trenches did not define Befland, nor did they define experience. Large numbers of Beflanders never went anywhere near them: for each soldier in a fire-trench, for example, some five or ten were needed in support.[7] Those that did, primarily infantry- and artillerymen, experienced much else besides.

The 'trench', like the 'war poet', has overdetermined our image of the World War I in general and the Western Front in particular. Nor does the book exhibit any stable narrative focus, except for the dozen stories compounded of narremes. Instead readers will encounter the rushed and disorientate nature of experience – one thing following another; sudden changes of mood and voice; the absence of consummation; scrappy observations overtaken by new impressions as circumstances direct the eye and heart elsewhere. It might also be the case that fracturing the text into narremes mimics the fractured nature of real-time experience, whether processed in the heat of the moment or called to mind long afterwards. Individuals too, those undergoing experiences, are encountered only fitfully. We bump into them without introduction or foreknowledge, just as we would if we too were in Befland for a little while, and we get to know them, if at all, only haphazardly and incompletely.

Graphomaniacs are a godsend to historians. Generalized graphomania, however, presents us with real difficulties. What should be researched, what selected? Aside from the official histories, the single novel and a handful of published diaries and memoirs, I looked in depth at a small sample of the IWM's files: thirty-two Beflanders – men and women, officers and other ranks, front-line soldiers and 'back-area' denizens – who transcribed their experiences during and after their time in the colony. Of them other ranks and women make frequent comments and observations, but male officers speak loudest. This cannot be helped. On the whole they were better educated and more disposed to write extensively and confidently. Within the officer cohort there is a bias towards artillerymen; a deliberate choice, partly because they interacted with Befland's vast population of horses and mules rather more than others, partly because they tended to stay longer in one place and therefore had more time, or were more inclined, to describe and reflect. Chinese labourers, Americans, Portuguese, Dominion troops and subjects of the Empire – Indians, Africans, West Indians, etc. – appear only insofar as the selected Beflanders refer to them.

The obvious objection is that all this leads to a partial view of the Western Front experience, but the objection only stands if we can reference the whole. Part of the underlying contention of this book is that we cannot, or rather that the problem is wrongly formulated. There is no whole to be partial about because the 'Western Front experience' *qua* event never existed.

William Sewell argues that historical events exhibit 'a fractal character . . . Each might well be said to be composed of a series of events . . . And each of these sub-events is itself composed of a series of smaller but significant ruptures'.[8] If Sewell's characterization is allowed we see that what are commonly understood to be events (the assassination at Sarajevo, the Battle of Cambrai, the October Revolution) are really 'event packages' made up of countless divisible substructures, and of course any substructure only becomes a 'significant rupture' when someone (in Sewell's case an implied omniscient narrator) imposes meaning. In contrast a life might be imagined as a series of experienced moments strung out across time. Such moments are of indeterminate duration and significance, at least in memory: some might seem to have lasted for no more than a few seconds, others for years; some might be construed as momentous, others might appear as inconsequential fragments, haunting nonetheless. The elementary moment, that which has no substructure, is perhaps represented by the firing of a single neuron within the brain.

Moreover, a given string of moments, part of an individual's life trajectory, is not the same as the trajectory of an event package, though the two can be made to intersect. As Paul Ricœur remarks, perhaps with unconscious irony, 'numerous reputedly historical events were never in anyone's memories',[9] and anybody of a certain age will be well aware that the narrative structure of their historicized past frequently bears little relationship to recalled moments of experience. It follows that although evidential traces of moments of experience certainly exist – evidence of a wound, for example – they do not become part of an event package until someone decides they are. Historians often fabricate event packages *post facto* by realizing them as text. In the process they may corral experience as evidence for their creations, in which case experience reappears in attenuated form, often as metaphor, metonym or synecdoche. Experience is lived – 'what I did in France' – and cannot be denied (though it may be interrogated), but an event package – 'The Battle of Cambrai' – is a construct. Here bits of experience are chopped up, edited, condensed and reformulated as elements of the event package which pre-exists in the mind of the constructor. To add to our difficulties events can be packaged and repackaged to make experiences appear or disappear, just as experiences can be packaged and repackaged to make events appear or disappear. The experience of a single wound is not necessary to the 'Battle of Cambrai' construct, for example, but on the other hand inserting the wound can change the nature of the package. A man may be said to have been wounded during the Battle of Cambrai and because of the Battle of Cambrai. Alternatively he may be said to have been wounded during an encounter with a shell and because of international capitalism, or during a journey from Doullens to Arras and because a troop train was running late, or during his twenty-second year and because his hearing was faulty, or during a cloudburst and because a gunner miscalculated. Imagined thus, the history of the Battle of Cambrai resembles a secular *paso*, a series of animatronic floats borne aloft by scores of shuffling historians. Each float claims to incorporate the same event but each is differently fabricated, differently packaged. And we can imagine other *pasos*, other possible histories that edit experience differently and thus represent France's Nord Department in late 1917 otherwise. Stories of lovers, for instance, or priests, or births, or harvests, or marriages, or communes, or gestures, or thoughts, or dreams, or conversations. The Western Front cannot therefore be an event-experience any more than it could be an experienced event. No story, no history, is imperative. None can obliterate the past by claiming to encompass it. There are many – one is tempted to say an infinity – of event packages layered in a given time and locale which might be immanent within the minds of historians.

This is not to say, of course, that the edited collection of experiences called (by the British) 'The Battle of Cambrai' is a counterfeit or illegitimate reading of evidence, but it is to assert that there are multifarious ways of construing the heap contemporaneous experiences that are sometimes shaped in that manner. Nor is it to say that experience is unproblematic or unconstructed. There is always a danger that writing individual experience lifts stories out of their socio-economic setting and lures readers towards contingency and the privatization of explanation. In the war between agency and structure the former gets prioritized and we are well on the way to a reactionary historiography. Constructs impinge on experience. Materiality, socialization and acculturation come into play here and interact in complex ways. The experience of soldiers in France and Belgium was smeared by what others said, did and saw, and, since they were in the main literate, by what others wrote.

The fact of literacy raises a particular problem. Joan Scott maintains that historians can't simply reference transcribed experience (in our case letters, diaries, etc.) because there's no 'literal transparency' where 'the visible is privileged' and 'writing put at its service'. Transcription is always ordered through an individual's insertion in and manipulation of existing discourses and ideologies: 'there is no unmediated relationship between words and things ... experience is a linguistic event ... it is not individuals who have experience but subjects who are constituted through experience'.[10] This argument strikes me as overly reductive, not least because it leaves unanswered the question of how and in what circumstances people generate new discourses or ideologies. Reconfigured dialectically we might suggest that people have their own experiences but are forced to realize them in discourses not of their own choosing. Experience and discourse remain in tension until a synthesis is achieved. Thereafter new discourses generate new tensions. Humankind is never free of ideology because in this sense ideology is consciousness, but when a break occurs other forms of liberation and oppression are written on the soul. Experience is therefore uttered in the space that lies between agency and structure, the devastated area where people struggle to give meaning to their lives. That area is a proper terrain for historians. An emphasis on experience may well lead to empiricist formulations, but Scott's inculpations notwithstanding, experience, not event packages, is our point of departure. Ingrained habits of thought make this idea hard to sustain in practice, but it underpins much of what goes on in this book. We might also note that if all subjects are constituted through experience then so are all theorists; prisoners, like everyone else, of conditioned and conditional credibilities and bearers of historically circumscribed *Weltanschauungen*.

According to War Office calculations British soldiers alone (excluding, that is, labourers, Dominion and Imperial troops and auxiliary volunteers of both sexes) accumulated two billion, ninety-seven million, four hundred and fifty thousand, five hundred and thirty-seven days' worth of experience (total days multiplied by total population) in Befland between 4 August 1914 and 11 November 1918.[11] Bizarre as this figure is (why not count the hours, the seconds?), it does serve to bring together the points about source selection and experience. Communality notwithstanding, people saw and experienced things in their own way – often quite different things – and even if we wanted to imagine that a complete in-depth review of the evidence was possible, sheer bulk would defeat us. Lambeth holds only a tiny fraction of the sum total of transcribed experience. Much more exists elsewhere, but it is still only an infinitesimal fraction of an infinite whole. All the rest is lost because it was never recorded, *could* never be recorded. As for what remains in documentary form, an army of research assistants couldn't get through it. Besides, when a file is opened and its contents examined who decides what to notice and what to ignore? So much depends on what arrests the individual imagination. If someone else were to try this again using exactly the same files they would come up with quite different stories, as would I. Historical texts, like the sources upon which they are based, are representations of moments in time. On the other hand if we knew everything history would become impossible. We would be obliged to render everything into some unimaginable utterance, beyond the scope of human power. The totality of joys, of sufferings and indifferences, of glimpses and impressions, of actions and of mental and physical states that comprise an event package, or a life, or a moment in time, of whatever duration, is ineffable. For historians and participants alike to notice, to record and to explain is to select, and to remember involves forgetting. In order to exist at all history, that most vexatious of disciplines, requires a condition of partiality and colossal ignorance. But then again nothing is easier than to undermine the ontological and epistemological foundations of any discipline. The point is to make something of it.

Editing the sources

Diarists and correspondents frequently misspelt the names of French and Belgian towns and villages or mislocated themselves. Where possible I have silently corrected them. Other misspellings have been left alone, as has grammar and punctuation, except where the sense seemed to require intervention. Square brackets mark interventions. In the case of Belgium and some parts of northern France I've stuck to the linguistic variants current at the time (e.g., Ypres not Ieper, Dranoutre not Dranouter, St Eloi not St Elooi). All Saint- and Sint- prefixes have been abbreviated as in Eloi. Because quotation is used extensively I have not adopted the usual practice of indenting quotes.

The war in the west

The campaign in Befland was the greatest military effort of Great Britain during the War. The first British contingent had landed before 16 August 1914, and after that date the British Army in Befland grew ever larger until at the time of the Armistice it represented nearly one-third of the total Allied forces in the Western Theatre.

The campaign, commencing with the retreat of the whole of the Allied Army to the immediate neighbourhood of Paris and the River Seine, was retrieved by the Battle of the Marne, which drove the enemy back behind the River Aisne, his further attempts to outflank the Allies were victoriously repulsed, and a connected front established from the North Sea to the Swiss frontier. The situation continued thus from November 1914 to March 1918. Various attacks on a large scale by both sides – in 1915 in Artois and Champagne by the Allies; in 1916 at Verdun by the Germans and on the Somme by the Allies; in 1917 at Arras, to the east of Rheims and in Flanders by the Allies – effected little material change in the situation. In March 1918 the enemy, reinforced by large contingents from the Eastern Theatre, attempted several large-scale breakthroughs, but was unsuccessful in defeating the Allies before the arrival of large American forces, coupled with the serious decline of enemy manpower, and the unity of command which had been realized, enabled the Allies to strike a succession of heavy blows, beginning from the middle of July, which in five months compelled the enemy to consent to a cessation of hostilities.

Adapted from *Statistics of the Military Effort of the British Empire During the Great War 1914–1920* (1922) 741.

INDEX OF STORIES

For any story, start with the first numbered narreme (e.g., 42 for Aspects of Identity). At the end of each narreme go to the number indicated by ⮑ and continue until END.

Annals and stories

Monday 14 July 1914 1

Edwin Hautenville Richardson, a police dog trainer since 1898, was in Russia judging a tournament of army dogs attached to tsarist regiments. The two other judges were German officers. Sweden, the Netherlands and Italy, he mentioned, all had canine military establishments, but Germany had much the most organized service of both military and police dogs, even though their training was 'mechanical' and ignored 'the psychology of the subject'.[1] During the War they were used as message and medicine carriers, livestock guards, sentries and scouts. Herbert Leland spotted one, perhaps a disorientated scout, when he arrived on the Somme in November 1916: 'A German dog turned up yesterday, and is now the pet of the Headquarters Mess'.[2]

The RAMC had a few 'ambulance dogs' in service a month or so before Leland's encounter,[3] but Beflanders only started exploiting dogs on a larger scale in June 1917, and then only on an *ad hoc* basis to relay signals for artillery turnouts clustered around Messines Ridge in Flanders. Thereafter the practice spread quickly. Messenger dogs were soon working for infantry units in trenches across the zone, but in November, because designated keepers tended to make pets of them, all training was moved to Étaples under the auspices of the messenger pigeon service. Meanwhile Richardson established a War Dog School at Shoeburyness artillery range on the flat, marshy land around the Thames estuary.[4] Dogs' homes, the police and pet owners under pressure from food shortages supplied animals.[5] Dogs unable to stand gunfire were consigned to lethal gas chambers, but after crossing the Channel many of the survivors had forgotten most of what they'd learnt. Étaples' 'Central Kennel' was therefore surrounded with bomb pits. Explosions were synchronized with feeding – 'in order to associate the noise with the greatest of their daily pleasures,' noted Richardson.[6] Once habituated Richardson's dogs were sent into the zone as message runners. Dogs were fast and had the advantage over pigeons because they could work at night. On the other hand their eyes were badly affected by gas and settlers found them hard to control under heavy shelling. Like pigeons, they fell out of favour in summer 1918. About 7,500 are thought to have died in Befland in 1917–18.[7]

A small spat broke out when Beflanders tried to take dogs home at the end of the War. Demobilization committees – mindful, perhaps, that settler patience was wearing thin over delayed decolonization – forced a reluctant RAVC to allow dogs through the entrepôts to UK quarantine depots. The Corps retaliated by charging £8 per dog.[8] Under pressure from the Army Council the RSPCA agreed to subsidize costs and set up a quarantine station at Hackbridge just outside London with space for 500 animals, though the Society had little success in raising funds from the public. Nevertheless Hackbridge proved 'more than ample' according to the War Office. On the whole only officers took up the places.[9] This may have had to do with money – £8 was a considerable sum in 1918.

Stray cats adopted by settlers – Leland, Garnet Durham, William Orpen and Ronald Schweder mention them from time to time – do not seem to have been quarantined, though they could be slippery customers. 'There is a trench cat, a strict neutral,' wrote Durham from La Bassée district in December 1916. 'We call him "Wilson" because we found him asleep on a haversack with a rat rifling the contents. "To proud to fight". He walks across no mans land [sic] at will and knows the meal hours on both sides'.[10] It's not clear when the cat appeared, but it couldn't have been named before10 May 1915, the date of the US president's 'too proud to fight' speech.⊃ 6

2　Tuesday 4 August 1914

Céline Williams arrived at Boulogne on her annual journey to see a friend living at Cheux, just outside Caen. After disembarking she went first to the *Sous Préfecture* to get a passport and from there to the garrison to have it signed by the garrison CO. Then it was off to the *Bureau Central de la Police à la Haute Ville*. As she didn't have her birth certificate she was directed to the British Consul. She returned to the *Bureau* armed with photos and the *Sauf Conduit* and got the *Laissez-Passez* for Caen, only to be told at the station that her papers weren't valid outside the Boulogne military district and that further signatures were needed before she could board the Rouen train. She went back to the station with yet more signatures, but her papers still weren't in order. 'I believe they were told to raise as many obstacles as possible, to discourage private travelling,' she commented later. All in all it took her five days to get from London to Caen.[11]

Befland didn't yet exist as a coherent geographical entity – Boulogne and the other entrepôts were still virtually unaffected by mass immigration, though, as Céline Williams found, bureaucrats were already making life difficult – but by the year's end nearly a quarter of a million male settlers were in France and Belgium: 190,000 from Britain and the Dominions, around 24,500 from elsewhere (mostly India and Africa) and 6,000 followers and labourers ('elderly navvies and tradesmen', according to Edmonds). Another source gives a lower figure (120,000) but probably counts only British settlers. Just over 600 women were there too.[12]

After the retreat-battles that more or less wiped out the Old Army – Mons and Le Cateau in August, Marne and Aisne in September – Beflanders arrived in Flanders and pushed forward in front of Ypres (First Ypres). By mid November the Flanders' zone was about 20 miles long. Between 4 August and 31 December there were 177,423 registered casualties of one kind or another.[13] ➲ 18

Sunday 16 August 1914   **3**

'A good place to loot,' remarked an old soldier to Frank Richards as they strolled around Amiens Cathedral. Richards was billeted in a school just outside the city,[14] but he didn't stay long. Like thousands more at this early date he and his companion were passing through as the Old Army retreated towards Paris, and thereafter to the Salient. A single ordnance depot in the suburbs was quickly abandoned.[15] Settlement and colonization only began in earnest the following year when the Somme region was incorporated into Befland.

Nevertheless the Army's movement officers had long had their eye on Amiens. The initial British war plan envisaged the formation of one large base depot at a French port and a sizeable advanced base at some convenient railway junction – Amiens, for example. From there supplies would be carried by lorry to 'refilling stations' and thence by horse-drawn wagon into the zone. But this clashed with French military practice. The French had no plans for base depots. Instead all railways were to be militarized on mobilization and war timetables run by French railway officials and staff officers. They would organize the direct delivery of material to *gares régulatrices* where bulk trains were divided and remade with the daily mix of supplies and ammunition needed at the front. As far as the French were concerned they would run the railways while the British made their supply requirements known through formal military channels. Eventually an uneasy compromise emerged. Amiens became a hybrid of French *gare régulatrice* and British advanced supply base. An Inspector General of Communications supported by thirty staff officers located himself at Amiens to liaise with the French, but things soon went wrong. By mid 1916 the 'Somme Crossings', a vital complex of junctions at Amiens,[16] was choked with British traffic running east-west from the entrepôts and French traffic running north-south from the mining and industrial areas of Flanders and La Bassée district.[17] The tens of thousands of Beflanders squeezed into the Somme needed one hundred 'regular' supply trains a day to in order to maintain themselves; these in addition to various 'irregular' ambulance, railway material, reinforcement and remount trains that, somehow or other, had to force their way in and out of the city. By summer two key junctions were struggling to handle one train every three minutes twenty-four hours a day. Problems were compounded later in the year with the annual surge of traffic associated with the local sugar-beet harvest and the extraordinarily hard winter of 1916–17.[18] As overloaded lorries broke up the Somme's roads – even the best had metalled surfaces only three inches thick and railheads were often fifteen miles behind the border – more and more material accumulated in the marshalling yards and in wagons backed up along the tracks to the depots at St Roch, Serqueux and Abancourt-Romescamps. Eighteen-mile queues of stationary trains were common, with predictable knock-on effects: at the entrepôts Canadian forage ships waited for over two weeks to unload. Meanwhile the average daily number of railway wagons entering Amiens rose inexorably, from 2,500 in January 1916 to 5,200 in December.[19]

In August Beflanders responded to the crisis by building lines east of Amiens and taking over French track in and around the city, but it was not until October, when the War Cabinet pushed aside the army officers and appointed Eric Geddes, Deputy Manager of Britain's North Eastern Railway Company, as Befland's Director General of Transportation, that some kind of order was restored. His staff officers and clerks – soon numbering 100 and 600, respectively – migrated to 'Geddesburg', a new town of huts and offices that sprawled around Monthuit Chateau, three miles from Haig's headquarters at Montreuil. Next month, following a great deal of wrangling in assorted committees and commissions, the French cancelled the hybrid arrangement that had caused so many problems at Amiens.[20] Thereafter, as the official historian of Befland's transport system laconically records, 'the various requests for assistance eventually amounted to one comprehensive claim, that the British should provide and do everything necessary to ensure the movement of their own traffic'.[21]

While all this was going on the usual plethora of hospitals, dumps, transit camps and supply depots associated with deep and sustained colonization grew up in and around the city. Some were unusual. An Army Postal Service unit staffed by conscripted postmen dealt with all 'cross-post' correspondence (letters sent from Beflanders to Beflanders). At the 'Special Works Park' 281 privates and NCOs and fifteen officers (three of them officially designated 'artists') busied themselves fabricating dummy heads, bodies, sandbags and trees, screening roads, painting buildings and providing camouflage for observation posts and artillery batteries. The local branch of the Army's Printing and Stationery Service, which liaised exclusively with the Royal Flying Corps, had its own electricity generators in case air raids disrupted the city's.[22] Beflanders took over and extended the local sawmills – 'from a single shed with one circular saw a great workshop would quickly arise', noted Edmonds in 1932. After processing timber felled by Canadian foresters in the nearby plantations at Ailly-sur-Somme, the mills sent planks, coffins, pit props and duckboards into the zone by canal.[23]

Amiens was also a kind of pleasure resort, just about far enough away from the eastern border to exhibit a carefree – not to say careless – air. 'One thing that struck me,' wrote Private Rogers in his diary as he arrived from the United Kingdom via Le Havre on 6 June 1915, 'was the lights of the station. There were dozens of huge lights brilliantly lit which could be seen for miles around within 15 miles of the firing line while in England everything was dark even to trains. No precautions were taken to protect the lights and [they] had never had an air-raid'.[24] Just under a year later Robert Cude and friends couldn't wait to bike there on a day pass from the marshes around Bray-sur-Somme. He had 'a grand tea' in a large cafe and then sauntered around the town centre – 'west end of Amiens in fact'. Shops were open, trams ran without interruption and the cathedral, well worth seeing, according to Cude, was the pride and joy of the townspeople. Aside from the odd bomb falling on the station 'they do not seem to know there is a war on'. As evening fell he and his companions fiddled around to delay leaving for as long as possible. When the party finally dragged itself away someone got a puncture. Everyone stopped to help with the repair (in fact they spent most of the time trying out their rudimentary French on the pretty girls passing by), but when the work was done the bike's owner couldn't find the valve, a fortuitous loss which gave everyone else an excuse to drift off back into the town centre. By now their sergeant was 'nigh on being demented', and it wasn't until 9.30 that he, aided by the military police, was able to round them all up and set off back to Bray.[25]

George Stringer wasn't so impressed by what he saw, or maybe he arrived just after an air raid. It was horribly cold in Amiens, he wrote on 1 February 1917 after getting off the Doullens train at ten o'clock in the evening, no shops or cafés open and the place as dead as a morgue.[26] William Orpen was rather more equivocal. While on the one hand he fondly listed the city's officer-only attractions – Josephine's (the little oyster shop off Three Pebbles Street), the Hotel du Rhin for breakfast; for dinner The Godbert, The Cathedral (hosted by the beautiful Marguerite), or the Hotel de la Paix (the latter with a night club attached) – on the other he was less than enamoured of the city's ambience. 'Amiens was the one big town that could be reached easily from the Somme front for dinner,' he remembered, 'so every night it was crowded with officers and men who had come back in cars, motor-bikes, lorries or any old thing in on which they could get a lift. After dinner they would stand near the station and hail anything passing, till they found something that would drop them near their destination'. Easy enough, since there was always an endless stream of traffic running towards the killing fields on the Albert-Péronne road. 'Amiens is a dirty old town with its seven canals,' he continued. 'The cathedral, belfry and the theatre are, of course, wonderful, but there is little else except the dirt'. As for the street life, 'one could hardly jamb oneself through the crowd in the Place Gambetta or up the Rue des Trois Cailloux. It was a struggling mass of khaki, bumping over the uneven cobblestones'.[27] ➲ 4

4   Friday 4 September 1914

During the night the contents of Le Havre's *Hangar au Coton*, a single nine-acre shed more than half a mile long and six hundred feet wide, were hurriedly evacuated to St Nazaire, just west of Nantes on the mouth of the Loire, only to return in November when Befland's eastern borders began to stabilize. It wasn't an easy task. The shed housed 20,000 tons of clothing, ammunition and a welter of other supplies, including tens of thousands of horse-shoes – thirty-four sorts in seventeen different sizes, some for the fore and some for the hind legs. According to the ordnance services' historian 'the articles were in miscellaneous heaps often buried under piles of forage'. More arrived every day.[28]

The British identified Le Havre as a potential depot before the War broke out, in part because it had ample dock space, in part because it had good rail links via Rouen with Amiens, earmarked as the main forward supply depot. After the September Panic it quickly emerged as Befland's main entrepôt. The *Hangar au Coton* soon stocked 80,000 tons of supplies and wargear. By October 1916 ships unloaded over 58,000 tons every week just for those settled on the Somme. Three months later Befland's first motor vehicle repair centre started work when settlers took over the Deutsch Company's factory. Over the next three years many more appeared, the biggest northeast of the docks in Graville district. Meanwhile stores and workshops exporting discarded clothing to Britain materialized in and around the town. All remounts entered the colony via Le Havre. Two veterinary hospitals and a base depot for veterinary stores were located there. By December 1916 Le Havre contained the headquarters of Befland's Service Corps, Ordnance Corps and Veterinary Corps, three general base depots, bases for the Third and Fourth Armies, the headquarters of the British West India Regiment and the West Indian Labour Corps (newly arrived from Egypt), a branch of the Army Postal Service and the headquarters of Befland's Army Printing and Stationery Service and its six sub-departments (printing and photography, publications, printing and stationery, typewriter inspection and repair, technical stores and a rubber stamp factory) which liaised with subsections at Rouen, Boulogne and Calais.[29]

Like Calais, Boulogne and Rouen, Le Havre was also a key medical centre and food supplier. In late 1917 it had five hospitals (three British, one Canadian and one for 'coloured' labourers), and three convalescent camps.

When ambulance trains arrived from the zone sixty-seven Red Cross and St John's ambulances took the wounded from the station to the hospitals or the dockside – hospital ships sailed from Le Havre to Britain. Le Havre's field butcheries slaughtered livestock purchased from all over Befland. By 1918 its bakeries produced 9.25 million pounds of bread a month and the town could feed 233,000 settlers a day. As in Boulogne, settler-built onshore cold storage depots handled frozen meat imported from around the world. As in Boulogne, Calais, Rouen and Étaples there was an army cookery school – between 1915 and 1918 the five schools trained over 25,000 immigrants. A complex of reinforcement camps spread out in the surrounding hills. Between January and October 1916 the main officers' shop, located in the town itself and open seven days a week, served close on 13,000 customers – an average of forty-two a day.[30] The first branch of Befland's Canteen and Mess Co-operative Society opened its doors early in 1915. Founded 'to protect the soldier against the exorbitant prices which the shops and cafés were beginning to charge' according to Edmonds, it soon had outlets in St Omer, Bailleul, Armentières and Poperinghe. All were supplied from Le Havre.[31]

Jessie Wilson commented favourably on what she saw as she entered the town in August 1915 – 'French "villas" like gaily painted dolls' houses standing within formal gardens on the left side'.[32] George Stringer looked on the bright side too. Walking to the top of the hill by camp number eight on 20 September 1916, a pleasant late summer's day, he saw infantry at work in the distance and had a fine view of Harfleur nestling in the valley below. Beyond lay the Seine estuary. All the camps looked spick and span. Those of the Ulster division had flower beds and a tennis court.[33] But no one else seems to have found the place particularly attractive. Ronald Schweder, camped there in December 1915, found it unspeakable; nothing but muck, rain and tents in a sea of mud.[34] 'Inexpressibly filthy' was Garnet Durham's verdict the following April,[35] and this from an officer of the Post Office Rifles after the battalion had marched from the quayside to the reinforcement camps: 'A wind piercingly cold. Rows of bell tents flapping and tugging at their ropes on a muddy hilltop whence a clear view of the estuary of the Seine dotted with shipping. A line of dejected horses securely tethered'.[36]

Things were no better two years later when war weariness pushed Beflanders towards outright mutiny. 'Never was more dissatisfaction expressed, never did we hear so much grousing,' wrote Jessie Wilson, recalling Harfleur's YMCA hut early in 1918.[37] After the Armistice Le Havre seems to have experienced much the same kind of turmoil as Calais [89]. Large concentrations of settlers awaiting demobilization were kept hanging about in the hills above the town. On 12 December a minor argument over food erupted into a major riot. Arrests were made and the mutineers flung in jail. The hundreds who gathered to demand their release looted food stores, set fires, attacked fire tenders and raided the officers' messes. The authorities responded by speeding up decolonization. By 15 December around a thousand a day sailed for Folkestone and the unrest subsided. Many erstwhile Beflanders tossed their guns and equipment into the harbour as they boarded ship.[38] ➲ 14

5　Monday 19 October 1914

'We had an excellent view of the country to our front, which much resembled Essex or Suffolk, being greatly enclosed and with many hedges and woods'.[39] This is what Ralph Hamilton saw as he stood looking towards the border from a hillock near Hooge, two miles east of Ypres along the Menin Road. George Stringer arrived in the same district early next year but could access no references, East Anglian or otherwise, to help him make sense of what he perceived. Farmsteads covered the land and all the artillery turnouts were in farm orchards, a little higher than the surrounding fields and therefore better drained. Rows of trees, invariably pollarded willows and usually a dozen or so per line, marked off the fields. But everything looked like everything else – 'there are no distinguishing features in the landscape'. It was a perplexing place in which to find oneself, and for newcomers all too easy to get lost.[40] Nearly five years later, on 3 April 1919, a tour group walked over the same landscape while the group leader jotted down a snatch of conversation: '"Yes", said our guide, "this was the chateau and stables of Hooge."' Then the leader paused and looked around. 'There is just mud, water and shell holes now,' she added. 'Derelict Tanks lay in all directions. Dead Trees. Rotting land and stagnant ponds'.[41]

The guide gestures at something nearby and transformed, in fact at something absent and irrecoverable but once known or imagined: Hooge Chateau and stables. The narrator, Lady Londonderry, carries forward his gesture in time with her now of mud, water and shell holes, and then raises her eyes to the now-vista of derelict wargear, trees, land and ponds. Beckoned by the narrator we step into the landscape and see (a) a non-existent chateau and stables, (b) mud, water and shell holes in the same place as the chateau and (c) a panorama of stagnant ponds, abandoned tanks and dead trees. But what do we really see? How are the chateau and stables erected in our mind's eye? Do the shell holes have any specific and agreed location or structure and would we all picture the same panorama? And what are those silent others seeing? – *our* guide, says Lady Londonderry. Finally, do we see things differently from the way recently departed settlers would if they were there (or here) with us because, with the possible exception of our guide, we're all tourists – sightseers?

'What makes the very first glimpse of a village, a town, in the landscape so incomparable and irretrievable,' wrote Walter Benjamin in 1928, 'is the rigorous connection between foreground and distance. Habit has not yet done its work. As soon as we begin to find our bearings, the landscape vanishes at a stroke like the facade of a house as we enter it'.[42] Just over forty years earlier Thomas Hardy jotted this down after visiting an Impressionist exhibition at a London gallery: 'what you carry away with you from a scene is the true feature to grasp; or in other words, *what appeals to your own individual eye and heart in particular* amid much that does not so appeal, and which you therefore omit to record'.[43]

Beflanders perforce paid a great deal of attention to the exact and visible disposition of things around them, nevertheless settler evidence for landscapes *per se* is more often than not surprisingly vague and equivocal. Even an apparently straightforward three-line description of the site of Hooge Chateau turns out to be far from straightforward. Why should this be so? We don't need to explore theories of perception to understand the simple but important points that habit obliterates notice (our guide?) whereas novelty strikes the eye (Lady Londonderry?), and that what settlers recorded was very much a matter of what appealed to the individual eye and heart at a given moment. 'What's that over there?' asks the lyrically inclined interlocutor in a Blunden verse about landscape and topography. The narrative voice, a busy infantry officer, replies, identifies the Somme's Thiepval Wood, and advises his companion to put away his notebook full of rhymes about woodland flowers and fairy queens and concentrate instead on the military features in front of him.[44] Similar equivocations and resonances underpin descriptions of La Bassée district. In 1918 Lieutenant Capron paused to watch a dogfight in the evening sky while manoeuvring guns into position south of Béthune. 'The better plane nosed down and hard on the tail of the vanquished and pouring a stream of bullets through the ripped fuselage – till a fatal flame shot up, licking hungrily back against a sheet of smoke, and the stricken plane spun dizzily down, while the darkling earth rushed up to receive its final fall'.[45] Nothing here is simple. 'Vanquished' speaks of patriotic schoolbooks and playing-field clichés ('vanquished foe'), the pathetic fallacy makes an appearance (flames 'licking hungrily') and the earth rises towards the falling aeroplane, while that recondite adjective 'darkling' (*Paradise Lost*, book 3, or possibly Hardy's 'Darkling Thrush', first published in the *Graphic* in December 1900) suggests that we are in the presence of an educated (or at least newspaper-reading) Edwardian.

All Befland's landscapes are landscapes of the mind; true features dependent upon a point of view. They are also landscapes of memory. Even Hamilton, standing right there in front of the landscape ('we had an excellent view of the country'), is looking up, observing, and then looking down and writing. A temporal interlude falls between observation and recording, and we might, for the sake of convenience, designate that interlude as the space in which culture operates. Between observation and recording the settler's referential system translates what's being observed into something seen, and therefore accessible, comprehensible and potentially transmittable. In fact we seem to be watching prose manifestations of what Keith Grieves describes as the 'propinquity of place', whereby Befland's countryside called to mind England's and reinforced patriotic sentiments.[46] Inevitably, of course, the colony's landscape is thereby lost. The sublime gets domesticated and reappears as cultural artefact or metaphor – Flanders resembling Essex or Suffolk or, if no translation takes place, Flanders resembling nothing at all, appearing instead as an instance of Schiller's 'spirited disorder',[47] a jumbled collage of tree-lines, orchards, artillery batteries, farms and pollarded willows with 'no distinguishing features'.

One day a few months after his arrival in Befland Stringer stood on Kemmel Hill, a low rise five miles or so southwest of Ypres which stands 500 feet above sea level and dominates the Flanders plain for miles around. From there he gazed down on the setting sun and the ruined towers of Ypres, 'rose-impearled' in the valley two miles or so below.[48] Those 'rose-impearled' towers probably reference Gilbert Frankau's 'The Inn of a Thousand Dreams', a Housmanesque verse eulogizing the Kent countryside.[49] But the poem wasn't published until early 1918 and Frankau's verse itself references the village of Neuve-Église, a couple of miles from Kemmel, as remembered in June 1916, as well as a series of other verses reaching back into the eighteenth century. As for Stringer's lines, they were written not in Flanders but in High Wycombe in March 1918. His health had collapsed the previous summer and he'd left Befland in August, never to return. But we can still stand on Kemmel Hill on a summer evening in 1915 watching Ypres' ruined spires catch the sun's last rays with the shadowed valley between. The temporal interlude has done its work. Landscape-artefact has overlaid countryside, thus rendering it transmittable, and there we are, via High Wycombe and Gilbert Frankau.

In fact Stringer was well aware of the difficulty of representing landscape. In another meditation from 1918 he acknowledged the failure that must result from struggling to render the true feature of what appeals to the individual eye and heart. And what he produces is not a vista at all, but a Flanders collage; eloquent, nostalgic, impressionistic: descriptions of billets, one of his bedroom in a house by the windmill at St Marie Cappel, another at Le Steent'je with a French pot stove in the kitchen; the convent wall at Fleurbaix with the battery in the garden surrounded by apple blossom and primroses; a stay at Armentières where he helped saw down telegraph poles for gun platforms; Kemmel Hill in springtime, its woods floating on drifts of anemones and cowslip; pandemonium and death at the École de Bienfaisance; a companion's makeshift grave; smashed greenhouses at Bedford House and reminiscences of the cellar where he slept. There were thousands more impressions, he said, but he kept diaries only fitfully and had no photographs to school and illuminate the past – 'Many of the pictures have already faded into the mist of forgetfulness. Even those which I can see can never be seen by any other eye but mine'.[50] ➲ 8

Saturday 12 December 1914 6

Captain Robert Bontine Cunninghame Graham – Hispanist, novelist, adventurer, political prisoner, quondam socialist MP, delegate to the Second International, co-founder with Kier Hardie of the Scottish Labour Party and friend of, among other notables, Joseph Conrad, William Morris, Annie Besant and Eleanor Marx-Averling – arrived in Montevideo with five officers and three vets to set up the Uruguay Remount Commission. A few weeks later he established his headquarters and collection point at Frey Bentos, a hundred miles up the La Plata, to gather horses from across the continent. Most were small, but they were, according to the RAVC's historians, exceptionally healthy. 'Little trouble or care in selection seems to be taken, a fact perhaps due to the state of political unrest hitherto existent in the country, the horses of which have been repeatedly liable to sudden seizure either by the government or revolutionary forces. This has caused complete disorganization of horse-breeding in a country naturally adapted for it, and the result has been the production of a class of horse indefinite in type and deficient in height, but possessed of good powers of staying, and meeting the requirements of the people of the country as a general utility animal'.[51] In 1915 Graham sent about 2,300 by train to Buenos Aires and Montevideo, an eighteen- or twenty-hour journey. From there they were shipped to Liverpool or Avonmouth, often in foul conditions. Russians and (after May 1915) Italians returning to Europe to join their armies managed the animals under the command of British foremen but frequently had little understanding of horses. Language difficulties compounded the problems.[52]

The Canadian Remount Commission, staffed in the main by 'country gentlemen, large landowners, and competent masters of hounds' according to the War Office,[53] started work in Montreal shortly before Graham arrived at Montevideo and bought horses from all over North America. By late 1916 there were purchasing depots at Lachine and Calumet (Michigan), Grand Trunk (Illinois), Rosemount and St Paul (Minnesota), Le Pestre Miller Stock Farm (Ohio), Green Island, Jersey City and Goshen in New York State (the latter one of the largest), St Louis (Missouri), Cedar Rapids and Sioux City (Iowa), Lathrop (California), Portland (Oregon), Newport News (Virginia), Chicago, Ogden in Utah, Halifax (Nova Scotia) and Toronto. Range-reared animals housed in depots with roofed pens, lighting and ventilation survived best. Those turned out *en masse* into winter paddocks after long train journeys and given no exercise often died from exposure. In Ogden sickness rates mounted as the pens became more and more infected. At Goshen horses shivered in open paddocks all day long in the cold and the rain. Night stabling was well away from the pens and there was little control over movement. A deep connecting gully turned into a vast slough of liquid mud and dung and so stables became damp and diseased. Lathrop,

Calumet and Cedar Rapids were similarly fouled and heavily infected and, as at Goshen, fodder strewn around outside spread contamination. That which remained clean may have had little nutritional value. Befland's vets considered North-American forage to be of poor quality, and sometimes downright injurious.[54] ➲ 17

7 Sunday 10 January 1915

Ralph Hamilton, billeted at Staple near Hazebrouck in Flanders: 'The country here is extraordinarily quiet and peaceful . . . except for the absence of able-bodied men, life seems to be going on much as usual. They are cutting the hedges along the roads and working steadily in the fields'.[55] Herbert Leland, also billeted in Flanders: 'My window as I think I have told you opens on to the canal', he wrote to his wife in October 1917. 'It is very interesting to see the barges passing up. Enormous things, like dismantled "Lusitanias". Several have just passed with horses, and others with cattle, packed like sardines. The whole barge family live on board, for there are women and children galore peeping out from the little portholes, and they all look so sleek'.[56]

Few descriptions of the French were as neutrally phrased as these. Almost invariably opinion interlarded observation or was baldy stated as the end product of a chain of reasoning or prior experience. 'We would, I think, have been more inclined to regard the soil of France, rather than that of our own country, as the ground of our defence,' concluded Richard Foot in 1964 after meditating on patriotism, and he did not find much to commend the French. Peasants living in the back areas around the Pas de Calais were unfriendly and repellent, while natives in provincial towns (Amiens and Abbeville are singled out) were concerned only to extract as much money as possible from the settlers dumped on them.[57]

When Beflanders entered into specifics they exhibited a mixture of curiosity, surprise, disgust, condescension, hostility and sympathy, often in the same person. In June 1915 Kitty Kenyon, yet to emigrate, got two letters from a male friend based near Étaples. 'I told you last time about seeing a dog pulling a dog cart,' he wrote. 'Well I saw them doing something else yesterday. I saw them making butter. They have a kind of a tread mill very much the same as the ones they used to have in English prisons . . . If they were to do it in England I believe they would be brought up for cruelty to animals'. The French are more religious than the English, he added, most houses have a crucifix and a statue of the Virgin on display outside.[58] In December Ruth Durst, living down the coast at Le Touquet, went to a concert. 'It was rather amusing . . . the mayor or someone got up and made a flowery speech after which a little band struck up the Marseillaise, playing very fast and everyone leapt to their feet'. Three years later she was inland, at St Omer. 'The French girls in the kitchen are rather a trouble . . . They haven't risen to the occasion and we are having changes. Then they are terrified of air raids and run to the cellars in the middle of washing up, often, and are awake half the night and then are tired the next day. It is a problem'.[59] Phyllis Goodliff on a day off in Boulogne, April 1918: 'The more I see of the French the less I think of them as regards getting on with the war. They seem to leave everything to us'.[60] The local peasants speak an impenetrable dialect, complained Stapleton Eachus from Pont-Noyelles on the Somme in 1916, are very dirty and scruffy (even though the women dress carefully), live in shoddily built mud huts, throw food on the floor, defecate in the yard and have the same reputation as England's Jews – tight-fisted, suspicious and ungracious. In addition they are hopelessly superstitious. The woman of the house never puts a loaf on the table bottom up because that might bring bad luck, and before cutting it she always marks a cross on the bottom with a knife.[61]

Horror of filth was uppermost in the minds of George Stringer and Charles Carrington when they first arrived in Befland. Flanders, March 1915: a dreadful billet, wrote Stringer. The natives live like pigs and he was very glad that he'd had a typhoid jab before emigrating.[62] 'After a short wait in the snow, billets were allotted in various scattered farmhouses surrounded by ancient dirt' (Carrington).[63] But two months' residence softened Stringer's attitudes somewhat. By 13 May he was talking about the distressing sight of natives leaving a farm just appropriated by his unit. As shells rained down at a nearby crossroads the farm children packed a few toys and left quietly with their parents. 'C'est terrible,' said the farmer's wife as she piled a *tumbrel* high with the family's clothes and belongings. French artillery officers hereabouts, he continued, could certainly shave and wash more often, but they were thoroughly decent, always polite and never neglectful of military courtesies. He and the village doctor – also thoroughly decent – made time every day to exchange local gossip and denounce the War.[64]

From spring 1916 till August 1917 Stringer was on the Somme, and by now generally well disposed towards the French, civilians and soldiers alike. One place where he stayed (Bavincourt, September 1916) was a particularly restful spot. Even though all the surrounding villages were within the easy range of German artillery it was much quieter than during a recent stay at Kemmel. Nothing much happened. All that could be heard was a continuous background roar away to the south-east. The natives had perfected the art of staying out of harm's way; as he wrote groups of peasants were busy harvesting fields just behind the gun emplacements. A train journey from Doullens to Amiens on 1 February 1917 elicited further complimentary remarks. Stringer's carriage was full of *poilus* (French slang for common soldiers; roughly equivalent to Befland's 'tommies') so he had to sit on his valise the whole way. They didn't get to Amiens till nine in the evening, but the *poilus* remained cheerful and steadfast, bore themselves well, were smartly turned out and to Stringer's mind more intelligent than the average tommy. As the train clanked along, for most of the time at no more than two miles an hour, they all got chatting about the War and chaffed him good-naturedly when they discovered that he was a 'commandant'.[65]

Others made a similar range of observations. The natives are 'mostly sociable and we can always buy homemade bread and coffee' (Garnet Durham, Estaires, March 1915).[66] 'One has only to knock and enter a French home, and one is made to feel quite at home. There is always in attendance the cup that cheers, "coffee", and one has to drink it, or else risk the displeasure of Madame' (Robert Cude at Nordausques on the Calais-St Omer road, Christmas Day 1917).[67] Like Eachus William Orpen found French working-class women 'clean, neat and prim . . . they never seem to tire and usually wore a smile'.[68] Like Kitty Kenyon's friend James Williams and Rowland Luther were struck by French religiosity. Williams, July 1917, describing a village near Arras: 'very old fashioned . . . a roadside Roman Catholic altar of which there are many here is dated 1801'.[69] Luther, in spring 1916, encountered a religious procession. An old farm track ran in front of the barn where he was on sentry duty early one morning. Suddenly, from the direction of the border, a light appeared, hovering ten feet or so in the air, and the tinkle of a little bell, and the sound feet dragging along the ground and a flicker of white cloth: 'I thought the dead had risen as ghosts'.[70] Like Stringer the Post Office Rifles' interpreter sympathized with natives caught up in the War and, like Eachus, noted an instance of popular religion. In January 1918 his battalion was at Bettencourt-Rivière on the Somme. Most of the men were housed in the ruins of a pencil factory. The owner, 'a sad-eyed middle-aged bourgeois' paid them a visit one day after walking from Bapaume to visit his little daughter's grave and look over what was left of the factory. The previous August, as the transport reached the battalion's billet at Hondeghem village in Flanders, 'a bright little girl of 8 stepped out of the kitchen, carrying carefully a bowl of Holy Water and a sprig of box. Gravely she proceeded to open each door or hatch in the yard and over the calf, the sheep, the pig, the rabbits, the bundles of flax and the sheaves of corn she made a large sign of the cross with the sprig of box dipped in the water; she then crossed to the empty barn awaiting the soldiers and blessed it too, just as the gate swung open and the tired teams pulled into the yard'.[71]

Ronald Schweder too had glancing moments of sympathy and admiration. On Christmas morning 1915 he went to Mass at Francières on the Somme. Women dressed in mourning filled the nave – a pitiable sight – and the sermon was deeply moving. In March the following year at nearby Mailly-Maillet he was struck by the sight of an old woman on crutches shuffling along the road while shells fell in the adjacent fields. She must have been used to it, he thought, or she couldn't have stood it. At Dranoutre in Flanders in February 1917 he commented favourably on the care French households took over their domestic economy. Back on the Somme nine months later he was one of a party that rode six miles in search of food. Eventually they found a farm, ruined but still working; cows grazing among shell holes and graves and a shanty containing three women, one old man, a child and two beds. This family had fled the area when the fighting started and then returned. All that was left of the original complex (before the War they had two farms) was a gate standing by the side of the road. The shanty was made of wood and sacks. 40,000 gold francs, buried when they fled, were lost forever, churned up by the shelling, but all the same Schweder and his companions were given excellent omelettes and decent coffee.[72]

Decades later Rowland Luther summarized what he saw of French life in and around Flanders, and reflected on settler-native interactions: 'I did not see the beautiful French girls that we hear so much about. The women I saw were not attractive'. On canal towpaths they were strapped into harnesses and dragged the heavy barges through the water while old men sat in the stern steering. Field women, ploughing or bent over the crops, often right in front of the guns, were dressed from head to foot in coarse, black calico. In the farmyards and barns dogs and horses chained to treadmills ground the corn. Other dogs, lashed together in teams, pulled little carts along the streets. Crucifixes at every crossroad and the sign of the cross from every passer-by. And they were quick to exploit incomers. 'Just out of sheer boredom' Luther and his companions would enter their filthy, tumbledown cottages to buy watery beer, brewed on the premises, or thin, weak coffee at a penny a glass. 'It is certain that they didn't love us, but now I understand why. We were the lousy soldiers of Britain, and there were thieves and scamps among us. It was their country, and not ours, and we were the disturbers of the peace'.[73]

It would satisfy the classificatory impulses of historians if we were able to differentiate these various responses and at the same time separate them out from the background susurrations of Francophobia and Francophilia, both well established in British culture. Schweder, Hamilton, Leland, Foot, Stringer and Carrington – all officers – spoke at least some French before they entered Befland, and we might expect of them a broad appreciation of French life. Garnet Durham, Robert Cude, James Williams and Rowland Luther – all other ranks – did not, and should have been more disconcerted by what they saw. Stapleton Eachus lived with a French family and tried to learn French, though judging by his diary entries without much success. Nevertheless we might quiz him on Beflander responses to the minutiae of French domestic culture. If class and location should have inflected observation, so too should have gender and location. Ruth Durst and Phyllis Goodliff lived exclusively in the entrepôts and back areas, not so the men (Eachus excepted). And to an extent it all works: Ruth Durst and the troublesome girls, Schweder and the cure's sermon, Stringer's conversations, Cude and the Christmas coffee, Eachus's housewife and the loaves. But some things stand out in all accounts, regardless of our classificatory impulses. Chance encounters and novel scenes coalesce into agreed images of the

French – poverty and squalor, equivocal attitudes towards immigrants, fortitude in adversity, dog carts and Catholicism, grief, the absence of young men and the burden on women. ➲ 11

8 Monday 1 March 1915

'Estaires is somewhat battered in places,' remarked Garnet Durham of the old linen town ten miles southwest of Ypres, 'the churches in particular being often like brickyards or quarries'. 'The people are cheerfully indifferent to the signs of war and are planting crops wherever they can,' he wrote in April, and he soon got used to the hordes of soldiers and the everlasting flow of traffic, taking it 'as a matter of course'. But in spite of it all he thought the little towns of Flanders looked 'very theatrical' under moonlight; 'one feels like singing the sentry song from "Iolanthe"'.[74] In July, somewhere a mile or so from Ypres, George Stringer's artillery unit was firing, but something had gone wrong. He pushed his way forward through the trees in front to investigate and strode across fields tall with the previous year's ungathered harvest. He returned by a different route. Here the corn had been cut. One field had been half ploughed and then abandoned. The coulter leaned in the furrow. 'I can see the peasant, surprised by the approach of the storm, throw the traces over the horses back & trot away'.[75] Two years later Ronald Schweder was struck by the sight of a traction engine and reaping machine quietly rusting away in no man's land. Later still he wrote to his wife from the southern slopes of nearby Mont des Cats, noting the corn ripening to waste and grumbling about the tare field they had to dig over to place the guns. But he omits to record what was happening to the landscape right at that moment, though we can hazard a guess. Judging by the lie of the land and the direction of the guns he was firing at Bailleul's St Amand's church, four miles away.[76] Its ruins are now a war memorial in the middle of a roundabout.

The settler doesn't record mud, shell holes, cannon, horse-lines, ammunition dumps, work routines, targets or other instances of the manifold activity associated with siege warfare that we might expect. Though striking to we sightseers, these are too commonplace to merit attention. Indeed, though observed, to some eyes such scenes might not really be seen at all (Durham's 'matter of course'). But novelty – moonlight over ruined towns, crops amidst war, inconvenient flora, that abandoned plough and the image of the peasant hurrying away as shells fell around him – stimulates the habituate eye.

Landscapes could also be pressed into service as devices for introducing vistas. In March 1918 Stringer recalled a day spent at Mont des Cats in June 1915. He rode up with Challinor, an officer friend, and met another friend, Brent, at the top, who gave them a substantial tea. They sat watching the old, brown-habited monks walk by along the upper streets and looked over the rooftops into the countryside below – 'one has a wonderful view from these islands which rise up in the sea of the Flanders plain'. All around them lay northern Befland, though mist obscured the distant seas. Southwards they could see right down into La Bassée district. The twin slagheaps just outside Estrée-Blanche caught his eye, landmarks passed two years later (March 1917) on his way to Witternesse, just north of Béthune.[77]

And here, a month or so after Stringer passed Estrée-Blanche, is another Flanders hilltop vista piece, this one from William Orpen. 'The road from Arques to the station at the foot of Cassel Hill was always lined on each side by lorries, guns, pontoons and all manner of war material. A gloomy road, thick with mud for the most part, if not dust. It was always a pleasure to start climbing Cassel Hill, past the seven windmills and up to the little town perched on the summit. Cassel is a picturesque little spot, with its glazed tiles and sprinkling of Spanish buildings, and the view from it is marvellous. On a clear day one could see practically the whole line from Nieuport to Armentières and the coast from Nieuport to Boulogne. At that time, the 2nd Army H.Q. were in the one-time casino, which was on the summit of the town, and from its roof one got a clear view all round'.[78]

We might wonder about the psychodramas played out in the casino, a hubris-inducing spot, surely, for the Second Army's war planners as they gazed out over northern Befland, but what they would see if they stood on the roof on a fine day in 1917 and turned slowly anti-clockwise is this: north-eastwards and twenty miles away Dixmude, which marked Befland's border with the tiny eight-mile Belgian-held enclave extending to Nieuport; to the north the wet Flanders plain, flooded in the distance and stretching sixteen miles or so to Dunkirk; to the north-west Calais, twenty-nine miles away; St Omer, ten miles west, and twenty-nine miles beyond that Boulogne; Hazebrouck, six miles to the south; Bailleul, eleven miles southeast with Armentières a further seven miles on, and finally due east Poperinghe, eleven miles away, and Ypres, seventeen miles distant. East of Ypres little of the Salient would be visible except, perhaps, a brown smudge overlaid with cannon smoke. Elverdinghe, Boesinghe, St Julien, Passchendaele, Zonnebeke, Hooge, Zillebeke, Hollebeke, St Eloi, Lindenhoek, Dickebusch, Neuve-Église, Dranoutre and a dozen other border villages which ringed the town a couple of miles or so to the north, east and south in this densely settled enclave would be quite invisible, either because they were too small to register on the naked eye or because, having already been obliterated, they existed only as map references or road junctions. The same would be true of numerous farms and chateaux contained within the Salient, many renamed by settlers (Woodcote Farm, Belgian Chateau, Bedford House, etc.).

'In Flanders fields the poppies blow / Between the crosses, row on row, / That mark our place.' / John McCrae's verse was published in *Punch* on 8 December 1915, but where Flanders actually was is a moot point, and readers of *Punch* would find nothing in McCrae's stanzas to help them find it. Like every other settler landscape this was a place of the mind, somewhere more or less vaguely defined whose true features depended upon a point of view. Certainly any Beflander standing on the roof of Cassel Casino would agree that all the lands to the east in what was notionally Belgium (principally the Ypres Salient) comprised part of Flanders, so too all the French lands between Cassel and the Salient, and everything stretching north to Dunkirk, south to Hazebrouck and south-eastwards to just over the old Franco-Belgian border at Armentières. Lands to the west and south were debatable. To the west everything up to Arques on the River Aa, a mile east of St Omer, would probably be included. But St Omer, along with all else contained within the rough square formed by Dunkirk, Calais, Boulogne and St Omer itself, a region of gently folding land slightly higher than the Flanders plain, was often described as part of the 'back area'. Cassel itself was one of those 'islands which rise up in the sea of the Flanders plain' that enraptured Stringer as he drank tea with Challinor and Brent on the Mont des Cats in June 1915. Cassel, Mont des Cats and Kemmel Hill were links in a chain of low hills that ran eastwards to the south of Ypres and then merged into Messines Ridge which curved northwards around the Salient. Looking south from Cassel (or Mont des Cats or Kemmel Hill) the viewer might glimpse, five miles or so beyond Hazebrouck, the silver sliver of the River Lys, which marked Flanders' southern border, or at least part of the southern border area.

The Flanders known to Beflanders was thus a low-lying plain bisected by an east-west range of hills rising south of Ypres. It was bounded to the north by the sea, to the west by slightly higher ground rising from St Omer, to the east by Messines Ridge and the undulating arc of higher ground which curved round the Salient, and to the south by lands around the Lys.

But Flanders's southern border was a matter of human rather than physical geography. The whole of eastern Befland's zone, which in summer 1916 measured some ninety miles from north to the south (Ypres to Bray-sur-Somme),[79] consisted of three distinct regions. The Salient, and Flanders generally, resembled the Cambridgeshire fens; flat and waterlogged. There zone dwellers more often than not lived in sandbagged alleys running above the ground rather than in trenches. In the far south the Somme, in Picardy, was an area of open, rolling chalk downland much like Wiltshire, which tumbled down to the river marshes stretching eastwards from Amiens. '"Going north" to Ypres, or "going south" to the Somme,' remembered Charles Carrington in 1929, 'meant a different kind of warfare and new discomforts'. Sandwiched between Flanders and the Somme stood La Bassée district, part of Artois province and a region characterized not by distinctive natural features (the Flanders' plain continued twenty miles over the Lys, through Béthune and on to the Notre Dame de Lorette and Vimy ridges, sixteen miles or so from the Somme uplands) but by a distinctive economy. Flanders and the Somme were agricultural, La Bassée district industrial, full of canals, coal mines and brick fields: 'like South Staffordshire,' remarked Carrington.[80] Grieves' 'propinquity of place' [5] worked the other way round too: England reminded settlers of Befland. ⮞ 9

Friday 19 March 1915 9

The Post Office Rifles arrived at Béthune, walked southwest out of the town and got their first look at La Bassée district: 'An eight mile march to the mining village of Auchel. Orchards by the wayside; well tilled fields; thickset thorn hedges . . . Mud-walled barns, the high pitch of the thatched or red-tiled roofs, the many ditches brimful of clear water, the rows of pollarded willows, the red-brick or white sandstone houses . . . The shrines at the cross-roads. The black pyramidal masses of the slag heaps looming on the horizon'. Three months later they moved east towards the border at Vermelles, twelve miles from Auchel and another of the numerous mining villages huddled to the south of Béthune. On 2 June one of their officers climbed out of the trenches and looked westwards, back over the landscape they'd just traversed. He saw a 'broad expanse of land and sky, a varied panorama of red brick corons [workers' cottages] clustering around the chimneys and towers of the pit-heads . . . dark woods clinging to the hills of Artois' and 'the sombre masses of the slag-heaps rising from the green plain'. To the east, and 'peeping above the rise' over the border, were the twin red towers of the Loos gantry, a well-known landmark. In August the battalion shifted two miles south to Le Maroc, a workers' settlement attached to Les Brebis village, but this time into landscape difficult to interpret and, to some at least, not only uncanny but also threatening: 'Painted cabalistic signs, circles and crosses' on the roofs and walls of the houses, clearly visible from the other side of the border, aroused suspicions. The rumour had gone round that these were secret codes meant for German eyes. When questioned the natives explained their function; they helped pigeons recognize their lofts.[81]

This wasn't the end of the battalion's local perambulations. Spring 1916 found them billeted in a knot of 'typical white stone built Artois villages' (Gouy-Servins, Estrée-Cauchy, Verdel and Villers-au-Bois) 'set amidst chequered fields, where the crops were all mixed up in patches of different shades of green'. These billets were six miles south of Les Brebis and about another five from the border villages (Souchez, Carency, Givenchy-en-Gohelle) that straggled around the Notre Dame de Lorette and Vimy ridges. When, as evening fell on 15 May, zone dwellers blew the mines they'd placed under Vimy Ridge, a 'picturesque sight' struck the chronicler standing in Villers-au-Bois. From Carency village, set in a nearby valley, 'danced the unceasing flicker of guns where the howitzers fired untiringly'. High explosive shells 'splashed' along the top of the ridge. Amid the uninterrupted 'barking' of the guns the 'dull roars' of three enormous mine detonations rumbled through the air and shook the ground underfoot. Verey lights 'soared in shoals', bursting green and red above the low blanket of smoke. Infantrymen standing in orchards and gardens watched the 'pandemonium raging across the valley in the calm spring air under the rising moon'. As work along the ridges continued into July he deployed new imagery – fireworks, phantom trees, inland lighthouses – in his attempt to translate what was observed into something seen: Every night saw 'a display of fireworks somewhere on the horizon'. Muzzle flashes illuminated 'phantom pine trees' as if from 'a revolving light-house lantern'.[82]

George Stringer arrived in La Bassée district the following April and passed through Béthune and Noeux-les-Mines on his way to Grenay. It was just like the Black country of home, he wrote, though there seemed little of the filth and squalor characteristic of the West Midlands: all the villages neat and tidy and all the workers' cottages relatively new. All around were *fossés* (collieries), again relatively modern, and their associated *crassiers* (slag heaps).[83] Those *crassiers* came in handy for artillerymen anxious to peer across the border.[84] They were particularly valued because naturally occurring high ground was so scarce. Richard Foot remembered that competition for space on the little hill at Givenchy-lès-la-Bassée was so fierce that spotters had to risk travelling by daylight in order to secure a good vantage point – the whole place was teeming with settlers squeezed into makeshift observation posts, dugouts and trenches.[85]

Béthune to Grenay was a journey of seven miles, and as he arrived in La Bassée district Stringer would have passed through Le Maroc with its strange, cabbalistic signs which had so disconcerted the Post Office Rifles two years previously. A month later, on 27 May, we find him at work in the south, close to Notre Dame de Lorette Ridge, and construing a landscape of contrasts. After shooting off number five gun to correct its sights he walked with two other officers for a meeting at the colonel's billet somewhere nearby. The wooded slopes were resplendent and the entire countryside superbly decked in vibrant greens, Vimy Ridge excepted. There, on the tumbled mass of brown and white scars caused by heavy shelling, nothing at all grew. But in the mining villages dotted around women, settlers and families promenaded along the streets in the evening sunlight – peace and civilization vying with desolation and destruction.[86]

Next morning he did something experienced by very few settlers and almost no other Edwardians outside Befland. Out from Béthune, turning south towards Arras, high over Noeux-les-Mines, Les Brebis, Le Maroc, Grenay, Vermelles, Aix-Noulette, Bouvigny-Boyeffles, Gouy-Servins, Estrée-Cauchy, Liévin, Verdel, Villers-au-Bois, Neuville St Vaast, La Targette, Mont St Eloi, Souchez, Carency, Givenchy-en-Gohelle and dozens of other mining villages; high up across the Notre Dame de Lorette and Vimy ridges, Stringer made his first flight across La Bassée district (and as it turned out his first and last in Befland). The novelty of flying remade the landscape, and we can watch the Edwardian body and mind adapting to and creating new vistas. Suddenly, as he left the ground, the world turned as 'flat as a billiard table'. Roads, trees, houses, villages, haystacks, men, horses, vehicles, shadows – all became miniatures of themselves. Everything stood out starkly, trenches in particular, and riveted his attention – 'My sensations were those simply of intense interest and I had not a quota of fear the whole time'. He did need a stiff whisky though, when, frazzled and frozen after flying some ninety miles in the course of an hour, he eventually landed back at Hesdigneul-lès-Béthune.[87]

Just as for earth-bound settlers landscape was function of body position, so too for aerial denizens. Trench dwellers had eyes level with the ground ('shellhole and trench have a limited horizon,' remembered Ernst Jünger, 'the range of vision extends no further than a bomb throw'[88]); crawlers (artillerymen edging towards observation posts) eyes just above it. For the most part both conjured landscapes from glimpses and hints; things obscurely observed through tangled barbed wire, grass or clumps of weeds. The standing body granted a broader canvas to the mind's eye, broader still the gaze of the tall horseman who commanded vistas. And finally the aeronaut, whose eyeline to the earth's surface ran at ninety degrees to that of the trench dweller; while the latter perceived the ground only horizontally, he saw it only vertically, a 'solar eye'[89] possessing the world below.

Thus Stringer the aeronaut. And now six weeks later that same landscape restructured by Stringer the horseman, commanding vistas of biblical proportions as one afternoon he rode up to Notre Dame de Lorette Ridge, though woods in full summer foliage and into the ruins of what once had been a pleasant little village. For some odd reason only the church was more or less undamaged. There were no inhabitants. Then on to Bouvigny-Boyeffles and along the crest of a hill overlooking the site of a 1915 Franco-German battle. He paused, looked and commented. The French had driven the enemy down Notre Dame Ridge, he tells us, out through the village of Souchez and up onto Vimy Ridge, but could get no further. He remembered hearing the dull rumble of guns when he was at Kemmel Hill, miles away to the north. Rumour had it that down in the valley the bones of the dead still lay scattered around everywhere. Urging his horse on he reached the end of the crest and dismounted. In front was Vimy Ridge, a naked scar of white and brown. In the hollow sloping down towards Arras rose the broken towers of Mont St Eloi abbey, destroyed in the eighteenth century. To his left stood Lens, Loos and the other mining towns and villages of La Bassée district. 'All the kingdoms of the earth seemed to be laid at my feet. Unlike Moses on his rock I looked on no promised land, but on the waste & desolation'.[90] ➲ 19

Monday 29 March 1915   10

From 2nd Lieutenant Grant Taylor's diary, somewhere in the Salient: 'In the evening a message came through that the C.O. wanted a patrol to go out and find out whether the continuation of the trench was held by the Germans. Then there was cursing and swearing. We knew as well as anything that the trench was held, and jolly strongly too . . . It was a full moon and not a cloud. It was absolute madness to go out there . . . There was a lot of wire and it was rather beastly. We wormed ourselves through the wood over stumps and spikes. We could see flashes from the German trench all right and there were also bullets coming over us from Cuxon's trench (we had omitted to warn them). We were creeping about in that beastly wood for about twenty minutes, and all the time it was getting quite light and impossible to go any further'.[91]

Rowland Luther, driving guns near Doullens, May 1916: 'We had been made up fully with horses and men from England [and] had marched about three hours when a thunderstorm broke out – the most violent storm I can remember. The lightning flashed, the thunder roared, and the rain came down in torrents'. Soon their heavy, unwieldy greatcoats became wet through, making it all but impossible to stumble forward. Lightning flared and sizzled along the metal harness clips. Trees crashed and toppled into the road. The horses, by now completely out of control, kicked over their traces and bolted away in every direction, flinging seething masses of limbers, guns and terrified drivers into deep roadside gullies brimming with rainwater. A few, tangled in the harnesses or trapped underneath the wreckage, drowned or were crushed – 'This was the nearest to the front that some ever reached'. Those that managed to struggle free joined the rest in trying to restore order, but many of the horses had broken limbs and had to be shot.[92]

Lieutenant Capron stalking his way around the Somme's high chalk downs, 9 September 1916: the journey was about five miles from the guns to the ammunition dump, a ten mile round trip. 'Not far in mileage, but plenty far done nightly over ground fought and refought over, and where no roads but only wandering tracks led vaguely into night. This area, when there is talk of the Somme, is what I recall – I learnt to know, if not every inch of it, at least every mile of it only too well – helped by intuition and instinct and sense of smell, for I mostly knew it in the dark'.[93]

We can imagine the zone traversed by Taylor, Luther and Capron – no man's land, the trenches, the devastated area, and the apparently inviolate landscape a few miles to the west – as places where settlers were obliged to wander for a while. On a quiet day the zone might look innocent enough. After all, in one way a muddy devastated landscape is just that, and viewed with your head just above the trench top in summer no man's land resembles nothing more than a meadow scattered with barbed wire, skylarks, waving grasses, rosebay willow herb and slight humps lipped with brilliant wild flowers. And the inviolate places seem inviolate – woods, streams, hills, valleys and peaceful villages. On 19 May 1916 Ronald Schweder visited a gun emplacement by the side of a lake near Aveluy Wood on the Somme – idyllic for the time of year; officers' dugout a riverside summerhouse sheltered by trees; other ranks bathing and messing about in homemade canoes.[94]

Zoom up above it all. Perhaps you're taking reconnaissance photographs, like Capron who glimpsed 'pygmy Arras' through a hole in a 'polar sea' of cloud in May 1918,[95] or maybe you're in a cinema this evening watching a film about the Great War with convincing special effects. What do you see? Green, squared-off fields, rivers, plantations, towns and villages, the little ruler-straight roads and the occasional wink of long-range artillery; the back-area landscape shading into the zone's outer belt. Next, to the east, and blurring into the outer belt, is Befland's devastated area; a long strip of green-brown stretching from horizon to horizon scrawled over with the intricate trench maze. And next to that another green-brown strip stretching into the haze; no man's land, dotted with glinting shell-hole pools. Go higher still, as if you're repeatedly clicking on Google Maps. Towns, cities, headquarters, chancelleries, cathedrals, slums, parliaments, factories, rivers, hills, forests, ships converging on the Channel ports and the white ribbon-smoke of trains inching to and from the zone, all disappear with vertiginous rapidity until you get to the space-station view. Below is the curve of the earth and the thin blue ecozone. At this distance you've gone back in time. There's Europe, mottled green against the seas, much as it looked after the last ice age. Viewed top west it's a gigantic fossil squashed flat by the weight of its own history. The Iberian peninsula marks its lolling, hydrocephalic head, the Pyrenees its neck, the Apennines and Balkan peninsula malformed limbs and confused abdomen, the white Alps and associated mountain chains its broken spine and ribs, Scandinavia its plate-ridged tail. Stretching from Befland to Russia is its humped back, the Central Russian plain a dragging skin skirt hemmed by the Urals. All is peaceful and unmoving, even the colossal weather systems. But as you fall forwards in time towards the past 1916 begins to reappear. Perched on the spine somewhere is Lenin, pondering over Imperialism's self-destructiveness, and fingernail's width away the Austro-Hungarian army, shattered by Brusilov's June offensive. At the top of the humped back the French are going through Verdun's meat-grinder, Haig is waiting anxiously for news of a breakthrough that won't come for two more years, General Rawlinson is trying to keep control of the Somme's Fourth Army and Eric Geddes is struggling to sort out the messed-up railway timetables. Look closer. All the while hundreds of little winding columns wander around in the landscape.

You're falling faster now – the zone's pock-marked skin rushes up to greet you, and when you gently come to earth and start walking it's best navigated warily. On night patrol the summer meadow hides bizarre horrors lying around that can ensnare you, blow you apart or poison you. The barbed wire will tear at your flesh. You'll set off rusty tin-can alarms and alert snipers. You'll lose your footing as you crawl, slip over the red poppy-lips and slide into the mouths of suppurating pools where you inadvertently embrace rotting, bloated corpses. You'll get lost, go the wrong way, mistake His star shells for your own, forget the password and find the top of your skull shot off. The devastated area isn't safe, even when the trenches are cushy and even though the machine-gun rattle can't reach you there. The villages, woods, streams, hills and valleys that form the zone's outer belt, and the encampments and billets situated therein, are subject to sudden, lethal bombardments of high explosive and gas. And lying around are lots of strange objects, wargear that can hurt you if you incautiously fiddle with it or inadvertently get in its way. The vast stacks of high explosive shells you walk by shimmer and weep in summer, forming a dangerous film which all too easily bursts into flames. Those imported from the United States are particularly dangerous. Flares decompose. Phosphorous bombs, shell fuses and grenades explode prematurely. Trench mortars are liable to fail after firing a few rounds. 'Flying pigs' crash down into your trenches instead of sailing safely away over no man's land[96] [42]. Like Capron you have to become an expert in reading the terrain: nose, ears, hands and eyes must learn to distinguish harmless smells, sounds, sensations and visions from deadly ones. You need a whole sheaf of what Ross Wilson calls 'mental maps'[97] if you want to increase your chances of surviving here.

The journeys detailed above might be classified as intrazonal (Taylor's trip into no man's land, Capron's extra-border stalkings) and lateral (north-south or south-north; Luther's battery moving just behind the zone). Both could entail danger and hardship. But not all were arduous or involved encounters with lethal artefacts; Befland was too unpredictable and settler lives too diverse for that to be the case, even when travelling deep in the zone – witness Schweder's visit to Aveluy Wood's canoeing artillerymen. And there were other journeys besides lateral and intrazonal ones: horizontal journeys between base and zone (west-east, east-west), journeys to and from the portals, journeys of arrival, journeys of departure (permanent or temporary), journeys for pleasure (tourism or 'joy rides'). And each might be essayed variously: on foot, by train, by lorry or car, by boat, by air (rarely) or on horseback. A comprehensive journey schematic might therefore appear as follows:

1 Extraterrestrial: air
2 Terrestrial:
   a) arrivals and departures (the portals, the Channel, leave)
   b) base-zone-base
   c) final departures (decolonization, New Befland)
   d) intrazonals
   e) laterals
   f) evacuations (wounds, illness)
   g) tourism

Though from late 1914 until spring 1918 siege warfare kept Befland's borders more or less static, and though static settlements developed across the colony, settlers were not static. They travelled everywhere. 'What a migratory existence,' exclaimed George Stringer as he left Hébuterne one day in March 1917, 'but extraordinary how one settles down & how one's servants fix one up so quickly'.[98] ➲ 34

Sunday 4 April 1915 **11**

From Grant Taylor's diary: 'We left the Château at 7:30 PM and arrived at Dickebusch at about 10 PM. The men got quite good billets, but we had a beastly place to go into. The house itself was all right but the people were I think pro-German. They made things frightfully uncomfortable'.[99] Ralph Hamilton laid the same charge in October after crossing from Loos to Watou, before going on to voice some general observations. 'The people of the farm are, of course, pro-German. I have no doubt they would betray us if they got half a chance . . . I am depressed beyond words at being back in this vile country: I hate the Belgians and Belgium. We are billeted in a filthy farm . . . It is like all the farms in Flanders, only a little worse . . . more flies to the square inch than any other place I have yet met; it is also dirtier and the children more noisy. Altogether, a more offensive place could not have been found for a rest camp in all Europe'.[100]

Suspicions of pro-German sentiment seem to have faded a few months after the Salient's foundation, maybe because the press highlighted enemy atrocities in Belgium, maybe because residence altered opinion. In addition diarists and correspondents were, on the whole, less curious about Belgium than France. They paid scant attention to cultural differences between Walloons and Flems, for instance. Perhaps this was because, even if settled early, the Salient and its environs comprised only a small part of Befland, perhaps because by 1916 comparatively few natives remained in the area, and perhaps because of language difficulties. Craig Gibson suggests that settlers picked up French and Flemish readily enough,[101] though it's hard to imagine that for the majority this got much further than a menu of fixed phrases, or that there was anything like equivalence in language acquisition. Beflanders could buy booklets like Frank Scudamore's *Parley Voo – Practical French Phrases and How to Pronounce Them, for Daily Use by British Soldiers* (1915) or get French phrasebooks free with packets of cigarettes, but nothing similar seems to have existed for Gaumais or Picard (spoken in Wallonia) or Tussentaal (colloquial Flemish, one of several varieties of Belgian Dutch). Nor does there seem to have been any provision organized by voluntary associations – nothing like the French classes for newly arrived immigrants put on by Jessie Wilson at Harfleur's YMCA hut, for instance.[102]

Nevertheless, for whatever reason, some continued to express a general dislike of Belgium and its inhabitants. 'This is a very flat country and my first impressions are that the farms here are dirty and the people ignorant,' complained Sidney Appleyard.[103] 'We are delighted to be in France again,' wrote Hamilton in spring 1916. 'The change from Belgium is very great. The roads and farms are so much cleaner and better looked after, and the people nothing like so repulsive'.[104] Ronald Schweder was more nuanced, though like Hamilton and Appleyard appalled by dirt. That August, at Hill 63 near Messines Ridge, he stayed in a farmhouse fifty yards or so from the guns. Hardly a secure location, he wrote. Moreover, the owners were still in residence and the whole building stank to high heaven. During the advance to victory he passed through Gheluvelt, east of Ypres along the Menin Road, and stayed at a peasant smallholding. The only remaining inhabitant was an eighteen-year-old girl – attractive, but in need of a good wash.[105] On the other hand George Stringer noticed the resilience displayed by Belgian women when, soon after arriving at Wippenhoek near Poperinghe in June 1916, he went scouting for a likely gun position outside the village. One field seemed suitable, though another battery five hundred yards to the rear had been inundated with shells. As he rode by three more came over in quick succession. Nearby an old woman was milking cows in a field. One shell dropped a hundred yards behind her, but she didn't flinch and just went on milking. Stringer panicked, put spurs to his horse, galloped away and glanced back over his shoulder: there was the cow chewing the cud and there was the woman quietly milking.[106] In October Herbert Leland surveyed the Salient's human geography and, like Stringer, commented on the fortitude of the natives: 'The towns and villages around here are in a deplorable state. All ruins. It is extraordinary how some of the old inhabitants stick to what remains. You see the old people working away in the fields ploughing and weeding, taking absolutely no heed of the bursting shells. Some of them have set up little shanties and sell things to the soldiers'.[107] ➲ 16

12 Thursday 15 April 1915

George Stringer picked spring flowers at the Lindenhoek crossroads near Kemmel in Flanders to send to his brother.[108] At Givenchy-lès-la-Bassée Irish guardsmen were busy transforming a midden at 'The Keep', a strongpoint, into an Italian-style garden. Bulbs, box plants and other shrubs looted from a nearby cemetery traced out the shapes of regimental badges.[109] Next March Ronald Schweder walked on carpets of primroses and wild violets around Aveluy Wood on the Somme.[110] In May Garnet Durham itemized spring flora on Ypres' ramparts. 'I am writing this on the windowsill of our "house", the window being no more'. Shells came over in pairs, but as the field outside was sodden most of them failed to explode. 'I will act as spotter whilst writing (two 120 y[ar]ds in front). We have a nice garden – lilacs in bloom, and cherries, quite large but not ripe. (Shrapnel 200 y[ar]ds behind. Put on tin lid [steel helmet])'.[111]

Spring came late in 1917, and very cold. Zone flora also had to deal with the effects of prior human activity, especially in southern Befland: gassed earth, polluted streams, root systems torn by shelling, bulbs trampled by hooves and feet or buried under collapsed masonry. Stringer and Herbert Leland on the Somme, March and May: 'At B[ucquoy] I was struggling over heaps of stones, bricks, etc., and suddenly felt myself held up by – a mass of snowdrops. It really was the most pathetic thing I have ever experienced. My groom, who was following me closely, absolutely wept, when I drew his attention to them, and I had a big lump in my throat myself. We did not gather them as it seemed like sacrilege. The wee white flowers sticking up and out of the chaos and desolation . . . Rank grass is showing up between the shell holes, but as these very nearly touch one another there is a very scant supply . . . what trees are left are coming into leaf, and here and there a cherry tree is in full blossom, but they are few and far between'.[112] On 22 March Stringer walked through Sailly-au-Bois. Heavy snow was falling. Virtually nothing was left of the wood or the village, but as he trudged along he spied bluebells, lamb's tails and primroses forcing their way up through the mould, the snow drifts and the debris. On 24 May he gathered blue iris in La Bassée district.[113] A few days before James Williams, breaking stones for road metal west of Arras, went for a walk through Aubigny-en-Artois and on to Béthune. 'Country simply lovely. Fruit trees growing[,] crops etc. all in full swing. Now it looks glorious after so much snow and slush. The guns were going very heavy away in the distance with several observation balloons in the air'.[114]

Schweder described flowers and gardens near Bailleul. Daffodils blossomed among the ruins of an abandoned house. One clump had pushed its way up through a rusty sewing machine and a baby's cot. He left these alone but took the flowers. No one else had picked them, he thought, because they were too close to no man's land. He'd even started his own private garden outside his dugout, though he feared that his trees (presumably looted) wouldn't survive, having been transplanted at the wrong time of the year. Growth amidst devastation caught his eye again the following spring on the silent uplands around St Quentin, east of Bapaume – bulbs sprouting in the gardens of shattered cottages, green box enclosing heaps of rubbish, roadside hedges putting out vigorous new shoots.[115] ➲ 47

Monday 26 April 1915   13

On a field somewhere east of Étaples Garnet Durham kicked a ball around with a troop of French Zouaves, before long-range shelling cleared the pitch.[116]

In or out of the zone other ranks played football, early twentieth-century Britain's working-class sport *par excellence*. Two years later Robert Cude recorded details of fixtures played near Boëseghem on the Flanders-La Bassée district border, about two and a half miles north of Aire-sur-la-Lys, one of many diary entries about the game. The cold March days passed one another in quick succession, and to help while away the time, and perhaps keep other ranks fit and busy, divisional staff officers organized a championship. The Buffs (Cude's regiment, the Royal East Kents) beat the Queen's and the West Kents and also saw off teams from the fifty-third and fifty-fifth brigades. The twelfth Middlesex battalion went down 2-0 but after that their luck ran out; they lost 1-3 to the eighth Sussex and then 0-4 to the Surreys in the semi-final. Rain and sleeting snow marred the match – 'Not bad though and Surreys easily deserve their win, hav[ing] several pros playing for them'.[117]

Cude doesn't mention the cockfights that went on a few miles south in Béthune's mining villages. Perhaps he never came across them, but other settlers did. GHQ issued banning orders in 1916, to no avail,[118] though it seems to have had more success in stopping other blood sports. In January 1916 Ronald Schweder and fellow officers rode out on a paper chase along the coastal plain around Cayeux-sur-Mer, a substitute for a day's hunting. They were out again in February.[119] A year earlier at St Marie Cappel, just east of Poperinghe, George Stringer came across a stray dog branded 'M' on the inner fold of the ear, doubtless, he speculated, from one packs started by settlers as the Old Army fanned out from the entrepôts. *Défense de Chasser* was a common inscription in the landscape, he continued, even though GHQ had forbidden hunting time and again,[120] though the inscription, of course, was probably intended to deter natives as well as settlers.

Officers imported the hunt in November 1914 when Befland's eastern borders began to stabilize.[121] It's not clear when, or even if, fox hunting died out in Flanders, or indeed elsewhere in the colony, but Stringer's remarks indicate that senior officers found it hard to suppress. Either way hunting was a minority activity. Even if other ranks could afford it – highly improbable – riding to hounds was the preserve of gentlefolk, a social category difficult to define but one that certainly excluded farm labourers and proletarians. Privates and NCOs might be found at other equestrian events, however, either as spectators or subordinate participants; drivers and grooms. Schweder took part in a divisional horse show near Bailleul in May 1917, a three-day competition with artillery turnouts watched by hundreds of settlers – 'the war had to look after itself'. He mentioned two more shows in 1918, both in places apparently unaffected by the Ludendorff Offensive and the drive to victory; St Quentin on the Somme and Foche Farm in the Salient. He played polo too, on the Somme plateau after the German withdrawal to the Hindenburg line and again in June 1918, just before the Foche Farm horse show. Fortunately he managed to stay in the saddle. Tumbling on to the dry, compacted ground, he wrote to his wife, would have been no fun at all.[122] ➲ 21

Monday 3 May 1915 14

'Lovely morning. Marched all party to docks for days [sic] work. Had a look round lovely sands. Tide out. Saw women shrimping'. A week earlier: 'Here with 60 men. Disused yard canvas village. Slept well. Started work on yard. Went on sea wall. Finished noon. In afternoon went into market for shrimps. Loaded ammunition at night. Finished 1 a.m. (complimented)'. 12 June: 'Rue de Cordenes. Boulogne. Better day, very uneventful. To Le Portel in evening. Rather dull. Procession of boys chanting. Fisherwomen buying candles'. 2 October: 'Turned out 11 [o'clock] to H.Q 12 [o'clock]. To other side of Le Portel in afternoon. Lovely Autumn, to market place full of Autumn French flowers. Saw Wyatt and later Lindrop in evening. Waited for troopers & turned in at 5.35 am'. 11 October: 'Lovely day. On sands in morning. Hammock in afternoon. Piper playing on Napoleon's rampart, I can't alas sense history. More men on leave again. Picked up a 5 fr note'.[123]

These terse, vividly impressionistic diary entries – there are one or two more like them – are the only record we have of Captain Newman's life as a dock administrator, probably an MLO, at Boulogne. He was sent there in April after falling ill in the Salient. In November he left for Rouen, later on he moved to Étaples, and then we lose track of him for good. But from these few fragments one glimpses a man diffident, introspective, reserved; damaged perhaps by what he'd experienced in the Salient, quietly ironic and self-deprecating ('I can't alas sense history'), sensitive to fleeting moments (autumn flowers in the marketplace) and accommodating enough when it came to the performance of his duties but weary of army life. With a little imagination we can see him standing on the quayside, slightly apart and self-absorbed, indifferent to the shouting and the imprecations, superintending the disembarkation of Robert Cude and his companions as, disgruntled and resentful, they stepped off the transport ship into Befland in the early hours of 28 April. They marched across town and reached a large camp at three in the morning. It was hard to sleep under the flapping canvas tents and there was little respite. At two in the afternoon, or 14.00 hours (Cude was just getting used to continental time), they were dragged out of the camp and marched back along much of the route they'd just traversed. 'Am not struck with the general appearance of the town,' he wrote, 'in fact, on first impression I think it is a filthy hole'.[124]

Aside from a brief moment during the September Panic when stores were moved to St Nazaire [4] Boulogne, along with its suburb Outreau and the little fishing village of Le Portel across the river and a couple of miles up the coast the small town of Wimereux, was from 1914 to 1918 one of Befland's main entrepôts. The docks also acted as a base depot and regulating station for Flanders and La Bassée district. As siege warfare intensified enormous quantities of imported wargear piled up on and around the quaysides prior to being loaded onto railway wagons destined for Béthune and Hazebrouck. In addition 'irregular' trains carrying miscellaneous equipment left the yards at the rate of four a day, though the French refused Beflanders permission to land petrol at the docks, perhaps because they were too close to the town.[125]

Late 1916 witnessed a further extension of the settler presence. By then quarries in Jersey and Cornwall were quite unable to meet the Somme's voracious appetite for road stone. Because material cut from pits near Corbie wasn't deemed good enough, Beflanders took over and vastly expanded those at Marquise, a village just outside Wimereux. 'Coloured' labourers and prisoners of war worked the quarries. Meanwhile back in Wimereux settlers and French *camoufleurs* established a factory attached to the local 'Special Works Park'. Shortly afterwards, at Pont-de-Briques, a little south of Outreau, a large group of army laundries started operating.[126] In Boulogne itself a degreasing plant extracted glycerine from food waste gathered from all over Befland; approximately 1,500 tons in 1917, sufficient to provide propellant for 15,000,000 shells. Far less was produced in 1918, only 870 tons. 'This drop may largely be accounted for by the decrease in the meat ration and the substitution of sausages and rabbits', noted the War Office's statisticians.[127]

But the town's chief business was the movement, repair and sustenance of the body. Aside from processing successive waves of immigrants and dealing with cross-Channel leave boats, Boulogne also absorbed much of the enormous backwash of injured and maimed settlers, including all those returning from Flanders and La Bassée district. By 1918 eleven hospitals were dotted in and around Boulogne and Wimereux – eight for whites, two for Indians and one for 'coloured' labourers – as well as two convalescent camps, each housing 2,000–5,000 inmates. Those who couldn't be treated locally were shipped to Dover and Folkestone. 129 ambulances driven by women volunteers ferried them from trains to the quaysides managed by administrators like Newman. The town housed an army cookery school. Onshore cold storage units and a vessel anchored permanently in the harbour handled the contents of refrigerator ships bringing meat from the Americas and the Antipodes. Dumps, depots, slaughterhouses and bakeries fed northern Befland's settler population. In 1918 Boulogne's 'daily feeding strength' (the number of settlers supplied from its warehouses every twenty-four hours) exceeded 670,000. Between January and November army bakeries at Boulogne and Outreau produced nearly twenty-two million pounds of bread. All porterage in the various dumps and depots was done by 'coloured' labourers and 'category B' whites (those too old or unfit for life in the zone), most of the paperwork and food preparation by the many hundreds of women volunteers coming from the United Kingdom.[128] Louise Downer was one of them. From October 1917 till June 1919 she worked as a dockside weigh clerk and lived – uncomfortably – in a large camp outside the town. 'The huts for sleeping in had about twenty four beds in & was warmed by a heated stove etc.,' she wrote in a little seven-page memoir. 'Each hut also had a number of wash places. (Icy cold & where one had to break the ice in winter before we could wash our face etc)'.[129] ➲ 22

Wednesday 12 May 1915   **15**

Grant Taylor at Hill 60 [42] during Second Ypres: 'Quiet again. I think the Huns must have taken all their big guns away. We haven't heard a single "krump" for the whole five days. The men in the snipers' houses get rather a rotten time. 12 men and four N.C.O.s (4 posts) are put among the ruins. The furthest advance post is only about 30 y[ar]ds from the mound. All round the house lay dead men, Canadians I think, and the hot weather has made them stink abominably. These men stay out for 24 hours, at the end of which time they are relieved . . . I visited them every night. So did Laird. It wasn't particularly cheering, crawling among the ruins and lying flat on one's stomach whenever a light went up anywhere near. Relieved later by the Royals. The march back to the huts was topping. The fresh smell of the fields was very welcome, and we heard a nightingale'. A week later he moved to a new position. 'The whole brigade waited until dark in a field just outside Ypres. The march through the town was most interesting – and exciting! . . . The cathedral tower still stands although it is riddled with gaping holes. Close by two 17 [inch] shells have opened up a great vault. The Cloth-Hall Tower has lost two of its pinnacles. All the houses round the square are razed to the ground. Dead horses lie about and the deathly stillness is only broken by the tramp of the companies of awe-stricken men and the falling of ruined houses. The Menin gate has received a direct hit from a 17 [inch]. Nothing remains of the gate itself . . . Just beyond the gate these huge shells have torn up a cemetery exposing coffins and decayed bodies. The smell is terrible'.[130] George Stringer was also in the Salient that spring. Modifying trench walls or parapets often mean inadvertently exhuming corpses. He remembered pulling a bayonet free of a rotting body. The awful smell stuck to his hands for days afterwards.[131]

Ypres and the Salient stank because both were sites of continuous settlement – thousands of zone dwellers crammed into trenches, ruins and dugouts – and virtually continuous conflict. 'How I hate guns, horses and human beings,' raged Ronald Schweder when he arrived there in 1915, out here they all stank abominably, and soon he would too.[132] John Bullock, the narrative voice in Henry Williamson's *A Patriot's Progress,* sniffed 'iodoform and gangrenous whiffs' drifting in through the windows as he travelled on an ambulance train west from Poperinghe in 1917.[133] Geography and climate also played a part. Flanders and La Bassée district, waterlogged and low-lying, generated and preserved rank vapours. Herbert Leland noted the 'unsavoury smell' emanating from the canals,[134] Stringer the welcome relief offered when a thunderstorm broke near Béthune one evening in May 1917. To the south guns rumbled away, flickering and flashing onto the gloomy skies. All around him heavy raindrops pattered on the ground, masking the stink of war and releasing sweet smells from the damp earth.[135] When the siege broke in 1918 other zone locations were, intermittently, less noxious. In August Schweder moved into the empty uplands around Bapaume – healthy, clean air and none of the fetid stench of the Salient.[136] Three months later Lieutenant Capron entered Sebourg village, forty miles east of Arras and free of 'nauseous smells', though he did remark on the odd dusty smell of smashed up bricks and cement when passing through the ruins of Quéant and Pronville in September.[137]

What couldn't be avoided anywhere was the smell of wargear and human excrement. Latrines situated close to cookhouses in the back areas made eating intolerable. 'Camp sewage . . . is richer in organic material than town sewage and frequently contains an excess of fat', noted MacPherson in the official history series. Lavatories built in summer might be too far from the compounds and become muddy and slippery in winter, 'with the inevitable result that fouling took place'. Further difficulties arose because sanitary sections exhibited a kind of craft culture: 'each . . . preferred its own system of carrying out sanitary measures, and its successor in the area was apt to discard some of the work of its predecessor'. Digging latrine pits – two and a half feet long, six wide and twelve deep – was nigh on impossible in eastern Flanders and La Bassée district's border zones because the water table was too high. Even where they could be dug the work might be interpreted 'as an offensive measure' and attract mortar or machine-gun fire. In any event many trench dwellers avoided the pits – snipers targeted entrances and exits – and shied away from defecating in specially designed latrine buckets, believing, rightly, that they could get scabies if they used them. Instead they improvised lavatories from biscuit tins, cresol drums and four-gallon petrol cans and flung their contents into flyblown shell-holes during the night. Where excreta couldn't be buried it was burned.[138] The stench from thousands of 'Bailleul incinerators' [67] drifted across the colony.

Wargear had its own special savour. Ralph Hamilton, caught out by an artillery bombardment at Dickebusch in the Salient one day in November 1915, was engulfed in 'an inky darkness that stank horribly of bitter fumes'.[139] Twelve months later Charles Carrington experienced the sights and odours of Mametz Wood on the Somme. 'Every yard of ground had been ploughed up by shellfire and was tainted with high explosive, so that a chemical reek pervaded the air. The smell of burnt and poisoned mud . . . was with us for months on end, and through it one could distinguish a more biotic flavour – the stink of corrupting human flesh'.[140] At Vimy Ridge in March 1918 Richard Foot commented on the 'smell of cordite fumes blown back from the barrel' when his gun teams opened the breech blocks to reload.[141] The previous summer Schweder described a rough night at St Jean in the Salient.

Everyone was in gas helmets from eleven until four in the morning – sore eyes and headaches, thousands of gas projectiles for miles in every direction and no wind to disperse the fumes. The whole area stank.[142]

Gas exhibited a range of odours. Phosgene made cigarettes taste and smell of rotten eggs. Lachrymatories reeked of ammonia, sulphur and bad apples. The smell lingered for days. Horses hated it.[143] The slightly pungent, mustard-like odour of dichlor-ethyl-sulphide was 'readily perceptible' on first entering a shelled area, remembered MacPherson. Settlers used chloride of lime – no less pungent – to decontaminate affected landscapes.[144]

Colour and sound are all around us. We can see red crosses, brown uniforms and green flares, pay attention to the hue of polluted skies and torn earth, translate the noise of towns and traffic into the clamour and shouts of entrepôts and back-area bases. Distant thunder and low-flying aircraft remind us of the rumble and scream of shellfire. Even the feel of Befland might, to some extent, be revived. We can touch worn leather harness straps, old steel and rusty barbed wire, try on heavy trench coats, handle a rifle, or a shovel, or a bayonet. Smell is different. Like sound, texture and the colour of things smell is a product of specific cultures and modes of production, but it is also fleeting. When one goes so does the other. Unlike colours, odours don't travel through time. Though the stench of rotting corpses in Befland was probably much the same as it is Gaza, Iraq or Afghanistan, transforming diet, hygiene, agriculture, production processes and the built environment changes the tang of people and things. Unlike sound and texture smell cannot easily be reimagined, whether by attention to the material world or through imitative acts. We cannot rebreathe the complex smells given off by trenches, dugouts, ammunition depots, native billets and zone villages, and this loss greatly diminishes our ability to recover the past. Smell is also different because it is the most suggestive of the senses, intimately bound up with moments of experience. In John Brophy's short story 'The Soldier's Nostrils' (1931), an ex-Beflander opens his pantry door and is immediately overwhelmed. The smell of food triggers a rush of associations: the peculiar greasy odour of bully beef, the gagging stench of rotting corpses, the taint of old gas which has drifted into shell holes and the thick pungency of damp trench coats drying beside field kitchen stoves.[145] The language of smell is a poor substitute for the extraordinarily evocative power of smell itself, but it is all we have. ➲ 23

Thursday 13 May 1915 **16**

'It was funny to see the boys sitting on the footplate while the train was moving, and to see the French peasants calling for souvenirs of bully beef and biscuits'.[146] Sidney Appleyard made this note while journeying from Rouen to Flanders. George Stringer had the same experience on the same line in September the following year. As the train rocked slowly along, moving at little more than walking pace, hordes of children ran up to his carriage yelling for food. France is overwhelmed with widows, he wrote, crowds of them in every village and town. Those near the lines of communication practically live on British army rations. The widows teach their children to run forward shouting for bully beef, biscuits or loose change.[147]

Interactions between settlers and natives can be classified as transactional, social or affective, though the boundary between each is, of course, often blurred. In the entrepôts and back areas, or when travelling across Befland, transactional interactions might involve gift exchanges, begging (Appleyard and Stringer) or straightforward hiring, buying and selling in billets, farms, shops and markets, or in estaminets and stalls clustered around depots and railway stations strung out along the lines of communication. Ronald Schweder bargained his way across the colony on a lateral journey from the Somme to Flanders in summer 1916: plenty of opportunities to buy food and drink; a shopping trip to Audruicq (the site of a large regulating station), and meals in native houses (Schweder took advantage of his French). He arrived in Belgium on 21 July and set up wagon lines at a farm in which nine nuns had taken refuge – all ancient and hideous, he noted, so there wouldn't be any trouble with his gun crews, but they might be persuaded to do his washing.[148]

Trade or gift giving generally invited little comment, except when things changed or something unusual caught the recording eye. In 1933 Frank Richards remembered passing through Rouen in August 1914, and the contrast with later years. 'In those early days British soldiers could get anything they wanted and were welcomed everywhere, but as the War progressed they were only welcomed if they had plenty of money to spend, and even then they were made to pay through the nose for everything they bought'.[149] Late in October 1916 Eachus carefully noted how he'd dodged regulations to help out a native colleague who'd sent three francs asking for some English cigarettes and tobacco. It turned out that regulations forbade such interactions, but a sympathetic junior officer arranged for the items to be delivered by a dispatch rider. Next day he grumbled about the vagaries of French wartime currency. Locally printed chits were beginning to displace coins. A fifty centime note marked *Ville d'Abbeville* couldn't be spent outside the town's environs. The same went for one marked *Chambre de Commerce d'Amiens*.[150] Three months later Schweder regaled his wife with details of a trading incident at Cap Gris Nez, north of Boulogne. A stout old lady walked twenty-two kilometres carrying a large bundle of English newspapers to sell to resident Beflanders. Schweder was so impressed that he brought up most of her stock and gave her a flask of port to ease the journey back.[151]

Innumerable small-scale transactions like these punctuated everyday life behind the zone, but since the back areas were sites of permanent settlement, large-scale transactions also obtained, but not without tensions. In August 1914 the French tried to impose tariffs on supplies landed at the entrepôts, though the attempt was soon abandoned. Thereafter, wherever possible, the colony's procurement agencies followed a policy of import substitution. This brought new problems. Between 1914 and 1918 Befland's medical and veterinary administrations purchased local food and forage to the value of some 162 million francs, but despite continual protests some communes and municipalities successfully levied the *octroi*, an internal customs duty, on most of this produce as it moved across the colony.[152] The means of transport – railways – were also at issue. Agreements made prior to August 1914 specified that Beflanders would be provided with native rolling stock as requested, but the arrangement soon frayed. In April 1915 Paris told GHQ that it would no longer supply the colony in full. London retaliated by announcing the termination of all payments to French railway companies until the end of the War. Next February, when Beflanders were short of 22,500 wagons, the French blankly refused to offer any at all. Nine months later Paris abruptly cancelled the pre-War agreement. Thereafter Geddes set about expanding the colony's network on his own initiative [3] while the Railway Accounts Office declined payment of mountains of bills submitted by the French and diligently filed them away until after the War, though some disbursements were made to civilians caught up in the crossfire.[153] ➲ 20

Thursday 3 June 1915   17

From J. N. Peterson's letter to his girlfriend in Newcastle: 'Somewhere in France ... Dear little friend ... you will know there has been a great demand for everything that is needed in warfare and amongst them horses is one. Well we could not get sufficient horses and so we have mules 6 in each waggon & I drive the lead pairs, and of course every man must look after his own mules and harness so you will see we have plenty to do. We do not go right into the firing line but only so far, about 6 miles behind it, and then hand the ammunition over to another column (who then take it right up to those guns you used to see at Brighton Grove) and then we come back and get another load ready for the next time'.[154]

Shortages of horses obtained everywhere across the colony, in part because like Peterson's unit the British Remount Commission couldn't always get what it wanted. English Coach horses, best for light-draught work (pulling an omnibus, for example) could trot steadily on hard roads at eight miles an hour, but even before 1914 they were being displaced by motor vehicles. Substitutes crossed from Shires, Clydesdales and Hackneys didn't have the same staying power and were more likely to die or fall ill once in Befland. As a rule, noted one veterinary officer, 'the heavier the class the heavier the mortality'. Cavalry class survived best, followed by artillery, heavy, and poorest of all the extra-heavy class.[155] The Commission requisitioned heavy-draught horses from the countryside (though East-Anglian farmers at least sometimes tried to conceal their animals[156]) and sent them to remount depots in southern England before issue to Befland, but the Army hadn't used them much before 1914 and so the problems weren't foreseen. Shires and Clydesdales were specialized breeds, added the officer, 'leading a relatively pampered life and therefore of a delicate constitution'. As a rule they were 'bred and maintained under localised tranquil conditions of environment and work' and abundantly fed compared with lighter breeds. Colonel Oliver, the Commission's Deputy Director of Veterinary Services, thought that these circumstances 'rather than any inherent weakness of constitution' caused their 'remarkable susceptibility' to respiratory disease.[157]

In 1915 a committee met in London to mull over the pros and cons of sending them to Befland. The vets were against. They argued that Shires and Clydesdales weren't useful because they were inclined to disease, consumed too much forage and water and couldn't stand forced marches. On the other hand, a pair did the work of four mules. The young and the old didn't do well and that limited the age range best suited for enlistment. Nevertheless, 'for an intermittent series of severe muscular efforts age is an advantage rather than an impediment, but prolonged continuous exposure to wet cold weather and unfavourable conditions of management were better borne and more quickly recovered from, by the younger animals'. By late 1915 mortality was more or less under control and thereafter siege warfare made the Shire's enormous hauling capacity useful. But as the vets predicted many died of pneumonia once in the colony, and if they didn't die their hairy feet and lymphatic constitution, when combined with Befland's mud and damp, made them prone to eczematous and necrotic foot and leg diseases.[158] Perhaps for that reason they were always in a minority; less than twenty per cent of the colony's horse population in October 1917.[159] ➲ 24

18   Sunday 1 August 1915

6,400 women worked for the army abroad, mostly in Befland. Towards the end of the year settler population stood at just over 662,000, concentrated in the entrepôts, along the lines of communication and in the zone now beginning to crystallize around Ypres and La Bassée district (First and Second Armies – volunteers and Old Army survivors).[160]

The Salient contracted in April-May (Second Ypres) but the zone, forty miles long by September, now reached down to Armentières and Loos. A major extension occurred in summer when the newly formed Third Army incorporated most of the Somme and the rest of La Bassée district into Befland. In three weeks 72,000 immigrants arrived on the Somme. By December the zone stretched about ten miles north of the Salient and eighty miles to its south. Casualties totalled 892,765,[161] which means either that the population declined, or that some were wounded or fell ill more than once, or that the 'throughput' population was larger than the total at the year's end, or that some combination of the three obtained. ⊃ 27

Sunday 12 September 1915   **19**

An entry in Private Rogers' diary after his twelve-mile overnight trek along the northern bank of the River Somme from Corbie to Suzanne, not far from the eastern border village of Bray-sur-Somme: 'It was a hard march over ploughed fields, ditches, hedges etc. always keeping a hill to our left as we were quite near to the firing line. The star shells looked quite nice as they floated slowly along and lighted up the country for a mile or so'.[162]

Rogers was among the first to come into the Somme, just after its official incorporation into Befland in July 1915. Despite the fact that General Allenby's Third Army had been formed that month specifically to colonize the area, large-scale immigration didn't really start until later in the year – it took time to ship the tens of thousands of Allenby's New Army settlers across the Channel. Thousands more joined them after the creation of Rawlinson's Fourth Army in February 1916. These met still more incomers – the thousands detached from the First Army and migrating southwards from the Salient.[163] But prior to summer 1915 the Somme was still French territory. In 1932 James Edmonds remembered that unlike Flanders the Somme had almost no isolated farmsteads. The landscape reminded him of Salisbury Plain, but 'on a larger scale [and] with the difference that the whole of it was richly cultivated'. There were also several large woods scattered about. Nevertheless, he found the Somme rather neglected. Many houses were 'of poor construction' and transport networks weak – few railways and only a single main road, the Amiens-Albert-Bapaume highway. Albert, the region's only large town apart from Amiens, and further to the west Abbeville, had just eleven hundred houses and a population of no more than 6,700.[164]

Though he didn't mention it in his diary Rogers' walk from Corbie to Suzanne took him along Befland's newly established southern border. In its meandering twenty-mile course west from Bray-sur-Somme to Amiens the River Somme cut a two-hundred foot deep valley, half to three-quarters of a mile wide, in the great upland plain which, to the north, slopes down to La Bassée district at Arras, thirty-five miles from Amiens. In the early twentieth century marshes, peat bogs and water meadows, the latter submerged in winter, fanned out on each side of the river. The valley's southern slopes, on the French side of the border, climbed away gently, but the northern slopes, those traversed by Rogers, rose steeply, and were broken by several small valleys running north-south; 'the spurs of them seeming to be buttresses to the plain', remembered Edmonds.[165] The largest of these was gouged out by the Somme's main tributary, the Ancre, twenty to thirty feet wide and three to four feet deep. After passing through Albert the Ancre wandered six miles southwest to join the Somme at Corbie. North of Albert it turned slowly eastwards and petered out after another six miles or so just over the border at Miraumont village. Numerous minor sub-valleys branched to the west, the largest towards Fricourt and Beaumont Hamel.

Rising from the Somme's steep banks around Bray and Suzanne a series of ridges undulated away northwards and formed the edge of a plateau running to the east. Of land to the west and below the plateau – after mid 1915 the area occupied by Beflanders – Edmonds noted that 'troops of all arms could move everywhere over it, except in the woods (which outside the rides had thick undergrowth) and across the Somme and Ancre flats, where no causeways and bridges existed'.[166] The plateau, about three hundred feet above the land below, and the western slopes of the ridges, were dotted with fortified villages and redoubts settled by the enemy: Fricourt, Contalmaison, La Boisselle, Guillemont, Longueval, Bazentin, Pozières and Thiepval. At Thiepval Ridge the land dipped into the Ancre Valley before rising again to meet another ridge, this one running northwest to Serre and Beaumont Hamel (heavily fortified) and, further over the border, southeast to Bapaume. Until summer 1916 the west and south-western facing slopes of all these ridges marked the Somme's eastern border, but even in 1915 work was in progress to annex them. A few hundred miners had arrived a month before Rogers to dig under Redan Ridge (west of Serre), Hawthorn Ridge (opposite Beaumont Hamel), La Boisselle, and 'The Tambour' (opposite Fricourt redoubt).[167] As more labour flooded in and work intensified the system of tunnels and chambers under this seven-mile stretch of the border became ever more elaborate. When the vast stocks of explosives buried under the ridges were blown at half past seven in the morning on 1 July 1916 – the most powerful man-made detonations prior to the Messines Ridge explosions of June 1917 – the landscape changed forever.

But that was all in the future. The Somme that Rogers entered in autumn 1915 was only just beginning to take shape in the settler imagination. Centred on Amiens, it ran twenty miles or so north-east to Albert and extended three or four miles north of the river. Later settlers talked about land out towards Doullens and Arras – respectively seventeen miles northwest and twenty miles north of Albert – as part of the Somme, but there were no hard-and-fast borders to this northern extension of the landscape of the mind. After the ridges were annexed in the second half of 1916 there was another expansion. When the Germans retreated to the Hindenburg Line in spring 1917 the entire eastern border shifted to include swaths of territory well past Bapaume and Péronne. Later still, when the settlers had gone and Befland disappeared, metaphor overwhelmed landscape. Like 'Passchendaele', 'The Somme' stopped being a place at all. Both morphed into reductive anthologies of the western-front experience or, to steal another phrase from John Goode, into 'parodic names which echo its petrification'.[168] ➲ 31

Monday 13 September 1915 **20**

Private Rogers' diary entry from his billet at Suzanne, a mile and a half from the Somme's eastern border. 'There were only a few inhabitants left but they charged exorbitant prices for everything'.[169] In January Frank Richards had noticed a solitary house standing right opposite a communication trench at the Bois-Grenier near Armentières. The old man who'd taken it over did a roaring trade selling beer and wine to settlers moving in and out of the line.[170] 'France is getting quite civilised,' wrote Ralph Hamilton on the 8th of that month, 'yesterday's *Daily Mail* and *Times* being brought round to the farms by an enterprising French boy, a halfpenny paper costing two-pence'.[171] This was at Staple in Flanders, about three miles west of Hazebrouck. South, in La Bassée district, native children walked up and down the front-line trenches selling newspapers to zone dwellers.[172]

That Rogers complained about high prices in the zone shouldn't surprise us. Natives were scarce close to the border and only the enterprising or the desperate would trade under shellfire. Lack of competition allowed them to push up prices. In addition, though stable enough during the siege years, supply chains were always at risk and might be very long. Estaminets could source some foodstuffs from whatever farms remained in the area – around Bray-sur-Somme farmers turned themselves into merchants to sell food and drink to Beflanders[173] – but coffee, tobacco beer and wine, or the ingredients needed to make them, would have to be imported from outside. Nevertheless for some the benefits outweighed the costs and risks. In Flanders, the same month that Rogers complained about prices on the Somme, Sidney Appleyard walked the two and a half miles from the St Eloi trenches to Dickebusch. 'It is surprising the number of people who remain in this village which is shelled heavily all the time – I noticed one old woman who must have been about 80 – but then they do a very good trade as most of us spend about 20 francs whenever we can get up there'.[174] Two years later Ronald Schweder visited a zone trader (she supplied food for the battery's mess) before dropping in to the officers' club at Bailleul. He was startled to find native entrepreneurs running army services. In January at nearby Dranoutre he came to a trading agreement with one of the few natives still in residence – seven francs a week for a log hut: a large living room, tables and chairs, curtains on the windows, a stove and four small bedrooms. Two servants took up residence with him to act as groom, cook and footman.[175]

Occasionally zone dwellers traded on their own account. A few days after the Armistice men in Schweder's artillery unit started renting horses to local farmers in return for supplies of fresh vegetables smuggled in from eastern Belgium (probably, in fact, from the Netherlands). They might also have been selling them: one Frenchman offered Schweder 2,000 francs for his charger.[176] In January 1919 Richard Foot, based just outside Cologne, quietly ignored the ban on civilian firearms; he allowed local gamekeepers to keep their shotguns in exchange for a weekly delivery of venison to his battery.[177] Three years earlier the Post Office Rifles' interpreter watched gunners dug into the deep gullies in La Bassée district's Notre Dame de Lorette Ridge selling rings made from discarded wargear,[178] but this kind of thing must have been unusual. Gunners living in the second and third transections [83] might stay in one place for months on end – those on Lorette Ridge had been there for nearly a year – not so peripatetic zone dwellers [49]. Infantrymen, stretcher bearers, working parties etc., moving in and out of the landscape, would have neither the time nor the means to establish manufacturing enterprises. In contrast Beflanders attached to base workshops crafted cigarette lighters and jewellery from cartridge cases. Some memorialized particular locations.[179]

Often the details of trading arrangements elude us. Who were those newsagent-entrepreneurs, for example? Who placed orders in Britain, organized shipments across the Channel and reception at the entrepôts? How was the old lady who walked twenty-two kilometres to Cap Gris Nez (almost certainly from Boulogne) supplied [16]? Who arranged distribution into Flanders and La Bassée district's trenches? Who provided the finance, loading dockets, clearance forms, passes, movement orders, etc., and how did child vendors manage to penetrate the DGT and FE lines? None of this could have happened without the formation of settler-native partnerships stretching from the zone to the portals and involving signallers, clerks, dockers, storemen, railway workers and wagoners in a complex series of illegal, or at least unofficial, transactions. And what of the Englishwoman mentioned by Robert Cude who, in 1917, ran a thriving teashop at Pernes six miles southwest of Béthune?[180] Who was she? Why was she there in the first place? How did she get her tea from Britain into Befland? Or Miss Boot, who by special permission of the French and British military authorities presided over a refreshment buffet at Doullens station?[181] All too frequently our sources fail just when we need them most. For a moment the dead beckon to us in life, and then recede back into the shadows.

Where there were no natives left zone dwellers resorted to looting, though once again resident gunners were better placed because they had more opportunity than peripatetics to ransack empty buildings. George Stringer recalled well-furnished billets and shelters at Lindenhoek (Flanders) in June 1915. At this early date dugouts were practically unheard of, at least for artillery turnouts. Looting expeditions into Kemmel village were common. Even though everyone knew that pilfering was a serious crime, the houses, stuffed full of useful gear and luxuries left behind by the fleeing natives, were too much of a temptation. Rumours abounded that the APM's men, under instructions from GHQ, were about to raid the batteries in order to put an end to it. Settlers became watchful and nervous, but the looting continued and no one came. He shuddered to think what would have happened had the police discovered the officers' lavatory seats, crockery, gilded mirrors, brass bedsteads and deep, billowing Belgian mattresses – and the neat, colourful flowerbeds surrounding the other ranks' huts shaped from plants lifted from the local gardens.[182]

Quite what would have happened to Stringer if he had been caught is unclear. Officially looting was a capital offence, but the regulation was obviously ignored. Fewer than 400 settlers were shot between 1914 and 1920, the vast majority for desertion.[183] In fact as early as 1915 Flanders' APMs and COs were turning a blind eye to theft from native premises or handing out merely nominal punishments.[184] At worst it's most likely Stringer and others would have been dispatched to less salubrious surroundings, a fate that very nearly befell Schweder at the end of the War. Tourcoing was 'bucking up,' he wrote to his wife in December 1918. Shops were opening and the street lights coming on at night. In another way it was all rather a nuisance. Returning natives wanted their homes back, and they were in for a shock. Some of the 'temporary gentlemen' were behaving like pigs and causing trouble; vandalizing houses requisitioned as messes (chopping firewood on the front-room carpets was a favourite trick), leaving fuel bills unpaid and generally making themselves objectionable. The natives must hate us, he said, and if this behaviour carried on everyone would be banished to the revolting farms scattered around in the district. Earlier that year he'd strolled along a stretch of hurriedly improvised trench near Mont des Cats. All the farms had been abandoned, but only recently. Everything – furniture, prams, sewing machines, etc. – had been left just as it was and was wide open to plunder.[185]

But with or without the threat of punishment all zone looters were constrained by secular convulsions within Befland. There were only two periods when well-stocked towns and villages lay open to them: late 1914 to mid 1915 (Befland's formation – Stringer's June 1915 experience) and spring to autumn 1918 (the Ludendorff Offensive and the drive to victory – Schweder at Mont des Cats and Tourcoing). In contrast during the siege years what was left of the built environment was picked clean by resident gunners and successive waves of immigrants. Peripatetics were therefore reduced to roaming the devastated areas for saleable commodities as and when opportunities arose. Brophy & Partridge record that settlers translated RAMC as 'Rob All My Comrades' because medics rifled the clothing of the dead and the wounded lying around in no man's land.[186] Clean-up teams toiling in abandoned battlefields were equally assiduous. William Orpen saw one busy on the Somme uplands in August 1917 after the German withdrawal to the Hindenburg Line: 'During the month or so they worked there, they dug up, identified and reburied thousands of bodies. Some could not be identified, and what was found on these in the way of money, knives, etc., was considered fair spoil for the burial party. Often, coming down Thiepval Hill in the evening, everything golden in the sunlight, one would come across a little group of men, sitting by the side of the battered Hill Road, counting out and dividing the spoils of the day'.[187] Herbert Leland and colleagues, also on the Somme uplands, specialized in excavating native ruins rather than rifling corpses. Over the course of two days in May 1917 they looted 10,000 francs from a ruined village near Bapaume. But it was hard work. The money was buried in cellars lying under tons of rubble which kept collapsing as they tunnelled in.[188] ➲ 29

21   Thursday 16 September 1915

In the afternoon, Ruth Durst, currently nursing at Le Touquet, went to see a tennis tournament just outside Étaples. On 27 May 1916 she'd watched a polo match and on the 28th the Royal Engineers sports' day. 30 May: swam in the morning, performed in a VAD concert in the evening. 'Crowds of people came . . . matrons and sisters from other hospitals and people from Étaples'. Afterwards they had a party in the tiny X-Ray department – 'found sandwiches and cherries and champagne provided by the MOs'. 8 June: a VAD tennis tournament. 22 July 1917, another tennis tournament: 'The MOs gave tea on the courts and there was a band and it was quite [a] gala. Hemphill was playing in the finals of the ladies singles but was beaten by the Massachusetts champion'.[189] Social life was much the same for Phyllis Goodliff, working a few miles up the coast at Boulogne's BRCS headquarters. 'I played tennis the other night & couldn't play at all at first but I expect I shall soon get into it again,' she wrote to her mother in March 1918. 'When you send my tennis shoes don't forget some "Blanco" & a few balls'. Four more extracts from Phyllis Goodliff's letters to her mother, sent during the Ludendorff Offensive and the advance to victory. 30 March: 'I have just been out to the market and bought a beautiful azalea, a pink one. We are so frightfully busy now that we have very little time for going out'. 4 April, after a concert: 'it wasn't half bad for the kind of men who gave it . . . Of course if they had pretended to be something wonderful we should have said it was rotten'. 9 August: 'We have had some ripping bathes lately. There has just been sufficient wind to make it rough enough to have some fun in'. 29 August, life in her third-floor apartment: 'the 6 people who occupy the rooms are always great pals together & have no end of a [?laugh]. Half the people in the house always wend their way up there at night as there is a soirée held every night in one of the rooms'.[190]

Back-area towns were sites of ease and privacy, not just for those who lived in them, like Ruth Durst and Phyllis Goodliff, but also for sick and wounded settlers evacuated from the zone, immigrants waiting in rest camps and travellers *en route* to and from the portals or from base to zone. In March 1915 Phyllis Goodliff attended a concert party given by the 29th division's 'Diamond Troupe'. 'They were simply splendid & all of them have been over the top [into no man's land]'.[191] 'It was a perfect day and lots of people were bathing', wrote Ruth Durst in August. 'Several patients from B[oulogne] were on the shore'. Two years later she watched a comic melodrama at Le Touquet's YMCA staged by machine gunners just out of the zone.[192] Autumn 1916 found Jessie Wilson convalescing in Étretat's Hotel de la Plage, worn out after months working at Harfleur's No.15 YMCA hut. 'All day long I lay on the shore watching the blue-coated red-tied Tommies amusing themselves throwing stones at other stones erected as targets'.[193] Those blue coats and red ties marked them out as seriously injured.

As the siege lengthened and colonization deepened hospitals and base units hired professional entertainers on long-term contracts and converted native buildings into cinemas. If a base moved entertainers often moved with it. Early in 1915 touring troupes arrived in Befland, the following year five complete repertory companies. These circulated around back-area settlements and travelled along the lines of communication to field hospitals, convalescent camps, regulating stations, dumps, depots and tented villages for contracted labourers – Chinese, Indian, West Indian, etc.[194] In August 1915 the Post Office Rifles were 'in reserve' at Labeuvrière in La Bassée district; warm, dry weather, drill and cricket, trips to Béthune, swimming in mine craters at Marles and Auchel, evening concerts in dappled orchards.[195] Nothing much came of 'firing line parties', however, unfit men gathered in troupes to tour the zone. Nine were formed in 1916 but within a year they had faded away, though a few single-handed entertainers lingered on.[196]

In addition to those supplied by the army (shows, tournaments) or created spontaneously by settlers (parties, shopping trips, solitary walks), voluntary associations provided geographical and temporal spaces for the exercise of ease and privacy. By 1918 there were around fifty YMCA centres in the colony's main towns and about 300 more along the lines of communication. Some 1,500 volunteers, mainly women, staffed them. Most centres were housed in large double or triple huts, most were open twenty-four hours a day and most had a canteen, a concert hall with a piano and gramophone, a games room and a classroom. All provided free cocoa, cheap food, tobacco and confectionery, though no alcohol. Most also had a chapel and quite room with free writing paper and newspapers. Salvation Army huts offered facilities similar to the YMCA's, less so Church Army huts: these were more overtly Christian – 800 with a staff of 2,000 by late 1918. The YMCA also functioned as a savings bank. Officers could get advances on post-dated cheques, other ranks were paid at unit level with special arrangements to draw cash at the entrepôts when travelling to the portals, but settlers attached to voluntary societies had to depend on Post Offices, Expeditionary Force Canteens or the YMCA for cash.[197]

Despite their ubiquity, or perhaps because of it, YMCA huts were not to everyone's taste. Robert Cude waxed indignant about high prices and the lack of alcohol [68], and Ronald Schweder couldn't bear the thought of them. A leave camp had been set up for officers just outside Boulogne, he wrote to his wife from La Bassée district in May 1917. 'I should imagine it will be awful, – full of Y.M.C.A.s, tinkling pianos, and parsons'.[198] Jessie Wilson was horrified by what she found when she took over as manageress of the Harfleur hut in August 1915; surly staff in grubby overalls, unruly customers, sawdust floors soaked in tea and cocoa slops, filthy crockery, mud everywhere, cigarettes, tobacco, cakes and soap heaped in disorder on sticky wooden counters.[199] ➲ 41

22   Tuesday 9 November 1915

'1 Ter[ritorial] Camp Rouen. Fair, pouring at night. On pass at 2 [o'clock] to Rouen. Visited Bonlecoeur [sic] Cathedral, soldiers in palace[,] tea American Bar, raining hard. Back by taxi to camp 8.40. Beautiful views from hill top. Pouring all night'. 16 November: 'No.1 Base. Fine. Camp in morning. Pass to Rouen afternoon. Jeanne d'Arc (Wed 30 mai 1431). Looked round town and saw where Jeanne was killed. Met Humphrys, had tea with him, walked round after tea, thick fog, back by tram. Moonlight at camp. To bed. Letter from Lill'.[200]

As well as functioning as a regulating station for the Third and Fourth Armies on the line of communication between Le Havre and Amiens, Rouen was a major colonial settlement in its own right. From 1915 onwards large quantities of ammunition were stored in and around the town and a few miles up the line at Grand Quevilly. In 1918 a local factory – one of three taken over by settlers (the others were at Calais and Wimereux) – was busy producing camouflage equipment. Between them the three factories employed one hundred Chinese labourers, 2,000 natives and 600 Beflanders. By then Rouen's supply personnel were sending out 1.3 million ration packs a day for settlers spread across southern Befland. Field butcheries set up shop in 1914.[201] On 1 July 1917 an anonymous diarist recorded that on the previous Sunday the town's army cooks had boiled 11,000 eggs. (Where did he pick up such curious information? Perhaps by gossiping with officers at the local golf club. He was still in Rouen, and familiar with the club, two weeks later: 'very handsome[,] spacious and in the pink of order – great sweeps of fair way – well kept putting greens – plenty of sport, and in a gorgeous scenic spot about four or five miles out of Rouen. A charming club house, plenty of members, the caddies much tidier than ours, all in becoming dark grey or black blouses'.[202]) Huts and tents spread across the hills and valleys outside the town housed infantrymen in transit to and from the zone, including those at No. 1 Territorial Camp where Captain Newman worked in between his visits to the Cathedral, the American Bar and Rouen's cafes. Other encampments housed black labourers. 'A small audience, composed largely of Jamaica Indians,' wrote the anonymous diarist after putting on a show in No. 2 Camp, 'very difficult to hold'.[203] Australian bakeries arrived in 1916 to supplement those already operated by British immigrants. Scattered around elsewhere were remount centres, mechanical repair depots, two veterinary hospitals (one for the Indian Army) and offices containing the records of all Befland's horses and mules.[204]

Like most large back-area towns, Rouen was also a medical hub. It had two big convalescent camps and fifteen hospitals; ten British, one each for Canadians, Australians and Indians, one for 'coloured' labourers and one staffed by the Scottish Red Cross. Only two were in permanent buildings. Many of southern Befland's wounded who survived battlefields, regimental aid posts, casualty clearing stations and the train journey from Amiens, eventually arrived at the railway station where ninety Scottish Red Cross ambulances distributed them to the hospitals.[205] Garnet Durham stayed in one after being shot in the spine in May 1915: 'the most disgraceful hospital I have seen yet'; dirty, incompetent and indifferent nurses; 'men with unhealed wounds sent out with pick and shovel on fatigues'.[206] ➲ 26

Sunday 14 November 1915   23

'I turned and started to go back, when suddenly I heard the ominous little bang, so faint that it is very hard to hear at all. Three seconds later I heard the shell coming – just a low murmur at first, gradually rising to a loud scream, just like an express train passing through a station without stopping. I flung myself down at the foot of "A" sub-section's pit and at the back of it. With a roar, it passed a few feet above my head and burst thirty yards away. The noise was horrible, and the ground shook like a person kicking a table'. The world seemed to end; then a crash, rushing wind and 'the sound of a thousand lashes being swished through the air' as great pieces of jagged metal flew about.

This was Ralph Hamilton's first experience of a near miss – 'nothing can be likened in any way that compares to the noise', he wrote.[207] The first shells that Lieutenant Capron saw (September 1916) appeared quite inoffensive, a burst of black smoke rising into the air followed by a jet of brown soil, suddenly thrown up and shaped like a cone, and finally a noise resembling tearing sailcloth. Things were otherwise after two years in the colony. 'A determined blotting out' was how he described incoming fire during an artillery duel near Arras in spring 1918. 'Faster and thicker whine down the shells[,] some well over, some fearfully upon us. The hideous energy, the dust and acrid fumy reek, the blast and fury of each down-rush makes us catch our breath . . . The ground heaves, and seems to sway'. Long-distance quick-release projectiles deceived the ears, he remembered. They arrived before the sound of their coming. Others deceived the eyes. A moment before earth shot up into the air the shell itself seemed to be visible above the commotion. Gas shells landed with a dull thump thud ('an unmistakable and very unwelcome sound'). They didn't explode, but would quietly release their poisonous fumes for hours at a time without anyone noticing.[208] Cowering twenty feet underground on the Somme in August 1916 Hamilton compared the noise of a sustained bombardment to 'the vibration of the screw of a ship intensified'.[209] A shell bursting in woodland, noted Richard Foot, 'sends a flight of splinters whizz-whizzing overhead, cutting branches and twigs and creating a much more frightening effect than if the same splinters were buzzing harmlessly through the air'.[210] Lost in the streets of Ypres one night in 1916 a padre found his way home by listening to 'the heavy thud of a "crump," (like some old and portly body falling through a too frail chair with a crash to the floor) . . . an unerring guide to the main square'.[211] Shells meant for other settlers hummed as they passed miles overhead, wrote Ronald Schweder from the Somme in March.[212] David Jones has us reaching for our spell checks as, two decades later, he struggled to characterize the sound and feel of a near miss. 'Out of the vortex, rifling the air it came – bright, brass-shod, Pandoran; with all-filling screaming the howling crescendo's up-piling snapt. The universal world, breath held, one half second, a bludgeoned stillness. The pent violence released a consummation of all burstings out; all sudden up-rendings and rivings-through – all taking-out of vents – all barrier breaking – all unmaking. Pernitric begetting – the dissolving and splitting of solid things'.[213]

Settlers deployed other lexical motifs when representing the din of shells leaving as apposed to entering Befland. Every night when the signal flares rose into the sky at about eight-thirty in the evening, wrote George Stringer from La Bassée district in May 1917, you could hear the settlers' shells 'screaming' overhead as they hurtled eastwards. In contrast the German response sounded like 'a deep chesty cough'.[214] French cannon whip-cracked as they fired. 'Not an easy noise to describe,' explained Foot, 'one has to have lived close in front of a 75 to know it'.[215] British sixty-pounders made an ear-splitting noise which gave you a headache, like being rapped over the head with a stick, complained Hamilton.[216] Capron remembered how eighteen-pounders 'spat out' their shells with a 'flash and slamming crack'. This was at Maing, forty miles southeast of Béthune and twelve days before the Armistice. In addition there were very many howitzers scattered to the rear, perhaps even one or two big dismounted naval guns. Their shells howled overhead, enclosing the battery in a 'roaring world'. Everyone agreed that open warfare was much noisier than trench warfare, when dugouts and gun pits muffled the cacophony.[217] Seven months previously Foot anxiously watched his gun crews at work on Vimy Ridge during the Ludendorff Offensive – 'flinging the heavy shell up the bore, ramming it home with a thud and a curse, slamming the breech on the cartridge with a clang, pulling the trigger with a yell . . . watching the piece run out again on its slides after the roar of the shot'. That evening he recorded tiny, intimate trade noises as the battery made ready to leave. 'Never was sound more welcome than the metal of the trail-eye dropping on the limber hook'. Drivers standing next to their nervous horses as the odd shell came over 'needed no order to mount. That sound, and the lift of the pole as the weight of the trail came on the limber, was sufficient'.[218]

In July 1916 Schweder listened to sounds around Aveluy Wood on the Somme. The guns and shells spoke differently. Some whizzed, others sang and exploded with a crump. Crouched at an observation post two months earlier he ticked off the minutes to the start of an artillery strafe, set to begin at nine in the evening: 'It will be opened by a bass overture from the gunner band, followed up by a tenor song from the machine guns, and then a treble crackle of rifles, etc.'.[219] All this was before the offensive proper. Eight and a half weeks later Rawlinson unleashed the Fourth Army's artillery. For the rest of 1916 *Trommelfeuer* – 'drumfire' – dominated the local soundscape: 33,300,000 shells fired off between 23 June and 31 December.[220] In La Bassée district next spring Schweder compared the sound of machine-gun bullets passing overhead to the noise made by humming birds, but Schweder's ears weren't the only ones attuned to the zone's complex sound world. On 22 April allied fighter planes attacked a big flight of German bombers as it passed over his unit. The day was clear so everyone stopped to watch. One gunner remarked that the machine gun rattle high overhead sounded like hands clapping in a theatre.[221] Bullets make a smacking noise when they hit a brick wall, observed Hamilton, shrapnel shells a tearing noise when they burst and a 'violent patter' in towns as their contents richoched along the streets.[222] In 1916 and 1917 Herbert Leland tried to express zone noises to his wife: 'the continual roar of the guns, the whirr of machine guns, the ground shakes as if by earthquake, and it never ceases day or night'. For three weeks he went deaf. After recovering he wrote about small arms' fire: 'it is absolutely beyond me to describe what it is like. The nearest I can get to it is – let loose a swarm of bees. Buzz, buzz; swish, swish; ping, ping; all day long, and never a moment's rest'.[223] As barrages ebbed and flowed, or rifle fire drifted away on the wind, animal and human noises impinged on the ear – 'the steady regular grunting, squeaking, and clicking of the convoy at my back' heard by Capron as star shells swished overhead one night in 1917.[224]

'During battle, even when the lines were not cut, only short messages could be sent on telephones near the front as hardly a word could be heard,' remembered James Edmonds, so settlers reverted to visual signalling; pigeons and coloured rockets. But still, now and then, unearthly sounds cut through the tumult: klaxons blaring from aircraft to infantry in no man's land on the Somme, eerie wailings in the air around Loos,[225] trench alarms improvised from spent shell casings. One night near Ypres a sentry tumbled into Schweder's observation post screaming 'Gas!' Schweder rushed out and heard the gongs echoing for miles round the Salient – 'it sounded most weird'.[226] When the front went quiet everywhere in the trenches would be the murmur of men's voices, names softly called, and the creak of footfalls on trench boards.[227] ➲ 25

24 Tuesday 30 November 1915

Of remounts purchased in North America over the previous seven months nearly 80,000 were too ill to be shipped to Europe and fifteen per cent died or were destroyed. Death and sickness rates for 1916 were much the same.[228] Other horses died or suffered injury or sickness during the long transatlantic voyage, on arrival Britain, or when crossing the Channel.

A typical journey from the prairie to the entrepôts involved many hazards. The first stage was by rail to a dealer's stockyard at remount purchasing centre. Horses often arrived in 'soft' condition; unseasoned, perhaps never before exposed to specific bacterial infection and unused to harness or restraint. At this stage, or in the immediate subsequent stage of onward transport to the ports, many died from pneumonia, known in the American vernacular as 'shipping fever'. Animals were packed eighteen to twenty per wagon. In winter train crews 'slatted up' the open cars, which reduced ventilation, often with fatal results. Prior to1914 most travelled for no more than twenty-eight hours before off-loading for rest, feeding and watering, but by 1916 this had been extended to thirty-six hours. Since most horses wouldn't eat inside the wagons and couldn't be watered while trains were moving vast numbers perished from exhaustion as well as disease.[229]

The bulk of horses arrived at the eastern seaboard after journeys of twelve hundred miles or so. Seventy-five per cent were reckoned to be in poor health. Pink-eye influenza (weeping and inflamed eyes, swollen limbs, stiff and sore joints) killed thousands, as did paraplegia (arched backs, hind legs drawn under the body, high temperature and lack of appetite). Thousands more suffered from acute tendonitis (infected fetlock sheaths). After 1915 careful management reduced the death rate somewhat, but exhaustion and shipping fever remained major causes of mortality: in spring 1918 the disorganization of the US railway network was so bad that thirty-hour journeys took eleven days, with predictable results. If they were properly handled at the Canadian ports – three to six weeks in covered pens was considered essential – the survivors recovered and built up immunity to infection, but rough seas and the failure of crews to isolate 'kickers' caused injuries on the transatlantic voyage and many fell sick due to poor stabling, lack of fresh air and water and general neglect.[230]

After disembarking at Liverpool, Avonmouth, Hull or Glasgow a horse encountered risks inseparable from a sudden change of climate: exposure to new infections, frequent changes of locality and wayward companions, 'any one of whom might take a sudden dislike to him (as horses will),' noted the RAVC's historians, 'and administer a kick or bite of which the effects might prove fatal'. Most were unshod, and restiveness during the unaccustomed business of shoeing might cause a newly trained farrier to misdirect a nail, with agonizing consequences. When issued to a new unit mobilizing under canvas staffed by barely trained personnel insecurely picketed horses might join a fatal stampede[231] – Rowland Luther saw one on Salisbury Plain in August 1914; 2,000 horses 'taking everything before them'[232] – or die of some intestinal disorder from over-eating during a nocturnal raid on an unguarded forage stack. Each animal was tested for glanders before travelling to Befland. Those infected were immediately killed, those clear of infection burned on the flanks with a broad arrow. Risks encountered on the Channel crossing were far from negligible. One vet recorded that of the 1,800 landed at Rouen between 1 February and 7 March 1915, 1,040 went straight to veterinary hospitals with colds or pneumonia. Most had picked up infections in England or during the crossing. The previous year he noticed that when two horses were housed in a single stanchion, a common practice on Channel steamers, they often attacked each other. Some were so badly bitten – large areas of skin sloughed off the side of the neck – that wounds that took many weeks to heal.[233]

Moving an artillery brigade from England to Befland – eighty vehicles, 600 settlers, 450 horses and mules – was a 'nightmare of paperwork', remembered Richard Foot in 1964, and could take well over a week. After being loaded and off-loaded at UK stations and ports and crammed into transport ships even the most biddable animal had reason enough to become skittish. There was no let up at the entrepôts. On one journey they had to march to the railway yards; not far, but tricky for all concerned. As they picked their way along dimly-lit streets tramlines and wet cobblestones tripped the horses, sending men and limbers tumbling to the ground, and there was always the chance of losing animals in the darkness and confusion. 'We were told that the Havre butchers were already sharply on the look out for the well fed British Army draft horses, but they did not get any of mine'.[234] Luther's memories were equally vivid. 'Impossibles', horses that refused to be led onto the steamers, were slung in hammocks and winched over the gunwales. Once on board the drivers took turns down in the hold; 'one hour on and four hours off – and one hour down that hold, with the heat and the smell and sweat was gruelling'. As Le Havre came into view they harnessed up the horses and when the boat docked tried to lead the first contingent one by one down the gangway. 'But they led us', he remembered. They'd scented water from a trough placed on the quayside, and despite shouted instructions from the officers all control went until, dragging the drivers who were hanging on to the bridles, they reached the trough and slaked their thirst. It was the same with the second group, 'nothing would stop this mad rush'. Then came the difficult business of yoking the jittery animals to wagons and limbers which, somehow or other, had meanwhile been hauled ashore. The turnout paraded on the dockside and set off, but soon 'all hell let loose again'. The horses slipped on the cobblestones, sparks flying from their hooves, and crashed down onto the ground.[235] ➲ 43

25 Saturday 4 December 1915

Billeted in the peace and quiet of Coquelles, Ronald Schweder heard cannon booming away in the zone as he sat writing to his wife.[236]

Coquelles, now a suburb of Dunkirk, was a good fifty miles from the Salient and La Bassée district (the Somme had yet to be fully incorporated into Befland and was still quiet[237]), which means that in 1915 the zone's sound world echoed out as least as far as Étaples, Doullens, Cambrai, Valenciennes, Brussels, Ghent, Brugge, and Flushing on the mouth of the Scheldt. Closer in the noise was omnipresent. A few weeks later Rowland Luther's unit pulled back to Watou, twelve miles east of Ypres – 'we could always hear the rumble of gunfire, but it was away from the danger zone'.[238] As the supply of artillery and shells increased so did the sound range and the volume. Early on the morning of 18 April 1917 Stapleton Eachus laboriously anatomized the resonance of distant artillery fire as he lay half asleep in bed. The tremors and shocks, he reasoned, were conveyed to his body via the earth, the house and the bedstead.[239] This was at Pont-Noyelles on the Somme, by now twenty-five miles due west of the front and thirty miles away from the only major offensive going on that week – the Battle of Arras. The sound of static explosions carried further still. Two months later at just after three in the morning Beflanders detonated nineteen gargantuan mine stashes buried under Messines Ridge, probably the biggest man-made explosion prior to the nuclear weapons' tests of 1945. 'I cleared everyone out of the dug-outs and was watching for it,' wrote Ralph Hamilton in his diary on 7 June. 'Never could I have imagined such a sight. First, there was a double shock that shook the earth here 15,000 yards away like a gigantic earthquake. I was nearly flung off my feet. Then an immense wall of fire that seemed to go half-way up to heaven'.[240] 10,000 Germans died instantly, vaporized by the blasts. Shockwaves reached Lille. People in London and Dublin reported hearing the noise.[241] Even if we discount the latter location the reach is impressive. London was 140 miles away. On this measure the Messines sound arc encompassed much of north-western Europe. Amsterdam, Luxembourg, Cologne, Paris, Le Havre and Brighton were all within range.

In such a world silence invited comment. On 2 July 1916, after the sound and fury of the first day of the Somme, two zone dwellers noticed a distinct change. Schweder awoke to a beautiful Sunday morning with barely any cannon fire.[242] 'I have just discovered it is Sunday,' wrote Harold Bursey. 'The firing has died down and except for a gun now and again everything is quiet and peaceful. Over the fields comes the sound of church bells. It is from Corbie, which is many miles behind us'.[243] In October Hamilton saw Malins' *Somme* [104] at a Boulogne cinema. He found it convincing enough – 'minus the noise'.[244] 'Things are quiet on this front today,' observed Herbert Leland the following January. 'It is a strange thing not to hear the roar of the guns. I suppose there is some mischief brewing. There is generally a lull before the storm'.[245] 'The silence, and the drips of rain on my face' was how Richard Foot remembered a quiet moment during uproar of the Ludendorff Offensive.[246]

The sound of wargear ceased for good only after the Armistice. On the evening of 11 November Foot was at Maubeuge in New Befland. 'It was a strange feeling to ride back to the Battery in the quiet that followed eleven o'clock. One had got used to the background noise of shell fire, which could often be heard as far away as the south coast of England. Near the front, it seemed a continuous orchestration of deep and echoing sound, punctuated by the sharper rat-tat-tat of rifle or machine gun fire'.[247] Next April Lady Londonderry took in the stillness of the Salient. 'No fresh green tufts of grass or bright hued mossy patches, only dull blotches of grey weeds . . . The dead silence of the evening seemed in keeping with the dead country, derelict and gloomy in the evening light'.[248] ➲ 30

Monday 13 December 1915   **26**

Ronald Schweder was billeted at Francières on the Somme. At midday he rode into Abbeville to do some shopping and lunched at the town's main hotel, the Tête de Boeuf. It was just like a film set, he wrote, a pleasant bustle impinged on the eye; Beflanders and French soldiers ambling along the streets, staff officers in cars tearing round corners, civilians going about their business. The town had a fine cathedral and plenty of shops. One could buy almost anything. He left about four in the afternoon, satchels and saddlebags bulging.[249] Six months on, at four in the morning on 7 June 1916, Stapleton Eachus arrived there on his way to catch the leave boat from Le Havre. Later in the day, after taking a look round the camp and watching Canadians playing baseball, he went in search of food, but he soon gave up and wandered off into the town; over 1,000 settlers were crammed in the camp and the queues were enormous. One or two things caught his eye: a church dedicated to St Vulfran (impressive from the outside, less so inside); a monument to a dead admiral in the main square (mildly interesting); the River Somme running through the town (not particular attractive); the canal running from the Somme to the railway station (nice walkways along the tree-lined banks).[250]

Eight miles from the Somme estuary and twenty-six southwest of Amiens, Abbeville had a population of about 19,000 before the settlers came. It quickly developed into a major back-area supply base and way station for ambulance trains.[251] When Eachus arrived it housed, in addition to a signals depot and transit camp, veterinary stores, No. 22 veterinary hospital, a School of Farriery (training 250 settlers at any one time; two months for 'cold shoers', four to six for shoesmiths), various labour company food depots (differentiated according to religion and ethnicity – British and

Dominion, Hindu, Muslim, Chinese, etc.), petrol stores, an Indian cavalry base, several horse and mechanical transport depots, three gas mask repair workshops employing native women superintended by Mrs Morgan, Miss Beavor and Mrs Barocchi, two hospitals, a central ambulance train store, the headquarters of the Matron-in-Chief of Befland's nurses, Dame Maude McCarthy, and immense dumps of barbed wire, sandbags, picks, shovels, timber and corrugated iron. Day and night freight and ambulance trains clanked to and fro from the marshalling yards into the zone. A few months after Eachus's visit army steam laundries started to operate, building work began on a forage depot in the suburb of Moutort and on series of huge ammunition dumps at Saigneville, a mile or so northwest of the town centre. Seven miles away at Noyelles-sur-Mer a fifteen-hundred-bed hospital for Chinese labourers *en route* to Befland was already under construction, along with another vast food store and an engineering store at the nearby port village of St Valery-sur-Somme. Even more dumps and depots appeared in spring 1918 when the Somme's borders collapsed and thousands of settlers fled westwards.[252] ➲ 35

27 Saturday 1 January 1916

The settler population now stood 987,200. Of them 138,000 lived the back areas, 849,200 in and around the zone. Boosted by UK conscription and Dominion immigration, the number rose to 1,426,000 in June. By August Befland housed over 125,000 medics and 15,000 women, the latter adding to the quarter of a million or so back-area non-combatants. 18,000 signallers and 25,000 miners arrived during the course of the year.[253] 'Great establishments, amounting almost to small towns, began to develop,' wrote Edmonds, 'buildings were taken over, and there arose military settlements of huts erected by contract with British and French firms, supplemented by marquees and tents'.[254]

Formed in March, General Rawlinson's Fourth Army soon took over most of the Somme from Allenby's Third Army. General Gough's Fifth or 'Reserve' Army appeared in May. Despite the Somme offensives Befland expanded eastwards by only six miles or so. Elsewhere borders remained more or less stable and as in 1915 the zone still stretched for about ninety miles, though according to a 1919 committee of the Army Council settlement had now entered a new phase. 'Trench warfare', initiated at First Ypres, ended on 1 July 1916. Thereafter 'offensive operations' characterized Britain's war effort.[255]

By December Befland accommodated between 1,330,000 and 1,400,000 immigrants, but these figures seem to undercount labourers and women and overlook casualties. We shall never know the exact death toll for 1916 (or, indeed, for any other year of the colony's existence), but official figures published in 1931 list approximately 107,400 killed outright and nearly 24,000 who died of wounds or disease, a grand total of 150,300. Total casualties (the dead, the wounded, those who fell ill and recovered and those made prisoners of war) numbered just under 1,300,000. Most of this happened on or around the Somme,[256] though as for 1915 [18] the 'throughput' population must have been larger than the 'static' total for December. Nevertheless the enormous number of casualties had major implications for immigration. 'Henceforth,' notes Edmonds, 'the history of recruiting was to be one long record of falling numbers and of a struggle to keep the Army in France – which required not only reinforcements but officers and men for all the new specialist units – more or less up to strength by tightening up the conditions of exemption, by combing out men from home industries and services behind the front; and, when a crisis occurred, by reducing the number of troops in the minor theatres'.[257] ➲ 80

Saturday 12 February 1916 **28**

'Things We Want to Know. The name of the brunette infantry officer whose man got hold of the carrier pigeons (sent to this celebrated Company Commander when his communications in the front line had broken down) and cooked them. Also who were his guests?' And a few weeks later: 'Military Definitions. BIRDS – Are of two kinds only. – The Carrier Pigeon (a delicacy for front line trenches), and the nameless, untamed variety usually collected by junior officers'.[258]

Riffs on food, as opposed to women, seldom appear in the columns of Befland's satirical press, but food was of perennial – not to say obsessive – interest to settler correspondents. Much of this was doubtless in response to anxious enquiries from wives, parents and girlfriends. James Naylor was only sixteen when he arrived in the colony as trumpeter to an ammunition column. Of letters written home to Baluchistan between August 1914 and November 1919, mostly on family matters, health, and his schemes for promotion, 173 survive in the archives. A typical extract, dated 11 May 1917, shortly after his becoming an officer, reads as follows: 'Dad, you asked me what sort of grub I am having now. Well we get the same as the "tommy" only we have a Battery Mess and so have a few extras, which we can get from the Expeditionary Force Canteens. So we have for breakfast Porridge, (bacon ration) eggs or tomatoes or sausages, toast & marmalade. Lunch, meat & vegetables (ration) either Roast, Steak or stew, biscuits & cheese (ration). Tea. Bread & butter, jam & marmalade. Dinner. Soup (meat & potatoes ration) and another vegetable, tinned fruit. Tea at every meal. Our messing comes to four francs a day'.[259]

If such detail is evidence of settler conversations with outsiders, this doesn't explain diary entries about food; diaries, after all, weren't necessarily meant to be read by anyone besides the writer. One possible explanation has to do with insecurity. Everything in Befland was provisional and unstable, and in large measure dangerous. People and things came and went with dizzying rapidity. No one stayed in the same place for long and nothing stayed the same for long. 'A generation . . . now stood under the open sky in a countryside in which nothing remained unchanged but the clouds,' wrote Walter Benjamin in 1936, 'and beneath these clouds, in a field of force of destructive torrents and explosions, was the tiny, fragile, human body'.[260] And that body had to be fed. In a landscape of insecurity perhaps food was a trope for permanence and normality? Perhaps listing menus and mealtimes helped to give structure to minds and bodies jolted by disrupted days and nights, by interminable journeys, by uncertain destinations, by uncertain outcomes?

On a more mundane level most Beflanders were young, physically active males, and therefore likely to be possessed of robust appetites. They needed to eat every day and they didn't always know where their next meal was coming from. In this sense obsessing about food was neither time specific nor place specific nor culturally specific. It was entirely natural. In all our myths the warrior feasts – food hunted, food stolen, food supplied, food grown, food bought, food sent. ➲ 40

29 Saturday 26 February 1916

From the *Wipers Times or Salient News*: 'Answers to Correspondents. ETHEL. – No, we have none of Kirchner's pictures in our editorial sanctum. This austere chamber still retains its scheme of simplicity. (But if you have any we have a friend, whose views are not our own, who might like them)'.[261]

Throughout 1916 and 1917 the *Times* and its successor publications, *New Church Times*, *Kemmel Times*, *Some-Times* and *BEF Times*, carried many spoof entries like this in its 'Lonely Hearts' column, and kept up a running gag about the 'Munque Art Gallery', the supposed repository of a fabulous collection of pornographic images drawn by Raphael Kirchner, one of *La Vie Parisienne's* main illustrators.[262] As Stapleton Eachus recorded – rather sniffily – after hitch-hiking across the Somme in April 1917, pornography cropped up everywhere in the zone. One lorry's front cab was liberally festooned with postcards of French nudes; just like all the billets and bivouacs inhabited by Beflanders, he added.[263] 'The pictures in our mess of nude ladies are much admired,' wrote Ronald Schweder from Dranoutre a month later. 'Orr has pinned them on the walls'.[264]

That sex was on the minds of the hundreds of thousands of young male settlers crammed into the zone should come as no surprise. Charles Carrington believed that siege warfare meant that most were 'sex starved', unless or until they could get to a nearby front-line town 'from which the lucky ones returned at midnight, not too drunk, and boasting of their sexual adventures'.[265]

Carrington's reminiscence is entirely plausible, but it's hard to get much beyond such second-hand generalizations, at least by perusing settlers' letters. Correspondents were unlikely to regale wives and girlfriends with details of their exploits. As for diarists and memoirists, Dennis Wheatley's fragmentary list of prostitutes hired in southern Befland in 1917–18 ('Havre, Tortoni's. Havre with [?]. Ronnie. Amiens, Collette. Amiens, Marie. Amiens, Big Fair. Amiens, Under Bombardment, Aumale with [?]'[266]) is exceptional. The rest shied away from chronicling personal encounters, doubtless because mainstream British culture refused to tolerate anything other than silent reflection on individual predilections. The same goes for homosexuality. Eric Hiscock's memoir, not published until 1976, references homosexual behaviour,[267] and Ross Wilson gives credence to one or two studies which speculate that homosexual relationships were present in the ranks.[268] In addition homosexuality informs the plotlines of several late twentieth-century novels about the colony, and homoerotic imagery can be discerned in the output of a handful of public school officer-poets. But it's difficult to cite all this as proof that gay sex was common in the zone. Carrington, a judicious observer of life in Befland, remarks that he saw no evidence of homosexuality.[269] After carefully surveying courts martial records Craig Gibson came to the same conclusion – no indication at all of widespread 'transgressive' sex anywhere in the colony.[270] It's therefore likely that the vast majority of sexual interactions, whether straightforwardly 'transactional' or exhibiting some 'affective' element, were heterosexual. Moreover, despite the fact that jaunts in the back areas gave zone dwellers the chance to seek out nurses and VADs (in summer 1915, for example, buses ran from soldiers' camps near Wimereux to the beaches where female auxiliaries went swimming[271]) most interactions, certainly most transactional interactions, probably involved native women rather than immigrants. When Jessie Wilson arrived at Le Havre with the YMCA in 1915 she was shocked to learn that the locals couldn't understand the presence of women volunteers in Befland and simply assumed that they were all prostitutes.[272] They were wrong. Though Some UK prostitutes might have migrated to Befland, there can have been no more than a handful. Few would have wanted to, or needed to. In any case the journey from portals to entrepôts and beyond would be fraught with difficulties. ➲ 57

Thursday 2 March 1916 30

'As soon as the bombardment began,' wrote Ralph Hamilton from Ypres, 'we saw the German S.O.S. going up all along the zone that was threatened. There were red rockets bursting into red stars. Soon after, rockets of all colours went up – white, green, red, golden rain, and even red golden rain'. Back in the Salient in June the following year he met a colonel hurrying along a sunken road pursued by gas shells. 'It was really extremely funny; as we walked (very fast) down the road, a gas-shell fell 50 yards behind us, and this happened four times in about two hundred yards. These gas-shells make very little noise arriving, and burst on the ground with a little "pop" like pulling the cork out of a bottle. It was the first time I had seen one burst, although I have heard thousands in the dark. There was no smoke, either black or white; just the dust thrown up by the shell striking the dry ground, and then a small cloud of yellow-green vapour – much the colour of jade'.[273]

A shared aspect of these two stories – flares rising in the sky and shells falling from the sky – might at first glance suggest affinities with 'sky awareness', a notion advanced by Paul Fussell. But the classification doesn't quite work. Fussell's primary interest is not in settler sensitivity to the sky and its doings *per se*, but in something more specific: in the ritual significance of the act of 'standing to' (the occupation by trench dwellers of assigned positions at sunrise and sunset), in overtly literary representations of the act, and in connecting such representations to Victorian aesthetics.[274] And since colour impinges only insofar as it references these aesthetics, the colour awareness displayed in Hamilton's texts needs some other framing device.

On 29 May, two months before Hamilton and the colonel fled the yellow-green vapour, Dennis Wheatley arrived for a course at Wendover's Anti-Gas School. When he returned to Befland on 2 June his notebooks carefully listed the colour-codes of the unexploded German gas shells he would find lying on the ground within five miles or so of the eastern border: '(a) Howitzer, 15cm, Grey, yellow head and yellow K, contains 2350cc Palite (K); (b) Howitzer, 15cm, Grey, black head and Black T, contains 2300cc 'T' substance; (c) Field Gun, 7.7cm, Grey, yellow head, contains 317cc Triphosgene, no leaden container; (d) Minenwerfer, 17cm, Grey, yellow bands, contains 7500cc 'B' substance; (e) Minenwerfer, 17cm, Grey, two yellow bands, contains 7700cc Palite; (f) Minenwerfer, 7.5cm, Grey, two white bands, contains 460cc Palite; (g) Minenwerfer, 7.5cm, Grey, three white bands and letter 'D', contains 663grms liquid phosgene'.[275] Five years later William MacPherson remembered the colours which impinged on resident eyes when the casings broke open and spilled out their chemicals, smearing the earth and staining the air and shell-hole pools: the intense, vivid yellow of picric acid; trotyl, off-white or whitish brown; astralite, yellowish grey; amatol, yellow or brown; dinitrobenzine and dinitrobenzol, pale yellow or nearly white when pure; trinitro anisol, a greenish-yellow mass of soft, greasy crystals, and finally the rich, oily sherry hue of dichlor-ethyl-sulphide – mustard gas before it vaporized. When chlorine was delivered by cylinders instead of shell-fire a gas cloud formed; thick, rolling banks of white condensation fronting the yellow-green poison moving across the landscape.[276] When shot at night black smoke was sometimes added to German phosgene shells in order to confuse recipients. In contrast British howitzer shells produced yellow-white smoke while the propellant, lyddite, released clouds of deep yellow.[277]

What does all this add up to? For settlers sky, air and colour fused into an 'imaginative topography'[278] of considerable power, acutely visualized and carefully annotated, because the colour of things falling out of the sky or drifting on the wind mattered greatly. Beneath the visible text in Wheatley's notebook lie invisible stories of fear and caution, and though Hamilton's blithe account of evasive action along a sunken road in the Salient is just what we might expect from a young man whose diary suggests that its writer possessed a sunny, carefree disposition, he and his companion were still jog-trotting away from death. ⊃ 33

Tuesday 14 March 1916   **31**

Units of the First Army completed their two-week journey to the Somme. In 1932 James Edmonds sketched the scene: 'After the dreary and depressing surroundings of Flanders, the new area, dry and bright, with No Man's Land a wide stretch of scarlet poppies, yellow mustard, red clover and blue cornflowers, was a pleasing contrast. The spirits of the troops rose accordingly, the ground seemed made for a successful battle'.[279]

At first glance Edmonds' surmises look plausible, but when we dismember the text they begin to fall apart in our hands. The flora-idyll is wrong. In Northern Europe poppies, mustard, clover and cornflowers don't bloom in spring, and anyway that March Befland's weather was unseasonably cold. As for what incomers felt, we can't assert anything with much confidence: charting variations in one settler's mood minute by minute over a single day would be impossible – no historical evidence exists, or could exist, for such an undertaking – let alone the mood of an entire army over fourteen days. Here rhetoric ('pleasing contrast', 'the spirit of the troops rose') masquerades as evidence of mass psychology. In fact it's quite possible that the final sentence wasn't intended to mean anything at all. Its function may be euphonic, a cadenced phrase half consciously inserted to round off and balance the passage.

A medley of Somme landscapes across the year 1916, starting with Ronald Schweder at Francières, five miles southeast of Abbeville.

1 January: 'I rode eight miles today to the field cashier to get pay for the men. I found him in a deserted chateau, where heaps of telephone wires stretched across the avenues threaten to hang you if you are on a horse'.[280]

Those wires were changing the landscape everywhere. Within months 43,000 miles of cabling had been strung overland on telegraph poles. As one moved east and into the zone 'airline' cables plunged into the ground; snaking lines of freshly turned chalk, criss-crossing the downs like streams of white bandages, showed where they had been interred at grave depth – a six-foot 'bury' in the chalk sub-soil supposedly guaranteed protection from shell fire. Placed end to end the white streams would have stretched for 7,000 miles. Still more cabling lay directly on the surface, fanning out from headquarters, dumps, stations and depots of every description and wriggling away in every direction.[281]

Cecil Lewis's multiperspective 1936 reconstruction of the Somme in springtime, as if from Lahoussoye aerodrome, twenty-five miles east of Francières. First view, as from the ground: standing close by a row of canvas covered hangars, each housing four aircraft. Behind, a small orchard and the squadron offices. Second view, in the distance, imagined: the border, fifteen miles away, hidden by undulating ground. Third view, a panorama, large vistas: the northern French countryside; wide, featureless, peaceful and intensively farmed, some fields brown, others greening into spring. Fourth view: the Somme valley, a mile or so south of the aerodrome. Fifth view, the Somme from the air, and also from the ground: 'The lovely river wandered, doubling heedlessly upon itself, through copses of poplar and willow, split into diverse channels where the water-weeds streamed in long swathes, lazily curling and uncurling along the placid surface, and flooded out over marshes where sedge and bulrushes hid the nests of the wild-duck, the coot, and the heron. It was always there on our right hand when we left the aerodrome for the lines, an infinitely peaceful companion, basking under a haze at midday, cool and mysterious when the mists stole out in the dusk'.[282]

17 June: Stapleton Eachus's first impression of the Somme. His train from Abbeville made an unscheduled stop by the L'Hallue stream: 'At the time I am making these notes we are halted opposite a sort of "Venice of kitchen gardens". Many acres of land have apparently been cut into allotments and separated by waterways. The gardeners may be seen coming along punting their gondola shaped boats, and others going away laden with vegetables and greens'.[283]

4 July: Harold Bursey camped at the foot of the Bois des Tailles near the River Somme: 'Our bivouacs will be lovely after this rain. The valley of the Somme where I am now and where all the fighting – or most of it – is taking place is a beautiful spot. It is dotted right through by little villages, modest hamlets of 50 cottages, which hug the green hill side right along, some of them lying between the hill and the marshland. We I regret to say are on the latter'.[284]

7 July: The same place, *in tenebris* and during wind and rain: 'Again the storm is raging. There is something awe inspiring in the darkness that closes in around these battlefields as the rain comes down from the dark clouds and the thunder vies with our guns in noise. In the distance one can see dark woods slashed with shell fire, further back men march wearily along in the pitiless rain. One can stand watching these scenes of war until the gloom and terror of it closes right about one'.[285] Did Bursey employ the pathetic fallacy consciously? Was he knowingly attentive to the sublime in the manner of an

eighteenth-century essayist? Or was the literary culture speaking him, and through him the landscape?

7 September: Ralph Hamilton on the road from Maricourt to Bray-sur-Somme: 'The five mile ride here was most amusing. We were on the main road that divides the French and British armies. They do not appear to have any road discipline at all. The motor-lorries race each other and dash past transport on the wrong side, etc. We had a great excitement when a convoy of immense motor-lorries came past at about thirty miles an hour. The French divide their wagons up into different convoys, each with a large picture of an animal. Whilst the monkey column was passing the elephant column came up behind. The result was a race in which the lorries cut in and out of the traffic with a recklessness that took one's breath away. I expected to be knocked down at any moment. They were ammunition wagons, both English and French. Blue French forage wagons with three horses abreast, Turcos and Senegambians, French cavalrymen and English gunners, all in a desperate hurry and all very cheerful, yelling to each other and generally driving at a gallop. It was just like a Derby Day'.[286]

11 November: The Somme observed from a distance; George Stringer on a gunnery course at St Pol, thirty miles north of Albert: 'A most peculiar phenomenon in the sky southwards last night as we were going to bed. A red glow which lit up the sky, waxed, waned & waxed again; also bright small flashes in the air as though anti-aircraft shells were bursting & occasionally comet-like streaks of light. We stood watching'.[287]

Christmas Eve: Herbert Leland, less than a mile from the border. Panoramic revisions of wintry desolation are not attempted, nor are there modulations between frontal and peripheral glances, as when a narrative shifts from fronting the landscape to representing motion within it. But the *genius loci* is deployed to articulate seasonal ironies – Leland's vignette might well be sketched onto the front of a Befland Christmas card: 'As I was riding back in a frightful hail storm I passed a weary looking Tommy who was carrying a very skinny plucked fowl tied over his shoulder by a piece of string'.[288]

Inferences from the evidence:

1   The more the shaping eye fashions genre landscapes (e.g., Edmonds' 1932 flora-idyll, Lewis's 1936 multi-perspective, Hamilton's Derby Day on 7 September), the more specific landscapes disappear; in 1916 the Somme 'looks like' this, but doesn't exist like this in any particular.

2   When specifically observed the Somme exists only within circumscribed limits (e.g., Schweder 1 January, Eachus 17 June, Bursey 4 and 7 July, Stringer 11 November, Leland 24 December). Fleeting time, fleeting mood or the eyebeam's narrow field of vision create unique and therefore unrepresentative landscapes.

3   Sometimes settlers generated landscapes that were unrepresentative in their specific reality; sometimes they strove for reality effects by making them generally unspecific.

4   No ur-Somme is available to historians. As with everywhere else when settlers described the Somme they inscribed themselves upon it. There are no landscapes in nature and no moments of vision outside the individual consciousness wrapped within particular discourses.

Everything said so far is credible – in a way – but the forgoing can also be read as a satiric lunge at what Antione Prost and Jay Winter call the 'de-materialization' of history production: 'a turn towards ideas and representations independent of material conditions. To escape from the naïve view that the superstructure reflects the substructure, many historians have ignored the substructure entirely'.[289]

Reading the Somme through the lens of de-based theory, in this case as deracinated cultural, linguistic or visual artefact, might be credible, but matters appear in a different light when the object of theory – this time of 'critical' theory – is the very society which extrudes such artefacts. Then their ideological and political character becomes apparent: the flattening of contradictions through mass gratification and the democratic abolition of thought, the displacement of transcendent meanings, the invalidation of subversive force and the suppression of monstrous content. All are facets of the decline of radicalism in hyper-capitalism and the expansion of repressive tolerance.[290] Hyper-capitalism extrudes such artefacts as superstructural agents that function as ironized counterparts to the *status quo*, representations that stimulate without endangering and congeal into just another media product. Materiality is foregrounded but materialism is denied and veiled. The mode of production gets hidden behind facades and surface sheens. Severing base from superstructure weakens consanguinity and cancels the connectedness of things. De-materialization means that we can no longer name that which is absent, nor can we utter offensive truths. We can't, for example, name the Somme as one more bleak manifestation of modern capitalism's immanent destructiveness[291] – consumption = commodities = expropriation = imperialism = war = consumption – nor can we point to the links in the imperialist chain which connect the Somme to the Suez canal, the canal to the Mesopotamian campaign, the campaign to the partitioning of the Ottoman Empire, and partitioning to greed for oil, unremitting intervention in the Middle East and the 'othering' of the Arab-Islamic World.

As for Beflanders, what needs to be said is that they spoke the world as they could. As with us temporality defined their lexis, but whatever the discourse the Somme was material and situate. Figures in a landscape under bombardment – men and horses writhing on the ground, a crushed skull oozing brains, the living flesh torn from the bone – are not mediated 'representations' of an unknowable reality but incidents which satisfy Engels' post-Kantian criteria for 'things-in-themselves';[292] really-existing moments of truth directly produced by the interaction of definite, concrete and knowable machines and power structures. ➲ 50

Friday 17 March 1916 32

'I don't call this life very exciting', complained Ronald Schweder from Aveluy Wood on the Somme. 'One never sees a German'. Up in the line a few days previously he fell into conversation with a sniper watching a gap in the enemy's trenches. The man said that a sentry was walking up and down on the parapet, handed his rifle to Schweder and invited him to try his luck, but when Schweder squinted through the telescopic sight he could see nothing. Then the sniper had a go but said he'd missed. What Schweder did see, however, were some cows grazing peacefully in field behind the German line, heedless of the shelling going on around them. Later, on 27 May, he seems to have fallen back on invention to fill in the landscape. Bored and fretful during a long and uneventful day an observation post – all he saw was the front number plate of a passing lorry, dutifully recorded – he fabricated two stories, one about women playing tennis behind the lines, the other concerning a German wiping his mouth as he emerged from a house seven miles distant. To his amusement the tennis match made it into the divisional 'comic cuts', settler slang for the weekly intelligence reports circulated to zone dwellers.[293] One day in 1965 Charles Carrington peered across the Berlin Wall. On one side everything was familiar and friendly, he wrote, on the other mysterious and threatening. Over there was a land inhabited by people of whom you knew next to nothing, except what could be gathered from vague stories cobbled together from rumour and surmise. It was just like looking across no man's land to the 'unknown world beyond' fifty years earlier.[294]

The phenomena of 'empty battlefield' and 'absent enemy' are staples of western-front history writing.[295] Befland's eastern border – flat, or at best gently undulating – offered scant cover from the fearsome destructive power of early twentieth-century wargear. Front-line soldiers on both sides lived troglodyte lives and journeyed into no man's land only for night patrols or during major offensives. Most who became casualties were killed or wounded at long range by gas, trench mortars, artillery or machine guns manipulated by invisible foes. The vast defensive system erected by the Germans on the Somme was quite invisible to zone dwellers, for example, as was its huge population.[296] It could be attacked only by lobbing howitzer shells miles across the border. In December 1917, whenever the big, nine-point-two inch howitzers fired, all the candles in Capron's dugout shook and went out. During daylight hours one could stand and watch their gigantic shells sailing away, high up in the sky, until eventually they turned and tumbled down towards German-held Inchy, far out of sight.[297]

Territorial expansion didn't change matters much. Absence in one form on another still obtained: on the one hand bodily absence – abandoned wargear or the deserted allotments and timber-lined dugouts noticed by settlers as they walked through the Somme a week after the opening of the offensive[298] – on the other absence of life; the dead strewn around everywhere. Neither did the breaking of the siege. Capron remembered a 'joy-ride' into Cambrai during the advance to victory. The Germans had only just left. He pulled up his horse beside an abandoned field gun straddling a gravel path in one of the town's public gardens. Alongside it lay a heap of spent cartridge cases. In the gravel he noticed the heel prints left by the crew as they dragged the gun into position one last time. After pausing before those heel marks he rode on towards Eswars, three miles to the northeast. There was nothing to see except field-grey corpses, some scattered in the fields, others close to the roadside.[299]

Zone dwellers might encounter the living as long lines of anonymous prisoners moving westwards (in which case they'd ceased to be a functioning enemy) or as rumour – prisoners taken elsewhere and recorded as merely another feature of the environment. In April 1917 Schweder heard stories of 8,000 Germans and 50 guns captured at Vimy Ridge, but he gave them no more than a passing mention before going on to scrutinize the weather: heavy snow, dreadful cold and the sun shining brightly at six in the evening.[300] ➲ 71

33   Monday 1 May 1916

'It was most interesting to see the effects of the gas cloud on the crops,' remarked Ralph Hamilton. 'It must have travelled in a straight line, as one could follow its path quite easily. We seem to have been just on the edge of it. There were large fields of clover that might have been divided in half with a ruler, one half bright green and the other a chocolate brown'.[301]

Sometimes, when describing the visual impact of wargear on earth, air and water, writers could almost be referencing artistic genres. Hamilton's depiction of a phosgene attack in the Salient invites the reader to step inside a futurist canvas slashed with bold, angular lines and muscular blocks of colour. In 1917 John Masefield remarked that in the blazing light of an August day the empty Somme battlefields resembled a patchwork table cloth of browns, greens, greys and yellows stitched with trench lines.[302] Other settlers assembled blurred, post-impressionist landscapes shimmering with bright, fresh pastels, or simply sketched a striking contrast. 'On the whole of this great undulating plateau there is not a single green tree or blade of grass, nothing but yellow earth and white chalk,' wrote Hamilton from Maricourt in summer that year.[303] 'Clothes, guns, all that had been left in confusion when the war passed on, had now been baked by the sun into one wonderful combination of colour – white, pale grey and pale gold' was how William Orpen saw it. 'The only dark colours were the deep red bronze of the "wire"'.[304] A few miles away Masefield looked around Quarry Valley – 'the many shell-holes are reddish all over it, though the red is mixed with dirty fragments of chalk'.[305] Nearby Hamilton stood among hundreds of French graves, each marked with a large tricolour rosette which contrasted strongly with the dusty white of the roads and the tall green weeds spread across the landscape.[306] To the north the French translator attached to a London infantry regiment watched settlers frolicking in Dickebusch Lake, previously a favourite bathing spot of the Ypres bourgeoisie. Churned by shell-fire, the once pellucid water was now 'reddish-yellow . . . the typical colour of the Salient soil . . . You could hardly see your hand a foot below the surface'.[307] In *A Patriot's Progress* Henry Williamson relates time to colour by directing the reader's eye towards the thousands of empty bully-beef tins scattered alongside the railway lines running east from Le Havre – 'some old and rusty, most of them blue, or with red and yellow labels curling on them'.[308]

Five more moments of vision: white chalk dust on khaki leggings in the blazing heat of a Somme summer; the dust turning translucent grey as rain fell;[309] guns flashing among the grey slagheaps, white trenches and green fields of La Bassée district;[310] the countryside 'lit with a red light like in a photographic dark-room' when the mines went up under Messines Ridge in June 1917[311] [25], and Lady Londonderry's diary entry for 3 April 1919, recording her impressions of the Menin Road when she visited the Salient's battlefields, now silent and practically deserted: 'The only signs of life were salvage parties of men exhuming dead bodies, or burying them, or else digging cemeteries. Two bright splotches of colour caught the eye in the near distance. Flags! Yes. They were Union Jacks which lay over the floor of two wagons, they covered poor shapeless lumps of clay carefully placed in sacks'.[312]

Finally a homological resonance with gassed earth. Kitty Kenyon, a VAD nurse at No. 4 British General Hospital at Camiers, just north of Étaples, picturing the surrounding countryside in June 1918. 'Mustard makes some of the fields a yellow glory'.[313] ➲ 79

Tuesday 16 May 1916   34

From Cecil Lewis's logbook: 'Machine, No. 5133. Passenger, L[ieutenan]t Brown. Time, 1 hour. Course, Lines; La Boisselle. Height, 5800 f[ee]t. Weather, perfect. Wind, West. Remarks, Officer to see segment of trenches . . . nothing of interest seen'. Later, on an aeronautical journey photographing the Somme, he did see something interesting: 'I saw something black ahead of the machine. It was a howitzer shell, one of our own . . . slowing up as it reached the top of its trajectory, turning slowly over and over, like an ambling porpoise, and then plunging down to burst'.[314]

The only way travellers could hope to encompass Befland in its entirety was vertically, but as the above texts suggest, it is novelty that arrests the memorizing eye. Was this just a matter of the way the mind preserves some images and forgets others? Not entirely, though in a wonderfully evocative passage Lewis shows that he was well aware of the damage that time inflicts. In 1936 he struggled to remember the life of twenty years ago. 'My logbook, where each separate flight is noted, shows what I was doing, but strangely evokes no answering ring in my memory . . . I am like a man on a rise, looking back over a plain where white ground mists lie, seeing isolated trees and roofs, upthrust haphazard, floating on the sea, without apparent connection with the lanes and fields beneath. I remember only incidents, and lose the vivid landscape of the time'.[315]

But for our purposes it is that logbook phrase – 'nothing of interest seen' – that holds the key. It's not just that the professional eye becomes habituated (like the infantryman and the artilleryman, what the aeronaut observes he does not always see); the aeronaut inhabits a specialized technology that transforms gruelling journeys through arduous landscapes into geometrical movements above levelled scenery, a point noted by Walter Benjamin: 'The power of a country road is different when one is walking along it from when one is flying over it by airplane . . . The airplane passenger sees only how the road pushes through the landscape, how it unfolds according to the same laws as the terrain surrounding it. Only he who walks the road on foot learns of the power it commands, and of how, from the very scenery that for the flier is only the unfurled plain, it calls forth distances, belvederes, clearings, prospects at each of its turns like a commander deploying soldiers at the front'.[316]

Lewis flying towards Befland; over the portals, the Channel and the entrepôts and into the back areas: 'It was a day of cloudless blue and summer haze . . . At the coast already I could see the beckoning patterns of the Flanders fields; below, the toy ships were ploughing the Channel; behind, London under a murk . . . Dover pier, with little dots of people on it, threads of white foam marking the surf . . . Slowly it fell away behind me. My eyes were set for St Omer, from that height seemingly only a stone's throw from the coast . . . There to the north was the coastline – unmistakable landmark – Boulogne, Calais, Dunkerque. Beneath were the straight French roads with their avenues of poplars. Calais itself nestled under the right wing-tip, compact and cosy, one tall church spire and ten thousand chimneys, breathing a vague bluish vapour which hung pensive in the sky. Beyond the harbour was the Leave Boat, starting for England: two white furrows and a penn'orth of smoke. An escort of destroyers flanked her; and beyond the steel-grey sea, almost hidden in the evening haze, was the outline of the Dover cliffs, white beyond the water'. Traversing the colony: 'I turned south towards Boulogne, climbing, always climbing. Already I was two miles above the earth, a tiny lonely speck in the vast rotunda of the evening sky. The sun was sinking solemnly in a black Atlantic cloud-belt. To the east, night crept up; a lofty shade drawn steadily over the warring earth . . . A patchwork of fields, browns and greys, here and there dappled with the green of spring woods, intersecting ribbons of straight roads, minute houses, invisible men'. Navigating towards the zone during the night was a hair-raising experience. The countryside was completely dark except for beacons winking Morse code – 'It wasn't at all easy'.[317]

Ronald Schweder was less elegiac when faced with the prospect of vertical journeys. A year after Lewis took Lieutenant Brown high above the Somme he wrote to his wife from La Bassée district. Chapman, a fellow officer, had gone up in a balloon. Dangling above ground in a basket under a 'maiden's dream' was distinctly uninspiring, he reported after coming down safely. More alarming was the unhappy experience of another joy-rider who'd gone up a few days previously. When he ascended a German aeroplane attacked the balloon, forcing both him and the balloonist to struggle into their parachutes and throw themselves out.[318]

Perhaps the difference between Lewis and Schweder was a matter of temperament, or spatial location, or simply a case of time and distance lending enchantment; Lewis's elevated style induced by professional and personal disassociation from Befland's surface and a twenty-year interlude between journey and textual reconstruction, Schweder's lapidary phrasing by the cautions of a body exposed to the zone's everyday earthbound hazards, and firmly anchored in everyday discourse – 'maiden's dream' was settler slang for the large condom-shaped balloon shroud. ⮑ 36

Friday 19 May 1916 **35**

'The houses around the "Grand Place" are flattened out and the town generally pretty well messed up,' wrote Ronald Schweder. Nevertheless a few natives were still in residence and one two shops were still open. He'd been to Albert's Grand Place three days previously during a spell of fine weather to get supplies for the mess. Nowadays most shopkeepers lived in and worked from their cellars, he noticed; trading above ground was too risky.[319]

There wasn't any other reason for Schweder to visit the town. Heavily shelled and twice evacuated and reoccupied, it was far too deep in the zone to serve as a permanent supply base or the site of more or less permanent settlement. On the whole Albert was a place of transience. In the second half of 1916 immigrants in their hundreds of thousands passed through it and under the 'Golden Virgin'. Popularly known as 'Fanny Durack' after the Australian swimmer, the statue leaned out from the cathedral's spire over the road running straight as a die to the killing fields a few miles to the northeast between La Boiselle and Pozières. Visible from a dozen miles away, shellfire had thrust it into its bizarre position in mid January 1915.[320] Settler superstition held that the war would end when the virgin fell. It eventually collapsed in April 1918. In Henry Williamson's *A Patriot's Progress* the narrative voice describes Albert in mid 1916 as 'crammed with lorries, waggons, ambulance convoys, soldiers, mules, dumps of grey barbed wire and shells by the railway sidings, hay, sandbags, and wooden trench-boards. German prisoners were scrapping the roads with shovels and iron mud pushers'.[321] Populated by settlers 'making themselves at home in empty houses, while a few wretched shops and cafes hung on in the main street to live on them' was how Charles Carrington remembered it.[322] On 17 October after a stint away to the north Robert Cude noted in his diary that the place was very different from the one he'd know a few months previously. Back then quiet, well-cultivated fields ringed the centre. Now tented camps, wagons lines and vast earthworks stretched out in every direction. 'Town itself is one moving mass of vehicles, and all along railway is [sic] huge stacks of food, grain and shells'. Virtually all the civilians had fled, he wrote, because the German bombardment never ceased.[323]

By late 1916 there was just a single casualty clearing station left in the town and very few resident Beflanders;[324] most had moved out as the border shifted eastwards. Only in 1917 did it begin to recover. Natives drifted back to trade with the thousands of settlers still transiting through. 'Albert, that deadly uninteresting little town, looked almost beautiful and cheerful,' recalled William Orpen of a trip there in August. 'Flowers grew by the sides of the streets; roses were abundant in what were once back-gardens; a hut was up by the corner of the Cathedral and Daily Mails were sold there every evening at four o'clock, and the golden leaning Lady holding her Baby, looking down towards the street, gleamed in the sun on top of the Cathedral tower. A family had come back from Corbie and re-started their restaurant – a father and three charming girls. They patched up the little house by the station and did a roaring trade, and some few other families came back. Once more a skirt could be seen, even a few silk stockings occasionally tripping about'.[325] ➲ 72

36 Thursday 25 May 1916

Farrier Staff Sergeant T. W. Girling's leave order from the Somme, written on a sheet of paper torn from an army exercise book: 'Fourth Army. XIII Corps. 30th London. No: 25/1305. Unit: No. 2 Company. Leave: from 31/5/16 to 9/6/16. Destination: Kettleburgh P[ost] O[ffice], N[ea]r Wickham

M[arke]t, Suffolk. Approved: Captain, DAA and QMG 30th Division [signature illegible], L[ieutenan]t-Col[onel], Command 30th Division Train [signature illegible]. I. You should be at HEILLY station at 9 a.m. on the day before your leave starts. II. You should be at Waterloo station at 4 p.m. on the last day of your leave. III. You should report to the office of MLO HAVRE both going and returning from leave'.[326]

Rowland Luther pausing at Waterloo station while travelling from Befland to South Wales, late 1916: 'As we reached the gates, we encountered some elderly people, wearing arm-bands marked: "Guide". Outside the gates, were a great number of women and girls, enticing the young soldiers to have a good time with them, with promise of bed for the night and fish and chips for supper, for just one pound. The old guides were hanging on to us, however, directing us to Paddington, and exhorting us to leave these waiting women alone, and return to our loved ones at home'.[327] Two other travelling scenes. Frank Richards at Victoria Station, June 1916: 'There were always ladies soliciting outside and I expect many young soldiers who went with them wished afterwards that they had been blown to pieces in France'. In the concourse he watched the enactments as Beflanders passed through to the emigrant trains; drunks dancing with girls, sober family men chatting with wives, relatives and offspring.[328] Richard Foot's memory of returning to Befland, November 1917: 'The journey back to the battery was always a strange emotional experience. It was a wrench to leave home and England, and the farewells at the crowded leave train platform at Victoria Station were heart rending'.[329] For a while the public were allowed onto the platforms but later, as at Waterloo, gates were put up; portals separating one world from another.

Did faces relax from grief into relief as the two cohorts separated – on the one side emigrant carriages pointing inexorably towards Folkestone, Dover, Portsmouth, Southampton and the Channel steamers, on the other civilian trains and buses dispersing friends, relatives, prostitutes and chance acquaintances into the London smog and the towns and villages beyond – or did the dissolving heterogeneous crowds and the ranked khaki-clad emigrants squeezed into their differently classed compartments revert to anecdotes which served only to disguise anxiety, loss and fear? Doubtless some faces did relax and others did not. Some disguised fear and anxiety, others felt neither. Some were glad to be gone or see them go, others were heartbroken. But the explanatory categories available to historians – class, gender, ethnicity, kinship, age, etc. – will not take us very far if we try to classify settler responses at and beyond the portals. Diversities of thought and mood, evident in diaries and letters, disrupt our taxonomic schemes and present us with an intractable difficulty. We are faced with a dialectical tension; fruitful in some ways, disturbing and dispiriting in others. On the one hand there is the irreducible but elusive factor of individual temperament, on the other the given but mutating structures of social being. We understand neither, and they interact in ways we can never hope fully to anatomize, let alone synthesize. Their final reconciliation always remains beyond our grasp. Writing history involves making brief, clumsily executed raids into a dark continent. We return with ambiguous fragments of evidence, artefacts that shimmer equivocally as we examine them. On this basis we hazard to reconstruct the past by pushing and pulling at language, but at the back of every historian's mind lurks the gnawing suspicion that he has got everything wrong.

Nevertheless we could at least classify Victoria and Waterloo as liminal places, locations that Beflanders passed through but did not live in. And we might go further. We could plausibly adapt Eva Illouz's suggestion, made in quite another context, that 'romantic travel' enacts three stages characteristic of liminality – 'separation, marginalization, and reaggregation'[330] – to the experience of these journeying settlers, though we might want to discard the appellation 'romantic'. For settlers bound for Befland Illouz's stages would entail first, separation at the portals, second, a sense of loss or marginalization on the platform and into the railway carriages, and finally reaggregation and reintegration into the life of the colony as the train and the talk and the anecdotes gathered pace. Inside a post-portal third-class compartment, from Henry Williamson's 1930 novel from experience *A Patriot's Progress*: 'Eight to a carriage. Packs and rifles on the racks and under the seats. Games of nap. Laughter, singing, fags. Looking out of the window and waving to every girl they saw'.[331]

Of course there were many more portals, in New Zealand, Australia, China, India, Africa, Canada, Newfoundland and the Caribbean, where just such enactments, just such responses might be seen, or others, according to circumstance and culture. And for British emigrants travelling in reverse, from Befland to London, the whole psycho-social drama might occur more or less in the same order, but with different moods and expectations. Ralph Hamilton, 3 April 1916: 'St James's Terrace. Home once more . . . We landed at Folkestone at 1 p.m. and after a little delay got off, reaching Victoria at 4.30. It is impossible to describe one's feelings of delight in living in one's own comfortable house once more. I have seven clear days' leave in London, but have a lot to do – new clothes to get, dentist, and a hundred little things wanted for the battery'.[332] ➲ 37

37 Sunday 4 June 1916

Stapleton Eachus left Southampton for Le Havre in bad mood. He'd crossed the portals at Waterloo, missed his wife and failed to see her on the quayside. The only refreshment he could find was a dreadful cup of tea, outrageously priced at thruppence plus a penny deposit on the cup. The boat finally sailed at five thirty in the afternoon and ran into choppy seas as it cleared the harbour. Then seasickness struck. Passengers threw up everywhere, not only on deck, but also down below. The filth – impossible to avoid – sloshed about in the holds. Eachus arrived at Le Havre wet through, covered dirt and thoroughly disgruntled.[333] Ronald Schweder, no less irritated but within a different class context: at nine thirty in the morning of 15 July 1917, a Sunday, he was stuck at Folkestone's Hotel Metropole all day until the boat went at half past six; nothing was open and there were not even any papers to read. It was tiresome in the extreme, he grumbled, to be kept idling around like this; boats and trains should be made to coincide.[334] Others endured longer voyages and delays, welcome or unwelcome. In September 1916 moving a division from Egypt to the entrepôts – c.200,000 tons of men and material on about thirty ships – took, on average, eleven and a half days, but in spring nine divisions took nearly four months to complete the journey.[335]

Regulations probably accentuated Eachus's discomfort. After 1915 portholes were kept closed because of the submarine threat to Channel shipping and because hammocks were in short supply a quarter of passengers slept outside. Decks were soon awash with vomit, urine and excrement. As for Schweder's complaint, specialist roll-on-roll-off ferries appeared after December 1917 but there were never more than four in service. Everyone else had to scramble off the trains and into the boats, though before the army put a stop to it in March 1917 wealthy settlers sometimes sailed across in their own yachts.[336]

Overall, between 9 August 1914 and 1 April 1919, about seven million embarked for France from the Channel ports – Dominion, Imperial and US troops, naval personnel, nurses, relatives of the wounded, Chinese and other contracted labourers, British drafts and reinforcements. Many of these, of course, travelled several times; just over four million return journeys for the British cohort alone. UK ports and sea-lanes were always crowded. By October 1918, apart from leave and reinforcement ships, some 400 barges, dredges and launches and over one hundred hospital ships, each capable of carrying between 800 and 4,000 wounded, plied between Befland and the United Kingdom. Crossing their path or merging into the stream were dozens of ocean-going freighters bringing supplies (85,000 tons a day in 1916), remounts and settlers from India, Africa, the Americas and the Antipodes.[337] Nowadays a voyage across the Channel is awe-inspiring, wrote George Stringer in September that year, 'the ceaseless activity & the dim shapes of the very numerous unlighted ships that pass by in the night'.[338]

Siege conditions and stable lines of communication meant that the regular pulse of arrival and departure, from Befland to the United Kingdom and back again, was kept up right through to 1918.[339] In February 1915 Stringer journeyed from La Bassée district to London. He left his unit for Estaires at half past one in the afternoon by general service wagon, hopped on a bus to Steenwerck, got the leave train, arrived at Boulogne at nine-fifteen, boarded the leave boat at midnight, sailed at four in the morning and caught the Folkestone-London train at six-thirty.[340] Sidney Appleyard went through the portals at Waterloo on 5 May, waited at Southampton and arrived at Le Havre on the 10th.[341] Captain Newman travelled to Boulogne via Victoria and Folkestone in one day.[342] 'It is hard to realise that only this morning I was in action!' exclaimed Ralph Hamilton in April 1916 after leaving the Salient and crossing Victoria's portals.[343] Two years later Lieutenant Capron got from Arras to Hathersage in the Peak District in three days – 'a warm clean bed with linen sheets at last!'[344]

In *The Great War and Modern Memory* Paul Fussell comments on the literary aspects of Befland's proximity to the United Kingdom[345] – as the crow flies Ypres was no further from Trafalgar Square than Sheffield, Amiens about as far away as Exeter – but it's worth dwelling for a moment on a few of the physical, psychological and social ramifications proximity engendered. This wasn't just a matter of the well-attested settler contempt for jingoistic civilians or the inability to describe to anxious, sympathetic faces what life was really like across the Channel, nor of the obvious attractions (for a minority) of a well-appointed bourgeois house – Capron's warm, clean bed with linen sheets at Hathersage. The shock of transition engaged the senses at every turn. On the one side those going on leave often carried the very texture of Befland with them into the United Kingdom. In February 1918 Ronald Schweder mailed his wife to say that he would be crossing the Channel after an overnight stay in Boulogne, an unwelcome delay though on the other hand it did mean that he wouldn't be arriving home dirty.[346] But many did. While crossing the portals at Waterloo two years earlier Rowland Luther noticed 'some dear old ladies who collected bits of mud from each soldier's equipment, for some obscure purpose'.[347] On the other side those returning might have to reorientate themselves physically and psychologically within the landscape. The colony seemed worse in every respect after a stay in England, and so much noisier, complained Schweder in May 1916. Eight months later he returned again, this time to Dranoutre in the Salient: 'Too depressing for words. Everything looks so squalid and beastly, far worse than when I left, and so infernally cold'.[348] ⤴ 38

38   Monday 5 June 1916

Stapleton Eachus, *en route* to the Somme, drew rations at Le Havre station and then boarded a train. There were no carriages for other ranks, only cattle trucks marked *Hommes 36–40 Chevaux (en long) 8*. Most were little more than wrecks. The track showed through the base where planks had been removed or rotted away. Open to the skies and slatted up only about half way up, each wagon was also awash with decaying vegetable matter. The night journey was far from comfortable. Next January he described the mood of settlers waiting to go on leave. All were unanimous in condemning the complete chaos to be found along the lines of communication and at the entrepôts, and utterly sick and tired of days wasted hanging about at regulating stations, junctions and docksides.[349] Some leave journeys might be reasonably quick [37], but by no means all.

The colony's entrepôts and railway lines were perpetually choked with supplies, wargear and travellers. For returning Beflanders entrepôt rest camps functioned as 'accumulators' until fifty or so wagons could be filled – trains ran on continuous circulation, full trains going 'up country' and then turning round and running back down. At Boulogne there was always a stampede for the carriages, remembered Richard Foot.[350] If settlers were late for their allotted train it left without them. All they could do was wait and try to squeeze on the next one in the stream.[351] It took Sidney Appleyard twenty-one hours to travel from Boulogne to Bailleul in May 1915 and Ronald Schweder ten hours to cover sixty miles to Dranoutre in December 1916, though the latter's mood lifted somewhat when he learnt that his servant had been waiting at Bailleul for two days to meet him – 'wasn't it decent of him'.[352] In August Lieutenant Capron endured a long journey across the Channel and from the entrepôts on towards the Somme. He left Southampton at seven-thirty in the evening as the sun set behind the Solent. A lone swan flew across the bows. Early next morning the harbour lights at Le Havre came into view. People woke up and stretched cold and cramped limbs (like many others, Capron had been forced to sleep on deck, surrounded by piles of valises). When the boat finally docked they stumbled ashore. 'Havre was peaceful, and we found our way to Tortoni's and a good breakfast of omelette and peaches'. Then came a stay in a transit camp in the hills outside the town – hot meals in the canteen and afternoons sitting in the summer sunshine – thereafter a grindingly slow train journey eastwards. As they neared the zone lights pulsed and shimmered in the night sky. Then a breakfast of bread, cheese and beer in an estaminet at Saint-Riquier, their detraining point, and the following day a final train ride on to join his unit.[353]

George Stringer, by now an experienced traveller, fared much better a month later, but was still delayed at the entrepôts and hung up on the railways. 21 September was a hot, sultry day. In the afternoon he walked into the centre of Le Havre and sat in the Hotel de Ville's gardens watching native children playing in the sunlit street. After an hour or so he ambled over to the British Officers' club at 17 Rue Jules for tea – a pleasant experience – read the London newspapers and wrote a letter to a relative, Mrs Tenel. Next came dinner at the officers' mess; no less enjoyable than the tea. Three days later he spent an agreeable night sleeping in a railway carriage. There was only one other person in the compartment; Johnson, a fellow officer. They were both killing time, waiting for the train to leave for Abbeville. As the night wore on Stringer's primus stove came in handy for hot drinks. The train didn't start till eight, leaving ample scope for morning tea and a leisurely stroll up to the engine. Like most French locomotives this one leaked hot water by the bucket load, making it ideal for extempore washing and shaving. Just before the train departed he slipped to an even more comfortable compartment, one technically reserved for *les dames*, but in this instance, happily (or perhaps not), there were no other passengers. More tea on the primus stove followed as the train inched towards Saulty, as usual at a snail's pace, before arriving at six in the evening. Stringer clambered out and got into a general service wagon that had been sent from the divisional ammunition column to pick him up. Things were less comfortable six months later, though he did manage to make the best of it. Abbeville was cold, frosty and foggy, and crammed with railway traffic, so he wandered about looking for an officers' hut to sleep in until the Doullens train left the following day. He got tangled up in a maze of railway tracks, however, and lost his way as first one goods train and then another lumbered across his path and forced him to make endless detours. In the end he gave up, dragged his baggage into a workman's hut and bedded down. It was warm in the hut, but whistling, shunting and shouting kept him awake for much of the night. On the 30 November he recorded details of a train crash in the district: a dreadful business, he averred. A friend told him that a leave train had collided with a freight train in thick fog just outside Doullens. It was still on his mind on Christmas Day, and into the new year. About half of the freight train's wagons had broken loose, hurtled downhill and smashed into the leave train steaming uphill. The impact caused some of the leave train's carriages to topple over and catch fire, pinning the terrified Beflanders underneath. Thirty-seven were dead or injured.[354]

Trains were shelled all the time in the vicinity of the zone, so why did Stringer ruminate on the Doullens crash? Partly, one suspects, because it was out of the ordinary. Beflanders were far more likely to be killed by shells than runaway trains, but the type of train might also be pertinent. For British settlers leave trains may have formed part of a psychological continuum running from danger to safety, from zone to home via the back areas, the entrepôts, the Channel and the portals. Michel de Certeau suggests that travelling in railway carriages soothes and lulls the body and the soul: 'Inside there is the immobility of an order. Here rest and dreams reign supreme. There is nothing to do ... Outside there is another immobility'; things go by 'detached and absolute'. The window glass and the iron rail separate the traveller from the world and make an 'exterior silence'.[355]

As is often the case with cultural theorists the perspective here is that of the well-heeled *flâneur manqué*; not much chance of rest and dreams for travellers packed in the corridors of third-class compartments, one suspects, less still for firemen shovelling coal on the footplate. Nevertheless for tired Beflanders of a certain social class used to sinking into daydreams as they left the zone the horrors of a crash might be imagined particularly keenly. In addition, all settlers inhabited a world quieter than our own, the zone notwithstanding. Forty-seven years after the event Richard Foot could still recall the shock he felt when a sudden explosion killed some of his colleagues. 'Today, a motor car accident is the most likely way to provide a traumatic experience: everything goes along smoothly and normally, when, suddenly, bang crash and there are people killed and wounded all over the place. The horse and buggy days could seldom provide such an event; perhaps that is why this occasion at Miraumont is still so vivid in my mind'.[356] We should beware, however, of theorizing on the basis of negligible evidence. The quirks of individual personality might explain things just as well. Stringer, for example, seems to have been sensitive to the feel of trains, and to their cultural resonance. 'A truly domestic thing are the railways of France,' he wrote a few months before the Doullens crash, 'not a thing aloof like ours, but part of the life of the nation'.[357]

For travellers returning to Befland further delays arose when they left the trains and moved deeper into the zone. Frequent lateral movements meant that in their absence units had often shifted away somewhere else. When Capron returned to Arras in January 1918 he discovered that his battery had migrated to Gauchin-Légal, eleven miles distant. When he got there he found they'd moved again, two miles north to Savy-Berlette.[358] 'In the course of the day we meandered on, passing through Marles[-les-Mines],' wrote Hamilton in May 1915. 'St Pol etc., and reached Béthune at 4 p.m. There I got out, extracted my kit with great difficulty, and found out where the 108th Brigade were. The R.T.O. said they were in action at Grenay, where I had left them, so I rang up the I Corps and asked if they could arrange to send a car for me. I was told that the brigade was resting at Fouquières[-lès-Béthune], only two miles southwest of Béthune. I waited about the station for some time, till I saw a likely looking motor, whose driver I bribed to take me and my kit out'. He had a similar experience at end of the year: 'I tried to borrow a car from the Red Cross to run me out to the brigade, but failed. So I sent a telegram through the signal people to say I wanted my horses and the mess-cart to meet me at Surques at 4.30 p.m. After lunch I took the metre-gauge train up-country and duly reached Surques at 6.30. To my intense relief I found my horses and the cart waiting and rode the 3 miles in time for tea'.[359]

All zone dwellers shared risks in common, but they did not share common discomforts when on leave journeys. We should not forget that most of the travellers cited in this narreme were officers. Other ranks would have a harder time traversing Befland: no access to officers' clubs at the entrepôts, no sitting in the sunshine in the gardens outside Le Havre's Hotel de Ville, no breakfasts at Tortoni's, no accommodating RTOs, no horses, not enough money to bribe drivers, no telephone calls to the officers' mess, no cars, no servants and no plush carriages. '1st class coaches are easily distinguished by their old English road coach appearance', noted Eachus, 'but of course such compartments are exclusively reserved for officers'.[360] ➲ 39

Tuesday 6 June 1916 **39**

After a rough night on a train bound from Le Havre to the Somme (hardly any sleep and wide awake from four in the morning) Stapleton Eachus looked out from his railway wagon. Beautiful countryside met the eye; attractive little villages tucked into the hillsides and valleys that stretched away on either side of the track. After a while the train jolted through Rouen station and crossed the River Somme, giving a fine view of Rouen cathedral, 'splendid' in the morning light.[361] Three days previously J. N. Peterson posted a letter to his girlfriend as he walked with his artillery unit from the entrepôts to the Salient. Inside the envelope he tucked something he'd picked up along the way. 'Although we pass through towns that have been shelled we don't come right up to the firing line or I would send you a better souvenir than the one I am putting in which is a Belgian Penny or what they call 10 centimes'.[362]

Slim pickings indeed, but since walkers and lorries shared the same space more generous foraging opportunities occasionally presented themselves, and not only for souvenir hunters. Until they were sealed after July 1915 walkers often raided army trucks as they rumbled along the roads, but most supplies were not so easily looted, at least while in transit to the zone. Apart from motor vehicles, heavy guns and turnouts, driven in or accompanied on foot, almost everything and everyone travelled into Befland by train.[363] 'You can follow the trail of the British army by the bully beef cans,' observed Garnet Durham as detrained at Pradelles near Hazebrouck in February 1915, 'right across France from St Nazaire'.[364]

By April 1916 lines of communication were well established. For the Second Army trains ran from Calais and Boulogne via St Omer and Hazebrouck to Poperinghe and Ypres. Both entrepôts also supplied La Bassée district's First Army; trains branched south at St Omer and headed for Béthune and Armentières. Le Havre served the Somme: Rouen – Abancourt – Amiens for the Fourth Army in the south (Eachus's journey); Abancourt – Abbeville – Frévent – Doullens and St Pol for the Third Army in the north. Hundreds of railheads clustered around these central detraining stations or straggled out along subsidiary lines.[365] A few miles beyond stood the border, but climate and technology severely restricted the possibility of further eastward movement, regardless of enemy action. Even when horses, mules and lorries were in abundance and the going firm, military planners knew that armies could travel only thirty miles in advance of their railheads. After that they were forced to stop, reorganize and resupply. In fact Beflanders rarely got that far, and not just because of resistance in and around no man's land. Thousands of reinforcements and enormous quantities of food, forage and wargear had to be ferried every day across landscapes churned into mud by rainfall, heavy shelling and heavy traffic. Tanks, horses, guns and men wallowed in the mire. Resupply involved undertaking major engineering works every few miles or so along the front – extending standard-gauge lines, resurfacing roads, bringing up guns and remounts and building tramways back from the trenches. Large howitzers took thirty-six hours to dismantle and needed several lorries and five huge caterpillar trucks to move at all.[366] When resistance crumbled in the final days of the advance to victory Beflanders could only infiltrate annexed territory, they could not settle it; borders melted away faster than roads and railways could be laid or repaired. By the Armistice some First and Second Army migrants were thirty miles east of their railhead, some attached to the Fourth Army fifty miles, and worryingly short of food and fodder.[367] One way or another Befland's offensives soon ran out of steam. Siege was inherent in wargear and topography.

To a limited extent travellers could access other means of transport. Canals fanned out from Calais into Flanders and La Bassée district, though provision was scarcer on the Somme. Nearly 550 vessels operated on Befland's inland waterways in September 1916, 718 a year later, 950 in autumn 1918 and just over 1,300 for the entire period 1914–18,[368] but barges moved much more slowly than trains and couldn't carry many settlers (a mere 60,000 in 1917–18[369]), and canals took much longer to repair than railways. The *Canal de la Somme* ran for ninety-seven miles, from St Valery-sur-Somme to St Simon, forty miles east of Amiens. There were sixty-nine locks along the way. When the Germans retreated to the Hindenburg Line engineers struggled for eight weeks to reopen a ten-mile stretch running from Frise to Péronne.[370] In northern Befland 15,000 Chinese labourers were needed to restore 200 miles of canals.[371]

Artillery turnouts, too heavy and cumbersome for trains or barges, walked towards the zone. Between 25 February and 4 March 1916 Ronald Schweder's battery slogged the fifty-odd miles from Cayeux-sur-Mer to Mailly-Maillet on the Somme. Along the way we encounter miscellaneous aspects of Befland's culture: the speed and frequency of the colony's postal service, the duties of officers, their obligations to and spatial separation from other ranks, the lively awareness of identity, the availability of newspapers, stray reminders of home embedded in the built environment, the look of billets, perceptions of the enemy, the importance of horses, weather and the time of year, the condition of Befland's roads, the difficulty of supplying travelling cohorts, awareness but not experience of the wider warscape, the curious nature of life in the zone and instances of what Tony Ashworth calls the 'live and let live' system obtaining at the front.[372]

On the first day they covered twenty-five miles. There wasn't time to describe things in detail, he wrote, because it was nearly seven in the evening and the post was just about to go, but deep snowdrifts had made the roads virtually impassable; men, horses, limbers, gun carriages and wagons had slipped and sloshed about at every turn. He'd spent most of the day at the end of the column encouraging the stragglers to keep up. They'd arrived at their destination at around five o'clock, but there was no rest for the officers: horses had to be fed, watered and picqueted and other ranks settled into billets before they could look to their own comforts. To cap it all there were no supplies, so they would have to stay where they were for the following day. Next morning a large group of medics, perhaps the staff of a casualty clearing station on the move, went slowly along the road – one of his men called out 'good morning poultice wallopers'. Someone told him that the

French army was in trouble and that troops were being sent from all over the country to bolster the defence of Verdun. Asquith's speech, reproduced in a newspaper he was reading, was 'less cock-sure than usual'. Later on, after they'd set off again, he noticed a house numbered 119, his wife's lucky number. That night the officers were billeted in an abandoned chateau. It was as filthy as a farmyard and notable only for its fine chandeliers and the gloomy portraits of ancient ancestors that loured down from the walls. The grounds were a sea of mud. Outside hordes of Beflanders tramped by incessantly.[373]

In the first few days of March comes a meditation on the activities and responses of French, German and Canadian troops at the point of destination, and on the aspect of the warscape. When the French were in residence they and the Germans had come to an arrangement – no shelling before ten in the morning. This allowed both sides to sit quietly on the parapets shaving and eating breakfast. One night the French left and the Canadians took over. As dawn broke they saw the enemy silhouetted against the rising sun and fired off a salvo of high explosive shells, perhaps out of spite, perhaps in ignorance of the arrangement. The furious Germans scrambled for safety and called down an artillery bombardment targeted right into the Canadian trenches. When Schweder's brigade arrived a gunner friend, Major 'Bubbly' Bolitho, made the same mistake – firing on a German trench which, by tacit agreement, was never shelled. Lethal retaliation followed. As for the position itself, nobody cared a hoot about camouflage or security. All night long lights burned unscreened and motor vehicles lumbered about with their headlamps on, illuminating the snow-covered landscape as if they were miles from the zone. Once at Mailly-Maillet, the nearest village to his gun pits, Schweder was surprised to find an abandoned house with most of the windows still intact and a functioning kitchen range – ideal for the officers. Mailly was 3,500 yards from the German trench system, he wrote, but it wasn't shelled very often because gunners living nearby had more cannon, and more of a heavier calibre, than did their German counterparts. Moreover, they knew precisely in which villages enemy artillerymen had their billets, and were quick to respond if disturbed.[374] ➲ 48

40 Thursday 8 June 1916

Billeted on the Somme in preparation for the summer offensive, Ronald Schweder had two cavalrymen to dinner at the officers' mess. To his delight they arrived carrying a brace of large trout they'd caught in the Ancre.[375] Eleven days later Stapleton Eachus spent a happy afternoon fishing in the nearby L'Hallue stream while guns boomed away in the distance.[376] During the mass migration associated with the drive to victory Lieutenant Capron passed through the village of Oisy-le-Verger near Cambrai. Fish abounded in lakes there. Capron caught them by lobbing hand grenades from the water's edge. For settlers on the move this must have been a popular ancillary use of wargear because later on banning orders were issued.[377]

Instances of fishing in siege landscapes are comparatively rare, however. Apart from the Somme and the Ancre, rivers were scarce in southern Befland and large areas of standing water almost unknown, and there was little chance of catching fish in the two other border districts where settlers congregated. The Belgian king's decision to open the sea-locks at Nieuport in October 1914 created a vast, impassable marshland in the northernmost corner of Flanders, while constant shelling in and around the Salient turned pools and water meadows to slurry. La Bassée mining district was too polluted with discarded wargear support much that was edible, though at Givenchy-lès-la-Bassée in 1915, before the dereliction took hold, after hours of fruitless angling Frank Richards did manage to catch fish by chucking Mills bombs into the local canal.[378] But on the whole it's more common to find siege settlers hunting birds and mammals. On 24 April 1915, when George Stringer was near Lindenhoek in the Salient, he and some other officers went out to check traps they'd set sometime earlier – a trick learnt from their cook. They came back with a two pheasants and a brace of partridge. To his annoyance feral cats dragged off the pheasants before the cook could get to them, but the partridge survived and made fine eating. On New Year's Day 1917, now based on the Somme, he took a stroll around the snow-covered fields outside Souastre on his the way to a forward gun position. There were partridge and hares all over the place, he mentioned, before calling to mind – and then dismissing – yet another order prohibiting the shooting of game.[379]

No one else seems to have taken much notice either. Wild fauna was fair game for Beflanders keen to supplement rations with fresh meat – even roe deer were on offer[380] – but social class determined the method. Privates and NCOs generally trapped animals, officers usually shot them, sometimes in organized shoots,[381] before handing them over to servants and cooks: 'no [shot]gun to shoot them, of course,' regretted Herbert Leland in October 1916 as he watched a covey of partridges settle a few yards away near one of the Salient's waterlogged trenches.[382] Next spring Schweder, caught off guard just outside Bailleul, couldn't disguise his irritation when class conventions were violated – other ranks shooting pheasants with rifles; a dangerous practice, he averred, because rifle bullets went a long way and the entire landscape was heavily populated with settlers. He was in mellower mood with a fellow officer on the Somme the previous May, however, even though troubled by hay fever and asthma. Unable to sleep after a bad night at an observation post he got up at three in the morning and paced round the ruins of a nearby chateau. On his way back he fell in with a subaltern looking for rabbits. They hunted together until the dawn mists cleared, but without success.[383]

The Somme's broad, rolling chalklands, and the narrow strip of marshland to the south where the river marked Befland's border with the French, offered game in plenty, probably because the natives had gone and so left the local fauna unmolested. Thirteen years later another settler recalled life just after Christmas 1916 on the border around Frise, Biaches and Cléry-sur-Somme. 'Between these villages was a gap in the trench lines for about three miles, where scattered outposts watched one another across the flooded marshes. Every morning flocks of wild duck rose from their nightly feeding ground, vainly pursued by a rain of machine-gun bullets from both armies'.[384] Garnet Durham too noticed the proliferation of game – 'partridges all through the trench area'. Collecting salvage along the road through Death Valley to Pozières in September 1916 he stumbled across a French battery about to unleash a barrage. Out of the blue a flock of partridges flew over an intervening ridge and settled down to feed a few yards in front of the guns, but on this occasion sentiment intervened. A kind-hearted colonel raised his hand. 'Attendez, mes enfants,' he said, and sent a gunner to shoo the 'oiseaux' away. Only when they'd flown off did the firing start. The birds wouldn't have been killed, wrote Durham, but they would have been stunned, 'for, of all the bitter barks, a French 60 has the wickedest'.[385] ➲ 51

41 Monday 19 June 1916

Stapleton Eachus was travelling east from Le Havre, an interminable journey, as it turned out, and tedious; he'd made the same trip only two weeks previously. His train started about midnight, passed through Rouen early next the morning and made a lengthy stop just outside the town. Most of the passengers, settlers bound for the Somme, got off and wandered over to some huts, probably run by the YMCA. During the lunch hour the canteen staff put on a service – 'Onward Christian Soldiers' and other hymns. After that there was nothing much to do. As the afternoon wore on men broke the monotony by playing cards or Crown and Anchor. They were ordered back onto the train at three in the afternoon, but had to wait another hour before they left. The train crawled along, jerking and stopping every few minutes. It finally ground to a halt in the middle of nowhere. A gang of French engineers were repairing the track. As night fell men leaned out of the wagons, chatting away with the natives and practising their rudimentary French.[386]

We might be able to elevate the cliché that war is a matter of long periods of inaction punctuated by moments of terror to the status of a kind of fact by measuring the duration of inaction, though we could be less certain about terror. Terror is a possible response to action, but it is not the only one. Some might be frightened, others emboldened. Inaction has two aspects as well, ease and boredom. Historians cannot easily discern the line that divides one from the other. We may recover the externality of things – this many people of this or that age, social class, gender or ethnicity precipitated into these or those circumstances – but externality will not tell us how circumstances were experienced. Even when people are acting in common experience is individualized, a point implict in Simon Schama's lament for the inadequacies of history. 'Historians are left forever chasing shadows,' he writes, 'painfully aware of their inability ever to reconstruct a dead world in its completeness'. This doesn't mean that we can't establish offensive truths, however; death tolls, for example, or Lenin's *kto kogo* ('who does what to whom'). History is not fiction because it is anchored in evidence. It can't just be imagined. But it does mean, to continue with Schama, that we have to accept our 'unavoidable remoteness' from our subjects: 'We are doomed to be forever hailing someone who has just gone round the corner and out of earshot'.[387]

Schama's melancholy reflections apply most forcibly to researchers abroad in fields where the vast bulk of the dead leave no traces in the historical record, but even when there is an embarrassment of riches, in our case the mass of diaries, letters and memoirs left by Beflanders, the problem reappears. Eachus's train was the exterior thing, as were the sung hymn, the games of cards and Crown and Anchor and the conversations with French engineers. We are fortunate indeed to have evidence like this, but all the same we cannot know how many passengers were bored and how many at ease, or who found the delays tiresome or welcomed them because they delayed precipitation into the zone.

Two other men on the psychological interface between ease and boredom. On Wednesday 11 April 1917 George Stringer was near Aire-sur-la-Lys in southern Flanders and troubled by an appendix operation that hadn't gone well. He awoke to a fine morning, but driving rain and snow clouded the afternoon. Guns, heard for the first time in many a day, boomed away somewhere in the distance. On Monday a note had arrived from a relative in England. To send a card to someone stuck in the wilds of the Befland countryside was too much, he complained. Out here the only hope of escape from the 'engulfing boredom' was the post. The body is free, he continued, one can move about, but there's nothing to do or see, no distractions and no conversation except repetition of the same old stale stories heard over and over again. Miserable and disgruntled, he retired to bed with an aching stomach. At Kemmel Hill two year's previously he'd spent most of early April sitting in the garden of his billet in the sunshine, aimless and mildly pleased with life.[388] Ronald Schweder, in action at Aveluy Wood on 9 March 1916, three months before the Somme offensive, commented on current realities: a great deal of leisure and hanging about in the cold, gunnery notwithstanding, and no fires permitted until after dark because the smoke might alert the enemy – 'very tiresome'. Next year, in September, ten months after the offensive and six months after the German withdrawal to the Hindenburg Line, we find him up on the plateau near Bapaume and complaining about isolation – no news, nothing to do except think about food and sleep and make the occasional trip to Amiens. If he kept a diary, he told his wife, there would be nothing in it except records of schemes for the disposal of horse manure. In December 1918 he was billeted in a street lined with workers' cottages and factories at Tourcoing in New Befland and enduring a boring morning routine of breakfasts, parades and stable inspections. Evenings and afternoons were frittered away riding round the district and visiting the local cinema.[389]

In one sense Eachus and his travelling companions were all of a piece; all males, probably drawn from the same social class, and all other ranks dressed much the same, paid much the same and subject to much the same discomforts and constraints. Stringer and Schweder were artillery officers, subject to other discomforts and constraints. In each case evidence defines their circumstances, but in each mood and temperament conspire to produce individual responses, and we can never be sure whether or not they are examples of some wider social phenomena. ⊃ 54

42   Wednesday 21 June 1916

From Stapleton Eachus's diary; Fourth Army headquarters at Querrieu on the Somme: 'in the absence of street names in the village, English ones have been put up, such as "Exchange St", "Cannon St", "Burton St"'.[390] Decades afterwards Sidney Appleyard recalled structures along Ypres Ridge in May 1915. Before colonization native railway engineers had excavated a cutting and deposited three spoil heaps. Beflanders named the highest one 'Hill 60'. Because of its dominant position – sixty metres above sea level and commanding Zillebeke village and lake – it was the site of fierce fighting. The other was known as 'The Caterpillar' because of its irregular twisting shape; the third, a cone-shaped mound, was called 'The Dump'.[391] At Acheux on the some in November 1916 George Stringer and a companion walked into the ruined village of Mailly-Maillet, then to the Quadrangle, past Bertrancourt, on to Shrapnel Corner, Burnt Farm, Grossville and then home to his billet. Next month he reconnoitred trenches around Souastre – Naked Street and Neverending Street.[392]

In 1930 John Brophy and Eric Partridge categorized aspects of Befland's argot – slang, marching songs, chants and sayings – though their taxonomy is haphazard and their etymologies sometimes questionable.[393] Toponyms, a means by which immigrants asserted their presence in the colony, are no less expressive of cultural identity. Though often duplicated,[394] there must have been many thousands of unique nomens. While conceding that his list is by no means exhaustive, Peter Chasseaud has identified over 10,500 trench names alone.[395] Those produced by Chinese, Indian, Portuguese, African and West Indian immigrants, largely illiterate, are lost to us, but a glance at a small selection used by the English speaking diarists and correspondents considered in this book suggests that, like songs and slang, place names can also be categorized.

1 Full or partial Anglicisms of native or German toponyms: Carnoy
Valley; Flers, Frankfurt and Munich Trench; Leipzig, Schwaben
and Zollern Redoubt; The Gird Lines (probably after the nearby
village of Gueudecourt), Lousy (Leuze) Wood and Trones Wood,
Montauban Alley.

2 Names suggestive of danger, disaster or ease: Blighty, Death and
Happy Valley; Casualty Corner, Hell Blast Corner, Hellfire Corner,
Shrapnel Corner; Deadman's Ditch, Death Way, Machine Gun Alley.

3 Topographical names: Angle, Basin, Oakhanger, High, Wedge and
Caterpillar Wood; Caterpillar Valley and Centre Way; Cliff, Orchard,
Sickle, Skyline and Straight Trench; Crucifix Corner, Hawthorn
Ridge, Pendant Copse; Railway, Transport and Station Road; The
Switch Line, The Chalk Pit, The Citadel, The Dell, The Park, Sugar-
Loaf Salient, The Quadrilateral, The Triangle, Y Ravine.

4 Toponyms linked with settlers' places of origin, or units, or unit
histories: Abbey Road; Avoca, Breslau and Scottish Trench; Black
Watch, Cornish, Danzig, Dinkum and Munster Alley; Gordon
Dump, Minden Post, Cross Street, New Welcome Street; White
City, Tara Hill and Usna Hill, The Pope's Nose (to be punched in by
Ulster protestants entrenched opposite).

5 Collocations: Mash Valley and Sausage Valley; the many binary Ale,
Beer, Pint and Hops alleys and trenches.

6 Places named after settlers, perhaps long forgotten by later
immigrants: Pilla Junction [50], Pinney's Avenue, Beadle's Trench,
Wing's Way (after Colonel Wing; only his name survived),[396] Dive's
Copse (a dressing station; Captain Dive was its first commanding
officer).[397]

Chasseaud suggests other taxa, though little is done with them.[398] In fact it
remains the case that considered as a world, a society or a civilization rooted
in situ, the trench system still awaits its historian. As yet no one has essayed
the kind of close social-geographical analysis we might expect of, say, a
thick description of early twentieth-century Spitalfields: places of meeting,
places of departure, places of sunshine or shadow, street corner histories and
resonances, patterns of life, social spaces, etc.

Anglicisms also inflected native settlements: 'About Turn'
(Hébuterne), 'Ballyall' (Bailleul), 'Eat apples' (Étaples), 'Funky Villas'
(Foncquevillers), 'Hazy-Brook' (Hazebrouck) 'Plugstreet' (Ploegsteert),
'Wipers' (Ypres),[399] Mucky (Mouquet) Farm and Waterloo (Waterlot)
Farm. In addition, as with toponyms, names for wargear were sometimes
locational. 'Lyddite' was a high explosive propellant first used on the Lydd

gunnery ranges in Kent. 'SK', a powerful lachrymator, originated in South Kensington. Other attributions, often ironic or grimly jocular, referenced inventors, progenitors, characteristics or familiar objects. In 1915, the same year that Captain Battye invented the 'Battye bomb', zone dwellers in Flanders and La Bassée improvised 'hairbrush' and 'jam-pot' grenades,[400] though these personalized tools fell out of use as mass produced ordnance flooded the landscape during and after 1916.[401] At Carnoy on the Somme one afternoon in October Sidney Appleyard watched gunners firing off 'Lloyd George stuff', a nickname for heavy shells.[402] 'Flying pigs' were ungainly, 150-pound trench mortars, first trialled in June 1916. 'Rum-jar' and 'oilcan' projectiles appeared the same year. 'Mustard gas' was so named because of its smell (French troops called it 'yperite'). 'Premature' shells (it's not clear if the sexual connotation was intentional) blew up close to or in the gun. Howitzer crews were known as 'suicide clubs', as were infantry patrols. Settlers called German high explosive shells 'Black Marias' or 'Coal Boxes'. 'Jack Johnsons', named after the black US heavyweight boxer, burst with a cloud of dense black smoke. Unexploded ordnance lying around in the zone was either 'dud' or 'blind'. 'Whizz-bangs' gave zone dwellers little chance of escape; because they travelled faster than the speed of sound their approaching 'whizz' was heard only as they detonated.[403]

Occasionally mordant shorthand bundled together entire process; time, landscape, materiality and failed endeavour. Before 1 July 1916 the Somme offensive was known as 'The Big Push'. Afterwards other ranks called it 'The Great Fuck-Up'. ➲ 44

43   Thursday 22 June 1916

Harold Bursey at the foot of a hill by the Bois des Tailles on the River Somme: 'As the shells were falling some of my ammunition wagons were returning into my camp and I could not help but admire the coolness of the drivers as they wheeled their horses about and <u>walked</u> quietly away from danger'.[404]

We came from far away. We are cold most of the time, and hungry, and sick. The fodder tastes wrong, and there are no green pastures. The air is different here, and often foul and burning. The ponds are polluted and poison us. Our feet rot in winter and in summer we are plagued by dust and flies. We are terrorized by the sudden onslaught of inexplicable noise and violence which blocks our ears and slashes our big, defenceless bodies. Afterwards our flanks quiver and we slabber, wide-eyed at the horror. Our memory is but a little space and so the horror is new each time. We endure endless journeys across land and sea. We are wrenched from our native places. This is my friend and this is also my friend. These small ones I do not know. They bear many brands showing their transfer from man to man.

I have noticed that the designs of some of them are very intricate.[405] *We are torn, shattered, blistered and killed many and many and often our carcases stink and sink in the mud. We haul things we don't understand, labour day and night, and are taken to places we don't know.*
We fear the flying steel, the blinding light.
We fear the falling stars at night.
We fear the cold barrel between our eyes when we cannot get upright.
There is no place of abiding for us. We suffer many cruelties. We do not understand the barked command or the jerked halter. We have a good eye for men,[406] *but if we could we would shun them. 'We hate their sudden uplifted arms, the insanity of their flailing gestures, their erratic scissors gait, their aimless stumbling ways, the tombstone whiteness of their faces'.*[407] *This is their steam age, but they couldn't manage without us. Mostly we live up to our knees in mud. We can stand exposure to the cold and the wet if we are loose and can turn our backs to the wind but soon waste away if we can't wander.*[408] *Sometimes women train us instead of men.*[409] *Sometimes we chew through our headropes and wander about at night. Idleness makes us mischievous and vicious. Herded together and tied up in unaccustomed positions, strangers to each other, we vent our frustration by spiteful attacks in crowded picket lines or jam-packed freighters. Every day we bruise and fracture each other. The squeamish mare is a special danger.*[410] ➲ 46

Thursday 29 June 1916 **44**

Harold Bursey sprained an ankle in the hills around the Bois des Tailles on the Somme. 'Fancy jumping ditches at 46. I ought to be locked up. It will be awkward riding but it must be done. Just heard that we belong to the 13th Corps!! That explains the accident. No. 13!!'[411]

Most Beflanders were probably unaware of corps and armies or, like Bursey, paid them scant regard if they did learn of them. These large organizations, formed and dissolved as GHQ allocated settlers to this or that campaign, exhibited no corporate identity. A few months before Bursey fell off his horse XV corps, also on the Somme, was renumbered XVII. An entirely new XV corps emerged in April. General Gough's 'Reserve Corps' was renamed 'Reserve Army' in June, only to reappear in October as Befland's Fifth Army.[412] The Fourth Army became the Second Army when that unit went to Italy early in 1918, but reverted to its original designation when the original Second Army returned in spring.[413] Divisions – more permanent and therefore more likely to attract notice – were objects of approbation, mistrust or vague surmise. According to Charles Carrington settlers placed the Guards top of Befland's league table, closely followed by the New Zealanders and the 51st Highlanders. Your division, he added, always ranked fourth.[414] In 1915 zone dwellers in the 48th South Midland division attracted the derisive sobriquet 'goalkeepers' because they 'received' shells but never did any fighting. Australian divisions were rumoured to have good rations but were suspected of rustling. Of individual corps and army commanders Ivor Maxse (XVIII corps) had a reputation for efficiency, but also for harrying his subordinates unmercifully. Lord Roberts ('Bobs'), a veteran of the Indian Mutiny and the Afghan and Boer Wars, was popular with Old Army settlers but was gone long before the colony took shape. He died of pneumonia at St Omer in November 1914.[415]

As for the discontents and jealousies wracking the high command, most settlers probably knew nothing of them and were therefore in no position to take sides, even if they wanted to. The rows between Lord Kitchener and Field Marshal Sir John French, tensions between Indian trained 'colonials' and 'Europeans' (graduates of Camberley Staff College), General Sir Douglas Haig's scheming to make himself commander-in-chief, and the bitterness engendered by the 'Curragh Incident' – the refusal of some senior commanders to countenance forcing Ulster into a united Ireland – would be unknown to all but the well-connected and well-informed.[416] 'Fifty years ago,' wrote John Brophy in 1965, 'not one person, adult or child, in ten thousand had any direct evidence from his own senses concerning the people who ran the country. The "average man" was aware of statesmen, land-owning dukes, financiers and manufacturers, bishops and bankers through formal photographs and caricatures reproduced in the press, possibly as brief flickers jerking across the primitive cinema screen, or on the stage as conventionalised types in farce or musical comedy'.[417] Even the Easter Rising – 24–9 April 1916 – seems to have had no resonance inside Befland,[418] though timing might be important. Had it occurred after, not before 'The Great Fuck-Up' [42], the response might have been different.

Zone dwellers identified with little beyond their sections, platoons, companies and battalions, averred Carrington, but these were not amorphous agglomerations of individuals, at least initially. Old Army regiments had long histories and established regional associations. The latter also applied to subsequent 'territorial' formations.[419] 'Pals' battalions, groups of volunteers attached to Old or New Army regiments, compounded the mix. Here men joined up not only by locale but also on the basis of association; by sports team, trade or social club – e.g., 12th battalion East Yorkshires (Hull Sportsmen); 23rd battalion Northumberland Fusiliers (4th Tyneside Scottish); 15th battalion Highland Light Infantry (Glasgow Tramways), 8th battalion London Regiment (Post Office Rifles).

Little of this survived the Somme. 'After July 1st, 1916, the system of restoring an invalided man to his own battalion or battery broke down,' remembered Brophy. '"Base Details" were sent "up the line" to those formations which at the moment were most in need of reinforcement. A man who enlisted in the Devons might, after being wounded or sick, find himself in the Border Regiment or the Northumberland Fusiliers, and, after another wound, in a nominally Lancashire battalion composed of former Munsters,

Scots, Fusiliers, Middlesex, Norfolks and possibly every other regiment in the Army'.[420] But sometimes accommodations failed, or perhaps officers' preconceived notions reinforced pre-enlistment identities. In 1964 Richard Foot characterized the immigrants he'd encountered. Proletarians who'd spent their boyhoods selling newspapers on London's streets or dodging red-hot rivets in the Clyde's shipyards were more likely to be quick-witted than those who'd done little more than walk behind a plough, he thought. He distributed them in the battery accordingly; the town-bred to the more demanding technical tasks, erstwhile farm labourers to work needing physical strength and stamina. Thus does power shape experience. But we should not underestimate the capacity to assume identities. A few pages on Foot recalled life south of Arras in spring and summer 1918 when manpower shortages caused the re-organization of infantry units. Battalions were merged and brigades reduced from four to three battalions. Settlers originally from London, Durham and Devonshire flooded into his predominantly Yorkshire division, 'yet it was surprising how the Yorkshire spirit stuck . . . all of them on joining, assumed a Yorkshire defiant and stubborn quality . . . and were proud of it'.[421] ➲ 45

Saturday 1 July 1916 **45**

Someone, probably an officer, told John Masefield what happened during the day. 'I noticed that several men were inclined to take off their clothes before the attack. It may be fear in some cases, but then it was very hot, and there was the feeling that one would advance better free. One wants all one's strength, and the things pressing on the body seem to choke you'.[422]

When journeying into no man's land during major offensives infantrymen carried bombs, grenades, bayonets, firearms, rations, knapsacks, sewing kits, respirators, rolls of barbed wire, a range of equipment for signalling, cutting and digging, planks, groundsheets, field dressings and ammunition. The total weight of all this gear often exceeded 110 pounds, around eighty per cent of the average settler's body weight. Clothing alone accounted for twelve to fourteen pounds, far more if it became sodden. Boots absorbed one-third of a pound of water and took three days to dry out, greatcoats six pounds. It rained during the night of 30 June in southern Befland, so on the first day of the Somme there was an additional incentive to throw off clothing. Some walkers may also have been aware that penetrating wounds became infected if dirty fabric was driven into the body.[423]

In their sartorial aspect advancing infantrymen were beasts of burden akin to Befland's horses and mules. Not so the officers who accompanied them, though they might look much the same. Well before 1914 the high-visibility clothing characteristic of open warfare and mass illiteracy – brightly coloured tunics itemizing rank and unit – had given way to a uniform khaki.

Headgear changed shape in 1915 and 1916. George Stringer remembered chucking away his stiff-brimmed cap and purchasing 'one of those execrable floppy creations, which were a "sine qua non" of the time'. Befland folklore held that German snipers had the stiff-brimmed variety in their sights.[424] By the following year all zone dwellers wore heavy, two-pound steel-magnesium helmets. To avoid the attentions of the enemy some officers further blurred their identity by covering their shoulder taps and adopting other ranks' dress. Leather jerkins and rubber knee-boots, issued freely in winter 1917–18, added to the disguise, but residual bodily paraphernalia still expressed leadership roles. Officers carried whistles (for the direction and exhortation of inferiors) and pistols (for personal defence, shooting horses or, *in extremis*, threatening subordinates). Double identity discs, worn by all settlers after August 1916, identified corpses by name, rank and unit.[425]

Reading bodies outside the zone was much easier. At the entrepôts, in back-area bases and at depots strung out along the lines of communication trade dress or flashes of metal or cloth were more in evidence. Epaulettes, chevrons, cap badges, medals, etc. signalled the wearer's rank, unit, country of origin and military history. Railway guards and brakemen carried heavy gauntlets. Bakers wore calico, cold-storage meat handlers and disinfectors white canvas. Moleskin waistcoats or cardigans identified those attached to escort, artisan or labour companies.[426] WAACs and other female settlers still wore long, sweeping skirts, medics white coats, nurses the same uniforms seen in British hospitals. In or out of the zone discerning eyes could also pick out high-status accoutrements available to all, if they qualified. In January 1918 James Naylor boasted about the long-service 1914 Ribbon he'd just sewn onto his tunic – 'Everybody stares when I am out'.[427] Two months later Ralph Hamilton tried to get one in Amiens, and hinted that not all wearers were *bona fide*: 'we tried all the shops . . . Apparently it is not allowed to be sold in England, but the enterprising French are making it and selling it to the troops out here'.[428] Other sumptuary laws impinged on identity. According to MacPherson in the official history series sanitary sections hated their yellow armbands,[429] while the blue serge uniforms worn by immigrant railway workers proved so unpopular – other settlers mistook them for conscientious objectors – that they were discarded after 1915.[430]

High rank and elite status permitted bearers to elaborate complex identities based on sartorial and deportmental idiosyncrasies. Correct dress for officers was to some extent a matter of taste.[431] Siegfried Sassoon noticed a 'tailored' uniform worn by one of his officer colleagues: cap too soft, shirt and tie too yellow, breeches to bright.[432] In February 1917 Major Neely led the Post Office Rifles into no man's land brandishing a hunting horn.[433] For eighteen months in 1915–16 Richard Foot was adjutant to Lord Exeter, an hereditary officer of the Royal Household and a Burghley Cecil. Exeter, apparently, had lived for a while in the North-American prairie states. In consequence he rode like a cowboy rather than a British officer, feet sticking out to the sides and stirrups lengthened. No less distressing to the military mind was his habit of carrying an umbrella at all times, whether to guard against the sun in Egypt, where he'd been stationed for a while, or to fend off Befland's driving rain. Only once did Foot see him disconcerted. Stomping down a troopship gangway one day at Le Havre he bumped into an MLO, an equally bizarre figure, an ex-Navy man now dressed as an army captain and sporting a beard. 'My God, Colonel,' said the captain, staring at the umbrella as he stood shaking his hand in the pouring rain, 'you're the first sensible soldier I've seen arrive in this rotten country!'[434]

It's unlikely that outlandish displays like this, or the one witnessed by the Post Office Rifles' diarist, would have been tolerated in junior officers, let alone other ranks. ➲ 56

Wednesday 12 July 1916   46

'My men and horses are out night and day', wrote Harold Bursey from the Somme, '4 teams with 18 pounder shells left last night at 11 p.m. and didn't arrive home until 5 p.m. this evening. The men and horses are fairly done. Have 30 lame already and a few wounded'. There were more casualties a week later. 'Some of my drivers were gassed last night. One gone away on an ambulance. The others fairly cheery. Some mules were gassed also. Poor creatures, they are coughing now from the effects of it and there is something human about their cough. They will probably not be worth much soon'.[435]

'The reasons for the evacuation of sick and wounded animals are the same as those for the evacuation of sick and wounded men,' noted Blenkinsop & Rainey in the official history series. 'Briefly they are: – (a) Humanity. (b) Efficiency. (c) Economy'.[436] In the zone horses and mules were assessed and given first aid *in situ,* sometimes by the unit concerned. When one of George Stringer's horses got stuck in the mud near Hébuterne on the Somme in March 1917 he tried to revive it by pouring neat whisky down its nostrils.[437] Lieutenant Capron treated his own horses too. In May his charger trod on a grenade near Arras. He couldn't ride him for some weeks, but pretty soon it was grazing happily, apparently untroubled by the little puncture hole disfiguring its face.[438] Serious cases were transferred to Mobile Veterinary Sections, usually twenty strong and staffed by zone dwellers assigned for field punishment, assessed again, and then sent to Veterinary Evacuation Stations before onward dispatch by road, train or barge to base hospitals. From late 1914 to early 1918 siege conditions and stable lines of communication meant that most left the zone fairly quickly, but when overwhelmed mobile sections tended to kill animals on the spot.[439]

Siege conditions also led to the elaboration of vast back-area treatment complexes. RAVC reception hospitals at bases or the entrepôts earmarked animals for retention, transfer or 'disposal'. Retention and transfer were sub-divided into retention (surgical, medical and convalescent), transfer (surgical and medical), and mange. At the beginning of 1916 hospitals existed at Boulogne, Forges-les-Eaux, Montreuil, Neufchâtel-Hardelot, Le Tréport, Wimereux and Dieppe, but by the year's end the number had expanded dramatically: twenty hospitals, in part supported by the RSPCA, each divided into units of 250 patients. The largest housed 2,000 horses and mules. In addition there were four convalescent depots staffed by farmers and grooms, eighteen evacuation stations, sixty mobile sections, two base store depots and one bacteriological laboratory. A scheme whereby each hospital was to grow its own forage on hundred acre sites came to nothing because the War ended first. Convalescent depots were situated in northern Befland, but after the disaster at Gornay-en-Bray's 4,000-horse 3,000-acre site, a kind of horse slum closed down in 1916 because of mud and sickness, care was taken to select well-drained locations. On discharge some animals unfit for zone life were branded and sent by the Remount Commission to work along the lines of communication. Most suffered from exostosis, bone or cartilage deformations, but some vets suggested they'd be better off in the soft mud of the zone because hard road surfaces exacerbated the condition. The rest were auctioned off to native farmers and breeders.[440] ➲ 55

47 Saturday 22 July 1916

Stapleton Eachus took a stroll from Querrieu on the Somme to the village of Daours, three and a half miles away. He was struck by the aspect of the countryside: every inch of soil cultivated; spring corn ripening, winter corn already under the scythe; fields blazing with dots of vibrant red poppies and clumps of pale yellow flowers floating above the waving oats.[441]

Querrieu was twelve miles from the front, but summer flora sprouted right up to the border, even in the Salient's wasteland. The following day, as dawn broke over Befland, Garnet Durham walked into trenches outside Ypres. Curiosity got the better of him and he risked peeping over into no-man's land. All was quiet and peaceful. '[A]cres of poppies and wild chicory made a wonderful contrast of colour and here and there barbed wire showed up through the long grass'. In the near distance he could just make out the shape of a trench parapet. The quiet didn't last for long, however. Suddenly he heard 'a whistle like a covey of partridges and the rifle grenades began to burst'.[442]

Zone flora in full summer flush, from north to south, 1915, 1917 and 1918, and interwoven with cultural resonances; this first record posted by George Stringer from Lindenhoek Chalet, not far from Ypres: 'Dear Father, Please send me out a pair of tinted spectacles either brown or green. The heat is terrific & the glare rather bad . . . I gathered a topping lot of poppies this morning'. June 1915 was beautiful, he wrote from High Wycombe after being invalided out of Befland, the fields were covered with poppies and cornflowers. There were always flowers in his billet and glow worms twinkled as the evening light faded, something he'd never seen at his home in the Midlands. Early most mornings, when summer mists rose into the air, he walked behind a crest that blocked the view of enemy snipers and picked wild flowers waving in abandoned cornfields. Everyone gambled for life and beauty amid the ghastly realities of war, he continued, but at this time of day, when both sides were exhausted by the night's travails, the 'brutal instincts' were in abeyance. In August he noted the tall, unharvested crops drooping behind the hedges and waded through 'breast-high blue-flowered stalks', beetroot run to seed that should have been cut a year earlier. At this time of year the broad sweep of the Salient presented an image of what he imagined the North-American prairies might look like.[443]

South to La Bassée district – lines, almost indecipherable, scribbled in the back of Stringer's army notebook; June and July 1917. It was a windy day, dappled by sunshine and rushing clouds. He strolled into no man's land from a trench junction, the 'Double Crossing'. Tall grasses and wild flowers of every description waved in the breeze. A sea of colour unfolded before his gaze. At Hirondelle Wood just outside Hébuterne he entered 'a miniature charnel house' overtopped by 'the rave of nightingales'. Suddenly it stopped. Gas rising from the ground had knocked the birds out of the trees. Yet he was grateful for the flowers which his servant placed in his dugout fresh every morning. They blazed in the sunlight filtering in through the entrance. As artillery smoke shrouded the countryside one evening in July he glimpsed trailing strands of honeysuckle, beautiful in the acrid gloom.[444]

Two years earlier other settlers saw tall grasses and weeds in derelict cornfields around Vermelles. Wild flowers crowded to the edge of the trenches. Gigantic cabbages running to seed shaded those in front of Les Brebis.[445] Gun crews around Arras decorated their dugouts with blooms taken from abandoned gardens.[446]

Lastly the deep south, devastated after the 1916 offensive. A walker in a ruined village outside Bapaume: 'It is very hot over here, and we have a thunderstorm every evening. The country is looking very nice. There is a wonderful growth everywhere and wild flowers in profusion. I have a big bunch of semi-wild roses on my table as I write, and they have a very sweet smell, perfume I suppose I should say'.[447] William Orpen remembering August: 'Never shall I forget my first sight of the Somme in summer-time ... no words could express the beauty of it. The dreary, dismal mud was baked white and pure – dazzling white. White daises, red poppies, and a blue flower, great masses of them, stretched for miles and miles'.[448] John Masefield on the road to Contalmaison, where established species jostled for space with colonizers: 'The grass and some of the hardier weeds have begun now to grow in some of those furrows; in others the earth seems to have been killed, like the men buried there ...This road was once hedged, but fire has trimmed the hedge. There are brambles in it still, and dwarf beech, young elm – which will never grow to be old – and the wayfaring tree . . . Now that it is out of cultivation, one can find wild flowers all over that battlefield. In July, when the fighting began, it grew the flowers common in cultivated chalk soils at that time of the year; the purple hardhead, pale purple scabious, pale blue chicory; and the common weeds of cultivation: yellow ragwort, red poppies, and blue cornflowers . . . On both sides of the road, but especially near the windmill, there are patches of strongly growing henbit. To the east of the road, on the plateau, and in and near the quarry and middle gullies, there are patches of speedwell, ground-ivy, dead-nettle of two kinds, one with pink, one with yellow flowers (which also grows freely in Mametz Wood). Among the grass one can also find dock, milfoil, starwort, stitchwort . . .Venus needle, daisy, field madder, Lamb's lettuce, a cut-leave wild geranium, a veronica, and the little heart's-ease pansy'.[449] ➲ 81

48 Friday 25 August 1916

Stapleton Eachus was working alongside labourers mending roads near the L'Hallue rivulet on the Somme. This was punishment for arguing with an NCO about rations. 'We content ourselves with consolationery remarks such as "roll on", sometimes "Roll on Blighty", and "Roll on that big ship"'.[450]

For the great bulk of uninjured settlers the 'big ship' – an enduring Beflander trope signifying an end to war, decolonization and the final voyage back across the Channel – sailed after the Armistice. For zone dwellers the Armistice signified something more; the beginning of the end of shuttlings back and forth from base to zone, but for the anticipated final journey they seemed to have been determined to disencumber themselves as much as possible. When the news broke Robert Cude found himself with an infantry battalion at Pommereuil, thirty miles east of Bapaume. 'I am up forward at the time, and the lads let off all their amm[unition], but at a target every time. The Artillery too do not mean to be saddled with spare shells, and so right up to the minute of the time fixed for the armistice, they are pumping over shells as fast as they can'.[451] Richard Foot, twenty miles away to the northeast, did the same, but most other batteries in the vicinity, he said, had ceased firing by around seven in the morning, four hours before the appointed time.[452]

In fact disencumbering went on for much longer, at least in northern Befland. 'During the afternoon, the German wireless makes a request of us to observe the terms of the Armistice,' noted Cude, 'as guns of both the 1st and 2nd Armies are still firing on points behind his lines'. Within a few minutes of the Armistice, however, zone dwellers discovered new encumbrances. As the bugle calls signalling and end to the War faded on the air crowds of allied prisoners, intermingled with hordes of starving civilians weighed down with bags and sacks full of belongings, streamed westwards across no man's land – 'some of the sights are terrible in the extreme', wrote Cude. The Beflanders among them, men who'd been put to work in the district, told him that their captors dissolved the working parties as soon as they heard the bugles because there was no food left in the camps or the surrounding villages.[453]

We catch a last glimpse of Cude at one of the entrepôts. 'Parade before doctor. No disease, so push off then into another camp. Stay the night here, and parade next afternoon for boat. Before parade, stock myself up with 1 thousand cigarettes. March through Dieppe and straight on boat. This place is gaily decorated by bunting, and a huge flag upon the embarkation point reads – "Goodbye Tommy, we shall never forget you"'.[454] But as the date of this diary entry indicates – 24 February 1919 – decolonization was a prolonged business. Lord Derby's complex scheme divided settlers into five main groups and numerous subgroups. Priority was given to 'demobilizers' (those required to staff decolonization centres in the United Kingdom). Next came 'pivotals' (those urgently needed for peacetime reconstruction). Group three, arranged into forty-two subgroups, included all Beflanders who had a definite promise of employment. Group four comprised men wanted to accelerate industrial production. The rest were to be released by trades in order of their importance. Age, length of service and family circumstances were deemed relevant only within categories. The scheme never worked. 9,000 miners jumped the queue and were gone by 5 December and discontents on both sides of the Channel soon put and end to it[455] [89], but in any event large numbers of settlers stayed in Befland to remove the huge quantity of material scattered across the landscape. Five days after the Armistice an estimated 2,500 trench mortars, 7,500, artillery pieces, 52,300 machine guns, just under 800,000 mortar bombs, seven million grenades and nearly sixteen million shells were lying about in or near the zone. 343 million rounds of small-arms ammunition were stored on the lines of communication alone. Initially Beflanders planned to move it all to the entrepôts and dump it in the Channel, but the Board of Agriculture and Fisheries objected. Eventually wargear and supplies were broken down and sold off. As late as October 1921 a few settlers were still in Befland dealing with native contractors.[456]

After the Armistice many settlers migrated into New Befland; 202,000 were in the Cologne region by August 1919.[457] Ronald Schweder didn't get that far. Post-Armistice the First and Fifth Armies were quartered around Lille and Valenciennes, clearing up the devastated areas and overseeing the vast numbers of labourers and prisoners engaged in that work.[458] He settled in Tourcoing, six miles northeast of Lille. On 11 January 1919 he lamented the loss of his horses, due to be shipped away the following week, and the disintegration of his unit, loving tended through so many adventures. The men too were going. Those that remained had little to do and he feared that discipline would soon break down. The yearning to be done with it all strengthened as the days passed. On 17 and 20 January he noted that everyone was sick of military life and that he hoped to be away in a week or so. Two entries, the last in his archival file, read as follows: '27 January: Telegram: Hotel de Mulhouse, Lille, Come at once to London, I start today. Telegram: Meet me Burlington Hotel, Friday. Crossing tomorrow. Have wired for rooms. Ronald'.[459]

But not everyone was anxious to be gone, or pleased that it was all over. On the evening of 11 November 1918 William Orpen wandered around a back-area town musing upon the likely effect of the Armistice. What would Beflanders do now that the general drama of pain had ceased? For many the final journey to Britain led only to unemployment – by 1919, 300,000 British ex-Beflanders were on poor relief.[460] 'Wending my way home through the blackened streets that night, I met a Tommy who threatened to kill me because of his misery'. Back at his hotel, Marthe, a serving-girl, was sobbing uncontrollably into her apron. All too soon her soldier-husband would be coming home.[461] ➲ 49

49   Friday 1 September 1916

During the night zone dwellers moved 1,934 tons of equipment forward to Delville Wood and Pozières Ridge.[462] In addition, right across the Somme on this and every other night, thousands journeyed within the zone. About a million Beflanders were directly involved in the 1916 offensives but at no point was there anything like a million combat troops resident in the landscape. Divisions from all over Befland came and went. Most travelled in and out three or four times. Only seven stayed for longer than two months at a stretch. An 'incessant interchange of formations' is how MacPherson put it.[463] 'Exhausted' units 'rested' on 'quiet' fronts before returning to the fray.

The popular image of large cohorts of immobile soldiers permanently facing no man's land is therefore quite wrong. Until spring 1918 borders were more or less static but infantrymen were not. They constantly travelled inside and beyond the zone just as they constantly travelled inside and beyond Befland. Frequently small numbers crawled into no man's land on night patrol. Less frequently large masses attempted to cross it, usually unsuccessfully – the thirty-odd major offensive battles listed by the War Office's statisticians in 1922.[464] But a stint at the front did not entail permanent residence either. In 1933 Frank Richards recorded the circular motions of infantrymen during battles around Loos in September 1915: eight days in the actual front line, eight in the front support line and eight resting in towns or villages near the FE line: 'I have seen the Battalion arrive at Béthune plastered in mud from head to feet, and twenty-four hours later turn out as clean as new pins'.[465] Next year in La Bassée district the Post Office Rifles worked on four-day rotations.[466] On average even the most battle-hardened infantryman spent no more than forty to fifty per cent of his time in the trenches.[467]

These excursions within the zone were little miniatures of the circular journeys from zone to home via bases, entrepôts and the portals, but intrazonal journeys could be much longer than those detailed by Richards. When Beflanders adopted a 'defensive posture' early in 1918 the 'front line' virtually disappeared. A few 'forward zone' troops lay scattered around in thinly held outposts. Ronald Schweder came across some on the River Scheldt one evening in October. Small rifle pits dotted the landscape. Resident soldiers drifted into nearby houses to drink coffee with natives, returning now and then to check that everything was still quiet.[468] Immediately behind the pits was a well-prepared support line, often with underground chambers. The forward zone and the support line were about a mile deep. Three or four miles to the west stood the main 'battle zone' – fortified keeps, dugouts, strong points and trenches fronted by huge entanglements of barbed wire. Communication trenches ran between the forward and battle zones. Further back still, two miles or so behind the battle zone, was the 'defensive line' (billets or huts).[469] The entire 'front' was therefore about seven miles deep, but there was no 'front line' as such.

As in other times and places infantrymen journeyed between the three zones and into the back areas on a regular basis, and this might help to explain why so much infantry memoir literature foregrounds experience at the front. Infantrymen encountered front-line trenches anew every time, and vivid memories measure the intensity and novelty of what was experienced there, not the duration of that experience. 'Probably the main thing that helped us Field Gunners to get through the stresses of war cheerfully was that we were constantly in action,' remembered Richard Foot. 'This sounds a paradox, but it has substance'. In his view, gunners suffered the same proportion of causalities as infantrymen, but not in the same way. Turnouts lost men gradually – one here, a couple there, week on week and month after month – whereas infantry battalions might lose half their strength in a mad slaughter lasting no more than thirty minutes. In addition, artillery crews tended to stay in one place for relatively long spells. They did not have to endure the regular 'nerve strain' of constant intrazonal, lateral and horizontal journeys; pulled out of the border in one place, sent elsewhere for rest, moved again into reserve or support and then flung back into the line to relieve another unit in a new and unfamiliar location.[470] Schweder made a similar point in 1917. He thought that most front-line infantrymen had only the vaguest notion of where they were in a given district and were 'quite foggy' even as to the disposition of their own trenches.[471]

'All day we are idle,' wrote Garnet Durham while policing the FE line at Ypres' Menin Gate. Very few wayfarers passed through before dusk fell, only individuals bearing urgent messages or men attached to carrier pigeon units, and these were strung out at two-hundred yard intervals to avoid alerting enemy spotters. 'But at night Piccadilly isn't in it'. Thousands choked the roadway. Guns and wagons were fed through at one per fifty yards or so and battalions broken down into subsidiary units, one platoon per hundred yards, shuffling forward in single file. 'We get lots of cursing but are usually obeyed as Shrapnel Corner . . . rarely fails to take its toll'. After about two in the morning the flow reversed, 'and needs no directing except for those who ask their way through the town'. Wagons and artillery turnouts careered through the Gate at a gallop, heedless of anyone who might get in the way. Lone walkers – deserters or spies, perhaps, more likely message carriers, zone dwellers on the scrounge or men visiting friends – were detained and questioned before being allowed on. 'About dawn there is no one going either way, except the odd ambulance, silent as a cat, creeping with the night's casualties'.[472] It was the same right across the Salient. Throughout the night intrazonal travellers thronged the roads and trackways: infantrymen going into trenches, infantrymen coming out of trenches, turnouts moving from one location to another, ammunition columns delivering shells, general service wagons bringing in letters, rations and supplies, ambulances removing the wounded. As dawn broke traffic subsided. Few ventured out till sunset.

Those moving about south of the flat land around Ypres were less exposed. On 13 April 1916 Ralph Hamilton was at Kemmel Hill. 'The trenches here are really very nice; there is no necessity to get one's boots dirty, and as we hold the top of the crest it is possible to walk up to the front line across the open with perfect safety'.[473] It was the same odd mixture of danger and relative safety, very much dependent on microgeography, for those travelling on the Somme. In mid 1916 only one intrazonal road, that running eleven miles from Contay to Aveluy Wood, could be used during the day. All others were overlooked from the eastern plateau and liable to shelling.[474] 'Flers Ridge was about half a mile from Trones Wood, or the cross-roads, [the] one leading to Péronne,' remembered Rowland Luther. A shallow valley divided the wood (or the remains of it) from the ridge with Befland infantry entrenched on the top and his artillery unit fifty yards or so on the reverse slope. He doesn't say what he was doing that day, but his job was an unenviable one. He was out alone, making his way back to the guns in full view of the enemy, when, as might be expected, a German spotter noticed him as he reached the crossroads. A shell exploded thirty yards to his front, and then another, just to the right – 'they had got the range'. He ran back into the valley, reached a dip in the ground by Delville Wood and then cautiously worked his way home.[475] Next spring, as the Germans retreated to the Hindenburg Line, Foot journeyed deeper into the zone and arrived next to Miraumont village. The walk from the village to his observation post was terrifying, he recalled, but he was fortunate as to the surrounding terrain; there was a steep hill in front of the enemy's guns.[476]

Twenty-one months later and ten miles to the northeast Lieutenant Capron watched a rare example of a successful journey into no man's land on a mass scale, but by then the siege was over, in part because Beflanders had found a way of reinventing cavalry in a form that could cross the killing fields. First came the customary *Trommelfeuer* – a massive artillery barrage that inundated the trench system in front of Capron's observation post – then the big tanks, slithering over the ground (in this instance the surface hadn't been churned up by shelling). Between their lumbering bulks light tanks ('whippets') darted about, spitting machine-gun fire. When the big tanks reached the far side of no man's land they stopped, made a ninety-degree turn, lined up parallel to the German trenches, angled their guns downwards and ground slowly along, pouring a deadly stream of explosive directly into the bodies of the helpless defenders. Capron saw the tank muzzles flashing amid the smoke but could hear nothing above the din of artillery fire which, by now, had moved on to pulverize the enemy's second line as well as the ground immediately behind the forward line, thus blocking the possibility of retreat or reinforcement. It didn't last long. No one could have stood it for more than a few minutes, said Capron. Very soon little groups of German soldiers staggered into no man's land; there was no other place where they might be able to stay alive. Most Beflander infantrymen were already out and about, running along behind the tanks, but their only real work was to gather up the surviving Germans.[477]

Successful movements into no man's land gave survivors the chance to stand upright on top of the landscape – not all sectors were 'moonscapes'; in cushy ones crops sometimes grew between the lines.[478] 'It was certainly pleasant to be on firm land again, instead of shell-hole mud', remembered Roland Luther of his part in the advance to victory.[479] Even when advances failed Beflanders might have the opportunity to scavenge off the dead before they were obliged to turn round and go back. Late on 1 July 1916, after the day's slaughter (57,500 settler casualties from seven-thirty in the morning onwards, including 19,250 deaths), Robert Cude walked a few yards forward of the old front line at Bray-sur-Somme: 'Plenty of souvenirs about[;] watches, purses, rings and brass hats [and] helmets are kicking around everywhere'.[480] ➲ 62

Tuesday 12 September 1916   50

The Post Office Rifles left their billets in Franvillers on the Somme at three in the morning, walked eight miles east to Bécourt Wood, arrived at eight o'clock and bivouacked behind Bécourt Chateau, a mile equidistant from Albert and Fricourt. 'The scene near Bécourt was an extraordinary one,' recorded their diarist. 'Piles of shells lay everywhere and great guns fired incessantly from scarcely concealed positions along the roadsides, in gullies, or out in the open. Light railways fed each battery. Straight, dusty roads crossed the countryside in every direction. Steam rollers puffed where roads were being re-laid. Horses and mules thronged water-points; large iron tanks fed by pipe lines. Horses stood tethered in rows, horses trotted round in rings exercising'. Some said that the place looked just like Epsom downs. Stretching away for miles in every direction were slopes and valleys overrun with wagons, limbers, dumps, stores, depots, pontoons, tents, bivouacs and makeshift shelters. Above it all giant observation balloons floated in a huge, arcing 'S' indicating the general location of the border. In the afternoon, after tea, hordes of newly arrived zone dwellers mooched about among ruined trenches and tangled lines of smashed barbed wire, or sauntered off to visit Fricourt and the giant mine craters at La Boisselle.[481]

Next evening Stapleton Eachus sat down in his room in the tiny village of Pont-Noyelles to write up his diary. He was twelve miles west of the Post Office Rifles at Bécourt. Eachus's housing arrangements were something of an anomaly. He worked as a signalman at Rawlinson's Fourth Army headquarters in the chateau at Querrieu, a quarter of a mile across the L'Hallue rivulet from Pont-Noyelles. Querrieu was no bigger than Pont-Noyelles, and certainly not large enough to accommodate all the headquarters staff. Even though huts had been built in the chateau's gardens to house low-ranking clerical workers, space remained tight. This might help to explain why Eachus, though only a private, got permission to lodge with a French family outside the chateau grounds. 'I would like to mention that I have been positively astounded on many occasions to find what the true feeling of the French people really is with respect to their views on the war,' he wrote. The first thing any native said was that the War had lasted far too long already. Six months was more than enough. They also had clear views on what they expected to happen afterwards. 'I found that some people have the idea that we shall even continue to hold the territory we now occupy and work the railways, which we have built, by erecting stations etc. There is by the way a single line railway running between Querrieu and Pont-Noyelles. I believe it comes from Fréchencourt and runs to Amiens. It was built by Royal Engineers, and the local people are very anxious that the line should be allowed to remain after the war'.[482]

Eachus was partly right. A single-track line, the Hallue Line, built in May 1916, did indeed run from Fréchencourt, two miles north of Pont-Noyelles, and through Querrieu, but it did not originate in Fréchencourt (settlers were using that village as a supply depot) and nor did it run directly to Amiens. The line started five miles north at Contay, in mid-1916 the site of a vast ammunition dump, and ran south through Pont-Noyelles and Querrieu to Vecquemont, then a loading point for ambulance trains. At Daours, few hundred yards south of Vecquemont, it joined the main Amiens-Albert-Arras line operated by the Rothschild's *Chemin de Fer du Nord*, known locally as 'the Nord Company'. In any event Pont-Noyelles' inhabitants, and others along the line, were to be disappointed. When the Somme border moved eastwards again in spring 1917 and Beflanders no longer had any use for the railway they handed the entire ten-mile line from Contay to Daours over to the Nord Company. It promptly tore up all the track.[483]

The Hallue Line was by no means the only one built by Royal Engineers on the Somme in 1916. What the Post Office Rifles' diarist saw as he arrived at Bécourt was but a small part of an entirely new railway system – some of it running on narrow-gauge track (one metre or sixty centimetres wide), some on standard gauge – spreading out eastwards from Albert across the devastated plateau. The system's spine ran east from Dernancourt Junction, half a mile south of Albert, to Longueval, a distance of eight miles. Along the way was a string of halts and stations – Ancre Sidings, File Factory Exchange Sidings, Méaulte North Tranship Station, Bécordel Crossing, Bécourt Junction, Fricourt, Willow Avenue, Bottom Wood, Caterpillar Junction and Bazentin – around which thronged stores, dumps, wagon lines, artillery emplacements, dressing stations, casualty clearing stations and first-aid posts. At Ancre Sidings there were two branch lines. One ran north for a mile or so through Vivier Siding to G Dump and S Spur. The other, much longer than the parent Dernancourt-Longueval line, meandered across the plunging slopes of the plateau's southern edge to Guillemont, and eventually to Ginchy. The first stop was Méaulte Junction. Here you could take a train along the little sub-branch running steeply down into Ancre Valley to the gun emplacements and engineering stores at Hill Top, MM Dump and The OV. After Méaulte Junction came Catch Siding No.1, Catch Siding No. 2, Pilla Junction (with yet another sub-branch, this time running south to the French railhead at Bel Air), Grovetown (site of Ford Spur), Happy Valley, The Loop (with a link to Bray-sur-Somme), Halt No. 5, The French Gun Spur, Plateau Station, Halts numbers 2, 4, 1, 3 and 6 (in that order), Trones Wood, and finally Guillemont and Ginchy. If you returned and continued along the Dernacourt-Longeuval line the next branch was at Bécordel Crossing (a single track cutting back to Albert), closely followed by one at Bécourt Junction – a four-mile line running north to Bécourt South, Bécourt Central, Chapes Spur Transit Station and Pozières. The fourth branch line ran south from Fricourt and cut down to Happy Valley and The Loop. At Willow Avenue, five miles out from Dernancourt Junction, another branch curved south, and then east and south again, through Mametz and Combles and on to Cléry-sur-Somme, post-July a border village though, as with so many other Somme villages, nothing remained of it except ruins. Two lines ran from Caterpillar Junction; one north to Contalmaison, the other – the Caterpillar Wood Branch – to The Quarry. A final branch line ran three miles northwards from between Bazentin and Longueval to Le Sars village.[484]

Back on the Nord Company's Amiens-Albert-Arras main line and just west of Dernancourt there were yet more halts and stations associated with the zone lines reaching out into the recently annexed plateau – Edgehill, Buire-sur-l'Ancre, Méricourt-l'Abbé, Heilly, Corbie – around which clustered supply depots and engineering stores. Further west still, to the north of the Hallue Line and well clear of the zone, Beflanders built two more systems. A seventeen-mile line ran east from Fienvillers and Candas, just outside Doullens, to Acheux, with halts at the villages of Le Rosel, Puchevillers, Belle Eglise, Léalvillers and Varennes. It was eventually extended several more miles to Colincamps and Albert, with a branch to Aveluy Wood and

Mouquet Farm. From there it crossed the Ancre River to Mesnil-Martinsart and Authuille, and terminated at the north-eastern corner of Thiepval Wood. In the far north of the Somme, near the border with La Bassée district, engineers built a series of branch lines running off the existing main line between Doullens and Arras. There were stops at Authieule, Mondicourt, Warlincourt-lès-Pas, Saulty, L'Arbret, Pommier, St Amand, Gouy-en-Artois and Wanquetin. All the halts and stations on these northern and western lines were surrounded by the usual paraphernalia of stores, dumps, depots and medical stations.[485]

Taking all the lines and sidings together, in 1916 Beflanders laid fifty-five miles of track on the Somme. Next to the tracks they built 4,900 square yards of ammunition platforms and dumps. These could process 873 railway wagons unloading simultaneously. As for the service, by late 1916 the Méaulte stations alone handled twenty-five trains a day, and on the entire Dernancourt-Longueval system thirty to forty per day ran in each direction, though not particularly safely – shelling, gradients and steep curves caused frequent derailments.[486]

Why should I itemize the apparently trivial in this busy landscape in such obsessive detail? After all, what wasn't torn up almost immediately – the Hallue Line, for example – was burnt, wrecked or shelled in spring 1918 when the Somme border collapsed and settlers abandoned everything east of Amiens,[487] so why bother? What's the point? If this were a straightforward military-economic history of the Western Front I would have no need to explain myself. The detail, though regarded by some readers as perhaps a tad excessive, would be used to frame a discussion of the consequences for the British high command of agreeing to undertake an offensive in Picardy in 1916. Since on the Somme railways were sparse and the few main lines congested with freight trains moving goods from the farms, mines and factories of the north to Paris and the French interior[488] [3], Beflanders had to build their own lines to make good the deficit. But this isn't that kind of text.

More to the point, in an essay on landscapes I could show how, right across the zone, from Dixmude in the north to Cléry-sur-Somme in the south, settlers changed things, not only by digging trenches and exporting shells (or receiving them) but also by building railways. And new railways not only changed the landscape in new ways, they also gave settlers a new way of seeing the landscape. 'And if you took this toy train up to the height of [the] land, the Somme country lay around you like a map,' wrote Charles Carrington as he recalled traversing the plateau on the narrow-gauge Willow Avenue branch line in November 1916. 'The countryside looked as if a tidal wave had flowed over it': flattened villages whose very names had disappeared except in the memories of longstanding zone dwellers, scorched hedges that would never bloom again, snapped tree trunks, their splintered ends 'like monstrous shaving-brushes', the only remains of the poplars that had once lined the roads.[489] Six months later, while walking across the plateau by the line branching from Bécourt Junction, William Orpen noticed how settler railways domesticated the colonized landscape. This wasn't just a matter of toponymic domestication (Bécourt South, Bécourt Central, Chapes Spur Transit Station) but, perhaps more expressively, of the very look of the built environment now just beginning to overlay the devastation. 'On up the hill past the mines to Pozières,' he wrote in April 1917. 'An Army railway was then running through Pozières, and the station was marked by a big wooden sign painted black and white, like you see at any country station in England'.[490]

So far so plausible. But there are other and perhaps more pressing reasons for listing the apparently trivial.

What if the past has no history, what then? If all our narratives are dubious; if notions development or directionality, which generate history by revealing structure and meaning in the past, are just the captious by-products of an Enlightenment fantasy, then the past may have no overarching story to tell and no particular point. Either way narratives exclude people, necessarily so: this or that argument 'about' the past and this or that destination signposted within the argument requires the prioritization of some facts and lives at the expense of others. Seeing the past as 'significant' (for us) or as adding to *our* understanding (not past understandings) only augments history's excluding impulse: the 'insignificant' gets eradicated. History might therefore be likened to a kind of weird, time-travelling creature that cannot help perpetrating acts violence against the past, or at least to one that so stalks the chambers of our imagination that it won't allow the past room to move or breathe – hence the formalized unreality of so much history. Maybe past lives go on when history is looking away? And maybe the evidential traces of past lives should be approached by us not as raw material for adventures in narratives but as found footage; a jumble of timeless moments, all equally present (or distant), from which sequence may be deduced, but not causation, and to which significance may be assigned, but not for us. For unlike history the past makes no treaty with the present.

Paul Ricœur writes of how the memory of having lived or travelled somewhere is 'particularly eloquent and telling'. In memories of this type, he continues, 'corporeal space is immediately linked with the surrounding space of the environment, some fragment of inhabitable land, with its more or less accessible paths, its more or less easy to cross obstacles. Thinkers in the middle ages would have said that our relation to the space open to practice as well as to perception is "arduous"'.[491] The Somme's railways were places of practice as well as of perception, and certainly part of an arduous landscape, one which severely tried the body, often to the point of its utter destruction. Beflanders lived and died on them, worked on them, characterized them. Bel Air was so named for its breezy location; Pilla Junction memorialized M. Pilla, the commanding officer of the French engineers who started work on the tracks before the settlers took over.[492] You might make life-long friends at junctions and halts frequently visited or lose them there in a derailment, or under shellfire. You might rest, leaning in the morning sun against the warm wood of a supply wagon at Cléry, with a cigarette trembling in your hand after a terrifying night's work in the trenches. You might be evacuated on one of the ambulance trains leaving Vecquemont with a smashed-in face that never healed, or with no legs, or no arms. Vecquemont might be the last time you were ever free of pain. If you got through it all relatively unscathed then names and faces milling around this or that siding, or incidents at ammunition dumps or gun emplacements, or the look of wargear piled by the trackside under moonlight, might stay with you for life so that if, in old age, someone were to say to you 'Bécordel Crossing' or 'Caterpillar Junction' or 'Catch Siding No. 1' you would be gone in a flash, back in the timeless moment which has now become present. 'I must go over the ground again,' wrote Blunden in the 1924 introduction to *Undertones of War*. 'A voice, perhaps not my own, answers within me. You will be going over the ground again, it says, until that hour when agony's clawed face softens into the smilingness of a young spring day'.[493] His last poem, 'Ancre Sunshine', describes a stroll across the old battlefields in September 1966.

Somewhere in Greece *c.*500 BC a boxer called Skopas organized a banquet and invited along the poet Simonides of Keos to sing his praises. Little more is known, but the story must have echoed around the Mediterranean littoral: about five centuries later Cicero and Quintilian mentioned that while Simonides was out of the room the roof collapsed, killing many of the guests. Their bodies were mangled beyond recognition. Sometime afterwards Simonides, who had a good visual memory, was called back in by the distraught relatives to identify the dead in relation to their exact location in space around the now vanished tables.[494] Contay, Pont-Noyelles, Ancre Sidings, Mouquet Farm, Bécourt Junction, Fricourt, Hill Top, Grovetown, Trones Wood, The Quarry . . . Stations in time which, like history, are now likely to have no destination, but significant locations in space for the once living, and thus not so trivial after all.⇒ 52

51　Saturday 28 October 1916

As the Post Office Rifles came out of the Salient's trenches, noted one of their officers, 'everyone who could get leave or find a pretext made off down the paved causeway past Shrapnel Corner to the Lille Gate and "Wipers" where they stared at the swans in the moat'.[495] The birds had been there for some time. Earlier that year, in May, Garnet Durham saw 'one wretched pair . . . the last of a big flock,' nesting by the Menin Gate. One day a settler tried to steal their eggs but ran off when bullets started whizzing past his ears. The sentries had made pets of them, wrote Durham, 'and would have shot him as calmly as not'.[496]

Clearly for some there were moral limits on what should be taken, but they do not seem to have applied to garden produce, regulations notwithstanding.

Horse Management and its Relation to Preventative Veterinary Medicine, a technical pamphlet issued to officers, had this to say on the matter: 'A man is observed to have a nosebag of distended and irregular bulk. Action. – Request that the nosebag be opened, when it will not unusually be found that the contents pertain to the man rather than to the horse. Enquire into the matter, and if it be found that the man should be carrying a feed of oats, report the fact to his commanding officer, informing him of the alien contents of the bag'.[497] If regulations failed to dissuade Beflanders local disapprobation sometimes did. A year before the Post Office Rifles walked into Ypres Sidney Appleyard returned to billets after a day's work digging trenches in front of Bray-sur-Somme: 'Morgan and myself went out after fruit (scrounging as we call it). We got over a barbed wire fence into a garden. We heard movements so went cautiously, but as soon as we shook the trees a voice shouted at us in French. This immediately put the wind up us and we retired in disorder'.[498] Sometimes scrounging operated on the set-aside principle, to save rations for others rather than satisfy immediate needs. In 1964 Richard Foot remembered that when the United Kingdom suffered dire shortages in 1918 most men hoarded little stashes of food – butter, scraps of bacon, twists of tea and sugar, whatever they could find – to take home with them on their next leave.[499] Phyllis Goodliff, a VAD working at the Red Cross headquarters in Boulogne, also tried to scrounge for her family in 1918, but without much success. She wanted to send currants, raisons and nuts back home to Huntingdon, but 'the censor told me today that he can't let it through as the French a fortnight ago made them contraband as so much was being sent'.[500]

Regardless of the motivation theft in one form or another inheres in colonization. Indigenous peoples are denied, expelled or subjugated, land and homes appropriated. Beflanders stole, among other things, food – pilfering farm produce was commonplace[501] – but their moral economy evinced distinctions, albeit loose ones: on the one hand scrounging (which could morph into foraging and scavenging), on the other looting (sometimes characterized as a species of scrounging). Neither was necessarily an affront to cultural norms, or even a military offence. Situational ethics applied. In 1915 GHQ instructed the moving mass of settlers to forage,[502] and any suspicion of hostility from the natives opened the door to feasting. On 22 April 1915 men of Garnet Durham's unit billeted at a Flanders chateau watched the owner frantically threshing the remains of the previous year's harvest as the guns boomed out over the fields. His wagons were already piled high with household belongings, and he was trying to get the wheat in before joining the other fleeing natives. But as evening fell they became suspicious; he seemed to be signalling to the enemy, so they dragged him away and shot him. 'We had his ducks for supper,' wrote Durham.[503]

In addition the chronological fact of two short bursts of territorial instability (August 1914 to spring 1915, spring 1918 onwards), punctuated by a lengthy interval of stasis, framed what was possible. Scrounging was rare during the siege, at least in the zone, because natives had long since fled and what they'd left had long ago been consumed by the initial wave of settlers. 'That week we lived like lords,' remembered Frank Richards, one of the first to arrive at Houplines in October 1914 as settlers flooded northwards. In kitchen gardens and farmyards ducks, chickens, pigeons and vegetables were there for the taking. Wines of every description could be found inside the houses.[504]

If looting from natives was rare during the siege there was, according to Charles Carrington, a vast amount of 'scrounging' within the settler community, but it was governed by 'a local code of ethics. To be "on the make" or to "win" more than you were entitled to, was in some strange sense a meritorious form of conduct, but only on condition that it was socially directed' – no stealing from one's comrades and the further the victim from your group the more blame shaded into approval. 'To steal a bottle of rum from the company that relieved you in the trenches might be thought rather near the limit of decent behaviour, but a bottle lifted off the dump at divisional railhead was a famous achievement'.[505]

There's something badly adrift in the following extract from Rowland Luther's memoir, apparently written in the 1960s. His source, *Behind the Guns*, doesn't seem to exist and his chronology and geography are all wrong: food wasn't particularly scarce on the Somme early in 1916, the time and place when the events described purportedly occurred, and there were no abandoned German trenches. Possibly he meant early 1917, when rations were indeed short and Befland absorbed around 200 square miles of territory pockmarked with deep German dugouts. Moreover, it's inconceivable that something as dramatic as a shadow army of deserters, invisible but omnipresent, rising silently from the ground after sunset to predate on the settler community, would not have attracted comment in the diaries and letters of my other sources. But the truth is not so important. The fact that Luther believed what may be no more than latrine rumour echoing around Befland – who knows what might be glimpsed or heard in the zone's uncanny landscape? – is beside the point. When food went missing settlers noticed it. *Behind the Guns*, read long after the War and written, according to Luther, by an Australian, told the story of a community of deserters and 'missing' men living in abandoned German dugouts and trench systems who supported themselves by raiding depots and wagons under the cover of darkness. His own unit, he recalled, lost rations, and so guards were detailed to watch over food and supply dumps. There were also stories that men from neighbouring units, and indeed from his own, had been stealing food, but he saw nothing himself and, as far as he knew, no one was ever caught. Apparently the deserter community survived until the Ludendorff Offensive of spring 1918. Thereafter, as the Germans swept over the old battlefields, men emerged from their dugouts and turned themselves into partisan army, attacking the enemy from behind.[506]

More credible, and supportive of Carrington's observations and Luther's prosaic explanation vis-à-vis his neighbours, is what is revealed in Robert

Cude's diary entry for 3 November 1917, written at Elverdinghe in Flanders. During one of their 'nightly rambles' he and some companions discovered a supply dump packed with food belonging to the Guards' division. Incensed by the knowledge that guardsmen got it all free while ordinary Beflanders had to buy it they broke in, stole ten cases of cocoa (forty-eight tins per case), gave some away to deserving friends, kept a good few for themselves and sold the rest.[507] The back areas were not immune from this kind of thing. In 1916 settlers regularly burgled Harfleur's YMCA hut to steal food and money.[508] ➲ 61

Wednesday 22 November 1916   **52**

Report on a landscape closely observed.

Garnet Durham was convalescing somewhere close to Notre Dame de Lorette Ridge. He was bored, and spent part of the evening letter writing and reminiscing. 'It is deadly dull here, no sort of diversion whatever except watching the millwheel, or the old cooper making barrels. In some ways the trenches are better fun'. One still, moonlit night, he continued, the most beautiful thing he'd ever seen appeared. 'We were on top of the ridge just behind Duffield Crater'. Behind him he could see the heaped, chalky rubble of what had once been the villages of Neuville St Vaast and La Targette, and a little further on, partly hidden in the mist, the ruined towers of Mont St Eloi abbey. Immediately to his front was the 'dead world' of trenches, shell holes and mine craters. It was an eerie scene, deathly quiet. There were no flares and the country was too brightly lit for men on either side to risk venturing out – Durham was one of several crouching 'behind the lip of the crater and partly concealed'. As the mist slowly thickened and rose a sheet of cloud formed over the landscape, resolving itself into the shape of 'a huge purple cross'. (The cross, added Durham, exited much comment later on and was assumed by some to be supernatural). 'For the time being everyone was looking at this curious cloud and the war was forgotten for some half an hour. Then our battery in Neuville fired their midnight salvo and went to sleep. A German machine gun fired a burst of fire over our heads and the war resumed'.[509]

We could treat this text as an archaeological find or a discovered fragment of text and try to pin it down; try to overcome the past and gain certitude.

Astronomical records tell us that a full moon rose over Befland on Thursday 9 November, thirteen days before the text was apparently composed, and another a month earlier, on Wednesday 11 October. The metrological artefact described in the text could therefore have occurred on either of these dates, or of course at some earlier date, though this seems unlikely: there's no record of anything called Duffield Crater in the district until late spring 1916 and mist rising in the evening suggests late autumn or early winter, which narrows things down to late 1916 (but no later, probably, than 22 November) and therefore makes either 11 October or 9 November strong candidates for the date of the artefact.

But if we can't be sure of the date we can be reasonably exact about timing and quite exact as to location. In Befland in October-November 1916 the sun set at around 16.00. On 11 October the moon rose at 16.38 and transited (crossed the prime meridian) at 00.02 the following morning. On 9 November it rose at 15.28 and transited at 23.34. On either day (or indeed on any other day in autumn-winter 1916) the mist which triggered the artefact would have formed shortly after sunset, probably between 16.00 and 18.00. According to the source 'we were on top of the ridge just behind Duffield Crater', but the recording eye couldn't have been on the top of Vimy Ridge – that five-mile long north-south rise was over the border until the following year. We do know, however, that a Duffield Crater existed on the west-facing slope of the ridge.[510] 'On top of the ridge just behind Duffield Crater' must therefore refer to a subsidiary ridge situated on Vimy Ridge's western slopes. Neuville St Vaast, La Targette and Mont St Eloi, still extant although reconstructed, are on the far side of a three-mile wide valley to the west of Vimy Ridge and to the south of Notre Dame de Lorette Ridge. If the battery at Neuville St Vaast fired at midnight the artefact which stopped work in the district for half an hour was certainly visible in the valley, looking west from Vimy Ridge, by 23.30.

We can't know how many people saw it, but in late 1916 there were several thousand Beflanders on or around the two ridges. A figure of at least many hundreds therefore seems plausible for a potential audience. But what they saw would depend on their point of view. Samuel Hynes speculates that if 'all the personal recollections of all the soldiers of the world were gathered together' forming 'one huge story of men at war' then we would have access to some kind of total truth.[511] But we wouldn't. It's not just that there would be no common viewpoint; the reality of moments experienced is contingent not only on bodily position but also on available superstructural moments. Elsewhere Hynes argues that 'no man will see much of the battle he's in; and what he does see he will not remember as other men who were there will.'[512] This is closer to the mark. The cross was and wasn't in the world; it could be observed only from specific external angles and seen only through an internal Christian sensibility. ➲ 53

53 Friday 1 December 1916

From the *BEF Times* and probably written by Gilbert Frankau, one of the paper's editors: 'Guillemont Hippodrome. This Week – Great Review. "Hullo Tanko". Famous "All Star" Cast, Bosch Beauty Chorus. Preceded by a lively curtain raiser, entitled "Zero Plus 5". Screaming farce, Entitled "It's The Way They Have In The Army". "No Treating" Order Absolutely

Ignored, and We still have a Promenade. Book Early. Prices as Usual'.[513] Eight months earlier Ronald Schweder wrote to his wife in London from Aveluy Wood on the Somme about a 'new stunt' he'd recently witnessed. Men in a division newly arrived in the district wore red and white ribbons on the backs of their tunics to distinguish them from other zone dwellers. Next morning the Germans opposite hoisted boards painted red and white above their parapets, just to show that they knew what was going on.[514] From Clausewitz's *On War*, first published in 1832: 'Theatre of War: This term denotes properly such a portion of the space over which war prevails as has its boundaries protected, and thus possesses a kind of independence. This protection may consist in fortresses, or important natural obstacles presented by the country, or even in its being separated by a considerable distance from the rest of the space embraced in the war. – Such a portion is not a mere piece of the whole, but a small whole complete in itself; and consequently it is more or less in such a condition that changes which take place at other points in the seat of war have only an indirect and no direct influence upon it'.[515]

All Beflanders performed roles, and sometimes articulated them as theatre,[516] but performance metaphors – show, stunt, theatre – remind us that Befland's wars can be represented as a kind of costume drama. Politicians and generals write a play and a set a stage. Figures assemble in a landscape and put on their uniforms. Directions are given to the *dramatis personae*, action commences, scenes and acts unfold until eventually the show is over, the stage cleared and the landscape reset for some other species of human endeavour. Thereafter participants, observers and critics assign tragedy, farce or romance to the performance according to what they've experienced, witnessed or researched, and to their various temperaments.

Sometimes in Befland's landscapes, when the stage was small and the play short, interested parties might find it relatively easy to agree. The unseemly jostling among the French knights for a 'position of honour' in the front rank, which dragged on throughout the morning of Friday 25 October 1415 just west of Tramecourt Wood, midway between Boulogne and Arras, was clearly visible to Henry V's war band and helped to turn the subsequent action into a disaster for Charles VI. The battlefield really was just a field, and everyone could see what was happening. In the early evening the French and English heralds, who'd watched the spectacle from a vantage point, agreed on the victors and the vanquished and selected a name for the battle – Agincourt.[517] Just over five hundred years later, on Thursday 4 May 1916, Garnet Durham found traces of another show once running in Befland – bones, almost certainly from the Napoleonic era, 'with rusty armour still clinging to them', unearthed from Ypres' ramparts as he helped a burial party dig shallow graves for Befland's dead.[518] In the last act of that drama, played out over the border at Waterloo on Sunday 18 June 1815, the stage had become too large for most participants to see or experience the battle as a whole. Nevertheless Wellington and Napoleon, directing from the wings, just about managed to keep the action in view, and after a long day (the spectacle lasted from noon till eleven in the evening) both were there to witness the dénouement.

Agincourt was performed on a stage about 500 yards wide and a thousand deep, Waterloo on one two and half miles wide by a mile deep. At Agincourt the English might have numbered 9,000, the French 12,000. At Waterloo Napoleon disposed of 69,000 troops, Wellington about 67,000.[519] The theatre of war and the cast of players were becoming ever larger, the props and gear ever more technically sophisticated and the stage directions ever more complex. By the early twentieth century railways, conscript armies and industrialization had accelerated these trends enormously, and professionals sensed what this meant for the future direction of things. In Lieutenant-Colonel Ernest Swinton's 1909 short story 'The Point of View', a general, having set his warplan in motion, goes fishing. There's nothing more for him to do and nothing for him to see. 'It was recognised that the days when any one man could by personal observation keep a grasp of the progress of the whole of a battle have gone,' explains the narrative voice. 'Modern fights may cover scores of miles, and no one man upon the scene can hope to obtain more than an infinitesimal portion of information by the employment of his own senses'. It was all, according to Swinton, 'a question of mental optics'.[520] *Field Service Regulations*, issued a year later by Haig as Director of Military Training, came to the same conclusion. Commanders should stay away and collate reports sent back by subordinates. Visits to the front would only skew their judgement.[521]

But it was not only directors who would lose any overall sense of a battlescape. Everyone would. In 1916 the theatre of operations on the Somme was fifteen miles wide and at least five or six deep – far more if one counted the back-area supply depots, Channel ports and United Kingdom, Imperial and American mines, factories and farms necessary to keep the whole show on the road. Like the 'First World War' (which can't exist pre-1945) the 'Battle of the Somme' is an abstraction, a retrospective generalization that had no reality in experience and could have no reality in experience. No one was ever everywhere all the time, nor could they be. In an important sense, therefore, neither ever happened. Some understanding of this last point is evident in the 1922 official history volume *Principal Events 1914–1918*. There Befland's heralds, the 'Historical Section of the Committee for Imperial Defence', were deliberate in their use of the plural – 'battles of the Somme' – as a prelude to their careful delineation in time and space of each unique stage and each distinct 1916 battle-act (each of which, of course, is itself an event package subject to further fractal disaggregation): 1–3 July, Battle of Albert; 14–17 July, Battle of Bazentin Ridge; 15 July to 3 September, Battle of Delville Wood; 23 July to 3 September, Battle of Pozières Ridge; 3–6 September, Battle of Guillemont; 9 September, Battle of Ginchy; 15–22 September, Battle of Flers-Courcelette; 25–28 September, Battle of Morval; 26–28 September, Battle of Thiepval Ridge; 1–18 October,

Battle of the Transloy Ridges; 1 October to 18 November, Battle of the Ancre Heights.[522] And no one, of course, experienced all of these, or any of them, all of the time. But so often historians prefer retrospective generalization to the concrete evidence of human presence in the staged landscape. In so doing they proceed by deducing the latter from the former, a reification that inverts the materiality of the past by assigning to the evidence of lived experience the role of shattered fragment of some greater abstract whole. When retrospection occurs, argues Wolfgang Natter, the meanings attached to evidence are analogous to Freud's idea of 'belatedness'(*Nachträglichkeit*) in his treatment of the relationship between initial event (*Geschehen*) and subsequent hi/story (*Geschichte*): 'Relating the concept of belatedness to the problems encountered in thinking about works that fictionalize or historicize the war', explains Natter, 'one might think of the undeniably real event as being less an origin from which interpretation proceeds, as it is already its result'.[523]

All this edges us towards revisiting the notion of *post facto* event packages mentioned in the Introduction, and we might start by considering Richard Lowenthal's statement on one aspect of the historical method. 'The actual past is beyond retrieval', he writes, 'all we have left are much-eroded traces and partial records filtered through divers eyes and minds'.[524]

Lowenthal's observation presupposes a past totality which could, in principle, be recovered, but even to say that we recover the past from traces embedded in sources elides the complexity of what's going on. This book, for example, might be considered as a secondary source for a study of World War I, but what is its date? A note on the verso of the title page says 2013 (though it wasn't written then), but it is, of course, billions of years older because it's composed entirely of elementary particles, or merely scores of years old because it's abstracted in part from carbon fixed in timber. But since it's also in permanent transition (decay), at any moment it's no more than a few minutes old. The onlooker has to choose a point of view to ascribe a date to it. Having failed to establish a chronological point outside the realm of human cognition we now turn to its purpose, use and meaning. For publisher and author it may represent exchange value: profit for the former, career advancement for the latter. In terms of use value it may function as doorstopper, firelighter, unread gift or child's colouring book. Considered from an engineering perspective it's an example of binding and print technology. To the student of applied arts it's an exercise in style and design. The chemist discerns the effect of one compound upon another; ink on paper. Just as its materiality nominates no stable chronology so as artefact it discloses no stable purpose or meaning. We bring time, purpose and meaning to it, and *may* decide to interpret it as a source for a study of World War I. So with any source-artefact. Its pastness is imposed by the onlooker. Like the past, all sources are equally present, or absent; necrologic scrawls only if we want them to be. The past is sustained through histories mediated via a collaborative troika of historian, reader and the vivified dead, but the historian initiates no linear time-lapsed sequential procedure of belatedly recovering the past from evidential traces embedded in sources. Instead there is a dialectical process of creating the past into history. Because the past doesn't exist someone has to think it into existence while simultaneously rendering it into media discernable to another. Historians shape products from raw materials imagined into being in the act of shaping. Viewed in this way the past is already the result of its own history.

None of this is to suggest that Frankau, Schweder and Durham, or anyone else resurrected in this or any other narreme, materialized in Befland *ex nihilo* at the whim of this or that historian. We should not forget that once we've got to the point of imagining artefacts as sources then the normal rules of historical enquiry apply. But the rules will snare us, if we let them. They insist that innumerable 'causes' – gender, place of birth, social class, family, character, the Neolithic Revolution, imperialism, industrial capitalism, politics, shipping and railway timetables, the stroke of a clerk's pen, tides, weather, etc. etc. etc. – placed Frankau et al. at that point in space at that moment in time. Experience is therefore at once a conclusion, a product, and a beginning. But when resurrecting past lives the concrete evidence of presence in the landscape is where we must start from, not the second-order phenomenon of retrospective generalization, which, if pursued, entangles us in *reductiones ad infinitum*. 'The concrete is concrete because it is the concentration of many determinations,' wrote Marx in 1857, 'hence the unity of the diverse. It appears in the process of thinking, therefore, as a process of concentration, as a result, not as a point of departure, even though it is the point of departure in reality and hence also the point of departure for observation and conception'.[525] ➲ 58

54   Monday 4 December 1916

George Stringer was on a course at the village of Lucheux, just north of Doullens. The mess was good and it was pleasant to sleep in a bed at last, and such a relief to get out of the zone. His billet, shared with Leuthwaite, a friend, was clean and comfortable. They had no arduous duties; nothing more than the odd spot of drill and afternoon parades for the camp's commanding officer. Dinner followed, and then four-handed bridge at headquarters. Lucheux lay at the base of a deep valley. Woods, now leafless, sloped up the valley sides. It would be a beautiful place when summer came, wrote Stringer.[526] A few miles away at St Pol's Third Army's mortar school Beflanders swam in an open-air pool warmed by water discharged from a nearby factory.[527] Grant Taylor, somewhere near Ypres, 23 March 1915: 'Today we were given instruction in bomb throwing and trench mortaring. Very interesting. In the evening there was an informal concert. It was really jolly good, considering'. Two days later: 'It has poured with rain all day and I'm feeling rotten again. We have just come back from the concert. It was awfully good, but the end was rather spoilt by a number of shells landing uncomfortably near the camp which caused all the big [?wigs] to go out, and us, being battalion on duty to follow suit. So far nothing has occurred . . . I got a parcel with a ripping mess-tin, my other tunic, handkerchiefs, figs and peppermint creams today from home'. Back near Ypres: 'Wednesday 9th June. The battalion moved off at 9 a.m. Dalziel, myself, Margetson Webster and four men went to see a demonstration of gas . . . The camp is pitched near a farm in a beautiful field. The officers have bell tents and the men are in bivouacs. Rumours of leave. My name sent in'.[528]

Grant Taylor's diary entries seem to be referencing courses for immigrants new to the colony, but many Beflanders experienced them, if only because the accelerating pace of technological innovation required constant familiarization with new types of wargear. But, like back-area locations, courses also functioned as sites of ease and privacy. Senior NCOs and young officers who did well in action were often sent on them as a perk, remembered Charles Carrington. At worst they were safe and comfortable, at best a binge.[529]

Thirty miles south of St Pol and nine months after Stringer's course at Lucheux, Ronald Schweder, tired out after months on the Somme, described the long summer days on a gunners' course at a large chateau. Here ease morphed into boredom and sleep. We see him lying on the chateau lawns on a hot afternoon listening to instructors droning on about mathematical calculations for artillery range finders ('$R \times D = A \times 60$; $4000 \times 90 = 600 \times 60 = 360/32$'). In the near distance is the pock-pock-pock of other inmates playing tennis on the chateau's hard courts. The marquis and his wife are having lunch. Their children pass by in a little carriage drawn by goats. Thirty German prisoners of war and several dozen settlers tend the well-kept gardens, and there are clean glasses and white tablecloths in the mess. Next day four officers sprawled in deckchairs will fall sound asleep during a lecture on the shoeing of horses.[530] ➲ 77

Wednesday 3 January 1917   **55**

Just after moving into rest from the Salient to Cap Gris Nez Ronald Schweder wrote to his wife about a recent acquisition, a beautiful chestnut horse; 'Policeman'. He chose the name because the animal reminded him of the mounts ridden by the police in London's Rotten Row. 'Policeman' had been with the battery for a while but had been lame for some time. Schweder spent a couple of months getting him sound, evading veterinary offices who wanted to evacuate him, and making sure that no one else rode him. Six weeks later we find him busy plotting against Brownlow, his commanding officer, whom he disliked, over an impending move. Schweder was sure that Brownlow would object to 'my horses and servants' going with him, so he approached the colonel first. The horses and servants were his, said the colonel. Early in June next year he asked his wife to send him two yards of white saddle serge – Murray, a servant, would know just what was needed – and bragged about another plot: he was after yet another horse, this one allocated to a friend who had too many and was obliged to surrender some. 'Policeman' crops up again in a letter sent from Tourcoing in New Befland in January 1919, just prior to Schweder's demobilization. His first charger was earmarked for transfer to the Household Cavalry. Policeman he could keep and take back to England. He might serve as a useful brougham horse, or maybe the other chestnut he'd had for years would do better.[531]

That Schweder should equate servants with horses in a row about moving from one battery to another its telling, as is his use of the possessive pronoun, but it would be foolish imagine that he believed both to be of the same order of being. All his gun crews were catching dreadful colds, he lamented in winter 1916, he heard hawking and sneezing all around him as he wrote, but at least the horses looked fit – 'One would get far more cursed for having poor looking horses than men, which to my mind, an un-military one, seems incongruous'.[532] Nor should we imagine that his servants didn't have some say in the matter. We cannot recover fully the ways in which patronage operated within Befland, the little daily understandings that allowed the colony's social system to function, but when a move was in the offing batmen and grooms might well prefer to stick with 'their' officers rather than go through the tiresome business of accommodating themselves to strangers. Nevertheless one can't escape the conclusion that Schweder's attitude to servants and horses was proprietorial, that he saw both as the necessary accoutrements of someone of his rank and class, and that the latter were objects of his particular care and affection.

Once can't escape the conclusion too that settlers, officers and other ranks alike, viewed horses and mules as blameless victims of a man-made disaster. 'Their rations of oats and hay were very poor,' lamented Rowland Luther, recalling conditions on the Somme in December 1916, 'and the poor devils with the mud on their legs and bellies now developed balls of mud which froze on their limbs'.[533] Similar sentiments are scattered around everywhere. George Stringer remembered life in his battery somewhere in Flanders during spring 1915. Most of the turnout's horses, robust and strong-boned farm animals, came from Lincolnshire. They were much prized by the drivers detailed to look after them, and horribly cosseted. During the night men on stable duty crept out into the farmer's fields and gathered armfuls of large-leafed clover. (French farmers hardly ever turn their cows out to graze, noted Stringer, most of the land was under cultivation and most of the clover was harvested in winter for summer feed). The stolen fodder was then quietly fed to the horses before the drivers turned in.[534] 'The poor old grey, my first charger, is in trouble,' wrote Harold Bursey from Bancourt (La Bassée district, September 1916). 'He was knifed by the vet as he had developed an ugly swelling on the near fore near the fetlock through a bad wound. I fear he is nearly done. He has carried me many miles in this country as well as in England and I shall be sorry to lose him. One develops a real affection for one's horses. He is such a handsome animal too, so upright and carries himself like a two year old'.[535] And finally Lieutenant Capron in front of Arras during the Ludendorff Offensive, March 1918: 'After the fume and fury it was relaxing and restful to see our horses as they brought the limbers up, winding between the craters up the slope. We rubbed their silky noses, quickly off-loaded the shell, and sent them safely homewards down the hill'.[536]

Some were also acutely aware of individual personalities, and inclined to anthropomorphize them in terms of race, class and gender. 'Like most territorial infantry battalions, the Post Office Rifles arrived in France with rather a mixed stable,' wrote their officer interpreter. '*Negress*, no weight carrier and calling for good horsemanship . . . she was so badly wounded by the same shell that killed young Moon, the General's groom, during the advance on Moislains in the summer of 1918, that she had to be destroyed . . . *Corah* was the Battalion Second in Command's charger, big and handsome like her master . . . *Nigger*, an ancient pony, sleek and fidgety . . . The trials of the campaign aged *Nigger* rapidly . . . *Bill*, a strong chestnut with a sprung hock in his rear hind, was the transport officer's mount during the first six months of the campaign . . . he was too nervous for night work in the forward zone . . . *Buchanan*, a showy, wild-eyed, big-mouthed but good tempered charger that came to the battalion with a large draft of Fusilier officers after Vimy in May 1916 . . . *Bess* was a solid "old thing" of the sort that do hard work willingly . . . A rolling gait, yellow teeth, a licentious eye, an iron mouth and a fashion for lowering her head when going at a fast trot, were her characteristics . . . *Bobby* . . . Gifted with a certain cunning, he always remembered a good billet . . . *Nell*, a big animal with a head strikingly like a camel's, succeeded *Nancy*, an iron-framed carthorse, as the carrier of the battalion Quarter-master. *Floss*, a beautiful dark chestnut, was the pride of two transport sergeants. She was wounded in the shoulder by a shell splinter near Dickebusch but recovered . . . *Sunstar* the gentlest, mildest-natured beast that could be, possibly a war-sacrificed lady's pet, withered under the strain after captivating the hearts of several company commanders'.[537] ➲ 59

Thursday 4 January 1917   **56**

At four-fifteen that morning at Souastre on the Somme an infantry officer disturbed George Stringer's sleep. A telephone rang. He tumbled out of his cot and grabbed the receiver. A voice on the other end of the line shouted 'Assist Z.1!' Bleary-eyed and disgruntled, scrabbling around for candles and matches and struggling into breeches, gum boots and 'British Warmer' (a fur-lined jacket issued to zone dwellers), he eventually pulled himself together and hurried towards the pits. No guns were in action, but Corporal Crosby had beaten him to it and was already out and about. Crosby was left in charge while Stringer ran back, cursing and swearing, to haul the other gunners, still sound asleep, out of their beds. In short order all four teams were in action, but to add to his annoyances number one gun failed completely after shooting only three rounds. Next morning they dismantled it and found that a faulty shrapnel charge had broken one of the recoil springs. No one had spotted it (though they should have) because the outer casing was hidden behind rope lashings. Amid the noise and confusion Stringer was called back to the telephone. A sheepish voice told him that it was all a mistake. What the infantry officer had meant to say was 'test priority', i.e., send one ranging shot over a particular enemy trench. Stringer was furious. He'd upset the battery, dragged everyone out into the cold night air and exported fifty rounds of high explosive costing £200 across no man's land for no good reason. At least three other batteries had responded in like manner – a total cost of some £800–£1000. Stringer called a halt and went back to bed, but he couldn't sleep. He'd stood too close to number three gun and his ears buzzed and throbbed. To cap it all the phone rang again at quarter to six, just as he was drifting off. This time another infantry officer ask him to bring down fire on a forward position because the Germans had unleashed a counter-barrage in reply to the settlers' earlier and mistaken bombardment: 'Silly devils serves them right – what can they expect if they suddenly let the peaceful & unsuspecting Hun have 200 rounds gunfire. Gave them 10 rounds HE & went to bed again'.[538]

Intersecting military and regional identities were those coalescing around work. Indeed trade identities probably strengthened as colonization and specialization accelerated. Gardeners, linguists, trench mortar crews, bakers, artillerymen, aeronauts, anti-aircraft and machine gunners, farriers, gas teams, sanitary workers, clerks, footplatemen, medics, policemen, clerics, drivers, bargees, signallers, electrical and mechanical engineers, drill instructors, butchers, printers, surveyors, vets, tailors, pigeoneers, cooks, fitters, miners, armourers, meteorologists, water tank assemblers – the whole bewildering panorama of trades on display in Befland, some nomadic, some sedentary, continued year after year, regardless of attrition. Itinerant riflemen might (or might not) feel part of an ever changing 'trench community', typists working at Boulogne month in month out might consider themselves members of quite a different community. Just as there was no uniform 'western-front experience', so was there no common Befland identity, even among white male immigrants from the United Kingdom. Each group led a life distinct, differentiated from others in innumerable ways, some significant, some trivial.

For outsiders other trades might be objects of rumour, pity, jealousy or contempt. Machine gunners were envied because of their relative autonomy and freedom from irksome discipline, for example.[539] For insiders life might be miserable or cheerful, depending on personalities and conditions. Trades might interact sympathetically, stroppily (Stringer at Souastre) or indifferently, according to rank, moods and phases. Ronald Schweder was ordered to visit an infantry headquarters on the Somme on 21 April 1916, in principle to foster good relations between trench dwellers and artillerymen, but in his view to act as a kind of hostage to ensure that gunners did their job properly. Either way he spent most of the day bored and idling about. Next morning he was in better spirits, having made friends with one or two battalion officers. On Wednesday, he reported, the entire battalion was to come back to the guns in shifts to watch an artillery shoot from an observation post. But he was thoroughly annoyed by outsiders one evening the following year, though this may have been caused in part by a move to La Bassée district. A pair of 'infernal Balloonatics' came to dinner, got drunk, bored everyone to tears and thoroughly overstayed their welcome. To add to everyone's irritation they boasted that they were paid twenty-eight shillings and six pence a day, and that bad weather had meant that in February they'd only worked for only four and a half hours. A stint liaising with native artillerymen near Bailleul early in 1918 prompted unflattering comparisons with immigrants, and the iteration of a prejudice common to many zone dwellers about staff and high-ranking officers: Frenchmen made fine soldiers, he thought. Their generals didn't have 'dressed up puppies' trailing after them, and unlike Befland's their staff officers behaved in a proper military manner.[540]

Royal Artillery officers trained at 'the shop' (Woolwich Military Academy) considered themselves superior to territorial gunners, wrote Richard Foot.[541] Stringer recalled an incident in the Salient in 1915. A cohort of newly-arrived infantry attached to his unit for instruction in the dos and don'ts of life in the colony objected to being taught by territorials – they were full-time professionals, they boasted, while Stringers' men were mere weekend soldiers. One of Stringer's NCOs was particularly incensed, and had to be physically restrained from running amok and assaulting the jeering regulars as they marched by on their way to the border. When they arrived vicious trench brawls ensued because the proximate unit in the line, a North Staffordshire battalion, was also territorial.[542]

In the back areas Le Havre's printers spent their time churning out not only the expected range of military paperwork (anything from battle orders to fake German pigeon message forms) but also profitable sidelines; greetings cards and programmes for divisional horse shows. On Christmas Eve 1917, for example, Ralph Hamilton spent the morning sorting through cards sent by sister battalions and brigades, and regretting the fact that he forgotten to order up some of his own.[543] Engineers were well paid but poor soldiers, grumbled Stapleton Eachus after a hard day's work at Fourth Army's signals office. They bragged about battles they'd never seen and were mostly concerned with piling up money at home.[544]

Highly-paid civilian platelayers working on three-month contracts were unpopular, averred Alan Henniker in the official history series. Perhaps for this reason they disappeared in 1916.[545] Charles Carrington pointed the finger at the likes of Eachus. He thought that signallers were 'privileged people ... [they] have a secret life of their own and maintain endless conversations full of technicalities and private jokes'.[546] They always knew when something important was coming off, remembered Frank Richards, in many instances before the company commanders did: 'A signaller's life on the whole was far more pleasant than a rifle-and-bayonet man's'.[547] According to Capron's recollection his signallers were tough, capable and quick-witted. If they were sloppy and dirty on parade (and at most other times, for that matter) the fault was forgivable in a generally cheerful battery.[548] Things were different for Schweder when he moved to a new unit in September 1916. The battery was completely demoralized; the NCOs not to be trusted, the officers unpleasant ('one ranker a stinker'), the commanding officer ill, and the chief clerk ('a fearful bounder') universally hated.[549]

Sometimes tensions went beyond inter-trade grousing, intra-unit squabbles, trench brawls or shouting down telephones. On 20 April 1917 Stringer was at Béthune. For the first part of the day he accompanied a group of settlers out on a reconnaissance exercise, then sat as president of a military court of enquiry investigating the circumstances surrounding the discovery of the remains of one Private Bradley. Bradley's body had been fished out of La Bassée canal somewhere outside Béthune. It couldn't have floated down from the border, reasoned Stringer, because the front was too far away – seven kilometres from the point of recovery to Béthune and a further six from Béthune to where the canal crossed into no man's land. Since he'd been shot in the back of the head he'd probably been murdered.[550] Stringer didn't say by whom, and no one seems to have been brought to book. Perhaps a native killed him; more likely a fellow Beflander nursing a grudge of some kind. ⊃ 63

Monday 15 January 1917   57

Ronald Schweder arrived at Dranoutre, a few miles southwest of Ypres, and rode out to check a farm earmarked as a billet for some of the unit's officers. A 'buxom wench' met him at the door and offered him her room. After a while it became clear that she didn't intend to leave. Since he didn't relish the thought of sharing it with a woman who spent her days with pigs and pigswill he arranged for a bed to be placed in the mess and sent another officer in with her. 'He liked it very much, so we were all pleased and friendly like'.[551]

It's not clear what we should make of this moment. Schweder's colleague doesn't seem to have paid for his night, if so 'affective' rather than 'transactional' sex may have occurred, if it occurred at all. But sometimes it certainly did. Later in 1917 Frank Richards revisited a village, also in Flanders, where a contingent of Indian troops had been billeted three years previously. 'I saw several half-caste mites playing in the street,' he wrote. 'One old Expeditionary Force man remarked to me that if the bloody niggers were no good at fighting they were good at something else that sounded much the same'.[552]

It's very probable that many sexual encounters in the zone were just like the ones we can infer from Richards' memoir; a fleeting series affective moments (Richards doesn't mention the Indians paying for sex) lasting perhaps for a day or two before units moved on elsewhere, sometimes leaving children in their wake. At Pont-Noyelles on the Somme in September 1916 Stapleton Eachus jotted down the text of a little ditty which, he claimed, the village youngsters sang: 'Après la guerre fini, tous les Anglais parti, Mademoiselle Francaise a pleure sauvenir un bebe' [sic].[553] Richards remembered the situation just outside Amiens in the first month of the War. Men gave their cap badges to local girls as souvenirs, 'and I expect in some cases had also left other souvenirs which would either be a blessing or a curse to the ladies concerned'.[554]

Direct evidence of transactional as opposed to affective sex is, if anything, more difficult to recover. Moreover, as with other forms of settler-native interactions, the boundary between the two was probably blurred. Charles Carrington was sure that there were no licensed brothels in what he calls the 'forward zone', by which he probably meant areas east of the FE line. When the Germans retreated to the Hindenburg Line they took all the natives with them, leaving behind a vast desolation. 'For the last two years of the war, half the British Army was living in the devastated area, an uninhabited prairie about as large as the county of Sussex, within which there was no activity other than military activity, and there were no women at all. Even the nurses were not allowed further forward than the casualty clearing station at corps headquarters'.[555] But this is not to say that prostitutes didn't work close up to the trenches. There's no doubt that settlers paid for sex while under fire, though given the reticence of diarists and correspondents (c.f. Rowland Luther's careful, and perhaps disingenuous, disclaimer of personal knowledge in the extract cited towards the end of this narreme), the evidence is no more than fragmentary. Craig Gibson suggests that as the siege developed and units stayed in position for months on end sexual encounters multiplied.[556] Schweder mentioned a 'glorious scandal' at Francières on the Somme in December 1915. Several officers (he doesn't say from which unit) had been arrested for having paid prostitutes to come into the zone. When discovered they were sent back to the town – presumably Amiens – under armed guard.[557] In May and July next year the *New Church Times* made sly references to 'Tina', a Belgian girl who ran what appears to have been an estaminet deep in the Salient, somewhere near the ruins of Hooge.[558] Reading between the lines she seems to have been a part-time prostitute as well.

Zone prostitutes are virtually invisible to us because they had to remain invisible. They had nothing to gain and everything to lose by risking exposure to the authorities. Detection meant expulsion and, quite possibly, incarceration, or even execution, for espionage. We might speculate, however – and it is only speculation – that siege conditions worked in their favour. It gave them time to elaborate strategies of concealment and establish regular work routines; habitation, perhaps as one of group, in a ruin or a cellar not too far from the trenches, working hours timed to coincide with those of their clientele, foreknowledge of military police patrols, etc. In 1918, when the siege gave way to mobile warfare and disrupted settled patterns of life, we might expect them to become a little more visible. Something like this could have been happening when William Orpen glanced out of his car window while driving along the Cambrai-St Quentin highway in October 1918 during the advance to victory: 'mud on each side and the usual rows of trees, then a dip down to the fields. These fields were full of dead Boche and horses. The road had evidently been under observation a very little while back, as the Labour Corps were hard at work filling in shell-holes, and the traffic was held up a lot. In one spot in the mud at the side of the road lay two British Tommies who had evidently just been killed . . . Standing beside them were three French girls, all dressed up, silk stockings and crimped hair. There they were, standing over the dead Tommies, asking if you would not like "a little love"'.[559] Seven months earlier, during the Ludendorff Offensive, we get a very rare glimpse indeed of camp followers deep in the zone. Luther's battery was in headlong retreat westwards from the Somme uplands, a welter of guns, limbers and exhausted horses and men. 'We pulled out of this, retired again, and began to make our way back to Montdidier. The Battery slept in an old barn that night . . . Outside were four "Red Lamp"girls. I had heard about these French prostitutes, but had never previously encountered them. They were retreating with us. The whole battery was soon awake, and had the girls inside, sharing them out'.[560]

What drove prostitutes to endure life the zone can only be imagined. Like so many of the oppressed and marginalized they leave no traces in the historical record. As in this narreme their silence calls into question the pages from which they are excluded. All we can conjecture is that some may have had nowhere else to go or were hopelessly traumatized. Others may have been driven east by oversupply (too much competition in the entrepôts, back areas and nearby towns), or by victimization: after 1915 APMs in the back areas could expel women diagnosed with venereal disease.[561] When the siege broke and shattered their lives they attached themselves to units like Luther's battery. There, for a little while, they could trade sex for a modicum of security – transport, food from the men's rations and somewhere to hide for the next few nights and days, away from the gas and the roaring shellfire outside on the unforgiving, malevolent plain. ➲ 60

Friday 19 January 1917 **58**

George Stringer, currently at Souastre on the Somme, took a stroll round the ruins of the nearby villages of Mondicourt, Hénu and Monchy-au-Bois. He went first to headquarters for tea and then on to a battery mess. A miserable walk, he noted, pitch black in every direction and hard to find one's way. The countryside was entirely overlaid with snow and frost. The only help came when a nearby unit let loose a sudden barrage – flashes from the gun muzzles were intensified by reflections from the surrounding snow – or when a 'kindly light', shot now and then from a Verey pistol, illuminated his track. One evening twenty-two months previously, on 8 March 1915, he was walking along deep inside the Salient. There he witnessed a sight 'which created a cheer from mile after mile of our trenches'. He'd been idly watching a German aeroplane making its way back across the border after a sortie into Befland. Suddenly, out of nowhere, appeared a British fighter. It tore down from above, machine guns rattling. As the German plane caught fire two or three thousand feet above ground its observer fell out of the cockpit and tumbled to earth. The dying pilot struggled with the controls but the machine slowly turned turtle, looped, lost power, glided upside down and crashed behind a ridge. Stringer couldn't see the wreckage – the ridge blocked his view – but the smoke of burning petrol hung in the air for long afterwards.[562]

The fusion of landscape and human geography determines the settler's point of view. The unity of perception apparent in the Salient ('a sight which created a cheer from mile after mile of our trenches') was a function of its shape. There Beflanders of all humours and conditions were crammed into a two and a half mile semicircular theatre centred on Ypres and shared the spectacle of falling observer, burning plane and dying pilot. No such event could take place on the Somme. The fifteen-mile linear front defined and structured perception differently. Here events appear only as a series of more or less discrete and disconnected vignettes in staged landscapes, visible to some but not to all, and often only to one. Even allowing for the time of day – evening in the Salient, night on the Somme – we can discern Stringer's feeling of isolation and disorientation in and around Souastre. The 'kindly' Verey lights and the sudden, brilliant gun flashes speak of a landscape that did not exist in the round. (The former, incidentally, provides a likely illustration of the way culture operates in the temporal interlude between observation and recording [5]: consciously or not Stringer was probably referencing John Henry Newman's hymn – 'Lead, Kindly Light' – sung in schools across England in the early twentieth century).

Either way that sense of isolated figures in a landscape and the absence of a defined whole, contingent upon the aforementioned geographies, is tangible in an extended prose meditation (almost a species of stream-of-consciousness writing) dated 24 March 1917 and describing a sector of the Somme's northern theatre after the German withdrawal to the Hindenburg Line. Stringer again, and like many other Beflanders he knew all about 'psychogeography', 'deep topography', 'edgelands' and 'liminal spaces' long before cultural commentators invented the jargon. The recording eye translates observation into something seen and creates landscapes out of such things as appeal to the individual heart.

He rode out at 11.45 in the morning, kitted out with sandwiches and a hip flask and accompanied by a groom, ostensibly to recover a director and director head (artillery aiming devices lost in the confusion of a recent battle), in fact to go for a joy-ride. At first, for some three miles on either side of the opposing lines, absolute desolation greeted the eye. The names of two fellow officers are called to mind; Lethby and Tortishall, killed at Bucquoy and up in that day's casualty lists. Thereafter comes a description of three lanes meandering off into the devastated area. They once connected Sailly-au-Bois, Foncquevillers and Gommecourt. For the first half mile or so you had to chose your path carefully because shells holes and wire threatened to trip and snare your horse at every turn. Most of the skeletal remains of North Staffordshire infantrymen, killed much earlier, had been buried, but bits of equipment and personal belongings – spoons, etc. – were still strewn about everywhere. Colonel Brooke's body had been found. Two German redoubts, the 'Big Z' and the 'Little Z', stood out jagged near the crest of a hill. Then follows an account of an exhilarating gallop across a mile-wide stretch of no man's land undisturbed by shelling and the crossing of the Hannescamps-Essarts road – little evidence of recent use and therefore in good condition. In contrast heavy shelling had made the road between the Hannescamps and Monchy virtually impassable. After riding along Sunken Road from Monchy Hill southwards to Monchy village he stopped, dismounted, ate some of his sandwiches, watered his horse at a shell hole, left it in the care of his groom and strolled about. A trench junction which had served as the battery's aiming point for calibrating artillery fire was soon located. What faced him as he looked up and surveyed the scene was a landscape transformed by the remains of an impressive feat of military engineering: a superb system of tunnels and dugouts reaching towards Befland, a vast sea of thick German barbed wire and sturdy rows of steel 'knife rests' (portable barbed wire entanglements placed along the parapets of abandoned trenches). All of it, he conjectured, was able to withstand all but the heaviest of artillery shells. He wondered how on earth Befland's infantrymen had ever managed to reach the trenches. To the left, a defensive track running back from Sunken Road had been dug at least ten feet deep and reinforced with concrete footings. Each sniper's bay had a small covered shelter and a steel loophole facing west.

After poking around for a bit longer he and his groom resumed their journey; first into ruined Monchy, where the tip of a well-known local salient had been all but destroyed, then along the Monchy-Bienvillers road, badly damaged, but now under repair by crowds of labourers. No one seemed in much of a hurry – 'we are an idle lot & really some of the men hardly earn their 1/- a day. I guarantee Mr Bosche gets more done with 10 men than we do with 20'. Next he turned into the road leading to Adinfer – little used, apparently, and everything in good order, perhaps because the Germans were short of petrol and relied on trench railways instead of lorries to deliver ordnance and supplies – then into Adinfer Wood and up to a place known to settlers as Ferret Lodge. Hoof marks and wheel-tracks cut by German limbers were still fresh in the mud. It was a bitterly cold day, clear with a piercing wind. Pausing at the Wood's edge he could see the highway running between Doullens and Arras etched sharp on the skyline with all the Beflander villages plainly visible and the spire of Pommier church thrust into the sky. To the north the country stretched for miles. Arras and its cathedral were easily discernable in the cloudless air. Trench railways criss-crossed Adinfer Wood with German signposts in profusion. Some were still standing upright, even though the Wood had been heavily shelled. One line ran to a gun position. All the dugouts were shell-proofed and carefully built – solidly timbered inside – but at least two pits had been completely wrecked and a third seriously damaged. There was a hole made by a nine-point-two inch shell a yard or so in front of the entrance. It was still smouldering. Cutting across country towards Quesnoy Farm he passed gullies and a warren of battery positions. Here the enemy had made no real attempt to protect against shelling – almost an impossibility, according to Stringer – but the crews had made themselves comfortable: weather-proof dugouts, wooden flooring in the pits and sturdy, well-built beds. Every pit, position and dugout was connected by a series of camouflaged trenches. It wasn't hard to find Essarts, the next village on the itinerary. All one needed to do was to cross the bridges and follow the sweeping line of shell craters made by allied gunners or trace the line of test boxes of the German telephone system – cables deeply buried, he noticed, to protect against all but the heaviest shells. But of Essarts itself nothing remained. An old Frenchman was busy digging in a chimney corner, probably in search of money he'd left there. Three women were standing nearby. He asked where their house was. They pointed to a mountain of rubble. 'C'est très [?terrible] pour vous.' 'Oui c'est ça'.

After Essarts Stringer turned west towards the old Befland border, past Pigeon Wood and on to his old battery position at Gommecourt, then along the road to Puisieux, past Nameless Farm and across a little track leading to Hébuterne – an unpleasant interlude; there was so much mud about that he feared might get bogged down. Dead horses and mules by the track. Carl Watson, he remembered, had been forced to drive his gun carriages over a horse stuck in the mud. He couldn't shoot it because no one was carrying a revolver. Like all the other villages thereabouts Hébuterne was derelict and deserted. Nothing lived, only a solitary half-starved cat. In the near distance he spotted a Royal Engineer officer quietly turning over the bodies of dead Beflanders. Perhaps he was looking for a relative or a colleague. Stringer got back home at about five-thirty. The road between Hébuterne and Sailly-au-Bois on the last leg of his journey was in a truly dreadful state.[563]

Next month Stapleton Eachus went from Albert to Carnoy to lay flowers on a relative's grave. As he walked along he was astonished to see what had changed since his last trip. There was virtually no traffic (hence little scope for hitch-hiking) and very few settlers abroad, just one or two solitary figures working away at some job or other. The main road, previously little better than a slough of mud, was now in good repair. A steam roller was busy resurfacing the last few yards running into Carnoy. A vast effort of reclamation had transformed the landscape. Everything had been tidied up. The only signs of war were rusting huts and earth churned over by shell fire. Huge quantities of rubbish and abandoned wargear – timber, tin cans, etc. – were piled into enormous mounds on either side of the road. 'The whole scene was one of quiet and terrible desolation'.[564]

In 1919 the French government wanted to plant forests right across the Somme, believing it impossible for the region ever to revert to agriculture, but the British refused to stop the natives from returning and so the landscape was reset as farmland.[565] Other plans which came to nothing included a scheme to construct a highway from the Channel to the Alps with triumphal arches memorializing various phases of this and other battle-acts,[566] but even without them evidence of settler occupation is abundant, on and beneath the surface. Chalk smears visible from the air and deep pools ringed with trees mark the sites of shell holes and mine explosions. Soil and vegetation still contain excess levels of iron and natives still plough up unexploded ordnance – the annual 'iron harvest'. Every year archaeologists dig up the fields and unearth traces of settler lives; animal and human bones, scraps of leather, trench systems, tunnels and dugouts, rusty cans, bits of abandoned wargear. 243 cemeteries hold the bodies of 48,000 Beflanders killed there in 1916. Edwin Lutyens' gigantic Thiepval Memorial, three-quarters of a mile east of the Ancre, records the names of a further 77,000 who just disappeared into the ground. Five other monuments to the 'missing' are scattered along the escarpment slopes.[567] Here landscape functions as obliterate tomb, not only by eradicating warscapes (levelled spaces, flower beds, lawns), but also by regulating identity through the permanent militarization of the dead (parade-ground rows of uniform headstones, columned name lists, regimental affiliations). **END**

59 Wednesday 24 January 1917

Ronald Schweder was living in a semi-fortified house taken over by settlers at Dranoutre in Flanders. In the morning while dressing he heard a bell ringing somewhere upstairs. He went to investigate. It turned out that an upper room was being used as a pigeon loft. A keeper was cosseting a flock of birds. The keeper explained that when a bird returned to the loft it triggered an alarm. Each bird now had its own smoke helmet, added the keeper, a great improvement over the previous year when all the birds except 'Alfred the Younger' had died from gas poisoning.[568]

Pigeons first appeared in Befland in September 1914 when the French handed over fifteen birds. They carried messages for all manner of reasons: to send individuals or groups on journeys, to ask for food or wargear, to bring down artillery fire or to find out what was going on in the landscape. Most flew for an average of ten to twenty minutes, but some were trained to fly from ships off Befland's coast, others to make long overland trips. Numbers expanded rapidly in 1915. Zone dwellers liked them because they didn't have to rely on telephones or climb out of the trenches to send messages.[569]

About 12,000 worked on the Somme in 1916. There, in the winter, mobile instead of fixed lofts were used: 110 vans with fifty to seventy-five birds to a van, scattered around the zone and dragged hither and thither by tractors or horses. For the early part of 1917 they were considered more reliable than radios or runners. In June one army corps near Messines Ridge sent out 532 birds in one day, but in winter fighting around Cambrai they rarely flew because local roads were so clogged with traffic that settlers didn't return pigeon baskets to the lofts. In addition casualties were high because lofts were often shelled. Maybe enemy skygazers saw modern incarnations of birds released by Roman augurs – a wheeling flight an omen, a threat? The chaos of spring 1918 caused more trouble. Mobile lofts proved to be less than mobile, birds couldn't find their way back to those that had been moved and many lofts were overrun – forty during the Ludendorff Offensive. Towards autumn an Anglo-French two-way pigeon service connecting Paris with the French and British GHQs and the headquarters of the various French armies was in preparation, but nothing came of it, and anyway by late summer pigeons were out of favour. Radios were now more powerful and besides the birds were unsuitable for anything besides static warfare, though in the Salient, where the zone was almost impassable, aircraft tried to parachute baskets full of pigeons to the mass of settlers moving eastwards.[570]

What were they like? Their historian, Raymond Priestley, found pigeon nature 'not unlike human nature . . . if cocks and hens were liberated together, the result, while it might ultimately increase the numerical strength of the pigeon service, was not liable to improve the time of the individual message concerned'.[571] They couldn't stay away for long without forgetting their way home, so if nothing availed after a couple of days they were released. Gunfire didn't bother them too much but they would sometimes shy away from heavily shelled landscapes and their lofts had to be kept at least five hundred yards back from a battle. If dressed in smoke helmets birds could stay in gassed areas for up to six hours, but on the whole they were less likely to be affected than humans and were virtually immune to lachrymatories.

Tanks carried them from mid-1917, though the birds disliked the noise, shaking, and stench of oil and grease, and they couldn't fly in heavy mist or at night.[572]

It took three or four weeks to habituate pigeons to a new district. 'Pigeoneers' learnt how to feed and handle the birds; a popular job, unsurprisingly given that pigeon keeping was widespread in the Edwardian working class. Priestley again: 'The care of pigeons became as natural to the men entrusted with them as horsemastership is to the men of a mounted unit. Whenever possible, men with previous experience of the birds were chosen, but whether this was so or not there was no difficulty in obtaining a sufficiency of enthusiastic volunteers'. The St Omer district, where in 1915 control over all Befland's pigeons was centralized, 'became famed for the keenness of its pigeon fanciers'. Perhaps they flew 'Antwerp Carries' or 'Belgian Voyageurs', the fastest breeds available in the early twentieth century. By 1918 there were some 20,000 pigeons in Befland, managed by 380 specialists and around 90,000 trained settlers,[573] but they were not always treated as wargear. Settlers spoiled them, or just ate them[574] [28]. Of those that escaped and survived the zone some doubtless fanned out across Europe's fields and cities. Their descendants do not distinguish between the statues of frock-coated politicians and the grey memorials erected to equestrian generals. ➲ 64

60 Friday 23 February 1917

Stapleton Eachus had a night off from his duties in the signals office at Querrieu on the Somme. He went into Amiens, five or six miles away, to hear a lecture. The night was cold; a slight thaw over frost and snow. He arrived in the town centre at six o'clock and wandered around – it was still too early for the lecture. Prostitutes were everywhere. 'In fact nearly all the women and young girls appeared to be in the streets for no other purpose. I was personally accosted continually. One woman grabbing hold of my sleeve, really would not let me go, at least for some time'. Disconcerted, he dived into a gaudily-lit dining room-cum-bar and was instantly buttonholed by a pretty well-dressed girl accompanied by an older women, probably the establishment's madame. 'Almost the first question put to me was a proposition of familiarity with Mademoiselle'. He was tempted, he admitted, but thought the better of it and asked for tea. There was no tea, but there was plenty of alcohol, explained madame, who then went on to enumerate a long list of fortified wines available for consumption. By now Eachus was thoroughly on his guard and determined not to be sucked in to some unedifying encounter. He settled, reluctantly, for a small tumbler of Benedictine (one franc), but within a few seconds felt horribly woozy – the Benedictine must have been drugged, he reasoned later – and stumbled out of the place, much to the annoyance of madame and mademoiselle. Outside three settler nurses were hurrying by. Snatches of overheard conversation suggested that they too were going to the lecture and couldn't wait to get clear of the unsavoury street life, so, unsure of his way in the darkened lanes, he tagged along a few paces behind. All along the route women flashed little torch beams into his eyes, signalling that they were for sale and available.[575]

Amiens was overrun with prostitutes, remembered Charles Carrington and William Orpen; working girls expelled from Rouen, refugees from the devastated areas, immigrants from Paris, 'the badly diseased from all parts of France' and the 'riff-raff that is always to be found at the heels of an army'. They 'hovered about in the blackness with their electric torches, and led the unknowing away to blackened side-streets and up dim stairways'.[576] Cecil Lewis recorded an encounter in his 1936 memoir – a rare instance of frankness from an officer. Spring 1916: 'She took off her hat and coat and shook out her bobbed hair . . . In the Mess at the aerodrome hung half a dozen Kirchner drawings . . . And she was like one of those drawings. She had the same disobedient hair, the same impudent nose and credulous mouth, the same large, blue-shadowed eyes'.[577] 'Wise' settlers, continued Orpen, went to The Godbert, The Cathedral or the Hotel de la Paix where, he hints, they might pick up a better class of girl over dinner – Madeleine at the Godbert, or perhaps Marguerite at the Cathedral ('the queen of the British Army in Picardy'), though these choices would have been restricted to well-paid officers. The breaking of the siege in spring 1918 had the same impact as in the zone. Everyone fled, but when the Ludendorff Offensive collapsed the town gradually repopulated. 'Even a few of the girls came,' noted Orpen, '"early birds"'.[578]

Amiens was unexceptional. All zone towns offered transactional sex. A popular marching song, heavily abbreviated and bowdlerized in Brophy & Partridge's collection, celebrated Armentières' prostitutes.[579] Rue de Aire, the epicentre of Béthune's red-light district, attracted vast crowds of zone dwellers.[580] Town Majors, officers responsible for order in settlements around the DGT and FE lines, sent regular patrols out onto the streets of Estaires. 'My so called rest is 14 hours of police duty per day,' grumbled Garnet Durham in April 1915, 'directing traffic, and closing out estaminets, and other houses less legal, in our country at least'.[581] Henry Williamson fictionalized a Poperinghe estaminet-cum-brothel in his novel from experience, *A Patriot's Progress*. 'She had thick ankles and legs in coarse black stockings. The room smelt musty. He wished he hadn't come. "Fife! [francs]" said Madame in her fat double-chinned voice. "Fife," holding up five fingers'.[582] The *Wipers Times* and *New Church Times* listed Ypres' brothels in their 'Things We Want to Know' column – The Fancies, The Château, The Poplar Tree and the Hotel du Faucon.[583] They seem to have functioned well enough even thought the town was, technically, closed to civilians.[584]

Things were no different further to the west. Indeed prostitution was probably more entrenched in the entrepôts, coastal towns and villages and along the lines of communication. The former were sites of unbroken settlement, from August 1914 until well after the Armistice. All Beflanders passed through them at one time or another, swelling the already substantial population of resident immigrants. As for back-area centres, few were seriously threatened by the Ludendorff Offensive. Life went on much as usual except for a few days' panic associated with schemes 'X', 'Y' and 'Z' [69]. (This in contrast to places like Albert, for instance, twice evacuated and resettled between 1916 and 1918). Frank Richards and his mate Billy had no difficulty picking up prostitutes at Rouen a mere six days after the outbreak of war. 'Booze and fillies' were in abundance, he remembered.[585] According to Carrington Boulogne 'swarmed' with prostitutes while Le Havre was 'wide open'.[586] Richard Foot was buttonholed there in September 1914. 'The war was not a month old, yet one of these ladies of the town had an accurate knowledge of the British Army's methods of paying its officers, through Army agents, who, over the years, had been brought up and amalgamated for the most part into Cox & Co. of Pall Mall. As we turned back towards the dock gates, keeping well to the middle of the street . . . she kept up a running commentary, in quite effective English, on her attractions and their price. By way of silencing her, I called over my shoulder that there was nothing doing, and anyway we had no money. She replied, "That's alright! I take Cox's cheques!"'[587]

Foot's comment on the girl's language skills suggests that prostitutes were quick to accommodate themselves to incomers. Stray bits of evidence support this assertion. Craig Gibson mentions that some native women went so far as to enrol on English courses,[588] though many were probably hoping to find jobs with army rather than augment their marketability as prostitutes. Orpen believed that by 1917 nearly every French girl in Befland could speak some English – 'great was their anger if one could not understand them,' he remembered.[589] In December the previous year George Stringer was on a course at Lucheux near Doullens; marching drill at nine-thirty in the morning and then a break in the mess to write letters. One day two French girls, presumably employed by the Army, were in there making a dress. As he wrote they tried it on and he caught scraps of their chatter – one said 'Plenty swank'.[590] ➲ 65

61   Saturday 3 March 1917

Stapleton Eachus woke up out of sorts and got up late. The day was dull and cold, but the shifts had changed – he was on duty from one in the afternoon until five – so he could spend the morning in bed. That evening he walked half a mile from his billets at Pont-Noyelles to the other ranks' mess at Querrieu, headquarters of the Somme's Fourth Army. Dinner consisted of stew, not especially appetizing but a welcome change from the never-ending diet of corned beef and biscuits. But there were no vegetables and yesterday's tea had amounted to one slice of bread and a smattering of soiled currants. Next day and for several weeks thereafter he complained about new restrictions on the sale of food [68] – village bakers found that setters were willing to pay over the odds and were thus depriving natives of bread.[591] A month earlier, near La Douve rivulet in the Salient, an area long settled by Beflanders and virtually devoid of natives, Ronald Schweder gave an example of how settlers overcame shortages. He'd just taken over wagon lines from 'Bubbly' Bolitho, as fellow gunner. Bolitho kept a pig, fed on camp refuse. He watched in amusement as the animal was crated up and carried away on the back of a wagon.[592] Further extracts from Schweder's letters reveal the seasonal and geographical dynamics of shortages, and of scrounging. In 1916, in a landscape already crowded in preparation for the summer offensive, he visited an infantry headquarters in Somme village laid flat by shellfire. The officers had a good mess, not least because they kept milk cows in a cellar, stolen from local farms and carefully fed and tended,[593] though they might have been less happy had they known that the cows were probably diseased. Because most native vets had been mobilized Foot and Mouth was rampant in Befland.[594] Near Bapaume in January 1918 he found food and drink hard to find. Village billeting, pleasant enough in 1916, wasn't fun anymore; the farms and houses were poorly provisioned and well past their best.[595]

In times of siege, and therefore scarcity, the settler nurses and protects his stolen livestock or goes without, but with mass migration and the attendant economic disruption opportunities multiplied. The Ludendorff Offensive forced Schweder's unit back from just below St Quentin to Aumale, west of Amiens, a journey of around sixty miles. They lived well. Chickens left behind by the fleeing natives were slaughtered and cooked in the empty houses. Everything was intact – stoves, crockery, kitchen ranges, fires still burning, cream and butter in the larders, feather beds to sleep on – and anything might be purloined. They took whatever they fancied because otherwise the Germans would have grabbed it, but when gunners and drivers started to lug out Ormolu clocks and other knick-knacks Schweder called a halt – it was no good encumbering the wagons with useless 'articles de vertu'. As they moved through the landscape foraging parties rounded up cows and pigs and dug up potatoes. Cows became unit property, herded back with the guns, but pigs were too troublesome and had to be butchered on the spot. And again in summer, when his unit was among the first to arrive west of the Salient in front of Mont des Cats: shelled villages, open empty country, abandoned farms, abandoned fields. Men were set to work harvesting peas, beans and potatoes. Others built a dining hut and filled it with crockery looted from a nearby village. Corn rotted in the ground. Schweder regretted that he had no yeast, otherwise he would have tried to make camp bread.[596]

Taking vegetables and livestock on the hoof to feed the 150-odd men of an artillery turnout when supply lines had broken down could be classed as scavenging or foraging, but the incident with the ormolu clocks smacks of straightforward looting, even though Schweder's objections were practical rather than ethical. During the rout others too hovered on the borderline between foraging and looting. Dennis Wheatley scribbled this down late one morning when his ammunition column halted briefly at Verlaines in March, *en route* from St Simon near St Quentin to Crèvecœur-le-Grand, south of Amiens: 'Saw the Vet he had just returned from Ham and says that at the Hotel de France they are giving away as much bubbly as anyone can carry rather than the Bosch should have it'.[597]

It's generally accepted that the relative abundance of food and drink in Befland played a part in the failure of the Ludendorff Offensive. Instead of pressing forward soldiers stopped to gorge on things unavailable in blockaded Germany, but the thousands of settlers streaming westwards through hastily evacuated towns and villages and unguarded supply dumps joined in the feast too. What Wheatley saw in that hurried moment at Verlaines wasn't quite scrounging, and not quite looting either (the champagne seems to have been given up willingly), but as the collapse accelerated outright looting spread. In Amiens, hastily abandoned as the Germans surged westwards, Rowland Luther saw signs posted up along the streets as his unit passed through – "Looters will be shot on sight". Luther kept moving, back towards the base camps 'where all the base "wallahs" had evacuated. Here were the YMCA huts, and the Army Church, stocked with cigarettes and chocolates, with notices everywhere: "Looters will be shot on sight". Just give it to the advancing Germans. It seemed daft, but it happened'.[598]

For Luther situational ethics may have operated ('if I/we don't have it then the Germans/someone else will'), but other factors came into play as well; resentment of 'base wallahs' – clerks, storemen, staff officers, etc., who had already made themselves comfortable – and if there's a hint of restraint due to the possibility of being shot it was not shared by everyone. Forty miles southeast of Amiens and a few hours after Dennis Wheatley stopped in Verlaines, Robert Cude entered the small village of Babœuf with what seems to have been an experienced looting crew: 'I send 3 runners back 3 [kilometres] to Noyon, to the E[xpeditionary] F[orce] canteen which has been evacuated, leaving a huge stock of eatables and everything that we could need. They return loaded up with cigarettes, biscuits and a bottle or two of whisky. All for nothing'. Soon German cavalry scouts began to appear in the distance, so before night fell they hurried on to Villequier-Aumont. Most of the village was in flames, but not the abandoned YMCA hut which they found stuffed full of cakes and cigarettes.[599]

Cude's diary – admittedly the testimony of young man with an eye for the main chance – not only records the relish with which he and his friends exploited the situation, it also reveals their awareness of what was on offer should the occasion arise. 'This place was well known to us as being a very high class place, and so we reckon that there must be a decent bit worth taking,'[600] he wrote a week later when they arrived, exhausted after a long trek across the dry plateau, at Villers-Bretonneux on the

Amiens-Péronne road. Depots and a casualty clearing station, all deserted, clustered around the railway sidings.[601] After soaking in tubs filled with scented water (Eau de Cologne) and stealing clean clothes they ambled down to the bonded stores, which they knew to be on the outskirts of the town. 'I had the surprise of my life, for tons of canned fruit, meat, and game were stacked up waiting to be eaten'. No less welcome were the copious supplies of wine. Champagne, twenty bottles to a case, caught their eye: 'We soon have reinforcements down with stretchers . . . Journey after journey we make and we have enough to last out a siege of a few weeks very soon, and then we turn our attention to the other shops and houses'. The prize find was twelve catering tins of cherries pickled in brandy. They did 'a roaring trade' and got busy with the champagne, secure in the knowledge that there was plenty more in stock, and then moved on to feast in the abandoned houses. When they became dirty plates and cutlery were tossed out of the windows.[602]

In the end even Wheatley resorted to pillaging. '3.30 sent Thomas and Arnold into the next village Cuvilly to get food and chocolate they return with tinned herrings 8 packets of chocolate and some honey cakes,' he wrote on 26 March. 'Rations for the day for horses and men have not turned up[;] am rather worried [about] afternoon feed[;] we use such oats as we have and some sugar beets that we find'. For the next week or so, until they finally halted at Crèvecœur-le-Grand, the officers rode out daily to get food and drink for their mess and fretted constantly about rations and water and forage for the horses. They avoided raiding native houses but felt no compunction about looting abandoned supply dumps. Champagne and chicken were favoured.[603] ➲ 66

Thursday 8 March 1917   **62**

Lieutenant Capron's unit, based at Robermetz in Flanders, received orders to move south to Grouches-Luchuel on the Somme. For the first night they stayed at Calonne-sur-la-Lys, a scrubby little village with inferior billets. Next came Witternesse, reached only after a long march and as the bitterly cold day drew to a close. But it was an agreeable spot, perched on the side of a valley, and they found good quarters for the night. After Witternesse they travelled to Bergueneuse and Boubers-sur-Canche – adequate accommodation in both – and then on to Grouches, where battered and filthy Nissen huts sunk in a muddy valley awaited them. As dusk fell the rain started.[604]

In the afternoon fifteen days later George Stringer ordered a harness inspection. The animals were perking up a bit, but frost and biting winds meant most were in a bad state and he was short of twenty-four horses. No remounts were available. This was a worry, because the rumour had gone round that the entire turnout was to move the following morning.[605]

Here he is navigating his six-gun battery across Befland, a medieval siege-band dragging itself fifty miles in five days, this time from the Somme to Flanders.

The trek began three hours after his six o'clock morning cup of tea. Hard frost, a fine clear sky and the rumble of guns away to the north greeted them as they set off. They passed the small village of Amplier, two and a half miles from Doullens, just after midday. As the afternoon wore on the cold intensified and the fine weather gave way to bitter, sleeting rain. But their billets that evening were excellent. Stringer slept on a bed high up in a garret. Outside snowdrops and single crocus poked through the snow-encrusted garden. Inside the pretty little daughter of the house said 'bon soir' in the most charming manner. Next morning they left late – it took until just after eleven-thirty to get everything organized – and were further delayed by interminable traffic jams at a railway crossing near Doullens; artillery turnouts, troops, lorries and wagons struggling to squeeze by in both directions. Driving rain and dreadful roads for the next thirteen-mile trudge, then arrival at Beauvoir-Wavans, their next staging post, somewhere around four-thirty, though it was eight o'clock before the battery could finally settle down for the night. Thereafter on to Fillièvres, a long, tiring march over difficult country; three valleys to navigate and three very steep hills to climb. On the final slope two of the limber teams very nearly ground to a halt. The horses could take no more. Stringer too was exhausted, and worried. He had no spare horses. Those not in harness were virtually incapacitated and the rest little better. Next day, on the approach road to Haute Maisnil village, he did manage to water them all during a ten minute break, but had to shoot one which had come down with colic. It was an eighteen-mile march, and there would be a further sixteen miles to cover tomorrow. His gunners were dog-tired. Heavy greatcoats and full kit wore down even the strongest man but there was no space for them to sit on the wagons and regulations prevented them riding the horses. Nevertheless, all things considered the animals had done extraordinarily well, he remarked, due in no small measure to the skill and unremitting work of Farrier Sergeant Taylor – not a single shoe thrown so far. But despite Taylor's efforts horses borrowed from the divisional ammunition column were below par. Most had become jaded. The following morning they started out at nine-thirty, fed and watered the horses at twelve (drivers had to struggle with petrol cans to fetch water) and got into Heuchin three and half hours later. The weather was fine most of the way, but a violent storm broke just south of the village. Lightning struck one of the battery's cyclists. Terrified horses reared and plummeted as thunderclaps echoed round the sky and hailstones pummelled their heads and flanks. That evening Stringer pulled out the Hazebrouck 5A map. It meant swapping the high chalklands of southern Befland for the flat marshes of Flanders. He didn't relish the prospect. As on the previous day they left at nine-thirty sharp. Gradually the downs sloped and faded into the Flanders' plain and they were soon in a landscape of dykes, tall poplars and stunted, pollarded willows. Now and then from vantage points along the route he looked back and saw the whole brigade strung out behind him. To the right reared the distant slagheaps of La Bassée district, rising darkly beside the collieries. Eventually, on 1 April, the battery marched into Witternesse, its final destination, after another gruelling slog of fourteen or fifteen miles which just about finished everyone off. Stringer breathed a sigh of relief. His horses were not of the best – in their clipped condition every blemish showed – but five days on the road with no shoes lost, not a single horse in reserve and no other trouble to speak of was nothing less than miraculous.[606]

Lateral journeys behind the zone – north-south, south-north; Flanders-La Bassée district-the Somme – could be no less trying than intrazonal journeys or journeys between zone and base. A brigade like Stringer's, comprising around 560 horses and 600 Beflanders, stretched for more than a mile and a half along the road,[607] with all the problems that entailed: food, forage, watering and billeting. But walkers at least had the comfort of knowing where the next feed and billet was, and the comfort induced by the mindless rhythm of marching: thirty inches per pace, 108 paces per minute or two and a half miles per hour – two and a half and not three because regulations allotted ten minutes rest time starting at ten to the hour regardless of when the march commenced, whether fifty or five minutes previously.[608]

Shortly after his appointment as Director General of Befland's transport in 1916, Eric Geddes proposed an ambitious plan of railway construction. Two great transverse lines totalling 240 miles were to run behind the zone. A series of spurs and sidings would connect the lines to each of the colony's five armies. Geddes asked for 800 locomotives, 1,000 miles of track, 2,800 wagons and 25,000 railwaymen. By the year's end engineers were laying four miles of track a day, but work stopped when the Germans retreated to the Hindenburg Line in February 1917. Construction started again in autumn but was finally abandoned the following spring when Ludendorff's offensive put an end to the siege – in the south the Germans wrecked what had been built and Beflanders destroyed over 300 locomotives and 2,000 wagons as they fled westwards.[609]

During and after the siege lateral travellers were therefore in large measure forced to rely on Befland's roads. They were not helped by the poor state of their repair. In October 1916 intrazonal roads consumed 13,000 tons of resurfacing material a day, but those around railheads and near the border received priority. Nevertheless twelve months later two officially designated 'back laterals' opened to traffic. These ran right across Befland; one for 'up' travellers, the other for settlers trekking north-south. Problems and dangers remained, however, despite the fact that both roads were signposted and supplied with traffic police. Some sections ran forty miles west of the border, safe enough for twenty-four hour travel, but others veered within ten miles of the front, and in parts of the south four miles; too close for daytime use.[610] ➲ 67

63   Tuesday 13 March 1917

'Ten minutes to one & the minutes slowly ticking away. Watch in one hand & telephone at my ear I'm waiting for the moment to begin the good work. I'm converted into a timekeeper having worked things out & given them to Geoffrey who is out with the guns. Some poor devils will be going West tonight I expect. My idea in writing this diary is to aid me to envisualize such scenes as this if one has the good fortune to get through – a stuffy middle-aged middle-class manufacturer in a plush chair, & probably with a cold or cough, reading a screed like this of the doings of his youth; after a high tea, & in a small stuffy room with a big fire, a pipe of tobacco & a w[hisky] & s[oda] etc. etc. Imagine it! Have just started the battery. The air [above] us reverberating with the noise of many guns & it sings in your head & is unpleasant. I'm 30 feet underground too & the whole place is trembling'.[611]

One day early in 1918 Jessie Wilson surveyed newly-arrived immigrants crowded into Harfleur's YMCA hut. 'Two pathetic youngsters linger in my memory,' she wrote in 1922, 'sitting in the Hut, with their arms round one another's necks like homesick schoolboys, in a strange and unfriendly land'.[612]

Most Beflanders were very young. Some, like the couple remembered by Jessie Wilson, were hopelessly disorientated and snatched at whatever identities time and the colony offered. As far as can be discovered all the diarists and correspondents cited in this book survived the War. The two exceptions are George Stringer's brother Guy, killed in the Salient on 17 June 1915, and Ralph Hamilton, killed by a shell on 31 March 1918 somewhere south of Amiens. Few in the heat of action were as reflective as Stringer, anticipating a future self while timing artillery fire thirty feet below Rossignol Wood on the Somme, but in later life many were well aware that Befland identities were functions of time and place, nothing more. 'There have been moments when, searching among disinterred shards of memory for human relics, I have wondered whether the boy I have re-discovered was anything other than a juvenile delinquent, whose characteristics were a love of ganging-up with the other boys, a craving to demonstrate his manliness, and a delight in anti-social violence'. Thus the sixty-eight year-old Charles Carrington.[613] 'I only tell this story to show that it is quite easy to remember the horrors,' wrote Richard Foot in December 1964 after describing a death in his unit. 'It took us hours to find enough pieces of Bombardier Lake to assemble them for a decent burial. But it is also the fact that memory is more inclined to bring up the pleasant, happy events than the horrors: mercifully, I suppose, the horrors seem to be tucked away in cells that are seldom opened, though they are there for the opening'.[614] In November 1921 Robert Cude wrote a short introduction to his Befland letters. They are, he admitted, 'very disjointed in parts', but were written 'in all weathers and in all moods, so I may be excused if at times I am venomous'.[615] Ronald Schweder penned a valediction to a dead self eight years later. His letters were written 'anyhow, anywhere, and at any time of day or night, therefore perhaps the views and expressions of mind upon human beings and affairs in general had best be regarded as youthful exuberance rather than mature consideration'.[616] 'It was a fine introduction to life,' wrote Cecil Lewis in 1936, 'but now, a step beyond the half-way house, that immense experience begins to fall into perspective as merely an episode . . . those lives are over. In London the April rain drenches the roofs. The curtains are drawn. Within my study all is quiet and peaceful. The paper on which I write lies in a little pool of light, and my hand moves laboriously back and across . . . Back and across the years! It is not easy. I kept no diaries, and memory, that imperfect vista of recorded thought, eludes and deceives'.[617] A few years earlier, probably in 1930, Stormont Gibbs compared now with then: 'many of the events of this period stand out from the rest of my life in high relief and everything else seems in a far away mist by comparison with it. August 1916 might be a month or two ago. I can be more precise about most of it than anything I did last August. And as to the rest of the war, my mind is a blank except for incidents sufficiently stirring not to be completely thrown into shadow by the bright light of that August'.[618]

Time is the shaper of memory. It creates images of things that might have been but never quite were. These may be realized in memoir, where we are often in the hands of unreliable narrators (though as all historians know, all sources are unreliable narrators). Graves' *Good-bye to All That*, for example, could be read as satire rather than factual recapitulation, and after its publication the author found himself entangled in accusation and counter-accusation on the veracity of this or that scene or incident.[619] As for novels from experience like Henry Williamson's *Patriot's Progress*, Jay Winter tartly remarks that 'they are never documentary, even though they may pretend to be so'.[620] The unadjusted impressions of diaries and letters have their own problems, as some of their authors (Cude, Schweder) knew perfectly well. The experiences they capture are facts (or more accurately evidential inferences), and have such status as historians usually accord them. But they too are only temporary facts, fleeting impressions of fleeting and impermanent selves. And impressions might not be unadjusted at all – perhaps cannot be – and may therefore disclose endogenous rather than exogenous facts. In 1915 and 1916, for example, Schweder stated quite bluntly that in their letters his gunners deliberately and consistently exaggerated the dangers to which they were exposed.[621] 'The Suffolks and Gordon Highlanders seem to have lost most,' remarked Ralph Hamilton in March 1916 after watching wounded infantrymen trudging out of the Salient. 'Some men of the former regiment said their battalion was wiped out; but men always say they are the sole survivors'.[622] Who was telling the truth? Who was lying? Was a putative sole survivor consciously or unconsciously deceitful? If he was evacuated on a hospital ship and never saw Befland again did he reiterate his fact till his dying day? Richard Espley is surely right to insist that 'we can never understand the many truths of a past moment'.[623] We might go further, and assert that such moments must be functions of subjects, not objects external to them, but the point cannot be pushed too far. To suggest that *physical* moments – wounds, illness, hunger and disease, for example – are necessarily endogenous, things imagined into being by autonomous subjects, is just plain daft. The same could be said of fear, or exploitation, or any crimping of body and soul produced by social, economic or political structures. Though we can't establish unequivocally the parameters of inhumanity, people do live inhuman lives made for them by others. To examine a source and encounter past truths and past moments is, therefore, to rendezvous with enigmas. And the difficulties multiply. If the relationship between truths and moments is problematic so is the relationship between experience and reality. Schweder's gunners might indeed have experienced real moments of fear, even if he didn't, but on the other hand both parties did experience real moments of truth. For us the problem lies in deciding what can be said, what can be reconciled. ➲ 82

64 Wednesday 14 March 1917

Lieutenant Capron arrived with his battery at Simencourt, south of Arras, after a lateral journey from Robermetz in Flanders. As he settled down the weather took a turn for the worse. Biting cold set in. To add to his miseries a second misfortune soon followed, this one the direct consequence of a recent 'insane' directive. Before he left Robermetz higher authorities – the corps general staff – had ordered that all horses and mules should be methodically clipped, not just below the level of traces and tackle (this to prevent sweat gathering under the animal's belly, cooling, and then causing illness), but shaved all over (manes excepted), like a hunter. In addition the forage ration had fallen from twelve to ten pounds of oats per animal per day, ostensibly due to supply problems. At least at Robermetz the wagon lines had been sheltered and protected but here, at Simencourt, there was no shelter at all. The valley bottoms, little more than muddy swamps, were impossible, so horses and mules were tethered on high ground exposed to the wind and rain. Cold and exhaustion took its toll. Simencourt did for many of the animals. When they moved again, this time towards St Pol, many more, including some of the best, collapsed and died as they struggled along the road – 'Most heart-breaking, worse than losses by shell, and all because of that Corps Order!'[624]

George Stringer was no less infuriated by orders from above. Two days before Capron arrived at Simencourt and eight miles to the south he was struggling to move a gun to Gommecourt near the Hindenburg Line. As he wrote – seven thirty in the evening – it was still stuck in the mud, so they gave up for the day and took the horses back to the wagon lines. The horses were in poor condition before they started, continued Stringer, a direct result of late clipping. If only they would clip in October instead of January then half the skin problems encountered in the zone would disappear. His pack horses were in no better state. They were quite unable to fetch the required number of shells up to the guns. So far today they'd carried a mere 170 rounds; quite insufficient for the night's work. Clipping, no stables and exposed standings, a harsh winter and shortages of fodder – all took their toll on the unfortunate animals. A move to La Bassée district next month brought no respite. 18 April: dreadful weather, rain and sleeting snow; thirty horses down and no inkling of any remounts; wagon lines on top of a hill exposed to the elements. The one bright spot in the all-encompassing misery was a row of chestnuts glimpsed in Béthune – huge swelling buds on them waiting for a burst of sunshine. The horses were starting to rouse themselves too, despite having been clipped in January when temperatures regularly fell below eighteen degrees Fahrenheit. If and when it finally came warm spring weather would thicken their coats and brighten their unspeakably dreary lives.[625]

Clipping was the standard treatment for mange, a skin disease caused by an arachnidan parasite. Mange was always bad in winter but the vets couldn't agree on what to do about it. Some held that clipping was better than the risk of mange, others that it was too chancy because it weakened animals. In winter 1914–15 clipping was left to unit COs in accordance with peacetime practices, but next winter mange caused so much trouble that GHQ ordered compulsory clipping for all units, only to reverse their decision the following winter. Confusion resulted. Most COs decided it should be done at once but that mules should be left alone unless there were 'veterinary reasons'. Moreover, a CO might be unconvinced by a 'clipping order' but had no further responsibility for the animal's condition if he was forced to carry it out. Veterinary officers, on the other hand, were bound to clip those with mange to control disease. In Flanders, where stabling and temporary shelters had been erected, horses didn't suffer much, even allowing for lateral and intrazonal journeys, while the beneficial results of clipping were, apparently, marked.[626] Ralph Hamilton, however, was having none of it. 12 May 1916, Kemmel Hill: 'I went round some of the horse-lines this evening – D, H.Q., and C Batteries. My black horses are beginning to look beautiful again. I refused to clip them all the winter and have had them standing in the open all the time, wet and cold included. I have not had a single cold among them, and, now that their woolly-bear coats are coming out fast, they are going to look magnificent, and, more important, are all in hard condition'.[627]

Things were different on the Somme, where by late 1916 the zone was practically a quagmire. Since there was no shelter or stabling clipping was abandoned because it seriously affected health. Moreover, the harsh winter of 1916–17 and the organizational inability to keep up with the massive increase in the animal population caused many that had been clipped to die from exposure and malnutrition (forage was in short supply and much was lost in the mud) and mange spread steadily until spring 1917. In autumn 1916 the vets finally agreed on a colony-wide policy for the following year:

all clipping was to be completed before 15 November 1917. They argued that clipping should be done in early winter because later on coats became matted with skin excretions and mud. Early clipping allowed for all-winter grooming which kept the skin reasonably clean and made it possible to do a second clip with the spring moult. In between animals were to be dipped in baths, a practice introduced by Canadian vets. Mules, on the other hand, should be treated differently. Most strongly resented clipping and since they rarely contracted mange and their coats were usually much finer than a horse's they could be groomed more easily. But the vets still equivocated. If stabling and rugs could be found, they said, mules would benefit from clipping, not least because they were so valuable to Beflanders. Mules stood up to shelling better than horses, were less likely to die from disease and could be kept in good condition on much less forage.[628] ➲ 84

65 Saturday 31 March 1917

A paragraph from a diatribe against Befland's officer class, written by Stapleton Eachus from his billet at Pont-Noyelles on the Somme: 'In fact British officers have the reputation of a notable lack of all the foregoing qualifications amongst the civilians in France, it would appear that they are looked upon as a sort of useless ornament with too much money to spend. I have heard many remarks to this effect and have even heard it said that the British officer is only fit for searching for the bodies of women. Which latter remark is of course based upon a good deal of evidence'.[629]

We don't know what prompted this outburst. Eachus seems to have been a difficult, humourless character, or at least one who chaffed under the restrictions of army life. Seven months earlier he'd been hauled up in front of his CO for arguing about food [48]. Perhaps he'd had a run-in with a junior officer earlier in the day. Possibly he'd fallen out with someone over a native girl. Whatever the reason his remarks introduce us to the problem of secular trends in supply and demand in relation to sex.

It is, of course, impossible to know how many natives engaged in sexual activity with settlers, but it is possible to sketch out a broad supply-side aetiology. Not all native women were necessarily looking for sex. Some probably just wanted company. For others war may have brought liberation from the constraints of provincial life, but Craig Gibson is surely right to conclude that vast majority of full- and part-time prostitutes working in brothels or clustered around the cafés, hotels and estaminets patronized by immigrants were driven by economic necessity.[630] Between 1914 and 1918 France and Belgium suffered a demographic catastrophe unparalleled in modern times. Husbands and fathers disappeared, families were torn asunder, towns and villages were obliterated or evacuated and entire economies disrupted. Bereft and destitute, many women had no choice but to sell themselves.

On the demand side we can identify antecedent cultural factors. 'Part of the attraction of soldiering,' averred Charles Carrington, 'was the unspoken assumption that on active service soldiers were released from the taboos of civil life'.[631] 'Like all young men,' wrote Cecil Lewis in 1936, looking back on the war years and referring to himself in the third person, 'he thought there was something magic about French girls. To him, Paris was not the beautiful city of elegance and gaiety, of palaces, fountains, and boulevards . . . No, Paris was to him a sort of gigantic brothel where women wore nothing but georgette underwear and extra long silk stockings'.[632] But it was not just Paris. For many Edwardians the country at large was a mythic site of spontaneity and sophistication, not to say loucheness and promiscuity. 'Each man had been issued with a pamphlet signed by Lord Kitchener warning him about the dangers of French wine and women', remembered Frank Richards, 'they may as well have not been issued for all the notice we took of them'.[633] In 1929 Robert Graves recalled a conversation with chapel-reared Welsh boy who'd just visited the *Drapeau Blanc*, a notorious Rouen brothel, sometime in early 1917. 'I never knew before,' said the boy after returning to billets, 'what a wonderful thing sex is!' 'There were no restraints in France,' commented Graves, 'these boys had money to spend and knew they stood a good chance of being killed within a few weeks anyhow. They did not want to die virgins'.[634]

We can't know how many settlers, neophytes or connoisseurs, engaged in heterosexual activity with natives, anymore than we can know how many natives traded sex, part time or full time. By their nature records of experience – diaries, letters, memoirs – will not tell us. We might infer from Eachus's comments that officers had more opportunity to buy sex because they had more money, but on the other hand prostitutes responded to the market. Carrington remembered that well-advertised brothels around Amiens' Rue des Galions offered two scales of payment, first-class for officers, second-class for other ranks.[635] In addition some Beflanders of all classes and ranks – again, we can't know how many – refrained from sex. Doubtless fear of the consequences held back some. Christian teaching or affective loyalties to wives and girlfriends probably deterred others. We could also point to the possible psychological effect of war. Eric Leed cites the opinion of German doctor who believed that trench life induced impotence and loss of libido,[636] though one could just as easily make the counter augment that, as in the case of the young Welshmen in Graves' unit, fear of death increased the likelihood of sexual activity.

If records of experience will not help us much neither will official sources or surveys. A great deal of transactional sex was hidden from view, a matter of brief encounters in bedsits and back alleys scarcely visible to statisticians. What did engage official eyes was 'inefficiency', the number of settlers who contracted sexually transmitted diseases. 'The only other prominent cause of inefficiency was venereal disease,' wrote MacPherson in the official history series, after discussing the high incidence of enteric fever and trench foot, 'for which special venereal hospitals had to be opened at the bases. As venereal disease cases were not permitted to be evacuated to England, these hospitals had to be greatly expanded to accommodate the large number of cases which accumulated in France'.[637] Graves mentions laconically that 'base venereal hospitals were always crowded'.[638] By 1918 there were four in Le Havre, one each at Étaples, Rouen, St Omer, Boulogne and Calais and two more elsewhere in the colony – 9,000 beds in total.[639] An entertainer touring Befland gave a performance at Rouen's hospital in July 1917: 'Made an appalling slip by telling the Tommies that it was an inspiring sight to see men from every corner of the British Empire all there "on the same job". They roared and roared with laughter and I capped it by saying "and I know you all mean to see it through" at which they could not contain themselves. Of course I did not know till afterwards that it was a V.D. Hospital. (380 Officers also down with it, alas! – 100,000 affected)'.[640] Admissions climbed steadily as immigration increased – 3,300 between August and December 1914, 17,500 in 1915, 24,100 in 1916, 48,500 a year later – as did ratios: 1.7 per cent of Befland's ration strength in 1914, nearly three per cent in 1915, a slight drop in 1916 (1.8 per cent), 2.5 per cent in 1917.[641] Much higher figures for 1918 may be connected with the furore surrounding France's system of licensed brothels. Until late 1917 GHQ more or less accepted Beflander patronage of *Maisons de Tolérance*; officers could consort with known prostitutes, for example, but weren't supposed to be seen with them in public.[642] Indeed the army ran its own houses in at least two locations, Le Havre and Cayeux-sur-Mer. In the latter town settlers had passes detailing the hours during which specified streets and premises could be visited.[643] Things began to change as manpower shortages reduced immigration and the Cabinet increased pressure on GHQ to tackle waste and inefficiency, and when the United States declared war. US military regulations treated VD as a disciplinary rather than a medical matter, a fact that boosted public and parliamentary hostility to organized prostitution. As a result, and despite resistance from the Army Council, in April 1918 GHQ put *Maisons de Tolérance* completely of bounds. Unsurprisingly, the ban drove men into the arms of prostitutes not subject to inspection. Infection rates soared – just over 60,000 in 1918, or 3.2 per cent of the ration strength.[644]

According to MacPherson overall Befland's VD hospitals treated some 400,000 settlers between 4 August 1914 and the Armistice, but there is a whole host of problems associated with infection statistics, at least insofar as they enable to estimate the number of demand-side encounters. In the first place – obviously – not all cases were diagnosed. Secondly, and equally obviously, not all encounters resulted in infection. Captain Deane, charged with inspecting Le Havre's *Maisons de Tolérance*, recorded that over fifty-seven weeks in 1915–16 171,000 settlers visited brothels in and around the town's red light district but that only 243 contracted infections. Similar proportions obtained in places like Rouen, he stated.[645] Thirdly, hospitals did not capture all those infected, even if already diagnosed.

Many were evacuated to Britain as a result of wounds or other illnesses before they could be admitted. Fourth, some were infected while on leave in the United Kingdom rather than in Befland.[646] Craig Gibson's analysis of VD statistics for Australian troops in July 1917 shows that in any given week about two thirds of infections were contracted in Befland. The rest picked up disease in Britain.[647] In fact Dominion settlers in general exhibited high levels of infection, despite the fact that preventative measures were enforced in ANZAC and Canadian units. On average ANZAC VD rates ran at a staggering thirteen per cent, probably because dominion immigrants were better paid than British Beflanders and never went home and so used prostitutes more frequently.[648] Finally, the figures include men who deliberately infected themselves, raising the possibility that an unknown number of apparently promiscuous settlers might have had sex only once. In May 1917 one medic stated quite bluntly that 'slackers' caught and nursed gonorrhoea to avoid duty,[649] a view supported by Rowland Luther as he crossed the portals in spring that year. 'The advice of the elderly guides at Waterloo and Victoria Stations was being ignored: Leave the bad women alone'. Many took no notice. In fact venereal disease 'seemed to be sought after,' wrote Luther, 'even if only to keep a man from the front during treatment'.[650] This option might prove ineffective, however. Later in 1917 base hospitals sent VD patients into the Salient to work as stretcher-bearers because casualty clearing stations were so short-staffed.[651]

Whatever its causes 'inefficiency' continued to vex the authorities, even after the Armistice. 'The very latest here is what I call "Venereal Madness",' wrote Ronald Schweder from Tourcoing in New Befland on 7 December 1918. 'Everyone in authority has gone quite potty about it & there are lectures by doctors on this entertaining subject daily'.[652] ➲ 70

Friday 6 April 1917 66

In the evening Ronald Schweder wrote to his wife about his current location, La Douve stream near Bailleul. All the units in the district, his own included, were busy with horticulture. His wagon line had a particularly large allotment under cultivation. On 30 May 1918 at Foche Farm in the Salient, peas, cabbages and lettuce, grown by the battery's other ranks, were his for the asking. His 'head gardener' enjoyed the work immensely; 'he seems to be more interested in the garden than in gunnery'.[653] Camp dwellers in the hills around Le Havre put on vegetable shows.[654] To the east 500 hectares of vegetable gardens were laid out around the Somme after the 1916 offensives.[655]

From Dennis Wheatley's diary during his retreat from St Simon to Crèvecœur-le-Grand, 23 March 1918: '5.30 arrive at Avricourt. Send Smith to secure what billets he can. Water and feed horses but had a row with an [R]A.S.C. Officer when I started to park my waggons in the square. He and his S[ergeant] M[ajor] created a scene. He said that he had been here six months and had to collect over 100 agricultural implements in the square before retiring. I put it to him that there was a war on and that the ammunition and waggons and the animals that were dragging them were of more importance at the current time than all the plough[s] and harrows under the sun and that for people who commanded sets of ploughs, the right place was the base or the other side of Paris as not only were they absolutely useless and moreover a confounded nuisance in a retreat as they [?tend] to block the roads, and delay urgent traffic'.[656]

From *Statistics of the Military Effort of the British Empire During the Great War 1914–1920*: 'Military Gardens and Farms. With the object of making the Army self-supporting as far as possible in regard to vegetables, and of saving transport from place to place, units and formations were specially encouraged to extend the area and scope of their cultivations. During the spring of 1918 great efforts were made in many directions, with the result that the amount of land under garden and farm cultivation by the Army was increased from 610 acres at the end of 1916 and 3,492 acres in 1917, to approximately 6,500 acres in 1918. Many units produced the whole of their green vegetables, and a certain amount of grain and forage was also raised on Army farms . . . The formation of the Army Agricultural Committee in January, 1918, centralized and co-ordinated the agricultural work of all our armies both at home and overseas . . . In France, at the end of 1918, the Army was practically self-supporting in vegetables, and had, in addition, saved large quantities of forage . . . departments of agriculture were established and machinery and seeds have been sent out in large quantities . . . a large proportion of the daily vegetable requirements of the Army was grown by the troops themselves. 20,000 acres of cereals, which would have otherwise have been left derelict, were harvested'.[657] Around Roye, just south of the Somme, GHQ earmarked 45,000 hectares for cultivation by Beflanders with tractors imported from Britain. Péronne became a collection point for a vast array of agricultural machinery. But the Ludendorff Offensive and the drive to victory put an end to it all.[658]

All these things might be construed as indices of the colony's partial rootedness, or as evidence of an interrupted transition from a world of warrior nomads to one of settled agriculturalists; a transition, in reverse of the normal pattern, that was finally halted not by defeat but by victory. Victory led to the evacuation and abandonment of the colony, not, as Stapleton Eachus's interlocutors anticipated [50], to its annexation and settlement. In this sense all of Befland was always a field of battle and everywhere always a front line. On the other hand it's just possible that buried somewhere in the National Archives is a speculative paper written by a forgotten civil servant on the desirability of incorporating Befland into the British Empire. Failed transitions notwithstanding, some ex-Beflanders may have felt a lingering sensation of loss. John Pegum suggests that at least some who revisited the territory after the War evinced a 'sentiment of possessiveness'.[659] If they couldn't occupy the land physically they went on holding it imaginatively. ➲ 68

Monday 9 April 1917   **67**

During the night Beflanders launched offensives at Arras and Vimy Ridge. By the month's end over 90,000 had been wounded.[660] Four months previously Stapleton Eachus had copied out a message (strictly against regulations) received at Fourth Army headquarters on the Somme from No. 39 Casualty Clearing Station. Since the last sick return three officers and thirty-six other ranks either had or were suspected of having dysentery. Ten more officers had been hospitalized – four with dysentery, two with measles – and a further 326 other ranks. Among these were one case of scarlet fever, four of cerebo-spinal meningitis, four with suspected diphtheria, twenty-one down with mumps, five actual or suspected typhoid carriers, thirty-two suffering from various forms of measles and thirty-four actual or suspected dysentery. Forty-six other Beflanders (officers and other ranks) were scheduled for immediate evacuation; twenty-five with dysentery, thirteen with diphtheria and eight with mumps.[661]

All zone dwellers ran the risk of injury. Bullets, poison gas, shrapnel, bombs, grenades, mortars and high explosive threatened dreadful wounds at every turn. Their treatment is described in horrific detail in MacPherson's contributions to the interwar official history series, and no less harrowingly in Leo van Bergen's 2009 history of World-War-I military medicine.[662] In addition all Beflanders were likely to fall ill. Bad diet, exposure, hard physical work and wretched sanitation weakened practically everyone at some time or another. The zone harboured other dangers to health, apart from those posed by wargear. Heavy manuring was practised across eastern Befland, though less so after 1915 as natives abandoned their farms. Wounds and clothing became infected with tetanus spores and anthrax bacilli. Both gave rise to gas gangrene (rotting tissue), a disease that often resulted in death or amputation, no matter how slight the initial injury.[663] Besides those listed by Eachus other common illnesses included bronchitis, diarrhoea, malaria, trachoma (eye infections), chicken pox, pneumonia, frostbite, famine dropsy (swelling of the lower limbs due to protein deficiency), flu, 'soldiers' heart' (cardio-vascular disorders caused by stress), impetigo, 'trench' or 'war' nephritis (infected kidneys), exhaustion, hysteria ('neurasthenia'), shell shock (sometimes described as 'Not Yet Diagnosed Nervous'), trench foot (swollen legs and feet, sometimes gangrenous), trench fever (lice borne), enteric fever, scurvy, assorted venereal diseases, rheumatism, pediculosis (skin infections, also lice borne), various undiagnosed fevers (pyrexia), pyoderma (inflammation of the tissue and skin), dermatitis and periodontal disease. In 1916 in the trenches alone 35,000 fell ill or were injured every month – 'wastage', in army-speak. Across Befland about 500,500 suffered wounds and 644,000 contracted diseases serious enough to merit hospitalization. Two years later the figures were 575,000 and just under a million respectively. Enormous numbers of the sick and injured travelled across the Channel: 66,000 in 1914, 252,000 in 1915, nearly 500,000 the following year, 670,000 in 1917, 640,000 in 1918 and 114,000 in 1919. Around fifty per cent returned to Befland.[664]

Those wounded in the zone typically endured a seven-stage journey: from injury site to a first-aid post, from there to a collecting post, then on to an advanced dressing station and casualty clearing station, from clearing station to the entrepôts via base hospitals, and from the entrepôts to the UK. But not all were evacuated. Policy changed late in 1916, due in part to the submarine threat, in part to GHQ's worries about wastage. Thereafter about half the injured and sick were treated inside the colony, but the new policy had unintended consequences. Since base hospitals were now inundated with serious cases medics dispatched the lightly wounded to the UK. For the 'retained' death – obviously – might occur anywhere on a journey from first-aid post to base hospital. Alternatively they might be classed fit for duty at any point along the continuum and embark on new journeys inside Befland.[665]

Late at night on 30 March 1918 and into the following morning, in the thick of the Ludendorff Offensive, a medical officer hurriedly withdrew his advanced dressing stations at Templeux-le-Guérard and Jeancourt thirty miles to the west. Ambulances got lost or were hijacked by fleeing settlers. A few days before another CCS travelling on the Somme ran into the Ludendorff Offensive. An X-ray unit, a complete operating theatre, a dressing room, sixty beds and mattresses, about 350 stretchers, dispensary equipment, medical and surgical panniers, 1,600 blankets, two large marquees and eight bell tents were packed into lorries strung out along the Beaulencourt-Edgehill road, then under shell fire. Two years earlier it took one hundred lorries to transport No. 45 CCS from Vecquemont to Edgehill. Others required 400 lorries – some stations even dug up and removed their own road stone – and when moved by rail a CCS usually needed the services of an entire train.[666]

Dressing and clearing stations, often with YMCA huts attached, were highly immobile because during the siege zone-based medical facilities burgeoned into what were in effect fully-equipped field hospitals. 'Forward echelons' were six to eight miles behind the border, 'back echelons' twelve to sixteen. First-aid posts were usually near an infantry battalion's headquarters, and when zone dwellers collapsed on journeys into no man's land stretcher bearers fanned out in an arc in front of the trenches. Walking wounded were expected to find their own way back. If the 'length of carry' was too great bearers parked the injured at collecting points, usually shell holes. From there 'reserve bearers' completed their journeys to the posts,[667] but no one could plan for the immense confusion of battle. Methodical evacuation proved impossible over night-time landscapes reduced to quagmires and rendered impenetrable by smoke, gas, shelling and machine-gun fire. Survivors might lie for days in the open before they could be rescued. On 11 January 1917 a medical unit resting at Abbeville returned the Ancre Valley. In April its commander, Colonel J. Poe, submitted a report on what he found. 'All the country in front of the line held on 1st July 1916 was impassable even for pack animals except on made roads . . . About 18th January, five weeks of hard frost commenced, and the whole of the wet mud froze to the hardness of a metalled road; this made transport much easier, but it made it excessively difficult to do any digging, and excavations for dugouts could only be made with the assistance of explosives . . . On 15th February the thaw commenced and the whole country-side turned into a sea of mud'. Recovering the wounded became ever more difficult as settlers moved east towards the Hindenburg Line. By 19 March lines of evacuation stretched for seventeen miles.[668]

Overall, between 1914 and 1918 sick and injured Beflanders made four million journeys from casualty clearing stations to base hospitals. Most travelled by rail. In the south six ambulance barges, each with thirty beds, plied the Canal de la Somme in 1916, but a swing bridge at Abbeville was in constant use and could rarely be raised for river traffic. Barge flotillas made nearly 600 journeys but evacuated a mere 17,000. By contrast each ambulance train – forty-three by 1918 – carried between 350 and 450 patients. Temporary ambulance trains, *ad hoc* collections of carriages and wagons pressed into service during major offensives, crammed in many more, often over 1,000. In 1916 trains made over eighteen hundred journeys in and out of Flanders, La Bassée district and the Somme, but delays were common. In June 1916 staff officers calculated that virtually all Befland's ambulance trains would have to be sent into the Somme in order to evacuate the expected rush of Fourth Army casualties. Though on 3 July – the peak day for rail evacuations – wounded settlers left at the rate of ten a minute, thousands waited under shellfire at casualty clearing stations around Corbie, Edgehill, Contay, Heilly and Vecquemont.[669] That month Jessie Wilson was at Étretat, a fashionable seaside resort fifteen miles north of Le Havre and the location of No. 1 British General Hospital. She watched the wounded coming off the trains: 'it must have been indeed a "radiant change" after the horrors of the Somme to look out on the blue sparkling water and to breathe the clear bracing air'.[670] ➲ 69

Saturday 14 April 1917   **68**

'We exist almost entirely upon bully beef and biscuits, except for what we ourselves buy,' grumbled Stapleton Eachus from Querrieu on the Somme. 'This however is considerably more difficult now owing to the new French regulations which forbid the selling of eatables and drinkables until after 4 p.m. We are not even allowed to enter any sort of shop until that hour'.[671] Two years earlier Robert Cude was also on the Somme, in billets at Morlancourt. He noticed something new. There were three churches in the village, one of which, badly damaged by shell fire, had been turned into a recreation centre-cum-canteen by a very young army padre ('no more than a boy') under the auspices of the YMCA. The padre kept a beady eye on what was sold – no alcohol, much to Cude's disgust – and also pushed up the prices; everything was much more expensive than in the divisional canteen which, unfortunately, was outside the village and currently out of bounds. 'It is the old story,' he complained. British newspapers were full of appeals for money to supply food and beverages to settlers, but to his mind the whole thing was a scam; 'one of the biggest swindles it has ever been my lot to run up against. The profits must be astounding'.[672]

Settlers living far from the zone in the west, at the entrepôts or along the lines of communication, purchased off-ration food in local shops, despite encountering linguistic difficulties and profiteering. 'There are no decent shops here,' complained Phyllis Goodliff to her mother from Boulogne March and April 1918, 'and a great many close during the lunch hour. One doesn't get a chance to say what one wants in French before they race off in most extraordinary English and they don't half put the price on . . . We get plenty out here of sorts, quantities of meat and margarine. There is heaps of butter too in the shops but it IS jolly dear, for the English to buy at any rate. Some girls I know have stood by a stall in the market and watched the people selling oranges to the French at almost half the price they try to sell them to us'.[673] In contrast, those living to the east bought from voluntary organizations (the YMCA denounced by Cude, the Church Army) which had set up shop close to the zone, from official expeditionary-force canteens, or from the ubiquitous estaminets (probably from the Walloon 'èstaminê', 'staminê'; a cowshed), makeshift cafés opened by natives as waves of settlers came and went. But unless they were travelling and so could visit farms and estaminets along the road, regulations constrained the movements of most privates and NCOs.

Officers, on the other hand, by virtue of their social and military standing, higher pay and ready access to the means of transport – horses – ranged far and wide and spent freely. Somewhere near Bailleul in May 1917 Ronald Schweder rode out to a farm in search of food. The inhabitants were just about to leave, sick of the constant shelling. He bought eggs and a dozen or so hens, the latter at three francs a head, so that the mess would have a steady supply of fresh eggs. If they were forced to move they could always kill the birds and eat them. Unfortunately the cows weren't for sale. Had they been Schweder would have purchased them too.[674] Officers could also access Befland's network of closed shops, the officer-only clubs. Many native cafés, hotels and restaurants were also closed to other ranks, either officially or unofficially; in the latter case by force of class convention, in the former by order of the local Town Majors, military bureaucrats responsible for billeting.

Frank Richards and two friends went looking for food and drink during the retreat from Le Cateau in August 1914. 'We entered a café, where there were a lot of officers from other battalions, besides a couple of staff-officers, mixed up with ordinary troops . . . This was the only time during the whole of the War that I saw officers and men buying food and drink in the same café'.[675]

George Stringer wasn't feeling very well in summer 1915 so taking his groom with him he left his artillery battery at Kemmel in the Salient and decamped to the wagon lines a few miles to the west. From there he spent the days riding around Flanders (Ouderdom, Dranoutre, Hazebrouck), visiting friends and dropping into Poperinghe for lunch. The dining rooms, run by girls who had a café in the main street until bombardments made it judicious to move elsewhere, were on the Rue des Cats. Pigeon was a favourite dish, washed down with copies supplies of one-star champagne (which tasted of gooseberries and went straight to your head) and finished off with a large cigar. Just under two years later and now right up against the border at Angres in La Bassée district, he rode to Béthune and back, a twenty-mile trip, to do some shopping for the officers' mess. Endives, cabbage, lettuce, a basket of strawberries, peaches, a pineapple at twelve francs and much else were handed over to the cooks. Despite its proximity he thought that Angres officers' club wasn't up to much – too dirty, hence the shopping trip. But he had eaten there two months previously, reluctantly and alone; everyone else had gone to Béthune. Dinner comprised soup, roast mutton with onion sauce (potatoes placed under the meat), cauliflower, stewed plums and a savoury.[676]

Between these three diary entries – August 1915, April and June 1917 – Befland experienced a massive population surge, the stiffening of the siege, the hard winter of 1916–17 and disrupted ration supply, factors reflected in another entry. 'They rob us do these French behind the lines,' commented Stringer after riding five miles from the tiny village of Lucheux to Doullens to buy chickens for the mess early in December 1916, 'one price for the French & one for soldat Anglais. It's worth it to feed well – cost what it may'.[677] Others too noticed that things had changed. 'We were lucky this morning in getting one dozen eggs, price 5 francs,' remarked Herbert Leland from the Somme a week later. 'I cannot think where they come from as I have not seen a fowl for ages'.[678] Six months on Ralph Hamilton returned to Reninghelst, a few miles from Poperinghe. 'Since I was here a year ago there has been a lot more damage . . . I bought a huge basket of excellent strawberries for 4 francs, which is the only cheap thing I have ever seen in Belgium. Everything has gone up to famine prices, owing to the enormous number of troops in Flanders now'.[679] Rising prices and a burgeoning population doubtless account for the growth in sales at Expeditionary Force canteens. Takings rose from 3.4 million francs in the first half of 1915 to just over 223 million in the last half of 1918,[680] though once again class inflected consumption. In a general rant against officers Stapleton Eachus fumed about expeditionary force canteens whose personnel catered exclusively to the whims of 'nonentities'. Most of the time it was hopeless to try even to get near the counters because of the enormous orders for food presented by mess orderlies. In time like this (March 1917), when food was so short, he continued, ordinary soldiers found it nigh on impossible to get enough to eat.[681] The Angres officers' club grudgingly patronized by Stringer offered its customers a take-away menu which included fresh asparagus and fish, green artichokes and black grapes.[682] Other ranks were not admitted.

Breaking the siege failed to bring much relief to officers deprived of their usual fare or forced to pay over the odds for it – unless one was looting, of course. The rations were good enough, wrote Schweder in April 1918 during his headlong retreat from St Quentin, but the little extras that made life bearable – potted meat and fish, biscuits, whisky and so on – were now increasingly hard to find. The expeditionary force canteens rushed off so quickly ('like whirl-winds') that one couldn't ride fast enough to catch up with them.[683] ➲ 75

69   Wednesday 18 April 1917

'We had the Navy round to see us today,' commented Ronald Schweder, 'an Admiral and several Officers doing a Thomas Cook's tour'.[684]

This journey was probably officially sanctioned, but the RASC's historian records that tourism, or something like it, caused tensions at the highest level. Shortly after Lloyd George put Eric Geddes in overall command of Befland's transport early in 1916, Long, Director Supplies and Transport at the War Office, resigned, in part in protest at Geddes' relaxed attitude to irregular travel. 'Very early in the War, casual individuals began to career about in motor cars behind the lines, choking the roads and making free with the Government's petrol and spare tyres. It was the nucleus of the rabble which always tends to infest the skirts of an army in the field. General Long put as peremptory a stop to this . . . by positively forbidding any motor car to be landed in France without a permit signed by himself. Of course he had to go through stormy interviews with indignant nonentities who boasted themselves to be somebody, but his answer, whether to duke or dustman, was the same, a very resolute negative'.[685]

Long's robust prescriptions probably did little to stop travel to Befland – from mid-1915 YMCA hotels at the entrepôts handled between one hundred and 150 civilian arrivals from the UK every day[686] – still less to prevent the well connected from making unofficial journeys of one kind or another inside the colony, before and after his departure. In November 1916 Ralph Hamilton travelled from Villers-au-Bois to Carency in La Bassée district. 'I rode over to Divisional H.Q., and had tea with the general and his brother the admiral. They went to Guillemont yesterday for a joy-ride, but said there was nothing much doing. I borrowed the general's car to take me to Gauchin-Légal and the driver was a gentleman who owns several cars of his own and who, not being medically fit for the Flying Corps, has come out as a sergeant on the Motor Transport. He has now been chauffeur to three C.R.A.s of the 24th Division – Sir Godfrey Thomas, poor General Philpotts, and General Sheppard'.[687]

For the less privileged joy riding and tourism seem to have been no less a part of everyday life, whether in the zone or the back areas. 'Most of our work at present is cycle patrol, hunting spies,' wrote Garnet Durham from Flanders in March 1915, 'and we go into the trenches at times out of curiosity'.[688] Charles Carrington recalled that 'the art of hitch-hiking (which in those days we called "lorry-hopping")' spread quickly, even though lorries were scarce and usually shuttled between railheads and the zone, 'which was not likely to be the way you wanted to go for fun'.[689] But these limitations applied only to the early years. Motor transport expanded rapidly, particularly after 1916. By the Armistice over 57,000 vehicles had been imported through the entrepôts.[690] They criss-crossed the colony in every direction, and there was plenty of scope for enterprising hitch-hikers to get further afield. 'Whilst Jones was awaiting his court-martial he told me of his wanderings in Back Areas during the three months he had been away,' remembered Frank Richards in 1933, 'and how he could have still been away if he hadn't got fed up and given himself up. He had gone back to Béthune and in two days was in Boulogne: he had a good time there and then went to Calais. He never walked far, always getting lifts with motor lorries and got more food than what he had had since he landed in France. He also had some glorious drunks with some of the men he had met and nobody ever pulled him up or questioned him'.[691]

At a quarter past nine in the morning of Friday, 21 July 1916, a group of settlers arrived at Fricourt Cemetery crossroads. Over the next twenty-three hours and forty-five minutes 26,536 walkers, 5,404 horsemen, 1,043 cyclists, sixty-three artillery pieces, thirteen gun carriages, eight machine guns, ten caterpillar tracked vehicles, 515 one-horse carts, 568 four-horse wagons, 1,215 two-horse carts, 1,458 six-horse wagons, 617 motor bikes, ninety-five buses and vans, 330 ambulances, 568 cars and 813 lorries passed in front of them. Between 09.15 and three in the afternoon motor vehicles and horse-drawn wagons went by at the rate of just under eight a minute.[692] Darkness and salvos of German lachrymatory shells interrupted the count – the census takers had to wear goggles from ten in the evening until 4 a.m. on the 22nd – but even so it's apparent that prospective tourists could access a wide range of vehicles and destinations. Since the lorries, cars and buses were on average travelling for fifteen miles practically all the Somme's main towns – Albert, Amiens, Doullens, St Pol; even those bordering La Bassée district – were within easy striking distance of Fricourt, as were the several hundreds of villages spread out to the north and west. Moreover, what the census takers recorded was only a small part of the total volume of motorized traffic abroad on the Somme. By late summer between 1,200 and 1,400 trucks were shuttling in and out of the zone every day, from Arras in the north to Cléry and Bray-sur-Somme in the south. Fourth Army headquarters at Querrieu alone controlled one thousand cars, two thousand motorbikes and nearly five thousand lorries.[693] 'Around the railway stations vehicles swarmed like flies', remembered James Edmonds.[694]

Tourists also exploited Befland's trains. According to Alan Henniker there were 'numerous unauthorized movements of parties and individuals – stragglers, joyriders and members of benevolent associations and others who professed to be travelling on the business of the British army or to be desirous of forwarding gifts or purchases to it'. As with lorry-hopping opportunities abounded for the confident and the plausible: 'at stations where there was no R.T.O. the French *commission de gare* was seldom in position to judge whether an *ordre de transport* chargeable against the British army ought to be issued for such movements or not'.[695] And as with motor transport the rapidly expanding railway system multiplied opportunities: 1,900 locomotives, 69,000 wagons and carriages and 3,900 miles of rails shipped to Befland by December 1918, to which should be added the British takeover of two extensive French-built networks around Hazebrouck and Doullens.[696]

On 10 February 1916 Schweder took a train from Cayeux-sur-Mer to Abbeville. He changed at Noyelles-sur-Mer and caught the Paris-Boulogne express, complete with dining car and wagon lits. He spent the journey gazing at the passing landscape and trying to imagine that he was a civilian once more.[697] It's not clear whether or not Schweder had a legitimate 'movement order', but if, like London's portals Befland's stations were liminal places [36], unlike the portals the colony's thresholds were most likely negotiated with relative ease. Complicated forms and a fourteen-page booklet – *Instructions for the Issue and Use of Ordres de Transport* – circulated to RTOs late in 1915 probably had little deterrent effect.[698] But we should enter a caveat which applied to every potential tourist. In Befland the inequitable and divisive workings of a social system defined absolutely by class fundamentally shaped all material distributions. 'I may say that I have never once seen a motor car stop to give a "Tommy" a lift if it contained an officer', wrote Stapleton Eachus in his diary on 31 March 1917. They rushed about the country in vehicles which they seemed to believe had been provided simply for their own private use. Weary settlers trudging along the lanes, burdened with kit and wargear, could expect nothing. But woe betide those who forgot to salute as some jumped-up subaltern swept by in an expensive limousine.[699] As far as the railways are concerned we can easily imagine RTOs casually disbursing first-class favours for fellow officers like Schweder while their clerks surreptitiously slipped third-class chits to fellow NCOs and privates, but here we should enter two more caveats. Sometimes, as in January 1917 when all internal leave was cancelled due to congestion on the railways, secular movements in the economy may have constricted opportunities. At other times geographical fluidity may have expanded them.

When Befland's borders collapsed in spring 1918 GHQ briefly entertained the possibility of completely evacuating the entire colony. In the end 'Scheme Z' was abandoned, but schemes X and Y, involving the removal of all settlers from the Amiens, Abbeville, Abancourt, Dieppe, Calais and Dunkirk areas did temporarily become operational.[700] As the thousands of back-area settlers hurriedly despatched eastwards to burn stores and destroy railway lines collided thousands more fleeing westwards it's hard to imagine that RTO staff, frantically elbowing their way along overcrowded platforms, could even begin to establish everyone's credentials, let alone issue properly constituted movement orders. ⮌ 83

Thursday 19 April 1917   70

Stapleton Eachus, on a day tip to Corbie on the Somme, stopped and bought presents for friends and family back in England. Afterwards he walked around the town, calling in here and there for tea and cocoa. In one café sat a group of Beflanders attached to the Guards Division, at another table two good-looking native women. 'The usual topic of conversation as in progress,' noted Eachus. After a while the guardsmen told him that five Corbie girls, each with a newly born child, had recently got married to English settlers. Eachus had meditated on the same theme a few months earlier. It was well known, he averred, that the number of marriages contracted between settlers and natives had been rising steadily since 1914 and had now reached a high figure. In part, he explained, this was because native women gained financially if they married British immigrants – twice the allowance offered to those marrying French soldiers – in part because they thought British soldiers cleaner and better paid than their French counterparts. The matter crops up again in a diary entry dated 13 September 1916. After noting that extra-marital affairs seemed common in the village (Querrieu on the Somme), that the local girls preferred Englishmen, and that settler-native marriage and cohabitation was widespread – 'a vast number of unsolemnised unions' – he related the story of a local girl and her settler 'husband' (the man was already married). As the husband migrated within Befland she followed, obtaining passports, permissions, rooms, etc. with the assistance of the French interpreter attached to the man's unit. According to Eachus this kind of behaviour was not untypical. In fact, it was a daily occurrence. 'I might mention,' he added two months later, 'that another soldier, while he is the fiancé of a French girl from Amiens, also spends a good deal of time at the same place [Pont-Noyelles, Querrieu's sister village] and we are a jolly party when together'.[701]

What Eachus provides us with here is clear evidence of 'affective' relations between male settlers and native women. Even though 'transactional' elements obtained these interactions clearly involved something more than straightforward prostitution. Though we don't have any figures[702] it must be the case that the number of affective associations of all kinds – marriages, cohabitations, understandings, friendships, casual liaisons – grew as Befland developed. In the west of the colony lives intertwined because permanent settlement and the material aspects of war threw people together. Between 1914 and 1918, for example, over 4,000 native women and girls worked alongside Beflanders in base stores and workshops.[703] At sites like these and elsewhere in the entrepôts, in the back areas and in zone towns, traces of what look like the beginning, end, or continuation of affective relationships abound, and of misunderstandings and moments that never blossomed.

While searching for billets at Cayeux-sur-Mer on 24 January 1916 Ronald Schweder wrote to his wife describing a farm just outside the town run by a woman whose husband was a prisoner of war in Germany, and risked a startlingly candid admission. She was showing him a loft when suddenly she leaned against the wall and gave him such a meaning look that he decided it would be best to depart post haste – her nails were dirty, and besides 'I don't like them fat'. Cayeux was a resort popular with holiday-makers from Paris and Amiens, he continued. Before the War about 3,500 people lived there, but recently the figure had increased to over 5,000, due in the main to an influx of refugees from Belgium. The men would soon make themselves at home, he said; 'never have I seen so many "Birds"'. It didn't take them long. Within a day or two gunners and drivers could be seen walking arm in arm with native girls in the evenings along the darkened streets. They all looked remarkably clean and tidy. In their letters they admitted to sprucing up in order to go 'square pushing'. Just under two weeks later he was sixteen miles inland, at a hotel in Abbeville. After lunch he went into the reading room. Three officers breezed in, closely followed by a group of native girls who pretended to be interested in paper and envelopes. In short order the men picked up the girls and off the whole party went.[704]

That July Eachus spent the early evenings sitting in the garden of his billet eating fruit gathered for him by a local girl.[705] Next year, on 2 April, George Stringer rode into Aire-sur-la-Lys in La Bassée district with two friends to collect money from the field cashier: other ranks had to be paid and they needed some for themselves. After stopping for coffee and cakes at an officer-only patisserie they bumped into a group of men from his unit and asked what they were up to. The men explained that they were going to visit girls living in Saint-Quentin, a suburb of Aire, where they'd been billeted fourteen months previously. Stringer returned to Aire two days later, this time popping in to a different tea shop. The pretty girl who served him spoke perfect English – she'd been to school in England, Scotland and Ireland, she explained – but when young officers came in he noticed that she reverted to her native tongue and flirted with them as they struggled with their schoolboy French.[706] Three weeks on Robert Cude cycled the thirteen miles from Béthune to Isbergues, departing at ten in the morning and arriving two and a half hours later. It wasn't his first trip; two girls were waiting for him and they spent the entire afternoon together before he dragged himself away, very reluctantly, at just after seven – 'I must go, as if anything has happened today, I shall be rumbled'. As he left they implored him to come back the very next time he could wangle some unofficial 'leave'. He would miss these girls terribly, he confided to his diary. They were extraordinarily pleasant and went out of their way to keep him amused. In all honesty he didn't think that he was worthy of so much warmth and attention.[707] At Rouen in July an anonymous diarist overheard a snatch of street banter between 'a Tommy who had married a French girl, as many of them have . . . "Garn, you saucy jade!" he said, and she replied, "Pardon, Je ne suis pas saucy jade"'.[708] To the north, at a Cassel hotel, William Orpen exchanged smiles with Blanche, one the owner's two daughters, popularly known as 'the peaches'. The other, Suzanne, wore an RFC badge on her blouse because she was engaged to a Beflander pilot.[709] 'It was after lunch one Sunday: I had just got back to my room to work there when there was a knock on the door, and in walked Madame Blanche, who, after much trouble to us both, I gathered wished me to go for a walk with her. Impossible! I, a major, a Field Officer, to walk at large through the streets of Cassel, 2nd Army H.Q., with a serving-girl from the "Hotel Sauvage"! I succeeded in explaining this after some time; and then, to my amazement, she broke down and wept. The convulsive sobbing continued, and I thought and wondered, and in the end decided that I was crazy to make a woman weep because I would not go for a walk with her. So I told her I would do so; and she dried her eyes and asked me to meet her in the hotel yard in ten minutes'. She appeared dressed in mourning. In the pouring rain they went to a cemetery where she put flowers on her husband's grave and prayed for about half an hour. 'It was a strange affair,' mused Orpen. 'I may be stupid, but I cannot yet see her reason for wishing to take me out in the wet'.[710] It doesn't seem to have occurred to this appalling snob that Blanche probably just wanted company on a lonely Sunday afternoon, or needed a gentleman to escort her in town heaving with soldiers. ⊃ 74

Friday 20 April 1917 71

Ronald Schweder read in a newspaper that the enemy was bundling corpses into parcels of three and shipping them back to Germany, there to extract fats for the manufacture of wargear. The residual matter, continued the report, was fed to pigs. It was all quite possible, he thought. On 8 May, after a particularly heavy deluge of incoming shells, he overheard men in his unit saying that it was all due to the corpse factory and the sale of the Empress Augusta's jewels.[711]

That Schweder and his gun crews fell victim to the 'Kadaver Fabrik' rumour, a notorious British propaganda scam bandied about in *The Times* and *Daily Mail* on 17 April, or at least gave it some credence, is to be expected. Prolonged siege, stable borders, the empty battlefield and the absence of a visible enemy invited speculation and surmise. 'The new recruits are very eager for tales of the front,' wrote Garnet Durham in March 1916, 'and we old timers give them good measure and are becoming accomplished liars'.[712] Like Schweder, Charles Carrington bought the corpse-factory story.[713] So did Rowland Luther, for a while: 'News leaked out that the Germans were starving, owing to the naval blockade, and the German dead soldiers were being taken back to fry down for fat . . . but then we soldiers would swallow any yarn that was spun to us'. It was either 'latrine news' or the newspapers.[714] Occasionally Beflanders thought the Germans were cannibals, eating unprocessed flesh.[715] In 'Rumours at the Front', a short story published in 1931, Stephen Southwold speculates on the origins of zone gossip. He describes key transmission points (latrines, mess tents, supply dumps) and essays a classification system based on the colony's 'early', 'middle', and 'late' periods. His taxonomy includes 'mad majors' rampaging in no man's land, settlers who saw or spoke to the Kaiser, 'lost battalions' on the model of Roman Britain's lost legion, cryptic signals of peace (rockets, falling landmarks), stories of the Germans conjuring up bad weather, tales of awesome new weapons of mass destruction and, of course, secret factories turning corpses into food or wargear.[716]

'He', the collective noun for the unknown, unseen other, could be superior as well as bestial. On the Somme in March 1916 Schweder estimated that a good half of the shells he fired across the border were duds, doubtless because so many of them had been made in the United States. The German's shells, by contrast, were magnificent. They never failed to explode.[717] Twelve months later George Stringer examined ground recently incorporated into Befland. Looking around he was impressed by what the enemy had left behind – 'The more I see of Hun handiwork the more do I admire him – his method, science & truly excellent workmanship'.[718] 'He' could also be omnipresent. In 1915 some immigrants new to Flanders regarded local farmers and pigeon fanciers as spies – witness Garnet Durham and the Post Office Rifles [9, 51] – and believed that enemy agents used windmills and the disposition of grazing cattle to signal troop movements and artillery layouts.[719] On the other hand 'He' might be construed as a kind of Old Man of the Woods lurking on the margins of the imagination, or indeed a real person, intimately aware of Beflanders and their ways and cunningly magicked across the border against all odds. Stringer recalled two incidents at Lindenhoek in the Salient in 1915. While sleeping out one night (it must have been summer) a bullet woke him up as it struck the ground just in front of his bed. He waited. After ten minutes another came, and landed in the same spot. Stringer picked up his bed and took it round the lea of a nearby wall. What was going on? It must have been 'an old Bosch with a white beard' triggering fixed rifles from each bay as he trudged slowly along his trench, he mused. One morning later on Stringer fell into conversation with a captain in charge of an anti-aircraft unit parked by the side of the Dranoutre Road. An aeroplane went overhead. They both looked up. It was well-known visitor, a German spotter that came over about this time every day. 'They say that's Hamel,' said the captain, '& we get £500 if we bring him down'. Hamel, explained Stringer, was an aeronaut who used to do a great deal of exhibition flying in France, Belgium and the UK. Stringer remembered watching him doing stunts in the skies over Warwickshire one summer's day as he was playing tennis in the village of Hartshill. On 23 May 1914 Hamel flew out across the Channel and disappeared.

It's pretty clear than Gustav Hamel, a pioneer aviator, was just one of several early-twentieth century adventurers whose equipment failed them. French fishermen working off Boulogne early in July found a badly rotted corpse with clothing that matched his, but in Befland rumour and speculation abounded. While some argued that he'd fallen into the Channel and drowned others insisted that he'd reached the French coast and then secretly flown to Berlin to offer his services to the Kaiser. Stringer half-believed it. He would have been a very useful addition to the German war effort, he remarked, because he knew Befland, and England, like the back of his hand.[720] (In fact despite his Teutonic name Hamel was English born and bred; educated at Westminster School and a founder a member of both the Royal Aero and Hendon Flying Clubs). ⊃ 73

Friday 27 April 1917 **72**

James Williams, a middle-aged Londoner reluctantly conscripted into a Labour Company, made his first trip to Arras. 'A very nice place but no signs of recent fighting. One would not think there had been big battles fought here it seems so quiet & serene. The scenery around is very beautiful at any rate from a tourists [sic] point of view but what with the heavy work & jolting of the motors it does not quite appear so to me'. Evidence of heavy shelling was apparent when he went back a month or so later. While picking up stores on a windy day he noticed sheets of corrugated iron blowing about in the now deserted main square.[721] By then thousands of settlers had taken cover in the city's dense network of medieval tunnels, crammed in among underground dumps, depots, command centres and field hospitals. Arras was the first big border town that Lieutenant Capron saw after arriving in Befland. Years later he remembered riding through it for the first time. It was more or less undamaged but empty of civilians; uncanny, like a ghost town. Late at night his horse's hooves echoed around the vacant streets as they struck the cobblestones. Now and then, high in the dark sky, salvos of enemy shells rushed and roared overhead. A few seconds later would come faint, muffled sounds as they exploded far away in the distance.[722]

There had been no significant Beflander presence in Arras until almost a year before. In February 1916 most of Allenby's Third Army started to move there from the Somme, and Capron's arrival coincided with preparations for a major offensive east of the city which lasted from early April to mid May and helped to extend the border a little, but apart from the capture of Vimy Ridge to the north not much changed until the advance to victory.[723] Above ground life was maintained by 'a handful of persistent residents,' remembered Charles Carrington.[724] James Edmonds records that there were also one or two YMCA huts that stayed open from 1915 to 1918. 'Tea, coffee, cocoa, bovril and oxo, with biscuits, cake and cigarettes, were the principal articles provided; and notepaper and a few books and old newspapers were available'.[725] In 1919, when it was all over, the Salvation Army set up a branch of the 'Relatives' War Graves Visitation Department' in the city. Its staff guided people to the region's cemeteries and photographed graves for those who couldn't make the journey.[726] ➲ 78

73   Friday 1 June 1917

'Dear Mother & Dad . . . You say why don't our fellows kill the Bosche instead of taking him prisoner. I think our chaps are "soft-hearted". The Bosche brings [out] a photo of his wife & family etc. as soon as he finds he is in great danger. <u>But</u> – lately the motto has been "No prisoners" (and a good thing too)'.[727]

As James Naylor intimates, killing close up wasn't always easy, physically or psychologically. 'When we tumbled in,' remembered Rowland Luther, 'I fell on top of some of the enemy, and one put his teeth in my cheek and held on'. There wasn't much room to move but he tried to push his thumbs into the man's eyes. That failing, he grabbed his neck, squeezed the throat until he let go and then clubbed him as hard as he could with a rifle butt. Of the eight Germans in the trench bay six were soon either dead or dying. The two others had given up the struggle. Luther stood up, felt blood streaming from his face and checked himself over. In fact he was the only one relatively uninjured; most of his companions had serious cuts or puncture wounds. Three, dead or unconscious, lay sprawled across the bodies of the enemy. Shortly afterwards more Beflanders jumped into the trench. An officer told those who could still walk to go back for treatment and take the two Germans with them.[728]

Even if they got across no man's land and into enemy territory – a rare event – most zone dwellers didn't directly encounter functioning opponents. Infantrymen, defenders and attackers alike, usually fought each other by lobbing bombs over traverses, kinks in the trenches that formed little defensible bays. Once round a traverse they were likely to find only the dead and the wounded. Luther's account (September 1915) shows what was involved if it did come to physical interaction with a living adversary; a frenzied struggle in confined spaces lasting no more than a few minutes. Of course it's dangerous to generalize from one incident. The memoir literature is replete with examples of settlers who went on killing, or murdered those who'd surrendered. Much would depend on circumstance and temperament, but in this case at least once the adrenalin rush was over the reaction seems to have been one of concern for the body and care for the wounded.

There were other forms of interaction apart from killing. Conversations, understandings and gestures calculated to keep the peace and signal awareness of shared discomforts and dangers. In June 1916 Harold Bursey noted down details of a written communication seen across no man's land not far from the Bois des Tailles on the Somme: 'The morning is beautifully fine. Guns are very quiet. Everyone is making preparations for the coming advance. The Huns put a board up yesterday in their front line trenches and on it was pinned a paper with the following. "We know you are going to attack. Kitchener is done, Asquith is done. You are done. We are done. In fact we are all done"'.[729] As for signals designed to make zone dwellers' lives bearable, or at least predictable, the 'Christmas truces' of 1914 and 1915 seem to have been only the most singular instances of the zone's 'live and let live' structure of behaviour. From a settler perspective behaviour may have been inflected through a rough and ready assessment of differences within enemy formations. In March 1916 the Post Office Rifles, close up against the border in La Bassée district, found Saxons ready to swap food and tobacco and to give warnings when the Prussian artillery was about to fire. The settlers opposite returned the compliment by blowing whistles before they launched trench mortars. Once, when they were idly looking at the German lines, they saw a staff officer poke his head above the parapet for a moment before instinctively ducking for safety. Laughter drifted over from the trench as the officer, blushing with embarrassment, stood upright and resumed his walk, accompanied by grinning soldiers.[730] Two other instances of ethnic stereotyping, both grounded in experience. Somewhere in Flanders in March George Stringer chatted to a man who'd just come out of the trenches. He described the set-up. The lines were close together and Saxons lived opposite. Unlike Prussians they weren't aggressive, so every morning officers on both sides would climb out their respective trenches, sit on the parapets and chat. It all came to an end when a pugnacious Beflander colonel got wind of it. The Saxons were given notice that artillery fire would commence in one hour's time.[731] Two years later Ronald Schweder walked above trenches near Bailleul. He wouldn't have done it, he wrote, had the soldiers opposite been Prussians, but they were Saxons – peaceable, by comparison.[732]

Ignoring understandings could unleash deadly reinforcing signals. 'It was not customary to "pot" at an enemy should he show his head as this tended to attract reprisals and disturb the peace,' remembered Stormont Gibbs.[733] 'Bubbly' Bolitho found this to his cost in March 1916 [39], and settlers seem to have known exactly how to read actions of this kind. Two months later Garnet Durham endured a sudden flurry of shellfire while on traffic duty at Ypres' Menin Gate, 'punishment' after a Beflander anti-aircraft unit had shot down a German aeronaut. The following January he was in La Bassée district, around Neuville St Vaast. A brief thaw had flooded the trenches, leaving zone dwellers with little option but to shift elsewhere. Little groups from both sides climbed onto their parapets. Soon the banter started (here the lines were only fifty yards apart). One German asked the Beflanders to identify the man who lobbed 'lollipops' (trench mortar canisters) at them, to which the settlers replied that they weren't particularly keen on him either, and that he and his friends could come and get him if they cared to try.[734] ➲ 99

74 Monday 4 June 1917

Ronald Schweder wrote home after lunching with natives in Bailleul. 'I had to exhibit your photograph and Anne's. In fact I made myself into a real "Arry après la guerre." [After the war] we are going to pay them a visit whilst making a tour of the battlefields of Flanders'.[735] Schweder already knew these people well. They'd first met in September 1916 when he went to buy linseed cake for the battery's horses. The old corn merchant and his wife asked him to stay to dinner. Regrettably, they said, their two daughters were visiting Paris. Nevertheless Schweder had a good time – plenty of wine and liqueurs, all mixed together in the traditional French way, and plenty of French conversation. He went back a few days later. By now the girls had returned from Paris and once more he was invited to stay. This time he joined the entire family for a substantial lunch. Madame he much admired. She was the butt the family's jokes and took all the joshing in the best of spirits.[736]

We catch glimpses of many more affective moments between settlers and natives – village girls in paper slippers chatting to gunners one morning as their artillery thundered out over Aubers Ridge, just south of Armentières (the Post Office Rifles, May 1915);[737] local boys thrilled to bits by the guns and helping with the harnessing (Schweder at Cayeux-sur-Mer, January 1916);[738] a unit at Bray-sur-Somme that refused to shell a German-held village because a local man's family lived there (Cude, March 1916); film shows and boxing matches organized by Cude's division to which natives were invited (May 1916);[739] Herbert Leland eating sweets in billets with a little girl who jabbered away at him in French (November 1916);[740] the old lady who saved bathwater for 'les Anglais' to wash in free of charge (the Post Office Rifles at Souchez in La Bassée district, July 1916);[741] CCS staff on the Somme treating wounded and sick natives (autumn 1918);[742] Hester, 'the wench of the farm', working alongside men cleaning Number 1 gun's breech-block while another girl lent a hand sawing wood for the gun-pits (Schweder again, this time near Gheluvelt, October 1918),[743] and Cude feeding civilians and repairing roads at Robersart near Le Cateau, also in October 1918: 'a labour of love ... every little kindness that we can show to them, is too much for them, and the tears roll down their cheeks'.[744]

But not all interactions were as congenial or easy as these. In October 1914 Frank Richard's mate Billy started throwing his weight around in a Rouen café, cursing the landlord in Hindustani. Richards told him he couldn't treat the French the same as 'Eastern races'. 'Look here, Dick,' said Billy, 'there is only one way to treat foreigners from Hong Kong to France, and that is to knock hell out of them'. That November they occupied houses at Houplines in Flanders, pulling women from their beds and driving them out into a snowstorm. When on Boxing Day women at Armentières got wind of the Christmas truce they spat and shouted as Richard's unit passed through the town: 'You no bon, you English soldiers, you boko kamerade Allemenge' [sic].[745] Returning to his billets at Dickebusch in the Salient one evening the following November Ralph Hamilton was incensed to find 'three unspeakable Belgians looting in the yard'.[746] Hamilton doesn't say what they took, but looting from the army wasn't uncommon. When settlers passed through village sanitary sections frequently left equipment behind for the locals. It was often pilfered.[747] After the Armistice natives around Ligny-Thilloy near Bapaume stole blankets from nearby depots to make clothes and blankets, though Cude understood why. Most villagers were dressed in rags.[748]

Elsewhere petty tensions fractured relationships. Just before Christmas 1915 Schweder found the peasants at Coquelles near Calais accommodating enough, but their forbearance didn't last long. Within a day or two there was a contretemps about gunners lighting fires in their cottages. Next month on the Somme he reviled Francières and its inhabitants. The village louts were shovelling in chits for damage so that they could rebuild their miserable little fleapits, most of which had been not been affected at all the presence of Beflanders.[749] At Herzeele in Flanders on a cold winter's night in January 1918 Cude and colleagues fell out with a local farmer because he objected to a fire they'd lit in the barn, their billet. Sparks might set the rise into the thatch and burn the whole place down. After a stormy argument they grabbed the man and tossed him into a ditch, warning him to shut up and stay away if he knew what was good for him.[750] Not all natives were discommoded when Beflanders occupied their property, however. In July 1918 George Stringer's NCOs briefly requisitioned a mean little cottage near Mont des Cats. When the owner popped in to see how things were he was delighted to find it stuffed with the possessions of his neighbours.[751] ➲ 101

Monday 11 June 1917 **75**

Ronald Schweder wrote to his wife, thanking her for the ox tongue she'd sent. It came at just the right time, he said, as they had no hot food and could do little more than boil water. Yesterday bunches of asparagus had arrived from Courtlands (a house somewhere in England, presumably the residence of people known to Schweder) but the tips were limp and mouldy; rather sad, since everyone had been looking forward to them.[752] In half a dozen letters home in May and June 1915 George Stringer's brother Guy asked his parents to pay bills at shops in Birmingham's Broad Street – Chattertons, Skae, Hammonds, Whites, Orsell & Harrison's – and to send out a cheque book, a pipe, tobacco, cigarettes, writing paper, Huntley & Palmer mixed and ginger biscuits, a mirror, razors, field glasses, a watch, almonds, raisons, sardines, cake and peppermints.[753]

During the siege all manner of Beflanders received food from the UK, though officers, generally from wealthier families, got more. Parcels amassed at the portals – Waterloo and Victoria – went on to Folkestone and Dover, crossed the Channel by steamer to the entrepôts and from there fanned out across the landscape by train, lorry and wagon. Sharing the contents could form an important part of establishing and maintaining friendships.[754] One morning in March 1917 near Bailleul Schweder had kippers for breakfast, sent from Newcastle. A week or so later a birthday party dinner included oysters, soup, lobster, mutton, peas, new potatoes, cherry tart, coffee, champagne, port and liqueurs – much better than anything that could be got in London, he thought.[755] ⮑ 76

76 Wednesday 13 June 1917

'We have just got a supply of vegetables from Amiens,' wrote Herbert Leland from Bapaume in June 1917, 'but they are very faded, having been on the journey about three days, but I have no doubt we shall thoroughly enjoy them. Lettuce, cabbage, young turnips and carrots, asparagus etc. etc.'[756]

Other elements of food supplied attracted adverse comment. Between 1914 and 1918 the 'full' daily field ration for zone dwellers fluctuated in energy value from 4,600 to 4,100 calories (3,472 for those 'in reserve' on the lines of communication[757]). According to the Army's Advisory Medical Board this was sufficient, but not everything was always available, even during the siege years when supply lines functioned properly. In winter 1916–17 flour and meat were so scarce that bread was baked with dried turnips and horsemeat replaced beef. The following summer the zone-dweller calorie count fell to 3,850. In the rear food shortages helped to precipitate the Étaples mutiny that September [92]. Fresh vegetables were a perennial problem. Army dieticians understood their importance, but despite the farms and gardens campaign [66] provision and distribution were never satisfactory.[758] Beflanders grumbled about tinned stew, finding it monotonous fare day in day out. Many preferred pork and beans, though the ration consisted chiefly of haricot beans and a small dollop of pork fat, so in reality they ate tinned baked beans, or rather gulped them down: 'many men swallowed the beans without chewing them and they appeared unchanged in the faeces', averred the medical experts. Too much beef was another complaint, along with ropy and stale bread and biscuits – the latter often tossed aside or forgone completely. But settlers liked bacon, even though there was slime in the borax packaging and rashers were coarse and fat.[759] They also enjoyed the occasional startling substitution. To Ronald Schweder's surprise in March 1917 oranges replaced the potato ration.[760]

During the siege Schweder commented on other ranks' attitudes to army rations. They tossed fresh meat on the ground, trod on it, and put unwrapped slabs of corned beef on dirty wooden shelves. The cooks were hopeless, capable only of ruining perfectly good food. From his first day in Befland he'd tried to make them save ingredients for stockpots and soups, but they never learnt. All they did was to boil up vile stews, day after day. Once and only once he'd forced them to cook a curry, but the men wouldn't eat it. They are 'just like a lot of children,' he complained, 'only they are full grown and can get into mischief more easily'.[761]

Seen close up the personalities of the dead, like those of the living, defy easy categorization. Quirks, habits, likes and dislikes show themselves in all their bewildering variety, so much so that in the end one almost despairs of finding any clear-cut patterns at all; not only within a social class, but even within an individual. The more historians step back and generalize the more they falsify; the closer and narrower their focus the more generalization dissolves into the particular. The most that can be said is that Schweder's tone of exasperated paternalism was not unusual. He was often like that, and we should expect a cultured, fastidious, conscientious, Eton-educated Edwardian bourgeois of independent means unexpectedly thrust into the role of Befland artillery officer often to be like that. But his letters also reveal a character by turns resigned, infuriated, happy, forgiving, solicitous, harsh, miserable, bored, excited, calm, agitated, optimistic, pessimistic, or simply indifferent, sometimes within the space of a couple of days. The superstructure disports itself in the tangled lineaments of the individual personality, but it does not wholly define it.

Schweder, moreover, had a discriminating palate, hence his annoyance at the cooks' offerings. For trench dwellers kettles full of stew were slung on poles and carried forward by ration parties. Soldiers filled their mess tins and warmed the stew over 'Tommy Cookers', small stoves powered by solidified alcohol. 'There was a constant demand for these cookers,' wrote MacPherson in the official history series.[762] But artillery batteries were never in the trenches. Early-twentieth-century military tactics dictated that cannon should always be kept well back from the front, so Schweder's cooks did not have to reduce raw ingredients to a pre-heated stew to be ferried across the zone.➲ 88

77   Saturday 16 June 1917

'We are enjoying glorious weather, about 80 to 85 in the shade', remarked James Naylor in letter sent to his parents in India.[763] In June 1915 J. N. Peterson wrote to his girlfriend in England: 'Somewhere in France . . . Dear little friend . . . Of course we are not in billets like St Augustine's Hall (Newcastle) but on a farm and we just sleep on the waggons or make a tent with our ground sheets which is 6 f[oo]t x 2 and when you put 3 of these together and get some straight branches of trees it makes a good place to sleep in. The weather out here is very fine and warm so we take no hurt through sleeping out'.[764]

Beflanders led peripatetic lives, zone dwellers in particular. Infantrymen – 'an itinerant community', remembered John Brophy[765] – were constantly in motion, making lateral or intrazonal journeys or travelling between base and zone or from the entrepôts to the portals and back again. Artillerymen might stay in one place rather longer [49], though they were still subject to the tyranny of movement, but when they arrived in the zone all Beflanders entered a world virtually devoid of shelter, figures in a landscape open to the skies. Few buildings withstood shelling intact. Bodily ease, and perhaps spiritual ease too, was therefore a function of weather. Winter 1914–15 was cold, wet and foggy; spring to autumn more or less fine. In May Richard Foot was at Givenchy-lès-la-Bassée – 'it was pleasant to sit out of doors in the evenings looking at the stagnant waters of the disused canal'.[766] The following winter was less severe; dry, clear and frosty for much of December, thereafter damp, but snow covered most of Befland throughout the terrible winter of 1916–17. In mid-January a hard frost set in and lasted for five weeks. Canals froze solid and roads turned into sheets of ice.[767] 'Weather makes an unimaginable difference to this life of ours,' wrote George Stringer from the Somme, It was freezing cold right through November until the beginning of April.[768] Summer 1917 was hot and sultry. In the Salient settlers wore cotton shorts instead of trousers and puttees.[769] In July and August thunderstorms piled up over the Low Countries and Northern Befland experienced its heaviest rainfall for thirty years, compounding the unspeakable misery of Third Ypres. One Sunday near Béthune Stringer turned out for Church parade. The previous night had been hot and sticky, making almost impossible to get any sleep. The day was sweltering. In the afternoon he went to divisional headquarters and sat in the shade of some trees, wrote a few letters, strolled into Bouvigny-Boyeffles for dinner and had an enjoyable evening sitting in the gardens of a chateau chatting to a friend. Next day he got up at five in the morning and took some exercise, riding to a spur on Notre Dame de Lorette Ridge. He dismounted and grazed his horse for a bit before a violent thunderstorm drove him away. Then came tea and another ride, this time to Aix-Noulette to reconnoitre a possible artillery position, and then a visit to Souchez, just out of idleness. He thought that the village must have been an attractive place once. Now it was just a heap of rubble.[770]

Somehow or other, in Souchez and hundreds of other border towns and villages in the same condition, settlers had to cover themselves. In 1918 Befland imported 20,000 tarpaulins for sheeting down wagons, but they were often pilfered.[771] Two years earlier Ronald Schweder described how competing demands affected line officers. They were expected to show initiative in finding materials to build hutments, trench reverts and gun emplacements, etc. Many units boasted of their criminal endeavours, and glacial judgements descended upon the unenterprising and the slow witted. Any officer who failed was censured by his superiors. On the other hand orders had just been issued threatening cancellation of leave if officers condoned or were involved in stealing army property.[772]

Orders from on high were unlikely stop theft, but the opportunity to improvise depended on where you were. If we enter the zone as 'radical geographers' we find ourselves in a place transected by contours of material inequality, each shaped by the interaction of military role, social class and the lie of the land.

In the first transection – right up against no man's land, where nothing remained of the built environment and no one was likely to survive for long above ground in daylight – settlers could do little more than burrow into trench walls to ward off the elements. Nevertheless social and spatial demarcations were visible: officers' dugouts, NCOs' dugouts and other ranks' dugouts; officers' messes, NCOs' messes and spaces for other ranks to feed in. But the first transection was a site of transience as well as material scarcity. Though this or that 'funk hole' might be highly prized,[773] there was little incentive to invest time and effort in domesticating the environment because no one stayed for more than a few days.

A mile or so to the west, sometimes closer, sometimes further away, tucked behind heaps of rubble, half-ruined cottages, folds in the land or sunk into the ground, were cohorts installed around gun emplacements. These stayed longer, often for months on end. Time and landscape gave dwellers in this second transection the chance to improvise more or less permanent dugouts – timber, bricks and furniture dragged from shelled houses, tarpaulins and other material lifted from nearby dumps and depots. Nearly half a century on Richard Foot remembered the comforts of an extended stay (mid-June to mid-October 1917) just outside Noreuil village. Four months was long enough for the turnout to establish what was, in effect, a mini-settlement all of its own. The six field guns were dug into shallow pits, each protected by five feet of steel, concrete and soil. Ammunition, covered in the same manner, was housed in neat and carefully designed racks. Twenty stairs led down from each pit to the crews' quarters (bunks round the sides, mess tables in the middle). These quarters were connected by underground passages with junctions leading to a command post so that men could move around without exposing themselves to danger. Electric lights were strung along the passages. As autumn gave way to winter they built chimneyed fireplaces in the dugouts, also lit by electricity, to ward off the cold and damp.[774] Foot was in La Bassée district. Schweder describes second-transection living conditions (for officers) to the south and the north. On a warm day at Aveluy Wood on the Somme in April 1916 he was sprawled on a canvas roll directing the conversion of an ammunition pit into the officers' mess – looted furniture positioned seven feet underground and topped off with corrugated iron and sandbags. When that was done the battery's carpenter made an arbour with a rustic table down by the guns. Next March, not far from Bailleul in Flanders, he lived in a large hut with an entrance hall, a sitting room and two bedrooms. The officers dugouts were undergoing renovation. Warm weather and the sound of cuckoos added to his comforts. In July 1918, now in front of Mont de Cats, we find him ensconced in an abandoned house furnished with tables, chairs, beds and pictures lifted from other properties. Outside in the garden roses are in bloom.[775]

Behind the guns ran a third transection: dumps and depots, wagon lines and ammunition columns, temporary camps and billets and miscellaneous zone administrative units, all nestling, like those in the second transection, under whatever protection the environment offered, and all socially segregated. In farmhouses, for example, officers commandeered the best bedrooms and used the parlour for their mess. Sergeants took the farm offices. Other ranks slept on straw in the barns.[776] Nevertheless here all Beflanders were more at ease in the landscape, in particular those living just west of the DGT line where traffic could move around in daylight. Grant Taylor near Ypres in summer 1915: 'Thursday, 3rd June. Mollie's birthday. A beautiful day. The wood is charming. There is nothing to do. Shells go soaring over us, but never drop in the wood, and bullets occasionally come low. Headquarters moved to G.H.Q lines . . . We took over the H.Q hut, a most palatial affair made of logs with sandbags outside and with two beds, a table and 4 chairs'.[777]

Two other points on the Salient's third transection. Stringer, at Kemmel in late April 1915, luxuriating in agreeable billets and pleased to find a good place to park the guns. To add to his comforts there was very little to do. The previous tenants, professional soldiers, had even made gardens. Primroses and daffodils nodded in the spring breeze. All around were woodlands, as yet untouched by war. Most days he sat in the gardens, soaking up the sunshine, or took his turn at the well-appointed wagon lines; brick standings for the horses and for other ranks billets in a nearby convent.[778] Just over two years later, in July 1917, the Post Office Rifles spent six days near Dickebusch Lake, not far from Kemmel, helping to clear gassed areas and supplying fatigue parties to artillerymen and engineers who enjoyed a 'comfortable life' at a place called Chippewa Camp. Their headquarters was a wonder to behold. Inside, the kitchen was kitted out with a hen-coop, a meat safe and a slate-stone sink. Outside there were paved walkways, a pergola and a rock garden. Behind the garden and on either side of a broad oak tree were two wide shafts, both lined with concrete and each leading to the same destination;

a spacious iron-vaulted dugout-cum-air raid shelter. The tree roots, explained one of the camp's inmates, gave extra protection, while the boughs and leaves provided shade for those lounging about above ground.[779]

Lieutenant Capron was also at Dickebusch that summer, but soon left for the Somme. At four in the afternoon of 2 September he reached Bapaume. By the following morning all the battery's personnel was bivouacked on the grass-covered ground alongside the main road to Péronne – a pleasing prospect, the road was still lined with poplar trees – and there was abundant grazing for the horses and mules. Four days later his turnout upped sticks and moved half a mile or so northeast of Bapaume, not far from the ruins of Bancourt village. The officers lived in canvass huts pitched in a row under the lee of a high bank in sight of the wagon lines. It's not clear where the other ranks slept, but their billets were probably comfortable enough – Bancourt seems to have been no less salubrious than the grassy margins of the Bapaume-Péronne road – and the weather kept fine. Next day they scavenged the ruined village to make brick standings for the mules.[780] Two months earlier a travelling entertainer visited the nearby Hugh Taylor Veterinary Camp. He was much impressed by the staff's resourcefulness: '[Major] Hobday's Hut built of earth and wattle and the men's in many instances of old biscuit boxes . . . A very pleasant life for the men – the quarters gay with flowers and neat paths – grass lawns . . . almost everything utilised'.[781] ➲ 85

Sunday 15 July 1917 78

An English actor travelling in Befland to entertain the settlers (the archival file doesn't record his name) hurriedly jotted down his impressions of Abancourt as he entered the village: 'this amazing supply base from which nearly a million troops are fed – mountains of hay, bacon, jam, pickles, oatmeal, flour – Chinese, Kaffir and Jamaican native labour, also English. Saw the food specially imported for Chinese – nameless horrors of seaweed, dried cuttle fish. Quarters for Kaffirs lined with earth bricks – they suffer much with pneumonia in winter'.[782] In March the following year Colina Campbell went there to work as a YMCA driver. In a letter to her mother dated Friday 29th she described her living conditions: 'we live in the camp surrounded by huge dumps & engine sheds (this is a huge railway centre)'. Her room, eight foot square – basic furniture, mouse infested, damp floors and holes in the walls – once formed part of the officers' quarters, 'but I believe [they] were condemned as unfit for them so we have got them . . . our huts are connected by duck boards & at night walking to one's quarters one falls over rats & hears them gnawing at the floor'.[783]

Twenty-seven miles behind Amiens, Abancourt was a typical regulating station for trains carrying food, forage, petrol and veterinary stores from Le Havre, Rouen and Dieppe towards the zone. Settlers first arrived in

January 1915. By February 1916 the weight of traffic supplying the Somme's burgeoning population had grown so large that the station complex had spread two miles up the line to engulf the straggling village of Romescamps. From there, for an eight week period in 1916, labourers sent 1.3 million ration packs on twenty-two trains for distribution across the zone every day. Even in 1917, when the Somme went quiet, the Abancourt-Romescamps complex was still busy; on 16 February they loaded over 1.2 million packs.[784] ➲ 87

79 Friday 27 July 1917

An extract from the diary of an entertainer visiting Befland: 'One sees a terribly large number of widows in France. I was told the other day there are 400,000. They have a startling effect when seen in the street in their black and long mourning veils, which make them look very tall and weird – saw four together to-day – four long black figures outlined against the white houses as they passed'.[785]

A 1921 recollection from the historian of the Royal Engineers: 'The supply of black and white poles was part of the equipment of airline and cable sections . . . Where such cables raised to a considerable height off the ground would have been too conspicuous and likely to draw enemy artillery fire, the cable was run either along the sides of trenches or on short stakes at a height of a foot or eighteen inches from the ground'.[786] Three years on a senior medic recalled how zone dwellers fixed bandages to sticks to mark the site of first aid posts.[787] Garnet Durham noticed that most native horses around Estaires in Flanders were white; all the coloured ones, less visible to the enemy, had been requisitioned by the French army.[788]

Ralph Hamilton at work in Flanders on 14 November 1915: 'A lovely day, so like the proverbial Englishman, let us go out and kill something. Too bright to do much work at the position, as the air is humming with planes belonging to both sides. When I had digested my lunch and finished a cigar, I decided to go over to the OP and have a little battle . . . I fired on the Hollebeke Château, which is reported in the Corps Summary of Intelligence as being used as an artillery observation post. It has a nice white tower, which makes a beautiful dust when hit. After getting my lines exactly correct, with shrapnel, I turned on section salvos with high explosive. Made quite a good mess of it'.[789] Next September Lieutenant Capron was on the Somme. Most nights he saw eerie little flashes and sparkles running left and right along the length of no man's land, visual traces of machine-gun or rifle fire. Sometimes there would be a muffled bang as a trench mortar fired, then a deep boom as it burst. Occasionally Verey lights arced into the sky, fired off by jittery denizens of some outpost or other who thought they heard rustling and creeping nearby and believed they were about to be attacked by a raiding party. The light would hang in the air for a moment, illuminating the tortured landscape with a 'cold white radiance', before it flickered to the ground, 'to leave the blackness blacker still'.[790]

Black clothing silhouetted against white walls, the zone festooned with black and white stripped poles, white bandages fluttering in the breeze, a white light flaring over a black landscape, a white tower in the final moments of its existence, white horses in the fields . . . There's something familiar here. The restricted palette and the sense of things still and structured act as visual mnemonics, reinforcing our cultural memory of a frozen, monochrome world. We cannot, of course, gainsay the presence of flux and motion in three of these texts – the signal flare fluttering earthwards, Hamilton's 'beautiful dust' and the tall mourning veils perambulating weirdly along the street – but when movement, transformation and incongruity caught the eye they were more likely to prompt a colour response. The 'Golden Virgin', which crowned Albert cathedral's smashed basilica and leaned crazily over the settlers as they walked towards the trenches, is one of Befland's enduring visual clichés. Even in 1916 it was already a trope for suffering and futility. Nearby, Hamilton found another example of incongruity, albeit one less well known. 'I got lift on a motor-lorry that landed me at Carnoy, close to my wagon-lines', he wrote in September. 'I was much struck, in passing through Montauban, by a life-sized statue of the B[lessed] V[irgin] Mary which had been rescued intact from the ruins of the church there. There is not a house or even a wall left standing in the place. This statue seems to have been the only thing unbroken in the whole village. The men who had been collecting bricks for mending the roads had made a pedestal of timber 6 feet high or so, and put the statue on it, facing the road. The effect was very strange, as the pale blue and pink of her robes were the only touch of colour in the whole wilderness'.[791]

Was it the colour of the Virgin's robes that induced these settlers to drag the statue to the roadside and place it on a reconstructed pedestal? Did they want other settlers to see the colours? Was this behaviour unusual? We have no way of knowing, but in the zone the destruction of edifices, sacred and secular, was far more common than their reconstruction, and more commonly noticed. Blue, grey, red and pink; colours illuminating four moments of structural transformation on the Somme. On the 25 May 1916 Ronald Schweder was up early at an observation post looking out for a German working party, but it was too misty for him to see much. Annoyed by the waste of time, when the mist eventually cleared he directed a dozen rounds of high explosive into a German-held village. It was highly satisfying, he wrote, to see red dust from the shattered bricks drift about, though he did hope that no one had been injured.[792] Two months later John Masefield observed the results of a proximate bombardment: 'Then it would fall on village and wood in lines and simultaneous dottings of explosion, till a dull red, dirty haze covered the site of the village, and smokes and stinks of all colours and poisons smouldered and rotted in it'.[793] And finally two reminiscences from Capron. The first – late summer 1917 – colouring the impact of outgoing shellfire, the second – twelve months later – colouring incoming fire. In September he was positioned directly opposite German-held Quéant. As the early mornings mist cleared and the sun rose behind his back he could pick out details in sharp relief; red tiles, splintered rafters, smashed brickwork. A few moments later woodlands and fields further to the east emerged from shadow. A little blue wisp of smoke twisting up through the shattered roof of one of the cottages caught his attention. Someone was having breakfast. Capron told the signaller sitting beside him to send coordinates and instructions to fire. A moment later came the faint sound of guns opening up to the west, then the whistling noise of a salvo passing overhead, 'then oh joy three plumes and jets of ruddy brick dust and tiles fly up and gloriously close it seems to the little blue twist'. September 1918, 'receiving' fire in the ruins of Pronville, a mile west of Quéant. It was if a fast train hurtling towards him had abruptly entered a tunnel, smothering for a moment all sound. Then suddenly up shot 'a vast pink fountain, succeeded by a grey umbrella of dust and bricks and wooden debris'.[794] ➲ 104

80 Wednesday 1 August 1917

By now around 23,000 immigrant women lived in Befland, including 5,200 employed by the ordnance corps and 7,700 WAACs. Most WAACs worked in base depots, ports and along the lines of communication as drivers or nurses or in canteens and messes, but there were also clerks, typists, postal workers, chiropodists and piano tuners. Settler population stood at just under two million: 1,894,500 British and Dominion, 11,500 Indian, African and other troops, 62,900 followers and labourers.[795]

Chinese civilians on three-year contracts began to arrive at Noyelles-sur-Mer, their designated base depot, in April. Organized into battalions at Weihai, a British colony in Shandong province, most came from northern China via Canada, Liverpool and Le Havre. They were accompanied by their white doctors, most of whom had been medical missionaries in China. Numbers rose rapidly: 96,000 by mid 1918. South Africans, Indians, Egyptians, West Indians, Fijians, Italians and Portuguese soon joined them. The Indians – in the main Luseis, Nagars and Manipuris from the Eastern Himalayas deemed by their Imperial masters capable of standing Befland's damp and cold – came via Marseilles. By the year's end 102,000 'coloured' immigrants worked in harbours, dumps, depots, advanced bases and on the lines of communication alongside 310,400 white (mainly British) labourers. Sometimes they also dug trenches for zone dwellers and many Indians were put to work clearing up the Somme's devastated areas. South Africans and 'Cape Boys' settled near Rouen, Abbeville, Étaples and Calais. After February Portuguese troops attached to the First Army reached La

Bassée district. In 1918 they moved to Boulogne.[796] Only one of Befland's 'land drainage' companies remained, based in La Bassée district and staffed by East Anglian fenmen, but over 9,000 British bargees plied the colony's canals and rivers.[797] As the siege dragged on and technological innovation accelerated colonization broadened and deepened. In April Eric Geddes indented, apparently unsuccessfully, for further 94,000 non-combatants, including Australians, South Africans, Canadians and Portuguese, to help repair and extend Befland's transport network. A multi-national assortment of bureaucrats, administrators, planners, advisers, skilled workers, labourers and specialists of all kinds now comprised nearly a quarter of total settler population. The proportion rose to over one third in 1918.[798]

Late in February the Germans began their retreat to the Hindenburg Line. As they withdrew Beflanders moved eastwards and occupied the 1916 Somme battlefields. The retreat ended on 5 April. Bapaume was incorporated into Befland on 17 March, Péronne a day later. Armies were distributed north-south as follows: Second, from Ypres to Armentières; First, from Armentières to Arras; Third, from Arras to Serre on the Somme; Fifth, from Serre to the Somme's Transloy ridges; Fourth, from Le Transloy to just south of the River Somme at Roye. The zone now stretched for 110 miles.[799]

In 1917 there were nearly 1.8 million recorded casualties, mostly in Flanders and La Bassée district (battles of Arras, Messines, Cambrai and Third Ypres).[800] ➲ 102

Friday 21 September 1917   81

Ralph Hamilton rode out of Péronne on the Somme in the early autumn sunshine across ground thoroughly fertilized with blood and bone meal. The wild flowers of summer, annuals for the most part, had seeded and died back. Great swathes of agricultural weeds dominated the landscape. 'Never have I seen anything like it. The whole area for miles and miles in every direction is covered with a uniform green growth, which is from 3 to 4 feet high. The shell-holes are still there, but they are all hidden, and woe betide the person who attempts to leave the road. It is impossible to walk one yard in any direction without falling into a deep pit. And mixed with the vegetation in inextricable confusion are masses of barbed wire . . . I went along the sunken road till I came to the Quarry, but found it hard to believe it was the same dreadful place that I knew exactly a year ago. Gone were the thousands of empty shell-cases, and the many hundreds of dead – both British and German. Instead, there was a sea of rank vegetation waist deep, through which it was almost impossible to force one's way . . . The whole experience was weird in the extreme'.[801]

Like Hamilton, Lieutenant Capron was on the Somme in autumn, but on this occasion in 1916. The unburied bodies of horses and men hadn't yet rotted away and so the plants weren't so vigorous – 'short thistles and weeds, where I suppose two years before had been swelling cornfields'. He was back on the Somme in October 1918 during the advance to victory, this time twenty-five miles northeast of Péronne and in a very different phytogeography, though one still traumatized by war. He went through Aubencheul-au-Bac, a small village, still largely intact. Odd to be in unblemished countryside, he wrote, where most of the houses were abandoned and the hedges and fields blazed with autumn hues. But all around were indications of the Germans' recent retreat – orchards systematically ruined; roadside trees felled and dragged onto the highway to impede the advance.[802] ➲ 91

82 Monday 24 September 1917

Ronald Schweder spent the day dozing through lectures on the lawns of a chateau near Amiens. In the evening he anatomized the chateau's population: 'common' New Army officers, 'rankers' (subalterns promoted from the ranks) and regular soldiers. The commandant, a regular, behaved properly, but most of the instructors were rankers who cultivated *faux* upper-class accents. A previous group of 'coursites' had got horribly drunk and smashed up the chateau's tableware. The tone was all wrong. 'We shan't have any of that kind of thing, he sniffed.[803]

That armies reflect the societies from which they are drawn is a truism that requires little elaboration. A diagrammatic representation of Befland's population (albeit one restricted to British immigrants) would show clear intersections between gender and class in voluntary organizations and class and rank in military units. 'I would like to note here that all the Y.M.C.A.s I have been into so far over here are staffed with English ladies,' observed Stapleton Eachus in June 1916. 'They have to work all hours and very hard too. This type of English womanhood one cannot help but admire sincerely'.[804] In the military most UK officers were 'gentlemen', recruited from the landed classes, the middle and upper bourgeoisie or the liberal professions; most other ranks came from the rural poor, the proletariat or the lower commercial classes. But there were two groups outside the intersection: non-commissioned gentlemen and commissioned non-gentlemen. Most of the former probably chose their military identity. After 1906 public school, grammar school or university-educated youngsters could join the OTC and would be expected to accept commissions on enlistment.[805] The latter group, the 'rankers' and the 'common' New Army officers identified by Schweder's disapproving gaze, was a product of expanded settlement (the 1915–16 influx), attrition (Second Ypres and the Somme) and specialization (the demand for technically competent personnel as wargear became ever more sophisticated). For them changing identity meant changing diet, behaviour, speech, dress and bodily accoutrements. We can only guess at the psychological strains this imposed – in addition, that is, to those arising from life in the zone where officers were far more likely than other ranks to break down.[806] Though highly intelligent, remarked James Edmonds in 1932, New Army officers 'had not the native qualities which make leaders of men in the same degree as the original early volunteers'.[807] 'The offices are the most appalling set of men I think I have ever met', complained Colina Campbell from Abancourt during the Ludendorff Offensive. 'I have not yet met a gentleman[;] they are never sober at night & frequently not in the day. I'd enjoy the camp life if it wasn't for the officers'.[808]

But even if they did manage to fit in class would out. In December 1916 Schweder was detailed to conduct General Plummer, commander of the Second Army, on a tour of inspection. There was a dreadful fuss – 'Motors and red hats by the score'. Later Schweder learnt that his Brigadier thought that he hadn't been sufficiently 'obsequious', and had chatted to Plummer as a friend – 'but then our Brigadier doesn't know that we [are] both Old Etonians'.[809] Nevertheless some managed the transition easily enough, either through force of personality or personal circumstances. James Naylor enthused about his changed condition when promoted from the ranks in summer 1917, and proudly listed the military accoutrements he was now expected to buy – field glasses, protractor, compass, Sam Browne belt, etc.[810] But then he came from a military family. His father commanded Indian troops in Baluchistan.

There's nothing in the files to show how Naylor interacted with the privates and NCOs he'd left behind. Doubtless a degree of watchfulness obtained on both sides until the novelty wore off, but 'temporary gentlemen', officers promoted from the ranks or commissioned from the lower middle, or even working classes, often found themselves in a difficult situation.[811] In contrast regulars of all ranks were already socialized, territorials and OTC graduates well on the way to being so – like many other middle-class territorials Schweder was always ready to snub 'TGs' and 'common' New Army officers[812] [20, 82].

In the wider social sphere patronage and paternalism, immanent in Edwardian society and inflecting emergent military relationships, were evident in March 1912 when Richard Foot engaged gunners for the Hertfordshire field artillery. His job was to find men from Berkhamsted and Hemel Hempstead to crew two guns, and since he lived in Hemel his superiors assumed that he would know of any promising youngsters, and be able to select the right ones, even if as a solid member of the suburban middle classes the local tradesmen's underlings were more likely to know him than he was to know them. One day a Mr Mapley, no more than a teenager, stopped him on the driveway of his house. Foot had known him by sight for several years as the butcher's boy who biked up the hill to deliver meat, but that was all. Mapley asked if the turnout needed a butcher. The possibility had never occurred to Foot, but he recruited him on the spot. He made a fine gunner, he said, but it was only in Befland that he realized what a 'treasure' he'd stumbled upon; Mapely's brawn, conjured from indifferent army rations, was 'a chef's creation'. He lost track of him somewhere in the colony but hoped that he found a good unit elsewhere, or at least became a Sergeant Cook, a promotion that would have been richly deserved.[813]

But sentiment wasn't always a function of shared regional identity, nor was paternalism always quite so distanced. Custody presented itself differently. 'I admired Frank [Richards],' wrote Robert Graves in 1933, 'tall, resourceful, very Welsh, the company humorist – and became as friendly with him as a very young officer was allowed to be with a very old soldier. Indeed, the burden of keeping up military conventions fell chiefly on Frank'.[814] In 1965 Charles Carrington recalled his 'love affair' with forty Yorkshire miners under his command in England – 'the whole of my affection and concern'. Two days before they went to Befland he learnt that he was to stay in the camp. 'Well, I was still only eighteen years old ... Anyone would have been disappointed but I was more than that; I was heartbroken. When the battalion marched away to the station (27th August 1915) they sang a silly little chorus which still rings in my ears: "Kitty, Kitty, isn't it a pity, In the City you work so hard ..." As my platoon waved their good-byes I felt finished, disgraced, and my war over, though it had not yet begun'.[815] In January 1917 George Stringer regretted the loss of a batman found drunk for the second time because he feared the man's age and lack of education (he was entirely illiterate) might make other duties burdensome. But he expressed no qualms about the penalty dished out by the colonel – Field Punishment Number 1: up to two hours a day tied to a gun wheel or crucifix, perhaps within range of enemy fire. On the other hand he was deeply offended by the behaviour of a subaltern at Amiens railway station one evening a week or so later. As they stepped off the train the officer proffered a miserly tip, a mere half pence, to a Beflander attendant. The man refused. 'Oh then,' said the officer airily, 'put it in the war loan'. 'Curious how undiscerning some people are,' noted Stringer.[816] ➲ 94

83   Saturday 6 October 1917

'Just back at the wagon-line after a very pleasant trip,' wrote Ronald Schweder to his wife. It's not clear where he'd been, but he did the entire seventy-mile journey over two days with an overnight stay in Amiens, hitch-hiking all the way. 'I arrived back before my servant who came by train with my kit. He had a rotten journey, which I should have shared if I had gone in the manner prescribed'.[817]

Not all jaunts were by road or rail. In May 1915 George Stringer took a short stroll around the Flanders-La Bassée border. First he walked to an observation post to see a friend, Major Elliot, organize an artillery shoot. Major Crompton from the horse artillery joined them for lunch, after which they all went out to watch an expected German barrage, timed, they believed, for two-thirty, but nothing happened. Thereafter Churcher, another friend, accompanied Stringer on a visit to a siege battery. As they left a bombardment rained down on Laventie village, the place scheduled for tea, but it didn't put them off. When they arrived they found very little damage, just a few tiles scattered on the road.

By July Stringer had moved to Kemmel Hill, and in 1918 recalled making an extensive tour of the surrounding district. The day after he arrived two fellow officers, De Stage and Campbell, joined him on an afternoon ramble to Ypres, five or six miles to the northeast, ostensibly to buy crockery for the officers' mess. The first leg of the journey was via 'Railway Dugouts', bolt holes and shelters scattered alongside a metalled highway lined with trees. After a few minutes on 'Branden Road' they struck out across open fields, joined 'Raised Road' and then found the Lille Road – Stringer saw an eighteen-pounder battery dug into its western-facing bank. Lille Road led straight to Ypres' Lille Gate and the famous Cloth Hall in the main square. It must have been a wonderful structure before the War, he remarked. Repair work was underway. Some of the pinnacles had scaffolding round them. For a while they explored the cloisters, currently used as billets by zone dwellers (at this early date the Cloth Hall was relatively undamaged), there bumping into Basil Nicholson, a mutual acquaintance who also out 'sight-seeing'. The whole party seems to have spent the night in Ypres, setting out next morning for the border – east to dugouts cut into the embankment surrounding Zillebeke lake, over the little bridge at 'Moated Grange', past the Tuileries (a tile factory with its chimney and Hoffman kiln still in one piece), and on to 'Hell Blast Corner' and Zillebeke village and church, the latter now a fortified reserve post. De Stage found the parish registers and sent them on to the Belgian government. Outside, communication trenches overlooked by Hill 60 [42] ran across the street and towards the train station, skirting the graveyard with its grotesque wreaths and crosses. There they met Armitage, a medic, who'd just been to the forward line for a 'joy ride'. 'Maple Copse' and 'Sanctuary Wood' followed. In both hordes of infantrymen had felled pine trees to make shelters. More communication trenches (cut, noticed Stringer, in the gravel soil typical of the Ypres basin) led towards the front. The return journey was uneventful until they reached Manor Farm on the southern edge of Zillebeke lake. A salvo of shells crashed down, sending up huge fountains of water. In 1915, remembered Stringer, when natives still lived in an around Ypres, you could fish or bathe in the lake and hire paddle boats.[818] Within a year it was a slough of mud set in a landscape of utter devastation.

Most uninjured zone dwellers could, of course, walk. 'I went over to "Plugstreet" [Ploegsteert] to see my old battalion the other day,' wrote Garnet Durham from Estaires in April 1915, 'quite a long trip, partly under fire, and spend and hour with Bob Coull and other friends'.[819] But officers (Stringer) had more socially valid excuses for sauntering (crockery for the mess) than privates like Durham. In addition zone dwellers in the artillery (Stringer again) had professional reasons for being at large and unsupervised: a walk to the advanced base or the ammunition column could easily be combined with a pleasure stroll. In October 1918, shortly after the borders had moved away eastwards, Ronald Schweder was at Gheluvelt, five miles out from Ypres along the Menin Road. VADs and nurses were now to be seen in Ypres, he heard, and so the town had become a popular destination for male Beflanders living nearby.[820]

But walking took time and would only take settlers so far, a few miles at most for zone dwellers whose absence was likely to be noticed after an hour or so. To go further without deserting settlers needed legitimate access to a ready means of transport, commonly a horse, and preferably the financial means to make the most of things. Class and rank therefore determined the aspirant tourist's geographical range, and what could be experienced. From Ralph Hamilton's diary, 19 March 1916: 'I had been told that the colonel was in hospital in the Trappist Monastery on Mont-des-Cats. I rode over there, five miles, but found that he was not there. However, it was a lovely afternoon and I had a delightful ride up the slopes of the hill'.[821] On a summer's day two years later Schweder found himself at Foche Farm near Ypres. He and two other officers rode about ten miles to a nearby town, wandered round the square, visited the local church – cool and musty after the heat of the day – and dined in a restaurant with large windows overlooking a chateau garden where espaliers and roses grew on lattices. They discussed nothing but art and literature. All talk of the War was banned.[822]

Medium-range tourists also needed quasi-legitimate reasons for travelling, and once more officers were privileged: they had more scope for plausible invention, a point illustrated in an exchange of letters between Stringer, still resident at Kemmel Hill, and Guy, his brother. On 30 May Guy asked George to visit. After all, he was only eight miles or so distant. Perhaps they could both go into Ypres, he wrote, provided they weren't too busy. It's not clear what happened, but on 13 June George returned the invitation. Official cover might be needed, however, so he should come as if for training. Stringer could show him broken guns or the 'morning hate' (the ritual artillery duel as dawn broke along the border). 'I cannot say you'll get pheasant. You may get an obus [French for high-explosive shell]'. Did they meet? Stringer doesn't say, but it might have been their last chance. The *obus* quip turned out to be a grim premonition. Guy was killed four days later. Elsewhere Stringer records how earlier that month he used to get up at five-thirty in the morning, wash and shave, and then ride ten miles out from Dranoutre in the fine spring weather. Officially this was to exercise his horse before breakfast. In fact he often swung round to Bailleul or Ypres for a joy ride or to go shopping.[823]

There were constraints, however, even for officers. 'I'm bored of inaction,' complained Stringer a week or so before writing to Guy. Admittedly, his billets were good – a pleasant cottage set in wooded hills – but the quiet life had palled. Nevertheless he dared not escape: 'one is tied by the leg & afraid to go far away'.[824] And there were obvious risks for other ranks on the loose. 'A quiet day,' wrote Private Sidney Appleyard in his diary two weeks later and four miles away at St Eloi. 'Borrow had a nasty experience on his way to Dickebusch, which was, in fact, out of bounds. On the way shells fell on the road wounding a Belgian dispatch rider, leaving Borrow in an awkward predicament since he should not have been there in the first place. Fortunately for him, two other Belgians arrived and took their comrade to the dressing station'.[825] And not all Flanders joy rides were undertaken illicitly, or willingly. In April 1916 Garnet Durham was ordered out as a tour rep. 'We took a ride into Ypres one day as I had been detailed as a guide to show the boys around the country and acquaint them with the roads. I took them through Ouderdom and Kruisstraat, at odd spots shells came over and I showed the boys how to take shelter, rather needlessly at first as I had lost my ear for them and the boys began to laugh at my precautions. But coming back through Kruisstraat Heine sent over some big ones, just as we got to the houses, and I found it very hard to pry the newcomers off the cobbles and get them out of danger'.[826] ➲ 92

Friday 9 November 1917   84

Somewhere near the Salient Herbert Leland chatted with a veterinary officer about eye disease in one of his horses. 'He was . . . unable to diagnose the exact reason for the blindness. He told me, however, that very many horses were suffering from the same complaint. He thinks that it is a form of Ophthalmia imported from the Argentine'.[827]

Specific Ophthalmia was first diagnosed on the Somme in December 1916. Its cause was a mystery but was thought to be mud-borne. On the other hand, as Leland's interlocutor suspected, it might have been due to bad sanitation in South America, though other vets pointed to poor conditions in North-American depots. Other common illness included Glanders (highly contagious and marked by swellings beneath the jaw and discharge of mucous matter from the nostrils), necrosis (the death of a circumscribed piece of tissue or bone), Strangles (an infectious febrile disease caused by the bacterium *Streptococcus equi*) and Lymphanagitis (inflammation of the walls of the lymphatic vessels). Apart from Specific Ophthalmia two more new diseases made their debut in Befland. Necrotic or gangrenous dermatitis, in which rubbed or damaged fetlocks become infected and the flesh rotted away, was first identified in North-American remounts; Ulcerated Lymphanagitis (ulcers on mud-covered limbs) appeared on the Somme in summer 1916.[828]

Any journey within Befland – base to zone, lateral, intrazonal – might cause injury. Horses suffered from harness galls, developed strains and bit-injuries, became hopelessly debilitated or picked up nails and developed quittors (hoof ulcers). Nails lay around everywhere: wire nails pulled from

French packing cases and flung aside (the siege meant that thousands of re-supply points stayed the same for months on end, with huge build-ups of debris); nails in little fires lit all over the place by settlers trying to keep warm (Beflanders scavenged packing-case wood and the nails got scattered around); nails in the ashes of field-cookers dotted along the roadsides. In winter 1915–16 about 400 horses were admitted to veterinary hospitals with nail injuries every week, 500–800 a week the following winter. Mud softened their hooves and drove the nails into their feet. They were far more dangerous than 'caltrops', four pointed metal spikes thrown down in their thousands by retreating Germans over muddy tracks used by advancing horses. When trodden on the point penetrated the hoof and sometimes right into the bone, fracturing the navicular joint. 'Nail hunts', nail collection points, metal plates on horses' feet and electro-magnets dragged along Befland's road had little effect, and most newly-trained farriers didn't know how to treat injuries.[829]

During the siege horses and mules attached to artillery units spent long periods on the wagon lines and became weak from lack of exercise. When harnessed to guns and limbers they collapsed, pulled down the others in the team and broke their legs. General neglect and exposure killed many,[830] as did infections that emerged from the soil and penetrated tissues through skin lesions hidden beneath thick layers of mud. When cold and hungry they started chewing their handlers' tunics, remembered Rowland Luther. Chains attached to their noses and legs only caused them to chew each other and they soon became hairless – 'a pitiful sight'.[831] Horses also developed fistulous withers (puss-filled wounds and swellings between the shoulder blades), which took months to heal. Most animals also contracted mange at some time or other, and there was always the chance of injury or death from wargear.10,000 died or were wounded by bullets and shrapnel in 1916, 73,000 in 1918.[832] 'I never knew before that horses could scream', added Luther, 'but they can, in such conditions'. Others died of heart failure caused by the noise of exploding shells.[833] Gas masks, introduced in 1916, were always in short supply, largely ineffective and soon abandoned. Generally speaking horses could tolerate higher concentrations of gas than humans, but in the zone they suffered from chemicals that lingered in shell craters and the poisoned, impregnated ground. Fumes rose in the morning and blistered their feet, legs, mammaries and eyes.[834] ➲ 86

85 Thursday 29 November 1917

At Havrincourt Wood on the Somme Ronald Schweder bivouacked in the back garden of a demolished house. It must have been a garden, he wrote, because even though the house was no more a gate was still in place and strawberry plants were dotted about. There were remains of a garden wall too, which kept out the wind and made life comfortable. Schweder bedded down on one side of it, other ranks on the other.[835] In the winter of 1915 Captain Newman was living in farm near Poperinghe: 'Snowing hard ... went to next farm for eggs ... Quiet easy day, sent letter to Lill. Very comfortable in our billet'.[836] On 1 June Grant Taylor strolled into the town for a bath – 'a topping day'.[837] Three days later and five miles away at Kemmel, in summer country and with little else to do, George Stringer spent a pleasant evening scything meadow grass for the battery's horses.[838] In October, sixty miles to the south, Private Rogers was at Suzanne on the banks of the River Somme, a stone's throw away from the old front line: 'We had the day to ourselves and spent most of our time in the farmhouse by the fire drinking coffee'.[839] Robert Cude turned up in the village in March 1916. 'Weather has now looked up considerably, and time passes happily and pleasantly considering that we are at war. We have the canal running through the grounds, so that with a punt out now and again, when we feel like it, it is A1'.[840] In May, back in Flanders, Garnet Durham was living in a shell-proof culvert under Ypres' Menin Gate, a few yards away from the notorious 'Shrapnel Corner'. Just outside, where the stream fed into the Yser, he'd improvised some fish traps. Every day he played chess with a mate living further along the river – 'we communicate by semaphore'.[841] Five months on, in late September, Lieutenant Capron enjoyed a balmy afternoon camped near the ruins of Carnoy in the gently sloping chalk hills that rolled away north of the River Somme. By now the border was some four miles to the northeast. Broad sweeps of abandoned fields, some infested with weeds and rough grasses, others scarred by old shallow trenches thick with vegetation and topped with sprays of rusting barbed wire, lay between: 'things were comparatively pleasant in the early autumn evening sunshine, and peaceful'.[842] Finally Herbert Leland, a month after Capron's easy September afternoon and close to trenches somewhere in the Salient: 'I am still in the wood. Nuts and acorns drop round me, but it is quite warm and no rain, and really very comfy'.[843]

All these texts were written in periods when the War had gone away somewhere else – Newman between First and Second Ypres, Grant Taylor, Stringer, Garnet Durham and Leland after Second Ypres, Cude and Rogers before the Somme, Schweder and Capron afterwards – but even in the thick of major events, when the landscape was in uproar, zone dwellers experienced moments of ease. 'Looking at the battle from the top of the hill today I saw a man cutting hair, while a few hundred yards beyond him shells were bursting. Peace and war exemplified. Hear that the Bosch guns are not retaliating on our trenches and that our infantry in the 1st line of trenches are sitting on the parapets watching the shooting of our guns'.[844]

What Harold Bursey witnessed from the banks of the Somme happened four days before the infantry offensive and in the middle of the ferocious preliminary bombardment – 2,200 tons of shell fired every hour for eight days and nights without intermission.[845] During the advance to victory – no less ferocious – James Naylor snatched a moment to write to his sister Lely: 'We are having lull in the day's work. It's rather strange, during any old battle there is always about an hour when nothing happens, then nearly everybody sleeps or eats!'[846]

With sleep came dreams. At Francières on the Somme one day back in December 1915 Schweder spent an hour or two censoring other ranks' letters. One in particular caught his eye. The man mentioned that he'd fallen asleep while on picquet (watching the horses through the night) and dreamed that he was sitting at home in England in front of a table covered with clean linen. In came his wife with a piping hot apple pie. Just as he started to eat it he woke up and heard the horses munching away at their feed. Next month, on New Year's day, Francie, a fellow officer, told Schweder about a horrifying nightmare. He was alone in a battlefield with bullets flying around all over the place. Suddenly one struck him in the face. He awoke in terror. A kitten had crawled onto his face and was buffeting his nose with its paws. The purrs were the battle noises and the buffeting the bullets. Several months later, in 'rest' at Cayeux-sur-Mer, Schweder recorded details of a dream of his own. He'd been sent into the zone to relieve another unit. As he gazed around the countryside the unit's officers pointed to a hump in the ground. They all walked up to it together. It was the entrance to a lift in London's Curzon Street. The lift, explained his companions as they descended, gave access to a dugout. When they got out Schweder entered a windowless flat with a tiled bathroom, electric lights and a clean, well-appointed kitchen. He could barely contain his excitement, but did manage to steady his voice and ask – quietly, so as not to disturb his interlocutors – how far underground they were. '300 feet,' they said. His relief was overwhelming. He was convinced that he would live there for the rest of his Befland days.[847] On 17 August Herbert Leland wrote home from near Bapaume: 'I had a singular dream the other night. I dreamt that someone threw a bomb at me and it smashed the glass of my watch. I was furious, as I remember your telling me that the glass was unbreakable'.[848]

Eric Leed argues that on the Western Front 'immobility made movement a magical, fantastic possibility to be specified in dreams, legends and myths'.[849] That's not quite accurate. Borders were more or less immobile, not settlers. Better to say that settlers inhabited two worlds simultaneously. On the one hand each lived within the storied chambers of the imagination, on the other each life was framed by the brute facts of a shared material world. Dreamers synthesized both worlds and articulated common themes – fear of harm and a longing for safety, ease and privacy. When did this happen? For border dwellers at the close of the morning ritual. As dawn broke everyone 'stood to', remembered Charles Carrington, with rifles pointing into no man's land until it was clear that there was no likelihood of an enemy attack, 'whereupon all those who were not on sentry duty "stood down", snuggled up with a greatcoat in a corner of the trench, and got what sleep they could'.[850] ➲ 95

Friday 30 November 1917   **86**

Ronald Schweder, currently at Havrincourt Wood on the Somme, came to the end of a terrible day. Heavy shelling had plastered the wagon lines from nine in the morning, killing a charger he'd brought out with him from England.[851] Many decades later Lieutenant Capron recalled the effects of shelling on his ammunition column three months earlier at Dickebusch in the Salient. 'August 27th: No.1 Section lost 20 mules – we, No. 3, 10, including Driver Gilfrin's old wheeler "Whiskers" – "Old Bill" was blinded – Carter's chocolate tandem pair killed, also sadly Driver Rowley's famous "Lion"'. Thinking back after sixty years, he added, it was odd how little their training in the UK had equipped them for what they were to encounter in Befland. There was no instruction on how to deal with injured horses and mules, for instance, or how to kill those that couldn't be saved. The Somme in 1916 was no place for wounded animals and most of the time it was quite impractical even to think of transferring them to distant veterinary hospitals. The drivers tried their best to help them limp out of the zone, but often they had to be shot; a 'dreadful decision'. Revolvers were best for the job but only officers carried them. Rifles were too dangerous. Bullets might ricochet off the skull and injure the executioner. Capron, for one, couldn't face it. After the sun had set amid the mud and the shell holes and it was clear that nothing more could be done he'd hand his firearm to one of his 'efficient sergeants, who always rose to an emergency and seemed to know the answer every time'. But the decision was still his, and would have to be explained back at base. If the gun was held steady in the correct position – right over the star in the centre of the animal's forehead was favoured – then killing, he supposed, was 'mercifully painless'.[852]

If they survived the zone injured and evacuated animals might be killed in the back areas. 'The circumstances of a modern European war,' wrote Blenkinsop & Rainey,'waged on a large scale, with lines of communication in closely settled civilized areas, made it necessary, for sanitary and economic reasons, that there should be fully organized military arrangements for the disposal of carcasses of animals that died or were destroyed in veterinary hospitals'.[853] Horses and mules were first 'cast' in large numbers in winter 1915. The 'Disposal of Animals' branch at the RAVC's reception centres shot those too ill or too badly wounded to be worth treating or sold them to local butchers,[854] but there was no proper 'system', complained one veterinary officer. 'With a better organization at the receiving point it will be possible to weed out a good many animals of no further use and so relieve the hospitals where, once they are admitted, there is a tendency, a laudable tendency, to persist in treatment beyond what I consider is the economic limit'.[855] Organized, industrial-scale killing began the following year. In December 1916 H. A. Crowe, secretary of Harrison, Barber & Co., London's great horse-slaughtering firm, arrived in Befland to run the

RAVC's disposal branch. Within a few weeks he'd amassed a staff of 126 working in two 'Butchery Detachments' (Boulogne and Abbeville), the Paris Sales Detachment and eight 'Horse Carcass Economizer Detachments' (Le Havre, Rouen, Abbeville, Forges-les-Eaux, Neufchâtel-Hardelot, Calais, St Omer and Gournay-en-Bray). Wrangling over the profits to be made soon broke out. Just as Crowe started work Army Waste Products Ltd., a military trading company appointed by the War Council to clear up 'camp refuse', tried to take over animal disposals as well. The RAVC objected. Eventually a compromise ensued. Where Waste Products already had facilities in place it would take the carcasses. Elsewhere Crowe would deal with them.[856]

As in 1915 'Disposals' sold horses and mules to native butchers living along the lines of communication, but supply soon exceeded demand and surplus animals were sent to Paris. Vets slaughtered those too weak to travel at Boulogne and Abbeville. The RASC took surplus meat for 'coloured' labourers and prisoners of war. Animals unfit for human consumption were process by the Carcass Economizer Detachments – hair ripped out and dried, hides torn off and salted, fat and bones boiled down, flesh buried in manure dumps. Products were sold locally or exported. Hides, a profitable line, went to Hermann & Son of Bermondsey, Southwark. At one time a ban on exporting hides from the UK and the influx from Befland caused a glut on the London market, but there were also severe shortages of leather goods. The odd combination was due to the reluctance of British firms to tan horsehide. Later on Crowe imported plant manufactured by Industrial Waste Eliminators Ltd. These turned flesh into dried granules, another by-product.[857]

Over two years, from December 1916 to the Armistice, Crowe's organization sold nearly 53,000 horses and mules to native dealers and butchers, slaughtered 4,500 for meat and rendered down the carcasses of a further 7,000. Thereafter, as decolonization gathered pace, killings and disposals accelerated. Between 12 November 1918 and 31 March 1920, 238,000 were sold, butchered or sent to the economizer plants.[858] ➲ 96

87 Monday 17 December 1917

'Orders to go into action at Bailleul,' remembered Lieutenant Capron in 1986. They moved the next day. 'Dec 18 Tues: At 10 a.m. marched with my C[ompany] Sub[altern] to join the others already in action in centre of Bailleul village – very desolate – living in cellars. Close up to front line'.[859] Bailleul was even more battered than Ypres because it had been shelled continuously for four years, wrote Ronald Schweder to his wife as he returned there from the Mont des Cats in autumn 1918. It was a shock to see what had become of the place. Gone were the decent shops and the busy little streets. Now there were only smashed limbers, mountains of rubble and the rotting carcases of horses.[860] Phyllis Goodliff, initially based at Boulogne but by the War's end a nurse at the British Red Cross Society's Home for Convalescent Officers at Cannes, was equally appalled. When in January 1919 she travelled across Befland to visit a military cemetery near Bailleul she thought the place looked worse than any other settlement she'd passed through.[861]

In fact Bailleul was a small town rather than a village, right up against the border in La Bassée district and typical of the numerous frontier centres occupied, shelled, abandoned and reoccupied by Beflanders between 1915 and 1918. Though unremarkable in other respects it had one claim on the settler imagination. Many knew of it via the eponymous 'Bailleul incinerator', a bodged-up device for burning excreta invented by Major Smales, officer commanding No. 4 Sanitary Section, 'to overcome the great difficulty experienced in some parts of the French front with regard to material'. It was made of waste tins cans, clay and clinker.[862] ➲ 89

Tuesday 25 December 1917 88

Wancourt near Arras. Richard Foot and the other officers served the battery's other ranks Christmas dinner. 'Although dinner had to be served in two parts, one for the men at the gun positions, the other for those in the wagon line, both went off well, and without undue interference from the Germans'. A few days earlier he'd found a farm twenty miles away, haggled with 'a wonderful old bedridden lady' and returned 'in triumph' with enough turkeys to feed 150 men. Costs were defrayed by a whip-round among the officers. Beer, port and wine were purchased from the officers' clubs. Twelve months on, and now at Gemünd, southwest of Cologne and deep inside New Befland, the other ranks enjoyed slap-up Christmas dinner paid for by the officers in the village hall which had been requisitioned as a mess. Drivers and gun crews ate pork roasted in the local bakery, topped off with apple sauces and washed down with copious supplies of German beer. The villages watched through the open doors, astonished to see officers serving common soldiers.[863] On 25 December 1915, after eating tinned lobster, turkey and plum pudding and attending Mass at the local church (Francières on the Somme), Ronald Schweder, the battery's commanding officer and Francie, another officer, went to visit the other ranks: 'Poor devils,' he remarked. Their dinner wasn't up to much but they seemed to be in good spirits and paused for a moment to cheer the interlopers. After finishing their food the gunners, drivers and NCOs went outside to play football.[864]

This wasn't exactly Bakhtinian carnivalesque, temporarily overturning the social hierarchies of everyday life. The Victorian bourgeoisie's cultural hegemony was still far too deeply entrenched to allow space for such phenomena, except, perhaps, when the tectonic plates shifted temporarily during a looting spree. Nevertheless Army tradition stipulated, if not carnival, then at least a kind of paternalistic role reversal. On Christmas Day officers were supposed to feed and serve other ranks, but they didn't always do so: Schweder, the Major and Francie weren't the only ones to keep their distance in 1915. 'Christmas came,' remembered Rowland Luther of his time in the trenches outside Loos, 'and every man was given a present from the Queen – chocolates, dates and a small pudding. An officer took charge, and got every man to sign his name. Rations were supposed to be sufficient for every man, but there was a lot of thieving going on at base, and we never got our entitlements because of this'.[865] Deprived of seasonal fare in a base camp five miles from Le Havre where he was trying (unsuccessfully) to cut short his stay in Befland by getting himself demobilized, Robert Cude took matters into his own hands: 'Xmas day comes with bread and margarine for breakfast. [Lunch] 1 large tin of bully and 1 loaf for 8'. This, however, was mere ballast, just enough to get him and his companions through until the main business of the day. Climbing the camp walls as the afternoon light faded so as to evade the sentries they hurried to a town-centre restaurant where they ordered a seven-course dinner. 'Now I am broke. Spent night out. Came back sober however about midnight. Got in alright and laid in kip until 9 am, so lost breakfast[.] "A good miss too"'.[866] Down the road at Harfleur Jessie Wilson watched a 'never ending stream of sad, homesick men' pour into her YMCA hut. 'The Army provided a dinner and a tea but for the rest the action was the negative one of restricting fatigues to those absolutely necessary'.[867]

Elsewhere tradition was upheld. At Alquines, 130 miles distant from Cude's camp, the men of Ralph Hamilton's artillery unit had Christmas dinner in an estaminet. 'We got them two pigs and two barrels of English beer. They also had cigarettes, sweets and plum-puddings from the *Daily Chronicle*. I presented them with 3,000 cigarettes and cigars for the sergeants' mess. They had a glorious time, most of them being horribly drunk by 2 o'clock. However, fortunately, they behaved themselves and there was no crime. The poor devils have a dull time out here, and I am glad they should enjoy themselves for once'.[868] Occasionally patronage spread outside the settler community. Cude was at Nordausques on the Calais-St Omer road for Christmas 1917, and this time enjoyed a substantial feed. 'Dinner over,' he recorded after expatiating upon the relative merits of the French and the English (to the advantage of the French), 'the N.C.Os bring in almost the entire juvenile element of the village and they clean up the feast. Tea at 7 p.m., and supper at 10 p.m.'.[869]

One explanatory technique mobilized by historians is to infer the general from the particular. This can be done by citing what appear to be a convincing number of depersonalized 'macroscopic' factors and by gesturing with a few quasi-biographical 'microscopic' case studies. The aim is to persuade the reader to accept, if not laws of human behaviour, then at least predictive tendencies: because it happened here and in this way to these people then it is likely to have happened elsewhere and in the same way to other people. What factors might be cited and how might historians gesture with the examples given above to explain the behavioural variations exhibited in Befland on Christmas Day? We might start by suggesting that the artillery (Schweder, Hamilton, Foot) was more socially cohesive than the infantry (Cude and Rowland Luther). Certainly both infantrymen and artillerymen moved between units, but casualty rates of well over fifty per cent, frequent in infantry battalions, were rare in artillery turnouts. Living in the trenches, even if for only one week out of three, was far more dangerous than living a mile or so to the west, even if for months on end. Nevertheless infantry loyalties could be very strong. Robert Graves, for example, may or may not be an unreliable narrator [63], but it seems clear from his memoir that he loved his regiment (if not everyone in it) though its composition changed dramatically over the months, and that most of its privates and NCOs admired and respected some (but not all) of their officers, though few of them lasted for long. We might also suggest that infantry- and artillerymen had more in common with each other than with base-camp dwellers. There was little chance of 'charismatic communities' emerging from within an anonymous mass of settlers, officers and men, temporarily thrown together for a few weeks prior to dispersal elsewhere (Cude in 1915, for instance). Finally, we could cite the importance of antecedent wealth. Hamilton, the son of Lord Belhaven, was probably used to dispensing largesse to his Scottish tenantry and could afford to replicate the practice in Befland. On the other hand Schweder too was comfortably set up – a director of Waring & Gillow married to Andrina, patron of the Tate Gallery, sister-in-law to Walter Sickert and noted London socialite was not short of funds. But not all officers were rich. Foot doesn't seem to have been, though he did come from a military family and thus might have been more alert to informal obligations than, say, Schweder, so we cannot deduce behaviour from wealth, any more than we can from unit structure.

What seems apparent is that charismatic communities needed charismatic individuals to make them work, wherever found and in whatever geographical circumstances the moment offered. Hamilton and Foot did what was expected of them, the latter under trying circumstances (1917) as well as relatively straightforward ones (1918). Schweder, the Major and Francie didn't, and neither did Rowland Luther's officers. On Christmas Day in Befland the fickle sway of temperament and mood conditioned behaviour just as powerfully as the depersonalized factors of unit structure, wealth, socialization and geography. To adapt the lexicon of physics, though historians deploy the macroscopic and the microscopic to generate Newtonian predictive tendencies, at the microscopic level the quantum realm just keeps on encroaching, and you never quite know how the particles will behave.

Food hunted, food stolen, food supplied, food grown, food bought, food sent – where was it all consumed during the rest of the year? In a trench dugout near the border at Tilloy-lez-Cambrai one evening in summer 1918 Lieutenant Capron dined with a Middlesex battalion – 'officers of a good type, mostly London gentlemen . . . most anxious to keep up as far as they could peace-time etiquette'. They didn't 'talk shop' and the battalion silverware was carefully displayed on a cloth spread over the makeshift dining table laid out with soup, herring, mutton, vegetables, trifle, sardines on toast, coffee and liqueurs. The 'half-breed French Canadians' who came in to relieve them two days later were very different. They ate the same 'unvarying stew' from the same tins and in the same places as 'the men'.[870] At Fromelles one morning in October 1914 Frank Richards watched his officers eating breakfast at the end of the trench leading to 'their' bay while a servant milked a cow to make their tea. (The bay, incidentally, led to a nearby farm, thus ensuring that officers controlled access to the farmyard chickens).[871] Schweder was no less aware of social and spatial parameters. A gun pit at Aveluy Wood on the Somme on 5 April 1916 was miles away from the portals of a fashionable pre-war Knightsbridge restaurant, geographically and architecturally, but his referencing alerts us to the maintenance of social boundaries and liminal places. He was sitting at a table in what the officers called the 'Carlton Grill Room'. The carpenter had knocked up wooden flooring from abandoned packing cases and hung canvas screens in lieu of walls to keep out prying eyes. Beds, washstands, basins and bowls looted from nearby villages completed the ensemble. Servants prepared food on a primus stove and a brazier (hence the 'Grill Room'). Dinner that night comprised lobster, veal, beans, potatoes and plum pudding – mostly tinned, he regretted, but still, dining 'al fresco' was pleasant when the weather was good enough.[872] At Boulogne docks Louise Downer noticed how sergeants controlling the work of unloading took the best meat for themselves. Next in line came the officers, then the men, '& last of all we women'.[873] Perhaps this kind of thing led to the small rebellion organized by Phyllis Goodliff on the evening of 10 September 1918 at the Red Cross hostel up in the town: 'We are sending in a formal complaint about the food. I am typing it out first thing tomorrow & we are all signing it. Half a dozen of us composed it tonight as we sat on the bed of one of the victims'.[874]

Rank, gender and class generated segregated events (birthday parties, reunions – few could join Schweder when he took the evening off for an Old Etonian dinner at Amiens in May 1916[875]), and also segregated structures (canteens, estaminets, YMCA and Church Army huts, clubs, messes, cafés, hotels, restaurants – Stapleton Eachus called back-area officers' messes 'cosy retreats . . . 8 men and a woman to look after 7 officers'[876]). In their absence settlers consumed food wherever and whenever they could; in whatever interstices of time and place the colony offered. But as with the former so with the latter; at Fromelles in October 1914, Aveluy Wood in April 1916 and Tilloy-lez-Cambrai in July 1918, and in innumerable other places and moments, these interstices were themselves segregated. ➲ 93

Wednesday 30 January 1918 **89**

Extract from Robert Cude's diary: 'On 30th, we get a welcome change, for we have a large colony of Chinks in the vicinity, and they go out on strike. Will not work, neither will they move out of their camp to make room for other troops. Jocks were called out to quell the disturbance, and they soon get the beggars under, but not before they used the bayonet on some of them'.[877]

This was at Nordausques, southwest of Calais, and it was not an isolated incident. In December 1917 guards opened fire on Chinese labourers camped at Fontinettes just outside Calais, killing four and wounding nine.[878] Nor was violence and unrest limited to late 1917 and early 1918, or to one ethnic group. 'Demob is crawling on,' wrote Cude from Ligny-Thilloy near Bapaume in January 1919, before launching into a tirade against the entire, muddled process. Why was it, he asked, that jobs in and around London went unfilled, even though nearly three-quarters of the men in his division still stuck in Befland were Londoners? Immigrants from Lancashire, on the other hand, left more or less as they chose, no matter how long or short their stay in the colony. Discontents exploded on 28 January when most other ranks in the division's London regiments announced that they would do no more work until the matter was cleared up. They were joined by men from the local ordnance depot (the action was coordinated, said Cude) who decided that although they would continue to take food, ammunition and supplies into the zone and bring zone dwellers back, they would no longer move units camped at the entrepôts into New Befland or the devastated areas. There had been another big strike at Calais, said Cude, and news of an equally large one at Folkestone. These would increase pressure on the authorities and help a great deal.[879]

Calais and its environs was a back-area district *par excellence*, overflowing with settlers working in scores of offices, hospitals, factories, veterinary stores, ambulance centres, dumps and depots which sprawled out from the town into the surrounding countryside and villages. The ordnance and service corps were major employers. From 1915 onwards Calais' stores fed and supplied much of northern Befland – trains ran to Hazebrouck, Bailleul and Poperinghe. A large cookery school existed. In 1918 the town's army bakeries fed 600,000 settlers a day. Conscripted postmen dealt with all mail arriving from Britain. One of the six typewriter repair units attached to the army's Printing and Stationery Service was based at Calais. Travelling mechanics – each had a small workshop and a motorcycle (news and rumour mongers to a man, one suspects) – carried out running repairs on 7,200 machines scattered across Flanders and La Bassée district. A base mechanical transport depot with 20,000 square yards of covered storage, one of many in and around Calais, issued over half a million items for 377 different types of vehicle between August 1915 and December 1918. In the first ten months of 1916 alone Calais' storemen and storewomen sent into the zone 11,000 compasses, 7,000 watches, 40,000 miles of electric cable, 40,000 electric torches, 3.5 million yards of flannelette, 1.25 million yards of rot proof canvas, 26,000 tents, 1.5 million waterproof sheets, 12,800 bicycles, 20,000 wheels, 5 million gas masks, 4 million pairs of horse and mule shoes, 447,000 Lewis-gun magazines and 2.25 million bars of soap. In September 1915 settlers built what was then the world's largest boot factory. By 1917 the 800 Beflanders working alongside German prisoners of war, native women and specialists recruited from London were manufacturing 30,000 pairs of army boots a week.[880] The vast complex of salvage and repair centres at nearby Valdelièvres was the first to take on native women, 'not only in ordinary women's work, like sewing and washing,' records the historian of the army's ordnance service corps, 'but on jobs such as cleaning wagons and rifles or even unloading barges of barbed wire, long before women replaced men in England or the Women's Auxiliary Army Corps appeared in France. Girls who knew not a word of English actually undertook simple office work such as filing documents'. Others made things from scrap gathered from all over Befland. Old boots were used as fuel, solder was recovered from old tin cans, lead from the linings of tea chests, women made nosebags and cooks' clothing from old tentage, worn-out ground sheets and waterproof capes reappeared as ration bags and cap covers, old oil drums became braziers, kerosene tins fire buckets, petrol cans hospital baths, the spokes of old wheels legs for tables and chairs, while broken down lorries were converted into coal elevators and sent to La Bassée district where Beflanders requisitioned French coal to save congestion at the entrepôts. The RASC commandeered the blood of slaughtered bullocks to make paint.[881] All this, according to Ronald Schweder, was something of a spectacle. In summer 1918 one colleague went on a joy-ride just to see it all.[882] Native women and settlers also dealt with the vast quantities of waste paper and empty ammunition cases shipped back to Britain. In addition British immigrants manned the barges which ferried wargear from the docks through the canal systems of northern Befland, while hundreds of Chinese, Fijian and British labourers quarried sand along the coastline for railway construction.[883]

Calais' socio-economic make-up and geographical situation help us to understand why the unrest alluded to by Cude should break out in an around the town. Chinese and other ethnic minority populations, far from home, disorientated, poorly fed and housed, were subject to ingrained aspects of British and Imperial culture – overt racism and physical maltreatment. As for the British settlers, they had a good idea of what was going on in London and the Channel ports; frequent commerce between Calais, Folkestone and Dover saw to that. When after the Armistice soldiers in the UK demanded immediate demobilization, refused to board the leave boats returning to Befland and marched on London to press their case, an answering echo was heard in Calais. In January 1919 strikes and mutinies over pay, food, working conditions and delayed demobilization flared up at Valdelièvres and spread into and beyond the town. Most of Calais' settlers were proletarians, many had trades union experience and some were socialists; soldiers' committees were formed and copies of the *Herald*, a socialist newspaper, circulated freely.[884] These men were workers-in-uniform rather than soldiers. Few had been socialized into the zone's 'trench communities'. In addition close contact with the town's civilians might have weakened still further the fraying bonds of military discipline.

Cude's voice, like the voices of so many folded in the Imperial War Museum's archives, fell silent when he left Befland. We don't know what became of him. There is nothing more in the files. But we do know that before 1914 he was a skilled worker in the London engineering company C. Jamieson, Ltd.[885] Even if not an active trades unionist he would surely have been aware of working-class mores. Either way other extracts from his diaries reproduced elsewhere in this book suggest an individual contemptuous of authority and ready enough to bend life to his will when conditions permitted [e.g., 60]. Like all Beflanders he was his own man, but like everyone else he was also folded in his own time. He felt the same sense of injustice and frustration as the Calais strikers and mutineers and shared the same attitudes as those who turned their knives on the Chinese labourers at Nordausques. ➲ 90

Friday 15 February 1918 **90**

A walk from Camiers to Widehem village on a half day off: 'delicious day, sunny & sharp, & soft blues & browns, greens & greys over all the country, boys ploughing & a dozen magpies hopping round for worms in one place. Delicious tea & bought plants of primroses, ranunculus, & other flowers for the ward, out of the garden'.[886] The walker was Kitty Kenyon, a VAD nurse working at Camiers' No. 4 British General Hospital. She arrived there in March 1917 and left in August the following year.

Camiers was three miles inland from Widehem and three miles up the coast from the back-area town of Étaples. Kitty Kenyon's was not the only hospital in the district. Camiers-Étaples supported the largest base hospital complex in Befland; eight for British settlers, two for Canadians, Australians and white South Africans and four provided by the Red Cross and the St John's Ambulance Brigade. They treated causalties from all three Befland territories: Flanders, La Bassée district and the Somme, even though several were no more than sprawls of huts and tents. Étaples also had a large convalescent camp designed to stop bed blocking in the hospitals and prevent the emigration of those deemed lightly wounded. Inmates were subjected to a punishing daily routine of physical exercise. Alongside the hospitals were a series of reinforcement camps, also the largest in Befland, which processed 40,000 immigrants at any one time. The staff of a cookery school, bakeries, infantry base depots and a large ammunition dump and horse convalescent depot at Dannes, just north of Camiers, added to the population mix. Between June 1915 and September 1917 over a million settlers passed through Étaples. The local YMCA huts plied them with 200,000 mugs of cocoa every month.[887]

But it was for its training ground, the infamous 'Bull Ring', that Étaples was often remembered, and feared and hated. Immigrants and convalescing zone dwellers endured drill, simulated gas attacks and brutal forced marches across the dunes running between Étaples and Camiers. Terrorized and exhausted, many regarded the training as pointless and believed that the instructors, nicknamed 'canaries' by virtue of their yellow uniform flashes, had never been anywhere near the zone and therefore deserved no respect at all. And it is for the events of late summer 1917 that Étaples often crops up in First World War history texts. A railway separated the town from the training and reinforcement camps and settlers could only get to the bars and cafes via a single walkway, the narrow 'three-arch bridge' heavily patrolled by club-wielding canaries and military police. On the morning of Sunday 9 September rumours circulated that New Zealand inmates were planning to smash up the camp's police huts. In the afternoon police seized New Zealanders attempting to force their way across the bridge. These two events sparked a mutiny. 4,000 besieged the guardhouse and demanded the release of those previously arrested. Shots were fired. In the evening around 1,000 settlers already in Étaples, New Zealanders and others, attacked the police and surged through the town waving makeshift red flags. The following day there was more violence at the bridge, further demonstrations in the town and a mass meeting over the river on Le Touquet's Paris Plage. On Tuesday more than a thousand broke camp and there were more meetings on the Plage. On Wednesday cavalry detachments arrived to restore discipline. By Friday the mutiny was over.[888]

Local factors alone are probably sufficient to account for the mutiny. The Bull Ring was a brutal place and some settlers had reached the end of their tether. We might also point to the vanguard role played by New Zealanders. Dominion immigrants had a reputation for being less deferential than the British. Doubtless general weariness should be factored into the equation too. By 1917 the War seemed interminable. On a wider canvas events in Russia may well have had some impact. At least one participant's letter describing the events got through to the social-democratic newspaper *Workers' Dreadnought*,[889] and those makeshift red flags speak of a settler cohort aware of what was happening on Petrograd's streets and yearning, however fitfully and inchoately, for a radical end to the War. A few might also have remembered that six months previously a garrison mutiny had toppled the tsar.

In some ways it's natural for practitioners to focus their attention on things like the Étaples Mutiny. Often reputations are made by advancing new interpretations of event packages, and generally speaking historians are bored by continuity, excited by conflict and inclined to pass over in silence evidence that doesn't fit their bigger pictures. Moreover, the fame and fortune occasionally on offer to scholars, however fleetingly, can whet appetites. BBC Television's 1986 production 'The Monocled Mutineer', which dramatized the part supposedly played by one Percy Toplis (who might not even have been there) attracted a great deal of bilious comment from assorted right-wing politicians scenting left-wing conspiracies, and the furore doubtless did no harm at all to viewing figures and probably boosted sales of the book upon which the production was based. We can expect more (and more lucrative) opportunities to arise when the official pieties are bandied about during and after 2014, and as every writer mindful of consultancy fees and royalty statements knows, all publicity is good publicity. Indeed all histories, this one included, might be described as commodity-manifestations of Nietzsche's 'will-to-system'; attempts, never wholly successful, to gratify physiological needs by imposing order on a fractious and disorderly world via the stilling of time and the monumentalization of action, and then imposing that order on the consumer.

Apart from any cultural and commercial resonances, in its technical aspect what happened on and around the three-arch bridge, outside the guardhouse and in the town could be characterized as an event package fabricated by selecting evidence from the past, not as an essence awaiting discovery in the evidence. If this is so then the 'Étaples Mutiny' – an appellation that's far from uncontested – doesn't happen until someone nominates it, and it won't go on happening unless that nomination is sustained. Thus history is 'there' only if you want it to be, but the locational problem involves more than figuring out how to triangulate putative agency, presumed structure and disputed essence. It all depends on where you look for your history. In Petrograd as in Étaples quiet and ordinary lives ran their daily course; mundane to researches fleshing out a thesis, perhaps, but engrossing, perplexing and contradictory for the livers. While Red Guards forced their way along the corridors of the Winter Palace on 25 October to arrest the Provisional Government drivers from the city's working-class districts turned up for their shifts and ran trams up and down Nevskii Prospekt. In the evening Chaliapin sang as usual in one of the city's opera houses. While mutineers gathered for a second time on Paris Plage on 11 September, Ruth Durst, then at Le Touquet's No. 1 Red Cross Hospital, walked into Étaples for tea with Major Hewitt and another nurse. She noticed nothing unusual and nothing much outside her own life: 'Major Hewitt and I went to Paris Plage and did some shopping and then walked back'.[890]

Up and down the coast of Western Befland and a few miles inland were harbours, small towns, villages and one-time resorts overrun with camps, remount centres, hospitals, dumps and depots: St Omer and nearby Audruicq and Wardrecquers; Neufchâtel-en-Bray, Gornay-en-Bray and Blargies (midway between Amiens and Rouen); Rouxmesnil-Bouteilles,

Forges-les-Eaux and Dieppe (the latter a nest of intelligence men, according to Cude[891]); Cayeux-sur-Mer and Trouville-sur-Mer; Dunkirk (little used in comparison with the other entrepôts); Le Tréport; Coquelles and Zeneghem (both on the outskirts of Calais) and Frévent (northeast of Abbeville). There were scores more like them where life went on, uneventful in terms of large constructs, but full of incident nonetheless. In their own way they urge us to keep in view the teeming flatness of the landscape of the past and to turn our gaze from the imposing monuments erected therein by practitioners. ➲ 97

91 Sunday 24 February 1918

Templeux-le-Guérard, the Somme, east of Péronne. 'G' was the diarist's wife and the first of March their wedding anniversary: 'I went up to Farm O.P. this afternoon and got a bunch of snowdrops for G., which one of my young officers is going to take on leave tonight. I wonder if they will be fresh on the 1st'.[892] George Stringer saw snowdrops outside his billet in the Salient one February morning.[893] In the zone's winter landscape little else flowered. Indoor plants blown clear of shelled houses would die, even if their pots survived intact, though some may have been rescued by settlers living in deep dugouts, on the Somme or elsewhere. But winter gardens bloomed in the back-areas. On Christmas Day 1915 Jessie Wilson went to the allotment attached to Harfleur's YMCA and picked violets, primroses and polyanthus. For spring and summer planting she ordered seeds from Suttons of Reading; annual larkspur, mignonette and 'Rose Morn'.[894] END

92 Saturday 6 April 1918

Phyllis Goodliff wrote to her mother about a scandal at Boulogne: 'we are to wear our brassards always out of doors & carry our passports, identity certificates, and red passes. Two people were stopped the other day I believe & when asked to show their certificates couldn't & it turned out that they were not VADs at all although they had managed to get the clothes'.[895] Ronald Schweder mentioned two other security breaches involving females. Somewhere on the Somme in April 1916 the military police stopped couple of suspicious looking individuals dressed as officers. They were detained. On closer inspection one turned out to be a woman. They'd arrived by car and the excited policemen thought they were spies. In fact the female impostor was married to an officer currently resident in the zone. She'd been in the habit driving up to the border in disguise every fortnight or so to see him. Since the officer in question was the friend of a general, everything was hushed up. Eleven months later near Bailleul in Flanders two Canadian nurses got as far as the observation posts on Hill 63 on the southern edge of Messines Ridge, just west of the front line. They'd hoped to reach the trenches but no one was courageous enough to help them find their way in.[896]

It's impossible to know how many women managed to tour eastern Befland, but they needed a fair measure of audacity to get across the DGT and FE lines. Probably physical proximity helped. In June 1918 Phyllis Goodliff expressed real jealousy that a friend – 'lucky dog' – had been posted east to St Omer, fifteen miles from the border. 'They are nearer to the front than any other B.R.C. show & have to go through gas drill before they go & gas masks are issued to them'.[897] By then 'mixed parties' could go up to a line running through St Omer, Doullens, St Pol and Amiens, but no further. The War Office and Army Council declared that women had 'enrolled' rather than 'enlisted'. Legally, therefore, they were civilians.[898] Given such difficulties, and the gendered nature of the wartime landscape (almost all female immigrants settled in western Befland though some were sent to casualty clearing stations inside the zone[899]), it's likely that most contented themselves with day trips to places close to Befland's entrepôts and back-area bases. They were sometimes escorted by males, and we catch the odd glimpse of them at play. In June 1918 Phyllis Goodliff described a half-day trip with a major to nearby Wimereux ('we then went to the Club for tea & had it in the garden there – real butter'). For a second visit she and another girl lorry-hopped in an ambulance and took a stroll before going on to the town's nursing sisters' quarters for tea. Next month she went for an eight-mile walk and then lorry-hopped a further six to have tea in a village. The day before she'd sat with a friend on the sand dunes and walked in the woods behind the beach.[900] Ruth Durst, based at Le Touquet's No. 1 Red Cross hospital, day tripped in the opposite direction. In November 1915 she was struck by Boulogne's human show, 'gay little French women' mingling British settlers who'd just landed. One of them shouted out 'good old Sussex by the Sea' as he passed her by. 'Boulogne seems a weird place,' she remarked, 'full of English soldiers and Marines and Indians'. In July next year she and two other girls picnicked with two officers at the town's polo ground.[901] But even in the familiar environs of Befland's back areas touring women might have to negotiate patriarchy in order to make their way across the landscape. On 10 May 1918 Kitty Kenyon and friends travelled ten miles to Montreuil, the site of GHQ. They returned ten days later, but this time were detained and directed to the local military police office. After sneaking in a visit to a church they got to see the APM. 'I said we'd been told to report to him, & he sprang up (we'd both been fixing each other for a second or so) & said, "Yes, you're not allowed in here." "I know we're not," said I. He burst into a roar of laughter. "That's honest anyway" – waved his arms & continued: "there are hundreds of generals here, hundreds, thirsting for your blood if they saw you"'.[902]

Unremarkable little journeys perhaps, but in their way remarkable enough for young Edwardian women of a certain social class free from parental control, living abroad, hitch-hiking, meeting men unchaperoned, working with smashed up male bodies alongside male surgeons and generally paying their way. (Befland's immigrant women gained some financial independence; even Boulogne's lowly cooks earned ten shillings a week all found, a respectable wage for working-class women, though they had to work punishing hours[903]). Judging by their letters Ruth Durst, Kitty Kenyon and Phyllis Goodliff seem to have been passably educated. They may have known about the *fin de siècle* 'new woman' debates and would surely have been aware of the suffragist and suffragette movements, and alive to the fact that a few professions were just beginning to open up to middle-class women like themselves.[904] They might not have been feminists (though Phyllis Goodliff did once get into an argument with an officer who insisted that if women compete with men they must forgo various amenities and courtesies – 'I don't agree, naturally,' she retorted[905]), but they were a part of the restless spirit of early twentieth-century Britain, and doing something extraordinary. We do not need to validate their jaunts along the coast in terms of *nostalgie de la boue*, the emotional locus of so much western-front history production. **END**

93   Monday 22 April 1918

'A French mess is far more abstemious than an English,' declared Ronald Schweder after observing some untoward behaviour, 'they drink their wine with their meals and shut up, – there is no whisky soaking'.[906] A fiction of evening routines at company headquarters in trenches opposite Gommecourt on the Somme, autumn 1915: 'The quartermaster-sergeant, who has just come up from Bayencourt with the ration wagon, reports to the captain. He brings the officers' mail; parcels from home; yesterday's London papers . . . and the day's gossip. "Sit down Quartermaster, and I'll see if I can find you a drop of whisky. No, there's none left. Have you brought another bottle?" "Yes, sir, and a hell of a job I had to find it"'.[907]

Charles Carrington's nostalgic reconstruction of a brief encounter reads like a set of stage directions. The lights come up. Two men in khaki in a dugout, with much to endure before dawn, appear to us centre stage. They chat for a while, the lights go down, and they are gone. But the props remain in the mind's eye: a lamp, empty packing cases for chairs, a makeshift table scattered with paperwork, letters, newspapers and in the middle two cups and a bottle . . . for, of course, it is the alcohol to which our eye is directed. Another Somme stage set, this time written in dugouts at the foot of a hill on the edge of the Bois des Tailles by Harold Bursey on 26 June 1916. Once again alcohol, and something that might be nostalgia fifty years hence but in the moment is laced with hysteria. Off-stage thousands of cannons are roaring incessantly in preparation for the 'Big Push'. 'Half a case of Whisky came up today. Great rejoicings. But Lieutenant Tolpull thought it should be charged to individuals and not to the mess. "Don't be mean," said Nicholson. "Look here," said Lieutenant O'Grady, "if you object to pay for whisky, I object to pay for pickles." Roars of laughter from Nicholson and myself. (Tolpull is the only one who takes pickles). O'Grady is studying for law in Dublin. And he's mighty fond of whisky. As I am writing this he is holding forth. (The result of the 1st whisky)'.[908]

Just over 45,000 settlers were court-martialled for drunkenness during the War, but Schweder's admonitions on 'whisky soaking' notwithstanding, Beflanders probably weren't as drink-sodden as the soldiers of the Old Army, not least because many brought aspects of late-Victorian culture – nonconformity, the temperance movement – with them into the landscape: very few indictments were serious and 45,000 is less than one per cent of the total number passing through Befland between 1914 and 1918.[909] Nevertheless drink figures prominently in settler records; what was on offer, how to get it, its quality, taste, likely location, and most of all its availability. But as with food bought so with alcohol bought: class inflected consumption. Officers drank whisky, good wine, champagne, liqueurs and port. Some complained of a 'port famine' after migrating to Flanders in 1915 because they were now too far away from the Paris shops.[910] On the other hand privates and NCOs (unless on a looting spree) drank *vin ordinaire* and cheap beer. Natives caught selling whisky to other ranks risked a heavy fine, anything up to 1,000 francs.[911]

Standing on the Kemmel Road in February 1916 a military policeman watched locals selling beer and wine to settlers as, shift over, those still able to walk poured out of the Salient's waterlogged killing grounds.[912] No one seems to have stopped them. 'It is a desolate country and all very sad to look upon,' wrote Herbert Leland ten months later, 'but those inhabitants who remain do a roaring trade . . . There are also numerous estaminets rigged up where the men can get wine of a sort and a mild kind of native beer, which they abuse, but drink nevertheless . . . All the existing houses seem to be turned into estaminets'. The beer wasn't to everyone's liking. Leland couldn't bear it – 'like coloured water, and to my taste very nasty'[913] – nor was it always available, particularly in siege landscapes empty of natives or when large-scale military operations threatened: Bursey, two days before the whisky party – 'Am trying to get some beer up for the men but "nothing doing" as yet'.[914]

According to James Edmonds settlers frequently laced beer with the army's officially designated stimulant, rum. Carefully allotted at the rate of a gallon jar for every sixty-four men, rum came into the trenches every night, or was supposed to. Carrington marked down Lieutenant-General Haldane's VI corps as particularly dreadful because he refused his officers permission to issue the ration,[915] but even without the predilections of individual commanders a verse printed in the *Wipers Times* (6 March 1916) indicates that supply could falter: 'The corp'rl and the privit they / Was standing in the road. / "Do you suppose,' the corp'rl said, / That rum is "a

la mode?" / "I doubt it!" said the privit as / He shouldered up his load.'[916]
So does another of Leland's letters: 'The rum ration is practically done away
with,' he wrote to his wife in November, 'only half the original allowance
being given to the men who are actually in the trenches'.[917]

Could this be evidence of a 'rum famine', a subset of the intermittent
'whisky famines' to which officers frequently alluded between 1916 and
1918? In 'Narpoo Rum' (napoo/narpoo = there's none/there's no more;
corrupted from *il n'y en a plus*), a serial story running in the *Times* from
December 1916 until the following April, Herlock Shomes and Dr Hotsam
chase around the back streets of Hooge, Ypres and Zillebeke and fly to the
Somme by balloon in a frantic attempt to solve the 'Riddle of the Missing
Rum'. Eventually they discover it's all a function of a whisky famine – in
the absence of Scotch Befland's officers had drunk the lot. At the end of an
earlier dry spell (February 1916) the 'Things We Want to Know' column
asked readers to reveal the identity of 'the person who reintroduced the
sale of whisky in Pop[eringhe].' And again in March 1917, a bold-type
advertisement: 'Do You Like Whisky. If so send at once for a price list. We
have recently cornered all the stock in the neighbourhood, and are now in a
position to dispose of same on reasonable terms'.[918]

At a horse show near Ypres in July 1918 Schweder witnessed an example
of 'whisky soaking'. Fifty officers sat down to dinner in a large marquee.
Everything went off well enough until around 10.30 when the drink began to
take hold. Then the rumpus started – raucous speeches, bellowing, fisticuffs,
glassware smashed, tables overturned and chairs flung about. Eton was
'very quiet' in comparison, remarked a companion as they fled the
confusion.[919] In texts like these we are almost certainly witnessing the effects
of alcoholism, though it's impossible to quantify how many settlers became
seriously incapacitated. One wonders, for example, whether 'Bubbly'
Bolitho [39, 61] was so named for his sparkling personality or because he
couldn't keep off the champagne. Either way antecedent behaviour, along
with the strains of war and peer-group pressure – what we might call mess and
estaminet culture – surely took their toll, but the army refused to recognize
drink-related illness as 'contracted in service' and so deducted hospital costs,
two shillings and six pence per day for officers and seven pence for other
ranks, from the pay of those too ill to carry out their duties.[920] ➲ 98

94 Saturday 25 May 1918

Kitty Kenyon watched men digging trenches between the wards at Camiers'
No. 4 British General Hospital. 'The Chinks are very picturesque in their
bright blue suits & straw hats (like sailors) with C.L.C on the ribbon
whatever that may be . . . Young called me once to see a Chink in a "fancy
costume" & I looked out expecting to see a wonderful Chinese dress but it

was a slim Chink in the most nuttish of European clothes, straw hat, striped dark pants & spats, leaning gracefully back on his walking stick . . . I never saw people work slower'.[921]

For UK immigrants Befland society was divided by class, trade, rank, gender and region of origin, but it was also homogenous. However complex and contested, a British identity existed, and migrated across the Channel. Settlers outside the 'imagined community' were objects of fear, condescension or wonderment; in Kitty Kenyon's case, it seems, a mixture of the latter two. In part this was due ethnic and cultural differences, in part to racial segregation. GHQ corralled 'natives' in separate camps and units (CLC stood for Chinese Labour Corps), though both soldiers and labourers were scattered across Befland. In June 1917 Daryl Klein arrived at the entrepôts with a contingent of Chinese immigrants: 'It is the destiny of all Coolie Labour Battalions, once landed in France, to be divided into I don't know how many parts, and dispersed over a wide area of usefulness . . . Some are marching by the harvested fields of the Somme country on their way to chalk pits to dig ballast for light railways; others are on the docks in the great ports of the South, loading and unloading the cargoes of war; yet others are digging trenches within the sound of the guns, with 'planes droning overhead . . . A few on account of their special knowledge are retained at Base Headquarters, happy in the field office or the Y.M.C.A. canteen. And they are shod with heavy army boots and their shins are bound about with puttees. They sleep for the most part in huts and are well supplied with blankets. They have enough to eat and enough to do. And they are earning money'.[922] But not much. On 21 July James Williams complained bitterly about life in the Royal Engineers' 'slave ring', a vast depot south of Arras. 'Started on ammunition this time. More sweated labour loading up bombs, shells & cartridges. Worked right on till 4.45. 1/2 hour tea then until 7.30 p.m. Started again at 8 & worst of all worked in pitched darkness till 11.30 p.m. How lovely and as the song runs "All for a Tanner a Day". Hooray at least the Military Authorities have got what they wanted. In the evening 50 Chinese labourers came to help. Just suits the R.E. officials here, sweated labour at about 2d a day with 4 meals of boiled rice & biscuits & hot water'.[923] Next month James Naylor came across a group somewhere in the eastern borderlands, though unlike Kitty Kenyon he found them to be brisk and active.[924]

Poor conditions and harsh treatment probably account for sporadic revolts in the CLC during and after 1917 [89]. Rumours of revolt, on the other hand, may have been expressive of racial fears and fantasies rather than material events. Just before her departure to New Befland in 1919 Colina Campbell picked up a story circulating in Amiens. 'One rather cheery thing I heard of the camp I was going to work [at] is that it has a big number of chinese [sic] working there who are very fed up & not long ago they killed their O.C. & severed his head up at the officers' mess, this of course is not officially acknowledged but never the less is I believe quite true[;] one sergeant & a major took a hasty departure & are still missing. Two V.A.D.s were very nearly badly mauled by them'.[925] But the chief causes of fear and fantasy were geopolitical, not the product of Befland hearsay. Since Britain's empire was 'oceanic' very few Edwardians encountered its subject peoples directly. What they knew of them came via schoolbooks, the popular press and the music hall. All were sites of ethnic and racial stereotyping. Inside the colony these shaped perceptions of and behaviour towards 'coloureds', 'natives' and 'coolies', though sometimes contact induced, if not empathy, then at least sympathy. Between October 1917 and June 1919 Louise Downer worked as a weigh clerk at Boulogne docks. 'Chinese Labourers helping to carry out all the heavy Hinds & Quarters of meat etc. There were also Black Boys from Africa, but we had strict orders not to speak to them – We didn't like passing them so nobody need have worried – I felt sorry for them they looked so poorly clothed & looked frozen very often'.[926]

Only one cohort, Old Army settlers, could claim extensive association with peoples outside the metropolitan heartland. Some were profoundly changed by long periods of colonial residence. Early in 1916 a London Scottish battalion passed though Jessie Wilson's YMCA hut at Harfleur *en route* to the Somme. 'Never in all the course of my hut life do I remember the arrival of men with such a cowed air, as had those of this overseas draft. They had come from the heat of the East, from dry sands and warm winds. They found nothing but mud, bitingly cold winds and driving rain. They had, in many cases, hardly spoken to an English woman for years and the language they had picked up was a mixture of Greek, Arabic and Turkish, with a flavour of pidgin English'.[927] Browbeaten or not, garrison culture, vicious little colonial wars and years of lording it over indigenous populations reinforced racism. 'Native infantry were no good in France,' declared Frank Richards, a veteran of Burma and India. 'Some writers in the papers wrote at the time that they couldn't stand the cold weather; but the truth was that they suffered from cold feet, and a few enemy shells exploding round their trenches were enough to demoralize the majority of them'. Richards' observations should not be gainsaid – he was there and we were not – but the underlying assumption of racial superiority is evident. Moreover, while the Old Army's lexis was spattered with loanwords, this did not imply empathy or understanding. Most communicative acts probably comprised a cocktail of imperative-mood English interlarded with foreign locutions, grimaces, blows and gesticulations. One day in October 1914 Richards scrambled into trenches near Fromelles held by Indian troops. All their white officers were dead. 'One of the men told me later that the first night they went over they found the natives wailing and weeping; no one was on sentry [duty] and they hadn't attempted to remove their dead out of the trench. Our fellows cursed them in Hindustani and finding that of no avail commenced to kick and hit them about and also threatened to shoot or bayonet the lot of them if they did not put their heads over the parapet;

in fact, they put the wind up them more thoroughly than what the German shells had. It was quite possible that the natives might have hopped it in the dark, but if they had attempted to in the day they would have been mowed down by our own men as well as by the enemy'.[928]

Members of the Empire's administrative class abroad in Befland were probably no more forgiving of racial insubordination than Richards and his colleagues, but they were, of necessity, more alert to cultural difference. The colony could not function without accommodating a wide variety of ethnic identities. Because Chinese settlers strongly objected to post mortems, for instance, field commanders were told that in cases where a sick or injured labourer might die, two of his friends should accompany him to hospital to confirm that the body was treated properly. *Service Scales of Rations (40/ WO/5582)*, a substantial booklet, carefully detailed the dietary requirements of Indian, Arab, Fijian, West Indian, African and Chinese immigrants.[929] According to volume three of Forbes' *History of the Army Ordnance Services* finding the right cooking utensils for assorted food cultures was always troublesome. One telegram sent from a Marseilles supply depot to an Indian cavalry detachment somewhere in Befland on 24 November 1914 reads as follows: 'Mahomedan or Punjab Lotah has a spout, with or without a handle. Hindoo or Bombay Lotah generally of brass but has no spout or handle, is carried by lip. Hindoos and Mahomedans here both agree that a Katorah never has a spout but is a sort of metal bowl. Confirm that you want the spouted article for which the nearest substitute is enamelled teapot. These can be obtained locally, price three francs, also enamelled substitute for Parat, price between three and four francs. Delay in replying owing to communications with manufacturer in Belfort. May I purchase as order must be given at once'.[930] Perhaps officers consulted specialist followers to help resolve complex issues like this. Stapleton Eachus met one at Fourth Army headquarters on 10 July 1917, and gained a glancing insight into imperial tensions. 'Had a long chat this evening with a person who is attached to the Indian cavalry and is a sort of an agent, who buys the provisions for the troops. He speaks English well and also French . . . He told me that his sect was very rich as a whole and that they were called the Jews of India, he had not many nice things to say about our regular army in India and called them a lazy lot of fellows, neither did he speak well of the English middle classes he had met with'.[931]

Most British settlers probably considered 'foreign/white' immigrants superior to 'native/coloured' immigrants. There's no evidence, for instance, that Kitty Kenyon tried to interact with the Chinese labourers she saw digging trenches at Camiers, but she did talk to wounded Portuguese soldiers, even if communication was limited to sign language, a few Anglicisms – 'Sishte' (sister), 'no monnaie' (no money) – and one or two French loanwords. 'To make them shave – one strokes one's face – points at theirs, says "No bon" – they laugh, stroke their own & agree "no bon" – but "no monnaie", & [make] remarks about the barber'.[932] On the other hand her responses may have been a function of work, location and role perception; Chinese outside the ward and only labourers, Portuguese inside the ward, under her care, and soldiers. But one can't ignore the likelihood that race inflected response. Though culturally and linguistically distinct, Portuguese settlers were at least European. Helen Vincent, nursing African troops at a French military hospital, simply objectified her charges: Moroccans 'compare very favourably with Algerians . . . Patient Algerian & unusually vigorous . . . This Very unusual with an African patient . . . Patient a Negro (Mozambique) . . . Considerably more E[ther] required than for Algerians'.[933] But then again her phraseology, racist insofar as it foregrounds nationality and ethnicity, could also be a function of class and profession. Helen Venetia Vincent, Viscountess D'Abernon, daughter of the 1st Earl of Feversham and wife of Sir Edgar Vincent, governor of the Imperial Ottoman Bank, was a qualified anaesthetist, trained to objectify male bodies and socialized into distancing herself from inferiors.

Unlike Europeans, Dominion and other 'white' settlers shared a common language with British immigrants, but this did not imply shared identities. Charles Bean, editor of Australia's official history series, thought that Britain's rank-and-file soldiers were docile compared to Australians because a class culture of subordination induced feelings of social, moral and intellectual inferiority.[934] Widespread literacy, nationalism and, after the Armistice, frustrations over delayed decolonization, probably inflamed rivalries and prejudices, however configured. 'Contrary to general belief our chaps and the "Aussies" do not get along very well,' wrote Robert Cude from Flanders in August 1917. The reason, he said, was because anything done by 'colonials' was puffed up in the English press. If one went by the newspapers alone one would imagine that Canada and Australia were winning the War 'with occasional help from us'.[935] On New Year's Eve 1918 Ronald Schweder reported that the Australians billeted around Tourcoing in New Befland were becoming particularly violent. Rumour had it that there was to be a set to with his gunners. It would only lead to trouble, he feared, and result in everyone being sent into the devastated areas as a punishment.[936] A few days earlier, just before Christmas, Cude had wandered into an estaminet at Warloy-Baillon on the Somme, currently billeted with US troops. Unfortunately for Cude the bar's clientele turned out to be exclusively American. He was not made welcome and had to listen to the kind of abuse which, he said, even the Germans would not have used. But he gave as good as he got, announcing to all and sundry that 'the whole of the prisons of New York must have been emptied to fill the ranks of this Div[ision]'. A general brawl ensued. Thrown out and pursued through the village by livid Americans, he escaped further beatings by hiding overnight in a barber's shop, emerging the next morning only after he was sure that the Americans had gone. A friend, Sergeant Major Dick Wells, was not so lucky; a stab wound with two inches of the broken blade still buried in his neck. Wells and Cude were ordered into Amiens for treatment. The town was no less fractious than Warloy-Baillon – squads of infantrymen with loaded rifles patrolled the streets 'with orders to shoot first, and explanations afterwards', but Cude got his revenge. He and some others found a 'stray Yank', roped him to the back of a hijacked lorry and dragged him out into the countryside.[937] ➲ 105

Friday 7 June 1918   95

When the inmate stirs the birds retire discretely, and sing in green trees. Elsewhere strengthening morning light discloses a seed head to a drowsing watcher.

These two moments of ease – Ronald Schweder emerging from his billet at Foche Farm in the Salient into the dawn and the surrounding woods,[938] Lieutenant Capron watching the sun come up at from an observation post opposite Quéant on the Somme border[939] – enfold moments of privacy. It was the same all over Befland, except that for night-working trench dwellers dawn heralded the possibility of retreat into the self, for those isolated in observation posts the continuation of consciousness, and for back-area denizens on day shifts re-emergence into the dinning world of stores, depots, docks and regulating stations. The question then arises – how did settlers use such moments? The evidence suggests four overlapping modes of consumption.

The first is reverie – visions, anticipations, stray thoughts and a reassertion of personality. At five thirty in the morning of 2 April 1917 Schweder arrived at an observation post near Bailleul. It was like Christmas, he wrote; snow everywhere, red skies with flashes of gold and yellow in the clouds. No one else was around and there was nothing much to see because haze covered the ground. He was little more than a lone figure in the workaday hell of the War. But after a while about twenty Germans walked along a tramway. He thought of phoning the guns, but the Germans disappeared before he got round to it. The day wore on, still and uneventful. He was crammed onto a small wooden bench with his back pressed against the wall. On his left the large telescope which poked out of the slit window overlooking no man's land kept banging against his nose. Nevertheless, he soon drifted away. A fellow officer's birthday party, scheduled for the evening, is mentioned. He wasn't looking forward to it. By ten thirty in the evening he would be too tired and anyway such binges were too boring. Dressing up didn't appeal. Thereafter a few lines on food and drink. Broom, his servant, had sent up port with a message that the tea was undrinkable – horribly musty. The *Daily Mail*, he averred, switching tack, was the best paper to read in the zone. Its bold headlines allowed one to digest the news quickly. America was about to declare war. When his stint was over the map board on his lap would double up as a toboggan, etc. etc.[940]

Next comes the contemplation of quiet companionship, welcome or otherwise, in the context of shared comforts or discomforts. As dawn broke over Quéant, remembered Capron, you slid down from your bench in the observation post to eat the breakfast cooked by your assistant, usually an NCO or private, who'd attended you throughout the night-time vigil. A welcome interlude, even though the bacon and tea might be tainted by fumes rising from the little methylated stove.[941] One morning in April 1915 George Stringer walked past trench dwellers in Kemmel. Each man was silent, enclosed, but they all stood crowded together behind a wall of sandbags,[942] unity in isolation. 'I am alone in my forest now like a wild man of the woods,' wrote Schweder from Mailly-Maillet on the Somme the following April. He had no one to talk to, he lamented. This wasn't quite true: a servant accompanied him, but conversation didn't seem to appeal much.[943]

The third mode of consumption is reading. Throughout the siege the post came up daily with the rations.[944] Charles Carrington remembered how off-duty trench dwellers in cushy sectors crawled into the long grass of no man's land to smoke and read mail undisturbed.[945] In addition to letters Beflanders consumed publically available reading matter. Canadian and Australian units turned out newspapers tailored to their respective immigrant communities.[946] *La Vie Parisienne*, full of pin-up girls and mildly erotic stories, penetrated the zone, as did English-language newspapers and magazines, and Befland's satirical rag, published fitfully as the *BEF*, *New Church*, *Wipers*, *Kemmel* and *Some-Times* (sic). The *Continental Daily Mail*, printed in Paris, reached settlers on the day of issue, *John Bull*, *Bystander* and the London papers a few days later.[947] In 1916 Schweder asked his wife to send the *Daily Mail* every day. Earlier (December 1915) he'd requested weightier matter – two novels by Thackeray, *Henry Esmond* and *The Virginians* – and on 9 March the following year got through an entire book during a twenty-four hour stint at an observation post.[948]

Closely allied to reading, and encompassing all others in so far as they leave evidential traces, is the fourth mode of consumption: writing. Most white settlers could write, and even if they were not believers their consciousness was profoundly shaped by the protestant habit of self-narration. Literacy and a book-orientated Christian culture prompted many to textualize mental states and the surrounding world, either for the benefit of others or for the edification of some later version of the self [63], or just for the nonce. On a glorious day in July 1917 Stringer loafed about in woodlands near Béthune. When he reached the wood's margins the country lay spread out before him. A battle was in progress. He watched as the Germans shelled targets in the near distance, and watched and recorded himself – 'an aloof & disinterested spectator'.[949] Bureaucratized, industrialized warfare in siege conditions supplied the means of production for such compositions – paper and writing implements lay around everywhere – and for correspondents a sophisticated postal system operated within and beyond the colony. Indeed, without these particular expressions of privacy, generated by an historically specific combination of material and social factors, our ability to pry into settler lives would be severely constrained. ➔ 100

Friday 14 June 1918 96

Foche Farm near Ypres in the Salient. It was a fine day with nothing much going on so Ronald Schweder decided to spruce things up a bit. He mustered half the battery for inspection and ordered the gunners and drivers out for riding drill. What he saw appalled him. Though the men rode every day they couldn't sit upright and lolled and rocked about in the saddles – 'sacks of coal tied up with string is what they look like'.[950]

In 1986 Lieutenant Capron recalled the types of animals artillerymen encountered, and how they worked with settlers. First came team- and wagon-horses earmarked for 'field battery' work. These were 'light draft', in fact civilian carriage animals requisitioned by the army. The lightest worked as 'leaders' (those positioned in front of a team) and 'centres' (those selected for pulling power). 'Wheelers', a little heavier, and often used to pull milk floats in Britain, were placed on the outside, though in all cases mule teams were sometimes used instead. All three cohorts – leaders, centres and wheelers – had to be able to move rapidly and to respond quickly to orders. Horses detailed to haul 'Long Toms', enormous dismounted garrison guns left over from the Boer War, were heavier than wheelers. In addition every turnout had one four-wheeled general service wagon, much like a farm cart and drawn by two animals – Capron's had a gelding and a mare, both chestnut, both large and powerful and both probably brewery horses in civilian life – and one water cart, 'a huge barrel on wheels' pulled by a single horse or mule. Next came the individual mounts; officers' 'chargers', finer bred, perhaps originally polo horses or hunters, and 'outriders' ridden by various NCOs. A standard six-gun turnout therefore comprised around 140 horses and mules – six per gun (thirty-six), six for each of the twelve limbers carrying supplies, ammunition and other wargear (seventy-two); two for the general service wagon, one for the water cart, eight officers' chargers, eight NCO outriders detailed as grooms (one per charger) and twenty more for assorted sergeants and other NCOs. A divisional ammunition column, which supplied a group of batteries with shells, had about the same number. 'All these animals had four feet each,' observed Capron, 'continually on the go'. How were they managed and cared for? There was never much trouble, he said, because every turnout had plenty of skilled men who'd learnt their trades in civilian live – blacksmiths, farriers and saddlers were 'two a penny' in Britain. Now they were in Befland, carrying on the same trades.[951]

Schweder's brief comment on dodgy horsemanship was probably closer to the mark than Capron's fond recollection. Since 1861 the majority of Britain's population had been urban. Some knew how to manage draft animals, of course; horses and mules still thronged the streets of every city, but most New Army settlers, flooding into the colony during and after 1915, came from the UK's industrial centres and didn't know how to handle the thousands of animals arriving from Britain and the Americas – Rowland Luther, for example, was a South Wales miner who'd never worked with horses before 1914.[952] Vets were forced to run crash courses in animal management and issue instructional literature.[953] The authors of two pamphlets, *Sergeants A.V.C Attached for Veterinary Duties to Units and Formations other than A.V.C Units* and *Horse Management and its Relation to Preventative Veterinary Medicine*, complained that Befland's wagon lines were commonly crowded, dirty and disorganized, that settlers failed to separate out 'kickers' ('twenty per cent of all preventable injuries'), kept head ropes too short ('sixty-five per cent of preventable injuries'), neglected grooming and stabling, fouled ponds and streams by riding into them ('want of good watering and stable management is the direct cause of the majority of causes of poverty among animals in a Field Army'), exercised animals too slowly or too quickly and spread disease by scattering forage on the ground.[954] After Second Ypres a veterinary officer reported that 'loose animals, particularly when wounded, increase the disorder and want of discipline on a battlefield, a fact which tends to depress troops and cause straggling . . . There appears during an action to be too much galloping; quite a number of individuals can be seen at all times galloping as if carrying important messages, yet from time to time they can pull up to talk to a friend or watch the scene. Ammunition teams, also, in some instances travel long distances on hard ground at a fast gallop . . . It was very noticeable in the last action that galloping rarely took place in Old Army units'.[955]

Three years of siege only compounded the problems. During the advance to victory vets found that since most trench dwellers had no experience of mobile warfare animals suffered when forced out on long journeys. Special arrangements were made to attach skilled horsemen to infantry units as transport officers.[956] 'The tendency of the times is for the knowledge of animals in war to become more and more a monopoly of the Veterinary Service in proportion as the intelligence of the army as a whole is becoming increasingly concerned with mechanical means of transport and attack,' observed Blenkinsop & Rainey. 'It may be anticipated that in future wars almost the only knowledge of animals of any value will be the specialised possession of the Army Veterinary Service, who will carry on, until the last domestic beasts of burden disappear from the service of man, the traditions of animal lore which their predecessors have so painfully acquired'.[957] ➲ 103

97   Wednesday 26 June 1918

Ronald Schweder wrote to his wife from Mont des Cats in Flanders about a forthcoming leave. The date wasn't yet fixed but it would be in France. Could she come? It would have to be Paris, he wrote a few days later, the only city where spouses could stay with their settler husbands. Could she meet him at the Hotel Edward VII? It's not clear what happened, but the rendezvous doesn't seem to have been kept. Two weeks later, however, he mentioned a fellow officer, Broome, who'd had rather more luck. Broome's wife had sailed to Le Havre, met her husband on the quayside and then travelled on with him to the capital by civilian train.[958]

Paris wasn't part of Befland, any more than Cornwall's quarries or the North American plains [6, 14], but like them it was linked to it. Deep and sustained settlement meant that the colony connected itself in manifold ways to numerous external locations, economically, politically and socially. Orleans was the Indian Army's main camp and Marseilles its base depot (1918 daily feeding strength 58,400, hospitals attached; one for Egyptian labourers). The Midvale Steel Company's works at Bethlehem, Pennsylvania supplied ammunition to the zone's gunners. Canadian foresters cut timber for Befland in Bordeaux and the remote Jura and Vosges regions[959] and, as the above extracts from Ronald Schweder's letters indicate, Paris was a leave destination for Beflanders. Somewhere in the city was the little Princess Victoria's Rest Club for Nurses: thirty-three beds (always full), entertainment fund, excursions to places of interest, tickets for theatres and opera houses. It opened in autumn 1917, closed temporarily in March 1918 when all Paris leave was cancelled as Befland's eastern border collapsed, reopened in September and closed for good in April the following year.[960] There were many similar organizations.

But Paris was more than a just pleasure resort. 'If guns and wagons could be rebuilt in the country why send them to England?' asked Arthur Forbes, rhetorically, in 1929. 'If clothing could be renovated by cheap female labour in France why ship it home, where labour was so scarce, to be cleaned and mended? Then followed the havoc wrought on our mercantile marine by German submarines and the policy was extended to its upmost limits. With each succeeding year more and more services were carried out on French soil, where, moreover, the network of operations continually extended towards the front as rail transport was also scarce'.[961] Late in 1915 the 'Special Purchase Department' based itself in Paris and liaised with the French to secure forage from Orne (west of the city), Bouches-du-Rhône (on the Mediterranean coast) and Algeria, and paid for the hay pressing machines sent to each location. When submarines threatened ocean-going shipping it started to buy a wide range of supplies, not just forage, from Spain, Portugal and Italy. From 1916 the city housed repair shops for Befland's lorries and tanks.[962] The Veterinary Corps' 'Disposal Branch' [46] sold Befland's worn out horses to Paris's horse butchers – 37,000 between 1916 and March 1919. A 'Paris Sales Detachment' [86] ensured that agreements were adhered to, supervised slaughtering and made over half a million pounds from the trade.[963] In March 1915 the ordnance service contracted the Paris firm of *Joly Fils* to clean and repair textiles imported from Befland and leased a large warehouse and railway siding on the Quai de Javel. Debenham & Freebody of London hired premises to clean fur-lined items, but there was too much work and the French and British capitalists charged too much, so Beflanders set up their own shops and employed native women workers directly.[964] 'The capacity of Joly's laundry was quickly swamped and work found for many others in and around Paris,' noted Forbes, 'what was too badly stained was dyed blue for the use of Chinese labour or prisoners of war. It was found cheaper to carry out repairs in our own workrooms rather than by contract; and employment in fashionable dressmakers' shops being scarce, there was no difficulty in getting couturiers capable of even such a speciality as remaking kilts'. Between 1915 and 1918 the ordnance service's resident officers and clerks spent in excess of £400,000 on materials, labour and rent.[965]

Leave destination, financial centre, manufacturing and repair base; but there is one other way in which Paris probably served Beflanders – harder to detect but likely nevertheless. In September 1917 William Orpen visited the old sixteenth-century belfry in Amiens with a friend, the town's APM. The military police used it as a prison. He was introduced to a young man dressed in an officer's uniform with no papers found hiding in a brothel. He'd been living in the Hotel de la Paix for over a week and an abandoned motorbike was found in the street outside. The police discovered that he'd stolen the bike and uniform in Calais. Apparently depressed and riddled with venereal disease, he lied about everything. After a while they sent him to a hospital under guard, but he escaped. He was rearrested and sent to a detention centre in Le Havre, 'where I believe', commented Orpen darkly, 'no deserter has ever lasted more than forty-eight hours without telling the truth and nothing but the truth'. For a while nothing more was heard of him, but later on when Orpen was in Paris another friend told him of a dubious poseur – 'Lord X' – seen dining at a fashionable restaurant. Orpen caught a glimpse of him and believed him to be the belfry deserter.[966]

Was Orpen's deserter a chancer, an adventurer, mentally unstable, a sociopath, or just someone who couldn't take the strain of Befland any more? There's no evidence of political motivation, unless one considers desertion a political act in itself. Did he in fact exist at all? Masquerade, escape from a high place, hierarchy confounded, difficulties overcome, odyssey, satisfyingly subversive conclusion – we might be looking at a trickster-archetype, someone fabricated from rumour and wish fulfilment. One imagines zone dwellers chuckling as he bamboozles officers and policemen and fakes his way across the land before surfacing in triumph to live the life of Reilly. But even if he's the everyman-hero of a settler folk tale his geographical instincts were right. The seething anonymity of Paris doubtless provided better cover for deserters than a heavily policed Befland provincial town, a putative zone shadow army [51] or a back-area coastal settlement. In 1922 Jessie Wilson recalled talk in Harfleur's YMCA hut of four deserters who'd disappeared from under the noses of their guards at Le Havre sometime in 1916.[967] Perhaps they made it to Paris too. **END**

Saturday 3 August 1918   98

'There is a whisky famine in France,' wrote Ronald Schweder from Mont des Cats in Flanders, '& the British Army is quite upset about it. The Colonel has to drink lime-juice'. The junior officers weren't faring quite so badly, however. Henry, one of their number, had a friend working at base stores who ensured that supplies were sent up. Two days later Schweder visited four officers at the headquarters of an infantry battalion stationed at the front: they were 'piggish' and no better than 'ya-hoos', he averred, but like many others they too were victims of the famine, and it was a scandal that while whisky was plentiful in the homes of back area denizens who slept in clean sheets, none was available for zone dwellers who, more than anyone else in the colony, really needed their drink.[968] Others were less convinced. The liquors on offer in Befland might not be so efficacious as Schweder imagined. 'Amiens was a danger trap for the young officer from the line, also for the men', remembered William Orpen. '"Charlie's Bar" was always full of officers; mirth ran high, also the bills for drinks – and the drink the Tommies got in the little cafés was terrible stuff, and often doped',[969] something that Eachus for one had reason to suspect [60].

Mobile hygiene labs detected arsenic in beer sold to Flanders settlers in 1916–17,[970] but alcohol wasn't the only drink that might be poisoned. In September 1914 Frank Richards was billeted in a Marne village. 'Stories had been going round that the Germans had been poisoning the water in the wells and we had been warned to be very careful not to eat or drink anything where they had been. (To little effect, apparently: 'we never took much notice', added Richards[971])'. In March 1917, as he hurried into territory recently abandoned by the Germans, Georges Stringer received a message stating that all the drinking water had been poisoned with arsenic.[972]

Since armies had to move in order to contaminate wells deliberate and systematic large-scale poisoning could only have occurred during Befland's brief periods of territorial instability. Settlers were more likely to be infected by polluted rather than poisoned water, and in the zone clean water was hard to find. Artillerymen living around Givenchy-lès-la-Bassée in May 1915 looked on the nearby canal as a bonus because they could wash and do their laundry, but the water was lethal if drunk; 'putrid', it 'grew a vivid green scum when undisturbed by shell bursts, which, while they dissipated the greenery, stirred up the black and stinking mud from the bottom'.[973] Everyone in the trenches had to drink chlorinated ration water lugged forward in discarded fuel cans – it always tasted of petrol, remembered Carrington.[974] At St Eloi in the Salient in June trench dwellers had only one bottle per day per man,[975] and the natives guarded against scrounging; a few miles away and a few months later, while walking from Armentières to the border around Loos, Rowland Luther noticed that the villagers along the road had locked their water pump handles.[976]

In fact from mid-1916 onwards the entire zone, densely populated from the Salient through La Bassée mining district and down to the Somme, suffered so much environmental degradation that virtually nothing was safe. Flies hatched in rotting corpses bred in pools and water tanks. Settlers were poisoned by drinking from or washing in shell craters fouled by mustard gas. The chemical dissolved in the water, leached into the ground, and at dawn lingered a few inches above the surface as a toxic mist. Sanitation collapsed. The 'herring bone' system, a pattern of very shallow trenches designed to disperse the soapy residue from bathhouses and laundries, could not deal with the weight of numbers. Neither could 'grease traps', dug to drain away cookhouse waste. Latrines were neglected or churned up by shellfire. Night urinals made from old oil drums tumbled over. Faecal matter and all manner of filth leached into rivulets and streams.[977] A border conversation remembered (or perhaps invented) by David Jones: 'He was carrying two full latrine-buckets. I said: "Hallo, Evan, you've got a pretty bloody job." He said: "Bloody job, what do you mean?" I said it wasn't the kind of work I was particularly keen on myself. He said: "Bloody job – bloody job indeed, the army of Artaxerxes was utterly destroyed for lack of sanitation"'.[978]

Northeast of Amiens on 28 September, near Basseux, George Stringer lamented the combination of hot, cloudless skies and chalk subsoil. The little brook next to their encampment had run dry and they were forced to drink standing water from a nearby pool, itself shrinking by the day. Incessant thunder rumbling away in the distance was no harbinger of rain. Flashes of light cutting through the dusk told the story of yet another heavy bombardment on the Somme.[979]

As Stringer's dairy entry indicates, water was a particular problem in the south. The River Somme supplied few settlers because it formed Befland's southern border. The Ancre stretched northwards from the Somme but turned east at Albert and then crossed the border after only six miles. To its left a second tributary – L'Hallue, no wider than a ditch and reaching up a mere eight miles from the Somme – disappeared into the chalk at Contay, midway between Albert and Amiens. Further north a single rivulet, L'Authie, rose east of the border village of Gommecourt and meandered away towards the Channel coast. There were no rivers in the interior. Villagers inside the sparsely populated sixty square mile Amiens-Albert-Gommecourt triangle relied on wells driven deep into the chalk substrata, and it was into this area that settlers began to pour in the first half of 1916. One group of five hamlets housing 2,200 natives saw its population explode to 24,000, but there were only five wells, one for each hamlet. As thousands more immigrants fanned out into the triangle specialists transformed the landscape. 'Water Committees' mapped, tested and labelled all existing wells. Railwaymen shuttled water trains from Doullens on the four miles of track between Candas and Canaples. Engineers sank hundreds of new boreholes and installed imported steam-driven filtration and pumping plants in villages or on specially adapted 'filter barges' anchored in the Somme.

Mechanics established repair shops, laid six-inch piping with elaborate distribution networks which snaked for miles and erected numerous galvanized holding tanks. A 'water tank column' comprising 300 lorries lumbered around the encampments on fixed schedules. Each vehicle carried between 550 and 135 gallons and each had a purification engine. In addition the column provided 400 200-gallon water carts for the triangle's five army corps. By late June over 400,000 settlers had crammed into the area, producing 120,000 gallons of urine a day. Hundreds of sanitary units responded by improvising shallow soak-pits filled with stones, lose soil or abandoned wargear and drove tin cans into the sumps to bleed off methane gas. The excreta of more than 100,000 horses and mules added to the pollution risk.[980]

This stupendous effort, a direct result of the mid-Victorian revolution in the management of public health, was enough to prevent contamination while the population remained sedentary, but when the mass migration eastwards started on 1 July the largest dysentery epidemic in Befland's history broke out. As the offensive slid into confusion and more and more settlers were sucked into the maelstrom improvisation replaced routines and regulations – 'no drinking water obtainable,' complained Stapleton Eachus from Querrieu in August, 'and no effort has been made to procure any for the troops'.[981] Sanitary workers following the advancing settlers to incinerate rubbish and faeces, remove corpses and carcasses, fill in latrines and generally clean up the landscape, were overwhelmed or themselves became casualties. Pipe-laying teams could not drag their heavy equipment across the devastated border. Water wagons got left behind or sank in the mud. Everyone and everything was subject to constant shelling, machine-gun and rifle fire. Fear, exhaustion, wounds and shock, common enough on the Somme, induced thirst, and settlers had little choice but to gulp water from polluted craters and streams. Only in November, when the offensive finally ground to a halt and siege conditions returned, did the epidemic subside.[982] **END**

Friday 30 August 1918   **99**

'Yes the Bosche is a cad bombing our hospitals as he does, in fact he has nothing good to his credit, he certainly is a most unsportsmanlike fighter. We hear the Turks are cleaner fighters than the Bosche'. 12 December, writing to a sister after crossing into New Befland, *en route* to Cologne: 'It's awfully funny, we have to walk about in twos or threes and always carry revolvers, cos the Hun has shot at single British troops and enticed them away & knocked [hell] out of them. They are swines. But we just walk into their houses and say "I want to put 12 men in this room" and they start their horrible chatter. Jimmy looks and shows his teeth! – and they very much frit methinks. Their men have to raise their hats to our officers – and we see they do it too. Oh Eileen I hate them, I'm perfectly sure I'll never be able to be civil to them'.[983]

James Naylor's abhorrence was not shared by all Beflanders. Some were indifferent to their opponents, at least retrospectively. 'One only fought to orders,' wrote Stormont Gibbs in 1986, 'having I believe no feelings whatever of dislike for the enemy'.[984] On the other hand Robert Cude thought that antipathy intensified when the fighting stopped. The Germans he saw cross no man's land to fraternize with Befland's zone dwellers after the Armistice were given a very hostile reception indeed.[985] Naylor further records that when settlers arrived at Cologne Haig stood on the base of the Kaiser's statue, located in the main square, to review a parade. The troops, however, refused to salute as they marched past.[986] It's not clear quite how this should be interpreted – were they refusing to salute the statue, or Haig, or both? – probably the former. Later on they fired machine guns into civilian protesters, but then again some, billeted in villages just outside the city, slipped out after dark to meet the local girls, curfew notwithstanding.[987]

That attitudes could be unstable within the compass of a single personality, as well as within a single cohort, is clear from details to be found in eight of Schweder's letters to his wife.

At Mailly-Maillet on the Somme (23 March 1916) he described a trench raid led by grenadiers and mentioned that Rupprecht of Bavaria – 'your old pal' – commanded this section of the German line. (Did Schweder's wife really know the Crown Prince, soon to be placed in command of an entire German army group? It's possible: she was very well connected). Würtembergers were stationed directly across no man's land, he continued, cheerful and well-disposed. A few nights previously they'd captured a British lieutenant out on patrol and then hoisted a message above their parapet reporting that the man was safe and uninjured. On St Patrick's Day their regimental band struck up 'Old Erin' because they knew that Beflanders opposite hailed from Ireland. On 22 March a colleague in charge of 'D' battery let loose a desultory volley of high explosive in their general direction. After the first shots the Würtembergers signalled back a miss. On 16 May he reported shooting in response to requests from trench dwellers. An artillery duel ensued, but when after an hour the Germans gave up so did Schweder, but not before he'd given as good as he got, and killed and maimed men just like him and his gunners. Something similar happened at the end of the month, but this time involving infantry mortar teams. First one side fired, then the other – each giving the other time enough to get into their dugouts – before the whole thing petered out after an hour and a half or so.

By late summer he'd moved to Koudebeck in the Salient, and was bored stiff. The only amusement available, he wrote on 3 September, was shelling the line and watching debris flying about – and killing Germans; the water table was so high that trenches were no more than three feet deep. Walking back past wagon lines near Dranoutre after lunching in Bailleul just over two weeks later he came across a party of German prisoners mending the road, and struck up a conversation with one of them, a Prussian from Munster captured on the Somme. They both agreed that the War was 'sehr unangenehm' and wished that they were safe at home. At the nearby prisoner of war camp he watched the guards throwing cigarettes to the inmates from their watchtowers. He sympathized with the prisoners' condition. Though well enough fed and cared for they were stared at wherever they went, and often pelted with mud by 'gutter-snipes'. Many people in any country would behave no better, he said. On 28 September he witnessed an attack on a German observation balloon. In a panic the two observers parachuted out. One reached the ground safely but the other got tangled up in the shroud cords and hung there by one arm for eight hours as the balloon slowly lost height and drifted across no man's land. When it eventually came to earth in Befland a mounted policeman grabbed the balloonist, tied him to his stirrup and dragged him along the road. Schweder was appalled, but before he could intervene a group of officers rescued the exhausted man and took him to their mess for a stiff whisky and soda. Next year (28 March), and once again on duty at an observation post near Bailleul, he saw eight Germans walking by in the distance as dawn broke over the frozen landscape but decided to let them live. It wasn't worth rousing the battery, and beside killing them would do little good. That summer he watched in disgust as a padre and a doctor at a dressing station stripped wounded prisoners of cash and valuables. If the boot had been on the other foot, he told his wife, there would have been indignant reports in the *Daily Mail* about Germans robbing helpless Beflanders.[988]

Social class, education, rank and military role are obviously in play here, but the complex knot of attitudes was shaped just as much by passing mood, circumstances, individual temperament and the demands of the moment.

The attitudes of infantrymen and other ranks in closer contact with the enemy could be just as unstable. In 1966 Sidney Appleyard recorded details of trench raid at Carnoy on the Somme in 1915. Three of his friends, Nicholls, Stone and Borrow, the latter a German speaker, crawled into no man's land to drag back three wounded Germans. When they returned he lent a hand. The first German he encountered was in a wretched condition. 'He had two bad wounds, one in the side and another in the chest, and a large quantity of blood was soaked up in his clothing. After binding him up, we managed to carry him into a dug-out, and made him as comfortable as possible. Although our deadly enemies, one could hardly help sympathizing with this chap, for the weather was intensely cold and he must have been chilled to the bone, for his wounds prevented him from moving a muscle. He kept on groaning, and from what I gathered from Borrow, he said "Jesus, Jesus, this is more than I can bear!"' After a minute of two Appleyard scrambled round a traverse. 'The other two men were in a more pitiful condition than the first – one received four wounds and when he landed in the trench his insides fell out, and the other was shot through the mouth and died almost immediately. I then saw that I had done as much as I could so I decided to try and obtain a few hours sleep. I strolled off along the communication trench to find all sorts and conditions of men, all very excited and asking one another what souvenirs they had obtained. I then realised that I had forgotten to get a keepsake for myself, so I went back to the dying German, and got Borrow to ask him for his hat, which he decided to give me on condition that I obtained something warm for his head. This I did, and he passed over his cap which of course I considered my property, but much to my disgust the Officers collected all the souvenirs, as they were Government property'.[989] Next year Ralph Hamilton watched Beflanders escorting captured Germans after a fight near Guillemont, just north of Carnoy: 'The usual order is the Englishman limping along in front, carrying his rifle and smoking a cigarette, and talking to a Hun, followed by the rest of the party, two and two'.[990]

Decades later Rowland Luther recalled what happened after he'd killed a man in a vicious trench fight near Loos, also in 1915 [75]: 'We helped each other in field dressing, which every man carried in his jacket. We and the enemy were now humans again, and helped each other'. But he was no more averse to looting the dead and dying than the doctor, the padre, Borrow and Appleyard. Grenay village, La Bassée district, March 1917: 'We were here for about three weeks, and in that time I did quite a bit of trading, with articles I had removed from the German dead. Belts marked "Gott Mit Uns" could bring in five francs, German forage caps were worth two and a half francs, but the German spike helmet was more sought after, at twenty francs'.[991] **END**

100 Sunday 29 September 1918

'We have not been getting any mail from England for the last two days, owing to the railway strike,' complained James Naylor. 'All the soldiers get frightfully fed up about all these strikes'.[992]

Strikes notwithstanding, an enormous number of letters poured into the colony. In December 1916 approximately 572,000 mailbags arrived from the UK. Of these about three-fifths (c.343,000 bags) contained parcels, the remainder (c.229,000) only letters. The magnitude of the reverse flow is harder to gauge, but for seven days in December 1915 correspondents sent just over 5,100,000 letters via British army post offices around the world, the vast bulk of them to and from France. If we assume that Befland absorbed two-thirds of the total – not unreasonable given the scale of immigration – we arrive at a figure of 1,700,000. If we make the further rough-and-ready assumption that reciprocity obtained (about half incoming, half outgoing), then for that week alone Beflanders wrote something like 850,000 letters. In both years December was doubtless an exceptionally busy time ('Received our Xmas cards in the evening, which were ordered a few days ago,' wrote Stapleton Eachus from Querrieu on 19 December 1916. 'They depict on one side the village church and on the other the road which leads to Amiens with a transport column wending its way through the snow. They are both coloured engravings and make quite suitable a presentation to send to our people at home'[993]) but the total grew year on year, in or out of season. Ten months on from December 1915 the number of letters sent via the army postal service had more than doubled.[994]

Letters written in the zone were collected from field post boxes, dispatched to railheads and from there by lorry to the entrepôts, or if for delivery within Befland to the Amiens sorting office.[995] Just what was written, and how much, depended, of course, on social and individual factors – personal predilection and the correspondent's level of education. In November 1915 Frank Richards watched a Public Schools' battalion in literary action in the Salient – 'their mail was always twice as large as the rest of the Brigade's put together'. Fourteen years later Robert Graves recalled the tiresome business of reading other ranks' letters: '"This comes leaving me in the pink which I hope it finds you. We are having a bit of rain at present. I expect you'll have read in the papers of this latest do. I lost a few good pals but happened to be lucky myself. Fags are always welcome, also socks." Seldom any more, and signed "ever your loving husband", or "ever your respectful son"'.[996] Now and then the contents were livelier. One day in 1915 George Stringer copied out a verse from a letter he was censoring ('Nap' was a card game popular with other ranks): 'I'll go one said Austria; / I'll go two said France. / I'll go three said Russia, / For I think we have a chance. / I'll go four said Germany / And wipe you off the map, / But they all dropped dead / When Britannia said / "Gawd blimey! I'll go nap!"'[997]

Sometimes, in idle moments across the colony, correspondents tried their hand at verse parodies like this. 'Serious' poetry on the other hand, was by and large a high-status activity heavily imbricated with exploitation and inequality. In early twentieth-century Britain the majority lived lives disfigured by want, insecurity and illness. Most children left school at eleven and most women endured years of childbirth and backbreaking domestic work. Significant numbers of adults, the unemployed, were utterly destitute or on the brink of destitution – casual labourers. This 'reserve army of labour' held down the wages of the rest; men and women condemned to long hours of physically exhausting work and housed in noisome, overcrowded dwellings. Nearly a third of the nation lived their entire lives in slums which, according to Correlli Barnett, were in some ways no more salubrious than Befland's trenches.[998] Only those they supported were likely to have access to quiet and solitude, and time to spend learning how to play with words. These carried advantages accumulated at the expense of others with them across the Channel. The 'war poets' provide the best example, drawn in the main from the urban bourgeois and landed classes and in the main public school and Oxbridge educated. But transposing the literary fruits of such private moments as the colony afforded into the public sphere required something more than imported cultural capital; access to commercial publishers. Once more the 'war poets' provide a good example. Many were 'Georgians', in print before 1914. Those that weren't found sponsors from among their peers. For the less ambitious or the less well connected there was always the *BEF Times*, but on 20 March 1916 the editors issued a prohibition: 'We regret to announce that an insidious disease is affecting the Division, and the result is a hurricane of poetry. Subalterns have been seen with a notebook in one hand, and bombs in the other absently walking near the wire in deep communication with their muse. Even Quartermasters with books, note, one and pencil, copying, break into song while arguing the point re boots, gum, thigh. The Editor would be obliged if a few of the poets would break into prose as the paper cannot live by "poems" alone'.[999] The *Times* never printed 'serious' work (though it's unlikely that Graves, Owen, Sassoon et al. would have submitted copy). Nevertheless some verse parodies were rather good. 'A Dweller in Wipers' Elegy to That Town (With apologies to Grey)' takes us through a standard public and grammar school text, carefully preserving the original iambic pentameters throughout, and the lugubrious tone. It appeared two weeks before the prohibition, which, incidentally, had no effect whatsoever.[1000]

By copying out a soldier's verse Stringer alerts us to another aspect of inequality. Officers were on trust ('I am allowed to censor my own letters now', wrote a jubilant James Naylor the day after being promoted to 2nd Lieutenant[1001]) but censored other ranks' letters before they were posted. Occasionally they got a glimpse of farce or tragedy. In August 1916 an unfortunate Beflander sent two letters to England, one to his wife, the other to a girl with whom he was having an affair, but mixed up the envelopes. The blunder only came to light when the recipients replied. Ronald Schweder was aghast, and amused, ('What a terrible mistake!'), less so when confronted with a gunner desperate for leave because his wife had turned to drink. It was impossible, he told him, but suggested that he should stop her allowance and see what that did. Many married settlers complain that their wives don't write as often as they used to, he said, probably because they were too busy out and about frittering their money away on luxuries.[1002]

Non-combatants were censored too. Writing home from Harfleur's YMCA hut Jessie Wilson got into trouble for sketching an officer's personality. Naming officers was to be avoided, she was told.[1003] Phyllis Goodliff chaffed under the restrictions imposed at BRCS headquarters in Boulogne. 'At last I can write to you without visions of our rotten old censors prying into my letters,' she wrote in May 1918, before going on to pen acerbic vignettes of some of her colleagues – 'He is rather like Kitchener to look at & I should think rather aids the likeness . . . I don't know anything about the ways of Diana but Flora is an old tadpole . . . The other V.A.D. is Ross; she is a perfect dear, about 35, the ugliest person I have ever beheld, with teeth sticking out a mile, but she is awfully jolly & easy to work with'.[1004]

The only way subordinate classes could escape censorship, at least partly, was to get hold of one of the coveted 'green envelopes', something Phyllis Goodliff seems to have succeeded in doing. These were introduced in March 1915. The front cover reads as follows: 'On Active Service. A.F.W3078. Note. – Correspondence in this envelope need not be censored Regimentally. The Contents are liable to examination at the Base. The Certificate on the flap must be signed by the writer'. And on the verso: 'I certify on my honour that the contents of this envelope refer to nothing but private and family matters. Signature (Name only)'.[1005] Officers, of course, managed their distribution.

Letters, censored or otherwise, belonged to moments of quietude, but even in the thick of it zone dwellers wrote, albeit in a highly restricted format. During the slaughter around Messines Ridge in spring 1917 the YMCA, in co-operation with CCSs and field dressing stations, set up thirty-four small 'Red Triangle' centres where the walking wounded could fill in a field service postcard ('I am well/wounded' etc.). Those too badly injured to lift a pencil could ask the nursing staff to write for them.[1006]

If they tired of privacy settlers might ring up friends on army phones; rank, trade and opportunity permitting. Visual signalling virtually disappeared after 1916. By 1918 the thousands of telegraph and telephone poles connecting the zone with bases, headquarters and the entropôts stretched for fifteen hundred miles. Each pole carried about twenty wires, giving a total wireage of about 30,000 miles.[1007] Thousands more criss-crossed the zone itself [31]. Stapleton Eachus records that telephonists at Fourth Army headquarters worked on an eight-hour three-shift system, forty per shift, in order to keep communications open twenty-four hours a day. About 250 lines ran into the office. In November 1916 he and his colleagues handled, on average, 5,000 calls a day on thirty circuits connected to a host of units and establishments in centres like Abbeville, Amiens, Albert, Rouen, Corbie, Le Havre, Rome-scamps, Étaples, Boulogne and Paris.[1008] That settlers used phones for social as well as professional purposes, or at least were inclined to chatter, may be deduced from a reference to phone tapping. Sometime in 1915 the Intelligence Corps got wind of information leakage through badly insulated lines running close to the border. 'Policing by use of listening sets was introduced,' wrote James Edmonds in 1932, 'the organization being known as "I.T." It was regarded by the troops with considerable disfavour, and as the younger generation had a confirmed telephone habit, improvement in caution was very slow. In the month of September 1916, one single police set overheard within a radius of 3,000 yards, between thirty and forty units spoken by name, including an Army and several divisions; movements of troops were referred to, infantry operations discussed, whole operation orders quoted, positions behind the line mentioned'.[1009] But still, for some, the phone was an unwelcome intrusion into moments of privacy. 'One can't get away from the telephone out here', lamented Schweder from the Somme in March. 'It has rung up at least five times since I started this letter'.[1010] END

Sunday 3 November 1918   101

Robert Cude and six others, bayonets fixed and rifles at the ready, scouted a village near Le Cateau, some thirty miles east of Bapaume on the Somme.

He was very careful, however, because the Germans had settled the area since late August 1914. Everything seemed tense and eerily quiet, but it wasn't long before children's faces began to poke out from behind half opened cottage doorways, and within a trice adults were mobbing Cude and his companions as, by now quite unafraid, they made their way along the street or were pulled indoors by the ecstatic villagers. Cude couldn't believe it. At one house, full of teenage girls and young women, he was overwhelmed with kisses and plied with more than enough cognac before was allowed to move on – rather unsteadily, he admitted, but at least his kit wasn't nearly so heavy; he'd given all his food and rations away to the children and the girls.[1011]

It's understandable that affective interactions between settlers and natives surged during the final days of the advance to victory. Many village girls might feel themselves liberated, and be grateful, though some moved east as the advance gathered pace. In April 1917 Ronald Schweder heard rumours of what had been happening in French towns settled by the Germans; French women remarried to Germans and intent on moving to Germany after the War.[1012] Nevertheless incidents like the one played out in Cude's village were common enough, and parallel those seen at the entrepôts just over four years earlier. Céline Williams, travelling from London to Caen in August 1914 [2], watched French women waiting on the platforms of Boulogne station with flowers to welcome Befland's first immigrants.[1013] But the War's end posed a question for those who'd entered into long-term affective relationships. What to do next? Craig Gibson cites evidence, albeit patchy, suggesting that the rate of marriage between native women and RAMC, RAVC and pay corps men employed in Western Befland increased after the Armistice.[1014] This makes sense: many settlers in the entrepôts and back areas stayed put year after year and got to know the locals well – over 20,000 natives were employed by the British in France alone by May 1918.[1015]

But it was not only in the west that choices were made. A series of Schweder's letters posted from Tourcoing near Lille in New Befland and covering the period December 1918 to January 1919 show what happened in the east as the colony unravelled. Officers and other ranks in his unit started cohabiting with native women for the winter – two sergeants were particularly quick off the mark. Five days before Christmas Schweder went roller-skating with local girls, and on Christmas Day he and others invited girls from nearby Roubaix to the battery's dinner – an uproarious night. Other ranks brought their lady friends to the feast as well. Meanwhile an American revue troupe had arrived from Paris. Henry, a close friend, took up with one of the performers. By the end of the month they were living together in his quarters. Another troupe girl caught the commanding officer's eye but he made little headway, much to his chagrin. Meanwhile local girls and troupe girls were turning up *en masse* for lunch and dinner at the officers' mess. Only the colonel's adjutant seems to have objected to the invasion, but he was easily overruled. Over New Year rumours circulated that the troupe was about to leave, but on 5 January they were still there. That day, however, brought some distressing news. Henry's girl fell ill. The battery's medical officer diagnosed consumption. Three days later, on 8 January, a conference was held. The medic reported that the girl was infectious, but as the whisky flowed so did the talk and the sympathy. No one had the heart to throw her out and eventually all agreed that she could stay. She was still in residence a week later, and being cosseted by Henry's batman: he woke her up every morning, told her how she was looking, supplied tea in bed and ran hot water for her bath. 'Marvellous situation,' exclaimed Schweder, 'a soldier servant doing maid to a "cocotte"'.

In fact it's not at all clear that Henry's revue girl was a prostitute, but whatever the case on 16 January the party finally began to break up. Next day she left. Henry took her to the station to catch the Paris train. His servant carried her luggage. Schweder turned up with rice and an old slipper.[1016]

It would be pleasant to think that the rice and the slipper weren't just part of a blasé farewell, but the whole three-week episode seems more than tinged with hysteria; young men and women, lucky to be alive and perhaps unwilling to face the uncertainties of peace, grabbed at pleasure as and when they could. Had the colony lasted well into the 1920s then maybe Henry would have followed his girl to Paris, but probably not, though he cared enough to look after her while they were together.

Less exciting encounters – not necessarily less heartfelt – haunted Lieutenant Capron into old age. 'I have unearthed in one of my [diaries] under date 6th April 1918 a very faint Augusta,' he wrote in 1986. 'Just her name. They ran a good fruit and vegetable corner shop in Aubigny[-en-Artois] . . . I had one letter from her – in very correct English and saying that her mother approved her writing to me. But the letter hasn't survived. I expect many war-time romances did not survive the peace – backgrounds and upbringing such poles apart that it was [just] as well'. Earlier on he'd befriended another girl, Rose. They spent time on French-English conversation. Two teenagers, Yvonne and Marcelle, crop up in a wistful sentence about Christmas 1918 at Rouveroy in southern Belgium.[1017]

We don't know what happened to Yvonne, Marcelle, Rose or Augusta, or to Henry's girl from the Paris revue troupe. Everyone was young and unsettled. All we can say for sure is that transactional sex doesn't even begin to encompass the range of interactions between Beflanders, native women and others pitched into the colony. **END**

Monday 11 November 1918   102

Befland's ration strength comprised 1,202,000 'combatants' and a further 592,000 'non-combatants', a total of 1,794,000. Within a month numbers had, apparently, increased – 1,638,700 combatants and 625,250 non-combatants, a grand total of just under 2,264,000.[1018] The explanation seems to be that the Armistice Day figure excluded a substantial number of 'coloured' labourers. Variant figures for November posit totals of three million, 2.4 million or just under two million.[1019] Either way two million or so is similar to the 1917 figure, but the population was distributed differently between cohorts: the 1918 total disaggregates into 1,857,000 British and Dominion troops, 14,500 Indian, African and other troops and 117,800 labourers and followers – the latter figure representing a massive increase over previous years.[1020] In fact at one point in 1918 the number of West Indian, African, Chinese, Indian and Fijian immigrants attached to the Labour Corps may have reached a quarter of a million.[1021]

By autumn there were 25,500 women settlers, the highest level in the colony's existence, of which 6,700 were nurses (including curiosities like members of the Almeric Paget Massage Corps). There were also 5,100 military police, over 19,000 foresters, 394,000 printers, clerks and linguists churning out paperwork in English, French, Flemish and Chinese and Indian dialects (36,373 army forms alone in August), 89,000 transport labourers working on the railways, the roads and in the docks, 4,300 master farriers, saddlers and wheelers, 10,000–12,000 footplatemen and 1,700 assorted priests, clergymen, preachers and rabbis.[1022]

Early in 1918 Befland comprised a rough triangle running Roye-Dunkirk (about 100 miles), Dunkirk-Le Havre (about 150 miles) Le Havre-Roye (about 120 miles — Roye was just south of the River Somme). Its total area was therefore approximately 6,000 square miles, but the dissolution of the Roye-Dunkirk line during and after spring caused wild fluctuations. The zone's length fluctuated too, between 123 and sixty-four miles.[1023]

According to the medical authorities from 1 January to 11 November Befland suffered 2,060,250 casualties, far more than in any other year.[1024] This may in large part be accounted for by territorial instability, or what staff officers called 'the restoration of mobility to the battlefield': the Ludendorff Offensive and the advance to victory put more settlers at risk than did siege warfare. In addition the poor physical condition of many late immigrants may have increased sickness rates. Despite pledges to the contrary thousands raw conscripts aged eighteen or younger were hurriedly dispatched to Befland as the siege ended.[1025] ➲ 107

103 Saturday 7 December 1918

About 400,000 horses and mules lived in Befland, eight times the number for summer 1914 but significantly lower than the figure for 1917. That year the population stood at 436,000, a fourteen per cent increase over 1916 and the highest level of the war. In 1917 twelve per cent fell sick and thirty per cent died or were killed, due in large measure to food shortages, bitter winter weather, fighting around Arras and infections brought in by North-American remounts. Throughout the year Befland consumed, on average, 8,700 remounts a week.[1026]

Between 1914 and 1918 the colony imported 1,361,000 horses and mules. 605,000 came from Canada and the United States, 118,000 from South America and most of the rest from the UK, though a few came from Africa, Iberia and the Antipodes. Some 317,000 died or were killed. Hospitals and convalescent depots admitted 859,000 and discharged two-thirds as cured. In March 1919 only 14,900 animals remained. Twelve months later all the remount commissions were wound up. By then there were around 1,500 horses and mules left in the colony.[1027] ➲ 106

Tuesday 17 December 1918   104

Ronald Schweder reported on an 'epidemic' of photography going on around Tourcoing in New Befland. The day before all the officers of the Division's artillery turnouts posed for a group photograph, much to his irritation. Two weeks later he endured a group photo of his entire battery.[1028]

Moments like these weren't unusual, particularly as the War ended and 'temporary communities' began to dissolve. In addition Beflanders could have their photos taken when away from the zone. All other photography was strictly controlled. No reporters were allowed into the colony until May 1915, though a few had smuggled themselves in earlier. Thereafter accredited 'war journalists' – no more than thirty or so – took up residence at a chateau near GHQ, with their censors. 'They were given such information as was desirable, and paid visits to the front and places of interest', is the laconic note in the 1932 volume of the official history series, but unofficial photography was banned.[1029] Settlers weren't permitted cameras at all.

These restrictions notwithstanding, Befland was intensely photographed. By late 1916 all five army areas had their own workshops, each producing an enormous variety of plates, panoramas, mosaics and stereoscopic images recording the progress of the War and detailing trench systems, artillery emplacements, camps, towns, villages, railway lines, troop concentrations, depots, aerodromes, canals, woods, rivers and streams, and a host of other natural and man-made features. Formed in June, Befland's Army Printing & Stationery Service had a staff of 242 in August, rising to 752 in 1917 and nearly a thousand by November 1918. A subsection, the Printing & Photographic Company, handled images taken by aeronauts. In October 1916 a single workshop at Amiens turned out over 5,000 bromide prints from plates supplied by reconnaissance flights.[1030] Cecil Lewis worked for them in summer that year, photographing the Somme. 'Just above us the heavy cloud banks looked like the bellies of a school of whales huddled together in the dusk. Beyond, a faintly luminous strip of yellow marked the sunset. Below, the gloomy earth glittered under the continual scintillation of gun fire. Right round the [Fricourt] salient down to the Somme, where the mists backed up the ghostly effect, was this sequined veil of greenish flashes, quivering'.[1031] Next March Lieutenant Capron watched aeronauts fighting near Arras. His unit had reached the Pont de Jour just as dusk fell, making it safe enough to urge the wagons up over a nearby ridge – daylight travel on exposed skylines was too risky. Out of the east came a large group of enemy aircraft, droning westwards. Out of the west, hanging in the 'primrose sky . . . like a gauzy cloud of dragon flies' appeared a group of Befland aeroplanes, no less large. 'A spectacular airy fight' ensued. Even his drivers, nonchalant to a man, paused to watch and comment, 'slouched sideways on their saddles and heads craned skywards'.[1032]

Overall, the Printing & Photographic Company produced 25,000 images in 1916, just over two million in 1917 and 2,500,000 in the first ten months of 1918.[1033] These, along with privately taken portraits, are deeply embedded in modern British culture. Fading prints of young men in uniform posing stiffly in French or Belgian studios lie in thousands of family albums. Unit photographs – grey on black, rank on rank, three- or four-tiered, officers centre shot flanked by the NCOs – litter the archives. Zone scenes – grey corpses dissolving into grey mud, shattered grey trees, silvered shell-hole pools, grey smoke, dappled horses pulling gun-metalled cannon along white roads and the black and white stillness of destroyed villages – are reproduced by the million in every form of visual media. And everywhere the backdrop of blank, misty vistas and empty, featureless skies.

In contrast to photographic images films of Befland are less common and, since they were produced for propaganda purposes, of dubious veracity. Despite its promising title *Life of a WAAC*, commissioned by the Ministry of Information in 1918 to boost recruitment, was shot entirely in Britain.[1034] Much better known is John McDowell and Geoffrey Malins' hour-long *The Battle of the Somme*, filmed at the behest of the War Office, mostly over a two-week period in late June and early July 1916. Premiered in London on 10 August, *The Somme* was an astounding success, and remains so. By the end of October around twenty million people are thought to have seen the film, forty per cent of the UK's population, and virtually every TV documentary on World War I uses clips from it. But some of the imagery was staged. Scenes purportedly showing troops going 'over the top' surrounded by shell bursts on 1 July were in fact shot a few days later at the Third Army's mortar school near St Pol, miles from the battle zone.[1035] In any event, like the photographs, everything is in monochrome.

Contemporary culture experiences Befland in monochrome because it sees it through early-twentieth-century material culture, but it was not experienced thus by settlers. What we cannot in see in photos and films is their colour-world: the luminous strip of yellow and the sequined veil of greenish flashes glimpsed by Lewis on a reconnaissance flight over the Somme; the gauzy cloud of dragon flies against primrose skies watched for a moment by Capron and his drivers before they looked away and wheeled their guns into position. All of this can be apprehended, by us, only through words. And while we might regret the limitations imposed by monochrome technology – historians struggle hopelessly to convey the exact disposition of things in their vanished worlds – they do bestow a minor, or perhaps not so minor, advantage. When words substitute for images visual culture is thrown into sharp relief, because the vanished world is coloured, not by the impersonal operation of chemicals, but by the experience of its denizens. Befland's writers were their own war artists, shading colour onto structures, earth, air and water. **END**

Monday 30 December 1918 **105**

'It seems very vague about what kind of reserve force we shall have after the war,' wrote Ronald Schweder from Tourcoing in New Befland. 'If I could get a Territorial Field Battery I think I should go on with it, soldiering is now unfortunately ingrained in me. I'm afraid I shan't be able to get rid of it entirely'. Two years earlier he'd agonized over a forthcoming move – second in command of a six-gun eighteen-pounder battery. He didn't relish the prospect, promotion notwithstanding; a weak commanding officer and a ranker who was sure to be jealous and uncooperative – 'What do I care for a second pip? I'm not a soldier, – this isn't my career'.[1036]

Back in the late 1960s and early 1970s Franco Fornari, Peter Loewenberg, Arno Mayer and Richard Sipes advanced a range of theories about behaviour and identity in the Great War.[1037] One hypothesis suggests that, like sport and revolution, war generates spaces for the discharge of psychological drives that find no outlets in everyday life within stable societies. Another argues that war cannot be explained by referencing immanent drives. Soldiers are conditioned to particular forms of behaviour by identities inherited from the world they leave behind. In the Great War, for example, western males feared their own aggression as much as the enemy's because they were 'civilized' and therefore possessed defensive rather than aggressive personalities. In 1979 Eric Leed entered the fray. He argued that because conflict on the Western Front during the siege years favoured defence over attack, specific character traits were selected and strengthened. The 'official' persona, on display to outsiders, was patriotic and 'offensive'. Things were different when cowering in trenches liable to sudden and lethal mass bombardments. Because there was no chance of escape men elaborated 'clandestine', 'defensive' personalities, invisible to civilians and war planners alike. When in 1918 infantrymen abandoned their trenches – the Ludendorff Offensive and the advance to victory – the situation reversed. Among German soldiers at least 'neurasthenia' (generalized anxiety) declined markedly, even though the slaughter was no less fearsome than in previous years. A year later the psychiatrist Kurt Singer reported that his ex-soldier patients were leaving him in droves, 'cured' because the German Revolution eliminated conditions of powerlessness which had induced neurosis in the first place. 'The Revolution itself,' comments Leed, 'terminated the need for the neurotic complex as a protest of the inferior, the suppressed, the subordinated, precisely for the class of men who made up the main contingent of neurotics – the uniformed working proletariat. Those compensations for the feelings of inferiority, defences against medical opinions, flight into illness . . . were, suddenly, no longer necessary once the existing power relations were so radically transformed'. Leed further suggests that Germany's educated youth welcomed 1914 because the country had modernized late and rapidly. War released them from bourgeois constraints and offered an escape from humdrum modernity into a world of heroic sacrifice and adventure. Disillusionment set in when they found themselves proletarianized: modern warfare turned out to be no more than 'work' – impersonal, industrial-scale destruction. Real proletarians, on the other hand, had no illusions to shed. They were already slaves of the machine.[1038]

The trouble here is manifold. First, though no historian operates without theory, however vague or unacknowledged, theories are delicate creatures, easily discommoded when awkward facts clamber out of the sources. Moreover, the phenomena they claim to embody are always open to alternative explanations. Psychoanalytic labels, for example, are speculative and tend towards circularity – defensive actions are cited as evidence of defensive personalities because they are defensive. One might just as well use discourse culled from the official history series. Volume two of *Medical Services/Diseases* claims that while few men were outright 'malingerers' some lacked 'grit' because they were 'physical degenerates', 'neuropaths' or 'morose' products of unhappy families. Others, once 'sturdy soldiers', were 'broken' by wounds, illness or exhaustion.[1039] Secondly, generalizations based on modes of socialization peculiar to early twentieth-century Europe fall because it wouldn't be difficult to find evidence showing that some males enjoyed violence or feared the enemy's more than their own while others felt nothing much one way or the other. In any event plenty on all sides exhibited identities bound up with aggression and patriotism – in or out of the zone, before and after 1914–18, and regardless of rank, class, ethnicity, nationality or regional identity. Revolutions engender feelings of liberation, with or without antecedent wars. Drive-discharge doesn't work for the Classical World. Ancient Greece, that gallimaufry of quarrelsome city states, tiny republics and petty tyrannies, was hardly a model of stability, yet many of the peninsula's inhabitants relished sport and war, and adopted defensive military tactics as and when circumstances dictated. Much the same could be said of Dark Age or Medieval Europe. Germany may have modernized late, but 'modernization' is tricky concept, redolent of teleology. Large areas of the United Kingdom, to say nothing of France, were still agricultural, and some, particularly in France, were only patchily 'modernized'. Farm labourers in the former, peasants in the latter, comprised significant proportions of each country's armed forces. Educated German youngsters imbibed heroic stories inherited from Greece and Rome but so did the educated youth of all belligerent nations, and it is at least possible that valorizing male physical courage is *sui generis* to homo sapiens and not cultural at all.

Identities, and the feelings and behaviours we associate with them, are simply not amenable to reductionist explanations. They are too mutable and wayward. Correlations fail, palpably so once it comes down to individuals. By class Schweder belonged to the upper bourgeoisie. By region he might be classified as a Londoner with landed connections. By trade he was a gunner, but only in Befland, and – oddly perhaps – frightened of artillery fire. By military rank he was, respectively, a lieutenant, a captain and a major. In most of his letters home he complains about the army, the War, his subordinates and his superiors, or sympathizes, as the mood takes him. There's no overt patriotism but neither is there a sense that the War was futile, even though from time to time he'd had more than enough of it. There were many Schweders. Sometimes he's one thing, sometimes another. And cutting across all these affective selves bound up with trade, class, region of origin and rank was another: his vague all-encompassing civilian identity ('I'm not a soldier, – this isn't my career'), something that stood in apposition to the entire round of Befland identities.

Nevertheless we should beware of inferring a simple departure-return model of identity derived from apposition (pre-war civilian > Befland > post-war civilian), for Schweder or for anyone else. In the first place identity was fluid and dynamic. Neurons sparkle in the brain, become iterations ('I'm fed up/this isn't my life') and then ossify in the sources and turn into 'facts', but the meanings they convey may bear little relationship to the whirligig of emotions present in the mind at a given moment and may not resonate in the personality for more than a few minutes. Secondly, and to state the blindingly obvious, life changes people, especially in times of tumult, and life in the colony changed identities – 'soldiering is now unfortunately ingrained in me'. Thirdly, the vast majority of settlers were, if not citizens in arms (that appellation seems more appropriate for revolutionary armies), then civilians in uniform. Labourers worked on time-limited contracts. New Army immigrants signed up for 'the duration' only. Befland did not obliterate the past. Most of the settler songs collected by Brophy & Partridge, for example, are not 'martial' at all. 'I Don't Want to Die' is expressive of civilian longings; 'Fred Karno's Army' ironically celebrates military amateurism.[1040] Fourthly, leave journeys, the postal system and Befland's 'ridiculous proximity' to the portals (the phrase is Fussell's[1041]) continually dislocated military identities, especially those of British immigrants. Most Beflanders were never entirely severed from civil society.[1042] In one letter sent from Flanders in April 1917 Ronald Schweder sketched the evening scene in an officers' dugout. They all had dinner. Afterwards they sat up chaffing Francie, one of their number, about the family photographs he'd pinned on the wall; two each of his children and three of his wife, Freda. A telephone rang. Someone answered it. The staff captain wanted to speak to Francie. Francie took the message and put down the receiver. His mother had just died and he was to leave Befland next morning, catching the seven-thirty train from Bailleul. In the early hours Schweder could hear his servant stumbling about packing his valise. Thereafter details of Schweder's domestic arrangements: a thank-you to his wife for the torch refills (just received); not to worry about pyjamas (he would try to buy some locally); most recent pay cheque enclosed; commiserations over her bout of the mumps; assurances that he was in good health and details of the contents of a food parcel sent by an aunt.[1043]

Finally, for Old Army settlers Befland represented continuity, not change. They were soldiers before 1914 and some other colony might, or might not, claim them after 1918. James Naylor emigrated to Befland in August 1914 via Lucknow garrison, entered New Befland after the Armistice and left Tilbury for India in December 1919. Thereafter a fragment of correspondence places him at Simla. The next envelope in his archival file, postmarked 12 November 1922, is addressed to East Ilsley, Berkshire, crossed out, and redirected 'c/o Mrs Johanson, 1085 Great Western Road, Kelvinside, Glasgow'. Inside are two testimonials. 'Dear Naylor, I saw in the Gazette that you had retired; it was bad luck to have to leave the profession in which you had made start especially under the present conditions. I myself retired in June as it seemed no good waiting on longer on half pay. I am delighted to give you a testimonial as to your riding and hope you may get something to do in this line. H. Wayne, L[ieutenan]t-Colonel (late RFA)'. 'Dear Naylor, I was glad to hear from you, and enclose a recommendation as far as I can give one. The amount of riding that we were able to do in Germany was not very advanced, but I expect that after your time in India you have become quite experienced. I am sorry to hear that you have been "axed". Unfortunately many fellows have been also, and it is a hard job to find some means of earning their living. I hope that you will be successful in getting a job. I presume that you want to get taken on by someone, and are not proposing to set up a show on your own. That takes a little capital, and facilities for keeping a few horses during the course of training. I have 3 horses here, and am getting what hunting I can, in somewhat indifferent country. A.D. Musgrave, Brig[adier]-Gen[eral] (Retired)'.[1044]

We can press Naylor into service as an example of the 'temporary gentleman problem' anatomized by Martin Petter,[1045] Beflanders commissioned from the ranks who were unable to find their socio-economic footing after the War. But there were personal as well as professional disappointments, proto-civilian identity shifts never realized. In summer 1917 Naylor met Valerie Dove (Valgy) while on a course in England. On 30 August next year he wrote to his mother. 'I'll be 21 next Dec. & Valgy was 20 on August 20th. Mrs Dove says she is not to be engaged until she is 21, & she is not to encourage me because it is not fair to either of us, as we are so <u>young</u>. But we do like each-other tons, and always talk about what we will do when we come out to India for that holiday ... I don't quite know what to do. You see I'm very young & we couldn't live on a sub[altern']s pay here or in India. I expect she will get a little. You must tell me all about it. I suppose I must hang on & hope for the best eh[?] ... It's nearly eleven o'clock & there's another battle on to-morrow so I'll close. Tons of love Mummy, Always your Jim'. There were other letters, but he mentioned Valgy for the last time the following spring. 25 May 1919, somewhere near Cologne: 'Fraid the gap between my old lover is getting bigger, better now than later eh? Spose it was only a flash'.[1046]

It's hopeless to try to generalize, but somehow or other the attempt has to be made. Like everyone else Naylor's experience of the world was socially structured, but like everyone else born into the modernist ache it was also intensely personal and isolate (what landscapes of loneliness might lie behind that 'Spose'?) When he died (who knows where and how?) so did an entire world, *the* world. On the other hand as temporary gentleman, unemployed ex-soldier and failed lover he was no more than one among millions, a tiny fleck on that vast wave of sorrows, hopes and fears that washed over and reshaped post-war Europe. Both Naylors are real, and each demands reconciliation with the other. We historians struggle to do it, with him or with any other 'source', but we can take some comfort in pondering the fact that so does everyone else. **END**

Thursday 3 April 1919   106

As evening fell Lady Londonderry looked out over the Salient. 'We saw nothing alive the whole day except three wild duck in flight and a grey crow perched upon a tree. Even the insect life seemed to have departed'.[1047]

Everywhere Beflanders settled they changed the ecology. Dumps, depots, camps and hospitals favoured some species at the expense of others, but nowhere was the change so profound as in the zone. Every correspondent and diarist mentions the ubiquity of rats, lice and flies. Dung, excreta, food waste and rotting flesh allowed them to feed and breed in abundance. Lice survived for nine days when separated from the human body,[1048] ample time to find a new host. In 1915 Rowland Luther was in trenches near Armentières: 'All around us were ditches full of stinking water, and huge water rats would crawl out at night, in their search for food. Heaven help the soldier who had any food in his haversack: they would attack and crawl all over him'.[1049] 'They simply swarm and are huge beasts, more like rabbits than rats,' wrote Herbert Leland from the Somme in 1916.[1050] Zone dwellers fired ballisite charges to smoke out their burrows.[1051] When in February rumours circulated that the Germans were using rats to spread plague, trained ratters were let loose – a good dog could catch up to 150 a day.[1052] George Stringer remembered making his way down long-disused communication trenches in 1915. They were full of filth and corpses and buzzing with flies 'The flies were a plague – beautiful, incandescent. One eats them with one's food'. In Flanders mosquitoes swarmed and bred in stagnant ponds, sluggish water courses, and around dead livestock and piles of debris and refuse.[1053] 'They made a hum like one hears near telegraph poles', wrote Ronald Schweder.[1054] At St Eloi's trenches in July Sidney Appleyard described how flies 'swarm on the sandbags and in places collect in great black patches'.[1055] 'As we climbed over the heaps of corpses,' recorded Ralph Hamilton in his diary after walking on the Somme plateau near Maricourt in August 1916, 'they rose in dense black clouds around us, with a hum like an aeroplane'.[1056]

As rodent and insect life boomed so did predator species – owls, corvidae and migrant insectivores. Next summer on the Somme uplands William Orpen saw the sky 'a pure dark blue, and the whole air, up to a height of about forty feet, thick with white butterflies: your clothes were covered with butterflies ... Through the masses of white butterflies, blue dragon-flies darted about; high up the larks sang'.[1057] Swallows have appeared 'in great numbers' and nest inside trench dugouts, wrote Leland. On May mornings he watched magpies and crows quarrelling and nesting in shattered trees and abandoned sniper platforms in a wood near Bapaume – 'you would not believe the number of birds there are about'.[1058] 'Owls in the church tower and stray cats' was how Schweder described the deserted village of Mesnil-Martinsart the previous March.[1059] Both, presumably, stayed there to prey on the rats and mice that were no longer being controlled by humans. Later that year Lieutenant Capron walked into Death Valley with a carrying party. 'It was a glorious early autumn day, but as we penetrated further up the notorious Valley the beauty of the day fell away ... This had been very heavily fought over ground with dreadful casualties on both sides – and no burial parties had yet been organised. The flies were dreadful, and rose in clouds. Martins were "making hay"', gobbling down the flies 'and swooping everywhere'.[1060] **END**

107 Saturday 3 May 1919

655,400 settlers were still in Befland, down to 168,500 by 25 October. In 1920 the ration strength fell from 36,400 to 22,200, including 7,500 on what were once the lines of communication. Many Beflanders had moved to Germany as part of the 'Army of the Rhine'. In August 15,400 women settlers remained, falling to 2,900 a year later.[1061] By 1921 almost everyone had gone, though some lingered on well into the decade, and perhaps even until the outbreak of World War II. 'English is almost the dominant language of the new Ypres', noted Captain Taylor when he returned to the rebuilt town just before 1928. Because of the constant ingress of battlefield and cemetery tourists a British colony numbering some 450 lived around a group of buildings which constituted the heart of the British settlement: a British school with over one hundred pupils catered for the children of resident staff attached to the Imperial War Graves Commission, the British Legion, a 'British church' and the Toc H.[1062]

But even if this sub-colony didn't survive 1939–40 (and it's hard to imagine that it did) in a way settlers have never completely left: the War Graves Commission still manages over one thousand cemeteries on land granted in perpetuity to Britain by France and Belgium. Nor has the colony completely disappeared. In summer 1955 lightning strikes on pylons running across Messines Ridge detonated mines left over from the June 1917 offensive. Another mine stash, lying one hundred and fifty metres away from the explosion site, sleeps on undisturbed.[1063] Nearly half a century later, in April 2001, 15,000 villagers living around Vimy Ridge were evacuated when a huge deposit of buried wargear started leaking mustard gas.[1064] To the north a newly-constructed eighteen-million pound disposal facility a couple of miles east of Ypres at Poelkapelle (Poelcapelle), dealt with the 3,000-odd bombs, shells and gas canisters unearthed by the public that year. In addition the Belgian Army's bomb disposal teams uncovered a dump containing eleven hundred eight-centimetre British shells. 'Every year we find at least one storage site like this,' remarked Captain Luc Moerman, company commander of one of the teams. He went on to say that the annual volume of collections had remained stable for the last twenty-two years. 'We'll probably be at this for at least another twenty-two years,' he added. 'I'll be on my pension by the time we begin to resolve this problem.'[1065]

We can be pretty sure that overall the colony absorbed four to five million settlers, even if the exact figure is hard to determine. Four years after the Armistice the War Office stated that between one a.m. on 9 August 1914 and midnight on 1 April 1919 4,324,613 people travelled to Befland via the UK alone (including reinforcements, leave returnees and those coming from other 'theatres of war'), and that between 1914 and 1918 5,339,563 arrived via the UK *and* from elsewhere *and* settled for various periods of time (3,790,533 'combatants' and 1,609,010 'non-combatants').[1066] About twenty-three per cent of mainland Britain's male population went to Befland and six per cent of Ireland's (base line in both cases July 1914). For Australia, New Zealand, Canada, Newfoundland and white South Africa the percentage ranges between eleven and nineteen (base line in all cases July 1911).[1067] The official 1931 UK casualty figure for August 1914 to December 1918 is 6,218,581. This breaks down into 5,333,951 sick, wounded or injured (some more than once, therefore, and sickness and wounds covered anything from toothache to serious trauma), 381,261 killed outright, 183,454 who died of wounds, disease or injuries, 174,926 captured and 144,989 'posted missing'.[1068] Since the average desertion rate for 1914–18 hovered around one per cent[1069] we might hazard that only a tiny proportion of the latter were absconders. If so the number of 'military deaths' comes out at around 700,000–710,000, but again, as with immigration figures, it's hard to be sure, and we can't know how many more died from physical or psychological wounds years or decades afterwards. Some historians give figures significantly higher than those cited above, and some, doubtless, will go on arguing about it until their readers, and the profession, lose interest. Accountants, however, were preternaturally exact; fittingly enough, given the mode of production. For example in 1922 they calculated that the thirteen-day preliminary bombardment for Third Ypres cost, in 1917 values, twenty-two million two hundred and eleven thousand, three hundred and eighty-nine pounds, fourteen shillings and fourpence.[1070] Expressed in 2010 purchasing values this comes out at nine hundred and seventy million, six hundred and thirty-seven thousand, seven hundred and thirty pounds and eighty pence. But neither in 1922 nor at any time since has anyone been able to determine exactly how many died as a result of the battle. **END**

Maps

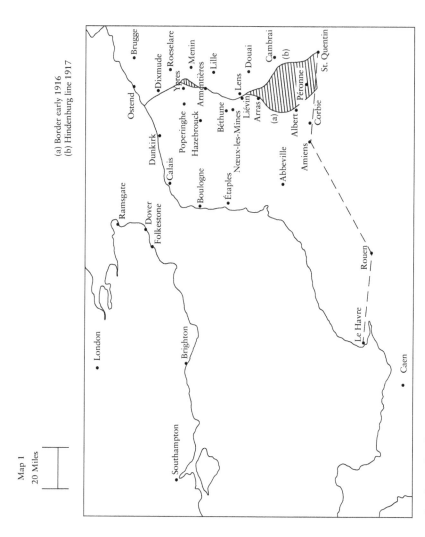

Map 1
20 Miles

(a) Border early 1916
(b) Hindenburg line 1917

MAP 1 *Approximate borders of Befland during the siege*

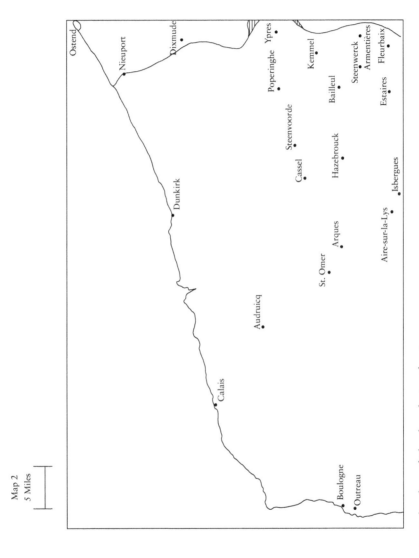

MAP 2 *Approximate borders of Flanders during the siege*

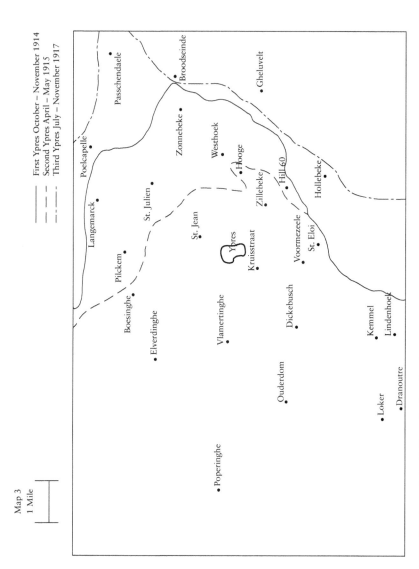

MAP 3 *Approximate borders of the Salient during the siege*

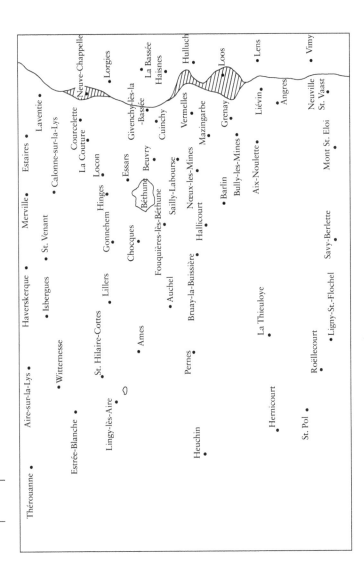

MAP 4 *Approximate borders of La Bassée district during the siege*

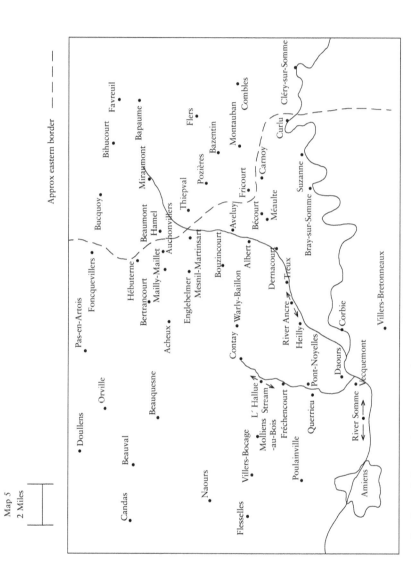

MAP 5 *Approximate borders of the southern Somme, late June 1916*

GENERAL GLOSSARY

advance to victory	Official term for the period from summer 1918 to the Armistice when Beflanders moved towards Germany.
ANZAC	Australian and New Zealand Army Corps.
APM	Assistant Provost Marshal. Military police officer.
Army	Group of military units. For most of its history Befland had five armies.
Army Council	Committee chaired by the Secretary of State for War that exercised political control over GHQ.
back area	Formally speaking anywhere not in the 'Zone of the Armies'. In settler parlance anywhere deemed far enough away from the zone to be relatively safe.
base	Back-area location, often in an entrepôt, from which a unit was administered and/or from which supplies and wargear were forwarded. 'Advanced bases' were subdivisions nearer to the zone.
battalion	Subdivision of a regiment (c.800–1,500 Beflanders).
battery	Artillery unit, usually comprising six guns, c.140 horses and mules and c.150 Beflanders.
Befland	B[ritish] E[xpeditonary] F[orce] land. Area of northern France and north-western Belgium settled by British, Imperial and Dominion immigrants and followers between autumn 1914 and c.1920.
Beflander	British, Imperial or Dominion immigrant to Befland.
Blighty	Settler slang for the UK.

Boche/Bosch/Bosche	The Germans; used mainly by officers.
BRC[S]	British Red Cross [Society].
brigade	(a) Group of three or four infantry battalions (*c*.3,200–6,000 Beflanders) (b) group of four artillery batteries (*c*.600 Beflanders).
British Legion	Ex-Servicemen's association founded in 1921.
CCS	Casualty Clearing Station.
Church Army	Anglican evangelical organization.
CO	Commanding officer.
colony, the	Befland.
company	Subdivision of a battalion (*c*.200–750 Beflanders).
corps	Group of two or three infantry divisions (*c*.36,000–45,000 Beflanders).
CRA	Commander Royal Artillery.
cushy	Settler slang for anything deemed easy or safe.
DAA	Director of Army Accounts. Accountant.
devastated areas	Official term for zone landscapes thoroughly destroyed by war.
DGT line	Director General of Transportation Line. Moveable internal north-south Befland border, usually two to four miles west of the zone, where nothing was allowed to move during daylight hours.
division	(a) Group of three infantry brigades (*c*.9,600–18,000 Beflanders) (b) cavalry unit (*c*.9,250 Beflanders).
entrepôts	Befland's ports, in particular Le Havre, Boulogne and Calais.
estaminet	Makeshift café run by natives for settlers.
FE line	Forward Examining Line. Policed intrazonal line in place during military operations.
First Ypres	'First Battle of Ypres', October–November 1914. Collision between advancing Germans and settlers which marked the Salient's foundation.
Flanders	Region of north-eastern Befland centred on Ypres.

followers	An imprecise term. Followers included (a) some but not all 'non-combatant' immigrants (labourers, etc.) (b) some natives more or less officially associated with the army's work (translators, etc.) (c) some natives and others who unofficially 'followed' settlers around Befland (traders, prostitutes, etc.).
GHQ	General Headquarters. Supreme military command of Befland's armies.
HE	High explosive [shell(s)].
He/His/Him	The Germans; used by all settlers.
Heine/Hun	The Germans; used by all settlers.
Hindenburg Line	Fortified line running from Rheims, south of Befland, to just north of Arras, to which the Germans withdrew in early spring 1917.
immigrants	See *settlers*.
La Bassée district	Region of east-central Befland located between Flanders and the Somme. Centred on Béthune.
lines of communication	Befland's formally designated supply routes, usually running from a base to the zone.
Ludendorff Offensive	Series of German offensives launched in spring 1918 which precipitated the temporary collapse of Befland's eastern borders and marked the end of the siege.
MLO	Military Landing Officer. Responsible for coordinating activities at the entrepôts.
MO	Medical Officer.
natives	Walloons, Flems and French; Befland's indigenous population.
NCO	Non-Commissioned Officer, answerable to an officer; Lance Corporal, Corporal, Sergeant, etc.
New Armies	Volunteer armies formed in the UK in 1915 and boosted by conscription in 1916 which arrived in Befland in 1915–16. Sometimes called 'Kitchener Armies'.
New Befland	Territory incorporated into Befland during and after the advance to victory.

OC	Officer commanding.
officer	Someone 'commissioned' with executive responsibility over settlers through a chain of command; Lieutenant, Captain, Major, etc.
Old Army	Pre-1914 regular army shipped to Befland in August 1914. Wiped out as a cohesive entity by late 1915.
old front line	The Somme's eastern border prior to dawn on 1 July 1916.
OP	Observation Post. Place from which an artillery officer directed his battery's fire.
OTC	Officer Training Corps.
other ranks	NCOs and privates.
platoon	Subdivision of a company (*c.*30–50 Beflanders).
portals, the	London's Victoria and Waterloo stations; Befland's gateways. More specifically the platform barriers.
Private	Lowest ranking Beflander.
QMAAC	Queen Mary's Army Auxiliary Corps.
QMG	Quartermaster General. Officer responsible for stores.
Quartermaster	Officer or senior NCO responsible to a QMG.
RAMC	Royal Army Medical Corps.
ranker	Settler term for officer promoted 'from the ranks'. Usually pejorative.
RASC	Royal Army Service Corps. Unit responsible for supplies.
ration strength	Measure of the number of settlers entitled to free army food.
RAVC	Royal Army Veterinary Corps.
RE	Royal Engineers. Unit responsible for shaping the landscape for war.
regiment	Designation of an army unit, usually infantry.
regulating station	Railway station where bulk supplies and wargear were broken down and repackaged for

	onward transit. Usually located between a base and the zone.
remounts	Replacement horses and mules.
RFC	Royal Flying Corps.
RSPCA	Royal Society for the Prevention of Cruelty to Animals.
RTO	Railway Transport Officer.
Salient, the	Semicircular border area a mile or two east of Ypres and everything contained within it.
Second Ypres	'Second Battle of Ypres'. German offensive of April–May 1915 which narrowed the Salient.
settlers	Beflanders plus immigrant followers.
shrapnel	Fragmentation shell(s) designed to shred the body.
siege, the	Period lasting from autumn 1914 to spring 1918 when Befland's eastern border was more or less static.
Somme, the	(a) Region of south-eastern Befland stretching from the River Somme to Arras and centred on Amiens (b) series of Beflander offensives undertaken in the region in the second half of 1916.
star shell	Artillery flare fired at night to illuminate the zone. Star shells burned white and drifted down on a parachute.
subaltern	Junior officer, usually a 2nd Lieutenant.
Third Ypres	'Third Battle of Ypres', June 1917. Attempt by Beflanders to break out of the Salient. Sometimes called 'Passchendaele'.
Toc H	Christian association founded in Befland in 1915.
turnout	Artillery ensemble; guns, horses, mules and Beflanders.
VAD	Voluntary Aid Detachment. Unit supplying nurses, mostly female.
Verey light	Coloured signal flare fired from a pistol.

WAAC	Women's Army Auxiliary Corps.
wagon line	Stables or standings a mile or so behind the guns for an artillery unit's horses and mules.
wallah	Settler slang. Pejorative suffix attached someone involved in some task or other ('base-wallah', 'canteen-wallah').
wargear	Artefacts designed to kill, maim or disable the enemy.
YMCA	Young Men's Christian Association.
zone, the	Area around Befland's eastern borders comprising no man's land, the trenches and land immediately to the west.

GLOSSARY OF DIARISTS, CORRESPONDENTS AND MEMOIRISTS

Appleyard, S. W. (Private): Diarist; infantry. In Befland April 1915–December 1917. Promoted to Lance Corporal November 1915.Wounded on the Somme July 1916.

Blunden, E. (2nd Lieutenant): Memoirist & poet; infantry. In Befland August 1915–November 1918.

Brophy, J. (Private): Memoirist & folklorist; infantry. In Befland November 1914–1919.

Bursey, H. F. (Captain): Diarist; artillery. In 1888 aged eighteen ran away to join the army. In Befland 1916.

Campbell, C. E. (Miss): Correspondent; VAD nurse. In Befland 1918.

Capron, J. T. (Lieutenant): Diarist & memoirist; artillery. In Befland August 1916–November 1918.

Carrington, C. E. (Lieutenant): Memoirist; infantry. In Befland 1915–1918.

Cude, R. (Private): Diarist; infantry runner. In Befland 1915–1919.

D'Abernon, H. (Lady): Diarist; BRCS nurse and trained anaesthetist. In Befland 1915–1916 and 1918.

de Caux, E. G. (Maréchal-des-Logis): Memoirist; infantry. Interpreter for the Post Office Rifles. In Befland March 1915–February 1918.

Downer, L. (Mrs): Memoirist; QMAAC. Clerk at Boulogne docks October 1917–June 1919.

Durham, G. W. (Private?): Correspondent, diarist & memoirist; infantry. Born in Scotland but emigrated to Canada before 1914. In Befland 1914–1917. Refused offer of commission.

Durst, R. (Miss): Diarist; VAD nurse. In Befland September 1914–December 1919.

Eachus, S. T. (Private): Diarist; signaller at Fourth Army headquarters. In Befland May 1916–January 1919.

Edmonds, Sir J. E. (Brigadier-General): Professional soldier & staff officer. Chief architect of the 'official history' series. In Befland 1914–1918.

Foot, R. (Brigadier): Memoirist; artillery. OTC graduate from a military family. In Befland August 1914 and March 1915–1918.

Frankau, G. (Captain): Poet & editor of the *BEF Times*; artillery. In Befland 1914–late 1916. Transferred to staff duties due to stress.

Goodliff, P. E. (Miss): Correspondent; VAD at BRCS headquarter Boulogne. In Befland March 1918–March 1919.

Graves, R. (Captain): Memoirist & poet; infantry. In Befland 1915–July 1916 and briefly in 1917.

Hamilton, R. G. A. (Lieutenant-Colonel): Diarist; artillery. Professional soldier. Arrived in Befland August 1914. Killed near Amiens in March 1918.

Hiscock, E. (Lance Corporal): Memoirist; infantry. In Befland March 1918–April 1919.

Jones, D. (Private): Poet & painter; infantry. In Befland December 1915–February 1918. Invalided out with trench fever.

Kenyon, K. M. R. (Miss): Correspondent & diarist; VAD nurse. In Befland 1915–August 1918.

Leland, H. J. C. (Captain): Correspondent; infantry instructor. Arrived in Befland September 1916, left in December 1917 following a mental breakdown.

Lewis, C. (Lieutenant): Memoirist & pioneer aviator; RFC pilot. In Befland 1916–1918.

Londonderry (Lady): (Edith Vane-Tempest-Stewart), diarist, Colonel-in-Chief of the Women's Legion, visited Befland April 1919.

Luther, R. M. (Private?): Memoirist; artillery. In Befland 1914–1918.

Manning, R. B. (Miss): Diarist; VAD nurse. In Befland September 1915–1919.

Naylor, J. W. (Lieutenant): Correspondent; artillery. In Befland August 1914–November 1919. Indian Army family. Commissioned from the ranks January 1917.

Newman, W. J. (Captain): Diarist; infantry. Arrived in Befland December 1914. Left the Salient February 1915 due to ill health. Thereafter a dock administrator at Boulogne and camp administrator at Rouen and Étaples.

Orpen, W. (Major): Memoirist; society portraitist and official war artist. In Befland 1917–1919.

Partridge, E. (Private): Lexicographer; infantry. In Befland 1916.

Peterson, J. N. (Private?): Correspondent; artillery. In Befland June 1915.

Richards, F. (Private) (Francis Philip Woodruff): Memoirist; infantry. Welsh miner and professional soldier. Arrived in Befland August 1914. His memoir was published with the help of Robert Graves.

Rogers, W. A. (Private): Diarist; infantry. In Befland September 1915–August 1918.

Sassoon, S. (2nd Lieutenant): Poet & memoirist; infantry. In Befland November 1915–April 1917. Declared unfit for service after publically denouncing the War.

Schweder, R. P. (Major): Correspondent; artillery. In Befland November 1915–January 1919. Promoted from 2nd to full lieutenant, then to captain and major.

Stormont Gibbs, C. C. (Captain): Diarist; infantry. In Befland 1916.

Stringer, G. E. (Major): Correspondent, diarist & memoirist; artillery. Arrived in Befland February 1915. Left on sick leave August 1917 and invalided out January 1918.

Taylor, H. A. (Captain): Memoirist; infantry & staff. In Befland c.1916–1917(?). Returned to Befland c.1926–1927 to research a tourist guidebook.

Taylor, R. A. G. (2nd Lieutenant): Diarist; infantry. In Befland March–July 1915.

Wheatley, D. Y. (Lieutenant): Diarist & novelist; artillery. In Befland 1915–1918.

Williams, C. (Mrs): Correspondent; civilian. Passed through Befland August 1914.

Williams, J. (Private?): Diarist; labour company. In Befland March–December 1917.

Williamson, H. W. (Private & lieutenant): Naturalist & novelist; infantry & machine-gun corps. In Befland August 1914. Invalided out late 1917.

Wilson, J. M. (Miss): Memoirist; YMCA. Manager of Harfleur YMCA hut. In Befland July 1915–November 1918.

ABBREVIATIONS USED IN THE NOTES

All dates are British style (e.g., 04/05/1916 = 4 May 1916)

Archival sources

Imperial War Museum (IWM) holdings are referenced by surname only, except where another source shares the same surname, in which case initials are added. The two anonymous Beflanders are differentiated by their IWM call numbers. See List of Works Cited for full attributions.

Published sources

See List of Works Cited for full attributions.

AOS	Forbes, *A History of the Army Ordnance Services.* (*Vol. 3*) (1929)
BEFT	*BEF Times / Kemmel Times / New Church Times / Some-Times / Wipers Times or Salient News*
MO1	Edmonds, *Military Operations. France & Belgium 1915.* (*Vol. l*) (1927)
MO2	Edmonds, *Military Operations. France & Belgium 1915.* (*Vol. 2*) (1928)
MO3	Edmonds, *Military Operations. France & Belgium 1916.* (*Vol. 1*) (1932)
MO4	Edmonds, *Military Operations. France & Belgium 1916.* (*Vol. 1. Appendices*) (1932)
MO5	Edmonds, *Military Operations. France & Belgium, 1916.* (*Vol. 2. Maps & Appendices*) (1938)
MSC	Mitchell, *Medical Services. Casualties & Medical Statistics of the Great War* (1931)
MSD1	MacPherson, *Medical Services. Diseases of the War.* (*Vol. 1*) (*c.*1922)

MSD2	MacPherson, *Medical Services. Diseases of the War.* (Vol. 2) (1923)
MSG1	MacPherson, *Medical Services. General History.* (Vol. 1) (1921)
MSG2	MacPherson, *Medical Services. General History.* (Vol. 2) (1923)
MSG3	MacPherson, *Medical Services. General History.* (Vol. 3) (1924)
MSH1	MacPherson, *Medical Services. Hygiene of the War.* (Vol. 1) (1923)
MSH2	MacPherson, *Medical Services. Hygiene of the War.* (Vol. 2) (1923)
MSP	MacPherson, *Medical Services. Pathology* (1923)
MSS	MacPherson, *Medical Services. Surgery of the War.* (Vol. 1) (1922)
PE	Historical Section, *History of the Great War Based on Official Documents. Principal Events 1914–1918* (1922)
RASC	Beadon, *The Royal Army Service Corps.* (Vol. 2) (1931)
RE	Priestley, *The Work of the Royal Engineers in the European War, 1914–1919* (1921)
SME	War Office, *Statistics of the Military Effort of the British Empire During the Great War 1914–1920* (1922)
TWF1	Henniker, *Transportation on the Western Front 1914–1918* (1937)
TWF2	Henniker, *Transportation on the Western Front 1914–1918* (*Maps*) (1937)
VS	Blenkinsop, *Veterinary Services* (1925)

NOTES

Introduction

1 White, H., *The Content of the Form. Narrative Discourse and Historical Representation* (Baltimore & London: The Johns Hopkins University Press, 1987).

2 James, H., *The Sense of the Past* (London: W. Collins Sons & Co. Ltd., 1917) 47–8.

3 Hardy, T., *The Life and Work of Thomas Hardy*, ed. Michael Millgate (London & Basingstoke: Macmillan, 1984) 239.

4 Alcock, L., *Arthur's Britain. History and Archaeology AD 367–634* (Harmondsworth: Penguin, 1985) 45–6.

5 Dorfman, E., *The Narreme in the Medieval Romance Epic: An Introduction to Narrative Structures* (Toronto: University of Toronto Press, 1969); Lindqvist, S., *A History of Bombing*, trans. Linda Haverty Rugg (Granta Books: London, 2002).

6 Goode, J., *Thomas Hardy. The Offensive Truth* (Oxford: Basil Blackwell, 1988) 3.

7 Bourke, J., *An Intimate History of Killing: Face-to-Face Killing in Twentieth-Century Warfare* (London: Granta Books, 1999) 6.

8 Sewell, W. H., *Logics of History: Social Theory and Social Transformation* (Chicago & London: University of Chicago Press, 2005) 260.

9 Ricœur, P., *Memory, History, Forgetting*, trans. K. Blamey & D. Pellauer (Chicago: University of Chicago Press, 2004) 497.

10 Scott, J. W., 'The Evidence of Experience', *Critical Inquiry* (vol. 17, no. 4, 1991) 775–7, 779, 796.

11 *SME*, 739, 742.

Annals and Stories

1 Richardson, E. H., *British War Dogs. Their Training and Psychology* (London: Skeffington & Son, 1920) 52–4.

2 Leland, 25/11/1916.

3 'The Dogs of Battle and Dogs of Mercy', *Vanity Fair* (September 1916) 76–7, <http://www.oldmagazinearticles.com/WW1_dogs_pdf> n.p.

4 *RE*, 221–3.

5 Evans, G., 'British War Dogs in the Great War', <http://freespace.virgin.net/ sh.k/wardogs.html> n.p.; Richardson, *British War Dogs*, 52–4.

6 *RE*, 223.

7 Morgan, T., 'World War 1 Trench Dogs', <http://www.roll-of-honour.com/ Bedfordshire/wardogs.html> n.p.; *RE*, 222–3; Richardson, *British War Dogs*, 88–90.

8 *VS*, 545–6.

9 *SME*, 187–8.

10 Durham, 22/11/1916.

11 Williams, C., 03/12/1914.

12 *MO3*, 66–7, 99; *MSC*, table 1/2–3, table 2/4–5; *SME*, 195, 197.

13 *MSC*, tables 1, 12; *PE*, part I; *SME*, 639–41.

14 Richards, F., *Old Soldiers Never Die* (London: Faber & Faber, 1964) 13.

15 *AOS*, 7–14, 26.

16 *TWF1*, ix–xii, xxi–xxii, 398.

17 *MO3*, 273.

18 *AOS*, 49; Grieves, K., 'The Transport Mission to GHQ, 1916', in Brian Bond, et al., eds., *Look to Your Front: Studies in the First World War by the British Commission for Military History* (Staplehurst: Spellmount, 1999) 66; *TWF1*, 136–7, 161, 242, 244.

19 *MO3*, 98, 277; Grieves, 'Transport Mission', 63–4; *TWF1*, xiii, 182, 243.

20 Grieves, 'Transport Mission', 64, 73; *TWF1*, xiii–xv, xxiii, 204.

21 *TWF1*, xv.

22 *MO3*, 83, 84n, 128–9, 132; *MSG2*, 69–70; *MSG3*, 33.

23 *MO3*, 279; *MSG2*, 138.

24 Rogers, 06/09/1915.

25 Cude, 03/05/1916.

26 Stringer, 01/02/1917.

27 Orpen, Sir W., *An Onlooker in France, 1917–1919* (London: Williams & Norgate, 1921) 16, 18, 25.

28 *AOS*, 7–14, 26, 30; *RASC*, 120.

29 *AOS*, 31–2, 90–1, 100–3; *MO3*, 95, 97–8, 114, 128–31; Gill, D. & Dallas, G., *The Unknown Army* (London: Verso, 1985) 89; *MSG2*, 142–3; *MSH1*, 321–2; *RASC*, 91, 93–4, 98–9, 104, 107, 109, 113–14; *TWF1*, 75, 93, 103–6, 187; *VS*, 19.

30 *AOS*, 90–1, 99n; *MO3*, 96, 99, 103–4, 106; *MSG2*, 65, 68–71, 84–6, 136–7; *MSG3*, 48–9; *RASC*, 87–8, 89n; *SME*, 580.

31 *MO3*, 133–4.

32 Wilson, J. M., 7.

33 Stringer, 20/09/1916.

34 Schweder, 01/12/1915, 04/12/1915.

35 Durham, 04/02/1916.

36 de Caux, 1.

37 Wilson, J. M., 69.

38 Gill & Dallas, *Unknown Army*, 102–3.

39 Hamilton, R. G. A., *The War Diary of the Master of Belhaven 1914–1918* (London: John Murray, 1924) 16–17.

40 Stringer, 15/02/1915.

41 Londonderry, 03/04/1919.

42 Benjamin, W., 'One-Way Street', in Hannah Arendt, ed., *One-Way Street and Other Writings* (London: NLB, 1979) 78.

43 Hardy, T., *The Life and Work of Thomas Hardy*, ed. Michael Millgate (London & Basingstoke: Macmillan, 1984) 191, italics in the original.

44 Blunden, E., 'Premature Rejoicing', in Edmund Blunden, *Overtones of War: Poems of the First World War*, ed. Martin Taylor (London: Duckworth, 1996) 98.

45 Capron, 26.

46 Grieves, K., 'The Propinquity of Place: Home, Landscape and Soldier Poets of the First World War', in Jessica Meyer, ed., *British Popular Culture and the First World War* (Leiden and Boston: Brill, 2008) 19–46.

47 Schiller, F., 'On the Sublime', trans. William F. Wertz, Jr. (The Schiller Institute, 2001), <http://www.schillerinstitute.org/transl/trans_on_sublime.html> n.p.

48 Stringer, 102.

49 Frankau, G., *The Poetical Works of Gilbert Frankau* (Vol. 2) (London: Chatto & Windus, 1923) 12.

50 Stringer, 24.

51 *VS*, 504–6.

52 *VS*, 504, 506–7, 643.

53 *SME*, 396.

54 *VS*, 62, 450, 452–4, 456–7, 459, 466–7, 473–4, 479, 482–3, 501.

55 Hamilton, *Diary*, 34.

56 Leland, 31/10/1917.

57 Foot, 72–3.

58 Kenyon, 19/06/1915, 20/06/1915.

59 Durst, 15/12/1915, 25/03/1918.

60 Goodliff, 06/04/1918.

61 Eachus, 03/07/1916, 26/09/1916, 10/10/1916, 04/12/1916.

62 Stringer, 22/03/1915.

63 Carrington, C. E., *The War Record of the 1/5th Battalion the Royal Warwickshire Regiment* (Birmingham: Cornish Brothers Ltd., 1922) 9.

64 Stringer, 13/05/1915.

65 Stringer, 25/09/1916, 01/02/1917.

66 Durham, 01/03/1915.

67 Cude, 25/12/1917.

68 Orpen, *Onlooker*, 33.

69 Williams, J., 11/07/1917.

70 Luther, 17.

71 de Caux, 36, 45.

72 Schweder, 25/12/1915, 12/03/1916, 10/02/1917, 18/10/1917.

73 Luther, 13.

74 Durham, 01/03/1915, 02/04/1915.

75 Stringer, 15/07/1915.

76 Schweder, 03/03/1917, 08/07/1918.

77 Stringer, 86–7, 21/04/1917.

78 Orpen, *Onlooker*, 31.

79 *SME*, 639.

80 Carrington, C. E., *Soldier From the Wars Returning* (Aldershot: Gregg Revivals in association with Department of War Studies, Kings College, London, 1965) 80–3.

81 de Caux, 1, 6–8.

82 de Caux, 17–18, 20.

83 Stringer, 19/04/1917.

84 Stringer, 27/06/1917.

85 Foot, 37–8.

86 Stringer, 27/05/1917.

87 Stringer, 28/05/1917.

88 Jünger, E., *Copse 125. A Chronicle of the Trench Warfare of 1918*, trans. Basil Creighton (London: Chatto & Windus, 1930) 263–4.

89 de Certeau, M., *The Practice of Everyday Life*, trans. Stephen F. Rendall (London: University of California Press, 2011) 92.

90 Stringer, 05/06/1917.

91 Taylor, 29/03/1915.

92 Luther, 22–3.

93 Capron, 5.

94 Schweder, 19/05/1916.

95 Capron, 33.

96 Capron, 4–5; Durham, 14/07/1916, 11/01/1917; *MO3*, 123–4.

97 Wilson, R. J., *Landscapes of the Western Front. Materiality During the Great War* (New York & Abingdon: Routledge, 2012) 114.

98 Stringer, 20/03/1917.

99 Taylor, 04/04/1915.

100 Hamilton, *Diary*, 87–8.

101 Gibson, C. K., 'Sex and Soldiering in France and Flanders: the British Expeditionary Force along the Western Front, 1914–1919', *International History Review* (vol. xxiii, no. 3, September 2001) 543.

102 Wilson, J. M., 16.

103 Appleyard, 15/05/1915.

104 Hamilton, *Diary*, 130.

105 Schweder, 13/08/1916, 22/10/1918.

106 Stringer, 83, 24/06/1915.

107 Leland, 23/10/1916.

108 Stringer, 15/04/1915.

109 de Caux, 2.

110 Schweder, 22/03/1916.

111 Durham, 07/05/1916.

112 Leland, 17/03/1917, 04/05/1917, 14/05/1917.

113 Stringer, 22/03/1917, 24/05/1917.

114 Williams, J., 21/05/1917.

115 Schweder, 29/04/1917, 11/05/1917, 14/05/1917, 10/03/1918, 14/03/1918.

116 Durham, 26/04/1915.

117 Cude, 25/03/1917.

118 Richards, *Old Soldiers*, 148–9.

119 Schweder, 29/01/1916, 06/02/1916, 21/02/1916.

120 Stringer, 25.

121 Gibson, C. K., 'The British Army, French Farmers and the War on the Western Front 1914–1918', *Past & Present* (no. 180, August 2003) 179–80.

122 Schweder, 02/05/1917, 07/05/1917, 09/05/1917, 17/03/1918, 24/06/1918, 01/07/1918.

123 Newman, 26/04/1915, 03/05/1915, 12/06/1915, 02/10/1915, 11/10/1915.

124 Cude, 28/07/1915.

125 *AOS*, 7–14, 26, 44, 90–1; *MO3*, 95; *RASC*, 87–8, 120; *TWF1*, xii, 93, 103–6.

126 *MO3*, 83, 84n, 96, 277; *MSH1*, 317–21.

127 *SME*, 580–1.

128 *MO3*, 95–6, 99, 103–4, 106, 271; *MSG2*, 65, 68–9, 71, 84–6, 136–7; *MSG3*, 48–9; *RASC*, 87–8, 89n; *SME*, 580; *TWF1*, xii, 103–6.

129 Downer, n.d./n.p.

130 Taylor, 12/05/1915, 28/05/1915.

131 Stringer, 102.

132 Schweder, 29/11/1915.

133 Williamson, H., *A Patriot's Progress* (London: Geoffrey Bles, 1930) 184.

134 Leland, 31/10/1917.

135 Stringer, 13/05/1917.

136 Schweder, 31/08/1917.

137 Capron, 40, 46–7.

138 *MSH1*, 7, 204–5, 185–212, 213–15, 218–19.

139 Hamilton, *Diary*, 110.

140 Carrington, *Soldier*, 127.

141 Foot, 80–1.

142 Schweder, 16/07/1916.

143 Hamilton, *Diary*, 80–1; Luther, 36; Schweder, 25/01/1917; Williamson, *Patriot's Progress*, 106.

144 *MSD2*, 425.

145 Brophy, J., 'The Soldier's Nostrils', in Conal O'Riordan, ed., *A Martial Medley: Fact and Fiction* (London: Eric Partridge at The Scholartis Press, 1931) 123–6.

146 Appleyard, 13/05/1915.

147 Stringer, 22/09/1916.

148 Schweder, 19/07/1916, 21/07/1916.

149 Richards, *Old Soldiers*, 12–13.

150 Eachus, 26/06/1916, 24/10/1916.

151 Schweder, 03/01/1917.

152 *RASC*, 90, 121.

153 *TWF1*, 85, 171–2.

154 Peterson, 03/06/1915.

155 *VS*, 56, 58, 482.

156 Blythe, R., *Akenfield: Portrait of an English Village* (London: Allen Lane The Penguin Press, 1969) 55.

157 *VS*, 516.

158 *VS*, 64–5.

159 *SME*, table (i) (a–d) 400–3.

160 *MSC*, tables 1–2/2–5; *SME*, 195, 197.

161 Brown, M., *The Imperial War Museum Book of the Somme* (London: Sidgwick & Jackson in association with the Imperial War Museum, 1996) 5; Carrington, *Soldier*, 80–3; *MO2*, 87, 87n; *MO3*, 19–20, 122; *MSC*, table 1, 12; *MSG2*, 343–4; *SME*, 639–41.

162 Rogers, 12/09/1915.

163 *MO2*, 113; *TWF1*, 84.

164 *MO3*, 247–8.

165 *MO3*, 246–7.

166 *MO3*, 247.

167 *MO3*, sketch 4 f73, 286.

168 Goode, J., *Thomas Hardy. The Offensive Truth* (Oxford: Basil Blackwell, 1988) 152–3.

169 Rogers, 13/09/1915.

170 Richards, *Old Soldiers*, 83.

171 Hamilton, *Diary*, 33.

172 de Caux, 9.

173 Gibson, 'British Army, French Farmers', 207–10.

174 Appleyard, 10/07/1915.

175 Schweder, 17/01/1917, 25/04/1917.

176 Schweder, 26/11/1918, 18/12/1918.

177 Foot, 113.

178 de Caux, 17.

179 Wilson, *Landscapes*, 106 fig. 4.6.

180 Cude, 27/04/1917.

181 *MSG3*, 30.

182 Stringer, 76.

183 Richards, *Old Soldiers*, 34; *SME*, table (vi) (a–b) 648–9.

184 Gibson, C. K., '"My Chief Source of Worry": an Assistant Provost Marshal's View of Relations between 2nd Canadian Division and Local Inhabitants on the Western Front, 1915–1917', *War in History* (vol. 7, no. 4, 2000) 435–6.

185 Schweder, 11/07/1918, 12/12/1918.

186 Brophy, J. & Partridge, E., *Dictionary of Tommies' Songs and Slang, 1914–1918* (Frontline Books: London, 2008) 169.

187 Orpen, *Onlooker*, 38.

188 Leland, 06/05/1917, 08/05/1917.

189 Durst, 16/09/1915, 06/08/1916, 22/07/1917.

190 Goodliff, 11/03/1918, 30/03/1918, 06/04/1918, 09/08/1918, 29/08/1918.

191 Goodliff, 11/03/1918.

192 Durst, 26/08/1915, 22/09/1917.

193 Wilson, J. M., 70–1.

194 *MO3*, 143–4, 57–154 passim.

195 de Caux, 7.

196 *MO3*, 144.

197 *MO3*, 108–10, 139–40, 140n, 141.

198 Schweder, 14/05/1917.

199 Wilson, J. M., 7, 19.

200 Newman, 09/11/1915, 16/11/1915.

201 *AOS*, 7–14, 26; *MO3*, 83, 84n, 95–6, 98–9; *RASC*, 87–8, 94, 98–9; *TWF1*, 75, 93, 103–6, 187.

202   Anon., box misc. 221(3180), 1, 16.

203   Anon., box misc. 221(3180), 10.

204   *AOS*, 31; *MO3*, 95–7, 99; *RASC*, 91, 104, 107, 109; *VS*, 19.

205   *MO3*, 95, 106; *MSG1*, 110; *MSG2*, 65, 68–71, 84–6, 136–7; *MSG3*, 48–9.

206   Durham, 07/05/1915.

207   Hamilton, *Diary*, 109–10.

208   Capron, 6, 22, 26, 31, 36.

209   Hamilton, *Diary*, 233.

210   Foot, 103.

211   *BEFT* (12/02/1916).

212   Schweder, 03/09/1916.

213   Jones, D., *In Parenthesis: seinnyessit e gledyf ym penn mammeu* (London: Faber & Faber, 1978) 24.

214   Stringer, 12/05/1917.

215   Foot, 92.

216   Hamilton, *Diary*, 203.

217   Capron, 44–5.

218   Foot, 80–2.

219   Schweder, 22/04/1916, 03/07/1916.

220   *MO3*, 302; *MO5*, 106.

221   Schweder, 08/03/1917, 23/04/1917.

222   Hamilton, *Diary*, 20–1.

223   Leland, 29/09/1916, 10/10/1916, 14/10/1916.

224   Capron, 12.

225   Hamilton, *Diary*, 72; *MO3*, 70–1, 89n.

226   Schweder, 03/09/1916.

227   Pegum, J., 'The Old Front Line: Returning to the Battlefields in the Writings of Ex-Servicemen', in Meyer, ed., *British Popular Culture*, 230; Taylor, H. A., *Good-Bye to the Battlefield: To-Day and Yesterday on the Western Front* (London: Stanley Paul & Co. Ltd., 1930) 51.

228   *VS*, 450–1.

229   *VS*, 478, 468–89.

230   *VS*, 451–5, 463, 468, 470, 472–3, 478, 491–3.

231   *VS*, 65–6, 476–7, 643.

232   Luther, 8.

233   *VS*, 564, 660–1, 672.

234   Foot, 20–7, 34–6.

235   Luther, 9–10.

236   Schweder, 04/12/1915.

237   *MO3*, 37–8.

238 Luther, 19.

239 Eachus, 18/04/1917.

240 Hamilton, *Diary*, 303–4.

241 Groom, W., *A Storm in Flanders: The Ypres Salient, 1914–1918; Tragedy and Triumph on the Western Front* (New York: Atlantic Monthly Press, 2002) 167.

242 Schweder, 02/07/1916.

243 Bursey, 02/07/1916.

244 Hamilton, *Diary*, 268.

245 Leland, 01/02/1917.

246 Foot, 92.

247 Foot, 107.

248 Londonderry, 03/04/1919.

249 Schweder, 13/12/1915.

250 Eachus, 07/06/1916.

251 *AOS*, 27, 90–1, 93, 104, 107, 109–11, 113–14; *MO3*, 98; *MSG3*, 48–9.

252 *MO3*, 95–6, 98–9, 106, 114, 116; *MSG2*, 54, 68–9, 71, 136–7, 160; *MSH1*, 317–21; *RASC*, 87–8; *TWF1*, 93, 103–6, 217, 392; *VS*, 19, 102–3.

253 *MO3*, 20, 20n, 72, 77, 94–5, 151–2; *SME*, 195, 197.

254 *MO3*, 95.

255 *MO3*, 18–19, 25–7, 32, 38–9, 102–3; *MSG2*, 342.

256 *MO3*, 95n; *MSC*, table 1/2–3, table 2/4–5, table 1/12, tables 1–2/148.

257 *MO3*, 153–4.

258 *BEFT* (12/02/1916, 20/03/1916).

259 Naylor, 11/05/1917.

260 Benjamin, W., 'The Storyteller: Reflections on the Works of Nikolai Leskov', in Hannah Arendt, ed., *Walter Benjamin. Illuminations: Essays and Reflections* (New York: Schocken Books, 1968) 84.

261 *BEFT* (26/02/1916).

262 *BEFT* (06/03/1916–25/12/1916).

263 Eachus, 03/04/1917.

264 Schweder, 01/05/1917.

265 Carrington, *Soldier*, 163–5.

266 Wheatley, n.d./n.p.

267 Hiscock, E., *The Bells of Hell Go Ting-a-Ling-a-Ling: An Autobiographical Fragment Without Maps* (London: Arlington Books, 1976) 75–7.

268 Wilson, *Landscapes*, 75.

269 Carrington, *Soldier*, 167.

270 Gibson, 'Sex & Soldiering', 536, 541, 563–6.

271 Schweder, 15/07/1918.

272 Wilson, J. M., 28.

273 Hamilton, *Diary*, 157, 353.

274 Fussell, P., *The Great War and Modern Memory* (London: Oxford University Press, 1975), 51–64.

275 Wheatley, 29/05/1917.

276 *MSD2*, 273, 279, 425; *MSS*, 584.

277 Carrington, *Soldier*, 5; Foot, 49; Hamilton, *Diary*, 185.

278 Leed, E. J., *No Man's Land: Combat and Identity in World War I* (Cambridge: Cambridge University Press, 1979) 121.

279 *MO3*, 37.

280 Schweder, 01/01/1916.

281 *MO3*, 69, 286.

282 Lewis, C., *Sagittarius Rising* (London: Greenhill Books, 1993) 81–2.

283 Eachus, 17/06/1916.

284 Bursey, 04/07/1916.

285 Bursey, 07/07/1916.

286 Hamilton, *Diary*, 245–6.

287 Stringer, 07/11/1916.

288 Leland, 24/12/1916.

289 Winter, J. M. & Prost, A., *The Great War in History: Debates and Controversies, 1914 to the Present* (Cambridge: Cambridge University Press, 2005) 26–7.

290 Marcuse, H., *Negations: Essays in Critical Theory*, trans. Jeremy J. Shapiro (Harmondsworth: Penguin University Books, 1972) xiii; *One Dimensional Man: The Ideology of Industrial Society* (London: Sphere Books, 1968) ch. 1.

291 Berman, M., *All That Is Solid Melts Into Air: The Experience of Modernity* (London & New York: Verso, 1983) 99–105.

292 Engels, F., *Ludwig Feuerbach and the End of Classical German Philosophy* (London: Union Books, 2009) part 2: Materialism.

293 Schweder, 17/03/1916, 27/05/1916.

294 Carrington, *Soldier*, 87.

295 Wilson, *Landscapes*, 94–5.

296 *MO3*, 248.

297 Capron, 21.

298 Gliddon, G., *When the Barrage Lifts. A Topographical History of the Battle of the Somme 1916* (Stroud: Alan Sutton, 1994) 293.

299 Capron, 43–4.

300 Schweder, 09/04/1917.

301 Hamilton, *Diary*, 184–5.

302 Orpen, *Onlooker*, 40.

303 Hamilton, *Diary*, 235.

304 Orpen, *Onlooker*, 36.

305 Masefield, J., *The Battle of the Somme* (London: Heinemann, 1919) 71.

306 Hamilton, *Diary*, 397.

307 de Caux, 35.

308 Williamson, *Patriot's Progress*, 48.

309 Hamilton, *Diary*, 224, 238.

310 de Caux, 3.

311 Hamilton, *Diary*, 303–4.

312 Londonderry, 03/04/1919.

313 Kenyon, 13/06/1918.

314 Lewis, *Sagittarius*, 67, 90–1.

315 Lewis, *Sagittarius*, 90–1.

316 Benjamin, 'One-Way Street', 50.

317 Lewis, *Sagittarius*, 56–7, 138, 251.

318 Schweder, 10/05/1917.

319 Schweder, 16/05/1916, 19/05/1916.

320 Brown, *Imperial War Museum*, 7.

321 Williamson, *Patriot's Progress*, 93.

322 Carrington, *Soldier*, 165.

323 Cude, 17/10/1916.

324 *MSG3*, 33.

325 Orpen, *Onlooker*, 37.

326 Girling, n.p.

327 Luther, 29.

328 Richards, *Old Soldiers*, 105–6.

329 Foot, 71.

330 Illouz, E., *Consuming the Romantic Utopia: Love and the Cultural Contradictions of Capitalism* (Berkeley: University of California Press, 1997) 143.

331 Williamson, *Patriot's Progress*, 38–9.

332 Hamilton, *Diary*, 167–8.

333 Eachus, 04/06/1916.

334 Schweder, 15/07/1917.

335 *MO3*, 7n.

336 *MSG1*, 114; *MSG2*, 93; 114; *MSH1*, 327; *SME*, table (iv) (b) 615.

337 *MSG1*, 110; *TWF1*, xviii, 103; *SME*, table (i) 510, table (iii) 613, table (iv) (b) 615.

338 Stringer, 18/09/1916.

339 Foot, 71–2.

340 Stringer, 22/02/1915.

341 Appleyard, 05/05/1915, 10/05/1915.

342 Newman, 06/07/1915.

343 Hamilton, *Diary*, 167–8.

344 Capron, 24.

345 Fussell, *Great War*, 64–9.

346 Schweder, 01/02/1918.

347 Luther, 29.

348 Schweder, 11/05/1916; 12/07/1916.

349 Eachus, 05/06/1916, 03/01/1917.

350 Foot, 72.

351 *TWF1*, 114–15.

352 Appleyard, 13/05/1915; Schweder, 07/12/1916.

353 Capron, 4.

354 Stringer, 21/09/1916, 24/09/1916, 30/11/1916, 25/12/1916, 02/03/1917.

355 de Certeau, *Practice*, 111–12.

356 Foot, 60.

357 Stringer, 23/09/1916.

358 Capron, 24.

359 Hamilton, *Diary*, 128, 281.

360 Eachus, 07/06/1916.

361 Eachus, 06/06/1916.

362 Peterson, 03/06/1915.

363 *AOS*, 29n; *TWF1*, 102.

364 Durham, 21/02/1915.

365 *TWF1*, sketch 7 f92, sketch 8 f93.

366 *MO3*, 274; *MO4*, 91–124; Hamilton, *Diary*, 171; *TWF1*, 123, 155.

367 *TWF1*, xix.

368 *TWF1*, xiii; *TWF2*, map 6; *SME*, table (iv) (a) 614, 740, 742.

369 *SME*, table (iii) 613.

370 *TWF1*, 174n.

371 Grieves, 'Transport Mission', 66–7.

372 Ashworth, T., *Trench Warfare: The Live and Let Live System 1914–1918* (London: Macmillan, 1980).

373 Schweder, 26/02/1916, 27/02/1916, 28/02/1916.

374 Schweder, 01/03/1916, 04/03/1916.

375 Schweder, 08/06/1916.

376 Eachus, 19/06/1916.

377 Capron, 42.

378 Richards, *Old Soldiers*, 170–1.

379 Stringer, 23/04/1915, 01/01/1917.

380 Leland, 17/11/1917.

381 Dunn, J. C., *The War the Infantry Knew 1914–1919* (London: Jane's, 1987) 64.

382 Leland, 03/10/1916.

383 Schweder, 22/05/1916, 23/04/1917, 29/04/1917.

384 Carrington, *Soldier*, 135.

385 Durham, 14/10/1916.

386 Eachus, 19/06/1916.

387 Schama, S., *Dead Certainties (Unwarranted Speculations)* (New York: Alfred A. Knopf, 1991) 320.

388 Stringer, 19/04/1915; 11/04/1917.

389 Schweder, 09/03/1916, 03/09/1917, 15/09/1917, 13/12/1918.

390 Eachus, 21/06/1916.

391 Appleyard, 2nii; Spagnoly, T., *Salient Points: Cameos of the Western Front, Ypres Sector 1914–1918* (London: Leo Cooper, 1995) 1.

392 Stringer, 30/11/1916, 22/12/1916.

393 Brophy & Partridge, *Dictionary*, passim; Partridge, E., 'Byways of Soldiers' Slang', in O'Riordan, ed., *Martial Medley*, 127–33.

394 *TWF1*, passim.

395 Chasseaud, P., *Rats Alley. Trench Names on the Western Front, 1914–1918* (Stroud: Spellmount, 2006) 230–416.

396 Wilson, *Landscapes*, 168.

397 *MSG3*, 18.

398 Chasseaud, *Rats Alley*, part 1.

399 Wilson, *Landscapes*, 104.

400 Brophy & Partridge, *Dictionary*, 130, 147; Foot, 3; *MO1*, 7n; *MO3*, 80, 80n.

401 Wilson, *Landscapes*, 183–4.

402 Appleyard, 27/10/1915.

403 Appleyard, 11/06/1915; Brophy & Partridge, *Dictionary*, 85, 122, 138, 196, 204; *MO3*, 61–2, 122–3; Foot, 33; Hamilton, *Diary*, 130; *MSD2*, 426; *MSS*, 15; Wilson, *Landscapes*, 209.

404 Bursey, 22/06/1916.

405 *VS*, 506, 675.

406 Pfungst, O., *Clever Hans. The Horse of Mr. von Osten*, ed. Robert Rosenthal (New York: Holt, Rinehart and Winston, 1965) 240–1; Wynne, C. D. L., *Animal Cognition. The Mental Lives of Animals* (Houndmills: Palgrave, 2001) 11.

407 Baker, J. A., *The Peregrine* (New York: The New York Review of Books, 2005) 95.

408 Carrington, *Soldier*, 27–8; *VS*, 549.

409 Stringer, 03/02/1917.

410 *VS*, 67, 548, 660.

411 Bursey, 29/06/1016.

412 *MO3*, 193n; *MSG2*, 344.

413 Wilson, *Landscapes*, 62.

414 Carrington, *Soldier*, 100–5.

415 Brown, *Imperial War Museum*, 9; Carrington, *Soldier*, 30–5.

416 Carrington, *Soldier*, 21–2, 36, 39–40.

417 Brophy & Partridge, *Dictionary*, 11.

418 Gill & Dallas, *Unknown Army*, 62.

419 Carrington, *Soldier*, 100–5; Foot, 1–7.

420 Brophy & Partridge, *Dictionary*, 17.

421 Foot, 8–9, 89.

422 Masefield, *Somme*, 11.

423 *MSH1*, 24, 304, 309–15; *MSH2*, 128–31; *MSS*, 26.

424 Stringer, 92.

425 Carrington, *Soldier*, 94; Foot, 74; *MO3*, 115–16n, 150.

426 *MSH1*, 304, 309–15.

427 Naylor, 10/01/1918.

428 Hamilton, *Diary*, 466.

429 *MSH1*, 9.

430 *TWF1*, 169.

431 Tynan, J., 'Tailoring in the Trenches: The Making of First World War British Army Uniform', in Meyer, ed., *British Popular Culture*, 79; Watson, J. S. K., *Fighting Different Wars: Experience, Memory and the First World War in Britain* (Cambridge: Cambridge University Press, 2004) 23.

432 Sassoon, S., *Memoirs of a Fox-Hunting Man* (London: Faber & Faber, 1954) 285.

433 de Caux, 31.

434 Foot, 30–1.

435 Bursey, 12/07/1916, 19/07/1916.

436 *VS*, 87.

437 Stringer, 12/03/1917.

438 Capron, 13.

439 *MO3*, 107; *VS*, 89, 91, 515, 549, 570–3, 637–9.

440 *MO3*, 95–6, 107; *VS*, 17, 56, 58, 62, 99, 105, 547, 563, 565–6, 570–3, 591, 629, 685; *SME*, 864.

441 Eachus, 22/07/1916.

442 Durham, 23/07/1916.

443 Stringer, 72, 08/06/1915, 11/08/1915.

444 Stringer, 19/06/1917, 13/07/1917.

445 de Caux, 6–8.

446 Capron, 12.

447 Leland, 13/06/1917.

448 Orpen, *Onlooker*, 36.

449 Masefield, *Somme*, 72–3, 77–8.

450 Eachus, 25/08/1916.

451 Cude, 11/11/1918.

452 Foot, 105.

453 Cude, 11/11/1918.

454 Cude, 24/02/1919.

455 Gill & Dallas, *Unknown Army*, 100–1.

456 *AOS*, 183–4; *SME*, table (i) (a–f) 405–7.

457 *SME*, 376.

458 *MSG3*, 325.

459 Schweder, 11/01/1919, 17/01/1919, 20/01/1919, 27/01/1919.

460 Higbee, D., 'Practical Memory: Organized Veterans and the Politics of Commemoration', in Meyer, ed., *British Popular Culture*, 200, 202.

461 Orpen, *Onlooker*, 96–7.

462 *TWF1*, 157–8.

463 *MSG3*, 14, chart f14.

464 *SME*, 640–1.

465 Richards, *Old Soldiers*, 138.

466 de Caux, 17.

467 Gibson, 'British Army, French Farmers', 179.

468 Schweder, 24/10/1918.

469 *MSG3*, 202, 229; *MSH1*, 281–3.

470 Foot, 121–2.

471 Schweder, 03/03/1917.

472 Durham, 02/05/1916.

473 Hamilton, *Diary*, 168–9.

474 *MO3*, 271.

475 Luther, 26.

476 Foot, 59, 62.

477 Capron, 40.

478 Wilson, *Landscapes*, 68.

479 Luther, 45.

480 Cude, 01/07/1916.

481 de Caux, 25.

482 Eachus, 13/09/1916.

483 *MO3*, 273–4; *TWF1*, 120, 125.

484 *MO3*, 273–4, 275n; *TWF1*, 120, 128; *TWF2*, maps 4–5.

485 *MO3*, 273–4, 275n, 279–80, 282; *MSG3*, map f233; *TWF1*, xii–xiii, 120, 125; *TWF2*, map 4.

486 *TWF1*, xii–xiii, xvii, 120, 126–7, 134, 138.

487 *TWF1*, 372–3.

488 *MO3*, 247–8, 271–3, sketch f271, 275; *TWF1*, xvii, 120.

489 Carrington, *Soldier*, 127.

490 Orpen, *Onlooker*, 19.

491 Ricœur, P., *Memory, History, Forgetting*, trans. K. Blamey & D Pellauer (Chicago: Chicago University Press, 2004) 148.

492 *TWF1*, 125.

493 Blunden, E., *Undertones of War* (Collins: London, 1965) 11–12.

494 Weinrich, H., *Lethe. The Art and Critique of Forgetting*, trans. Stephen F. Rendall (Ithaca & London: Cornell University Press, 2004) 9–10.

495 de Caux, 30.

496 Durham, 04/05/1916.

497 *VS*, 703 appendix B.

498 Appleyard, 18/09/1915.

499 Foot, 73.

500 Goodliff, 18/12/1918.

501 Gibson, 'British Army, French Farmers', 195; Richards, *Old Soldiers*, 27.

502 Foot, 39.

503 Durham, 22/04/1915.

504 Richards, *Old Soldiers*, 56.

505 Carrington, *Soldier*, 184.

506 Luther, 31.

507 Cude, 03/11/1917.

508 Wilson, J. M., 64–6.

509 Durham, 22/11/1916.

510 Thierens, M., ed., '7th Canadian Infantry Brigade. War Diaries 1915–1919. 3: 1917', <http://www.cefresearch.com/matrix/War%20Diaries/transcribed/.../bde7y1917.pdf> (2008) 6–7.

511 Hynes, S., *The Soldier's Tale: Bearing Witness to Modern War* (London: Pimlico, 1998) xii–xiii.

512 Hynes, *Soldier's Tale*, 14.

513 *BEFT* (01/12/1916).

514 Schweder, 02/04/1916.

515 von Clausewitz, C., *On War*, trans. James John Graham (London: N. Trübner, 1873) book V ch. 2.

516 Fussell, *Great War*, 64–9.

517 Keegan, J., *The Face of Battle* (London: Jonathan Cape, 1977) ch. 2.

518 Durham, 04/05/1916.

519 Keegan, *Face*, chs. 2–3.

520 Swinton, E. D., 'The Point of View', in *The Green Curve and Other Stories* (New York: Doubleday, Page & Co., 1914) 253–4.

521 Carrington, *Soldier*, 24.

522 *MO3*, vn; *PE*, Part I.

523 Natter, W. G., *Literature at War, 1914–1940: Representing the 'Time of Greatness' in Germany* (New Haven and London: Yale University Press, 1999) 5.

524 Lowenthal, D., *The Heritage Crusade and the Spoils of History* (Cambridge: Cambridge University Press, 1998) 106.

525 Marx, K., *Grundrisse*, trans. Martin Nicolaus (Harmondsworth: Penguin, 1973) 101.

526 Stringer, 04/12/1916.

527 *The Battle of the Somme – Viewing Guide* (Lambeth: Imperial War Museum Film & Video Archive, n.d.) 3; Orpen, *Onlooker*, 30.

528 Taylor, 23/03/1915, 25/03/1915, 09/06/1915.

529 Carrington, *Soldier*, 126.

530 Schweder, 24/09/1917, 25/09/1917.

531 Schweder, 03/01/1917, 20/02/1917, 14/06/1918, 20/06/1918, 09/01/1919.

532 Schweder, 27/10/1916.

533 Luther, 26–7.

534 Stringer, 65–6.

535 Bursey, 14/09/1916.

536 Capron, 32.

537 de Caux, 48–9.

538 Stringer, 04/01/1917.

539 Wilson, *Landscapes*, 187–8.

540 Schweder, 21/04/1916, 22/04/1916, 09/05/1917, 22/04/1918.

541 Foot, 64.

542 Stringer, 69–70.

543 Hamilton, *Diary*, 427; *MO3*, 131.

544 Eachus, 16/08/1916.

545 *TWF1*, xiv.

546 Carrington, *Soldier*, 93.

547 Richards, *Old Soldiers*, 109.

548 Capron, 44.

549 Schweder, 16/09/1916.

550 Stringer, 20/04/1917.

551 Schweder, 16/01/1917.

552 Richards, *Old Soldiers*, 39.

553 Eachus, 23/09/1916.

554 Richards, *Old Soldiers*, 14.

555 Carrington, *Soldier*, 163, 167.

556 Gibson, 'Sex & Soldiering', 545.

557 Schweder, 22/12/1915.

558 *BEFT* (22/05/1916, 03/07/1916).

559 Orpen, *Onlooker*, 91.

560 Luther, 43–4.

561 *MSD2*, 124.

562 Stringer, 08/03/1915, 19/01/1917.

563 Stringer, 24/03/1917.

564 Eachus, 03/04/1917.

565 Stormont Gibbs, C. C., *From the Somme to the Armistice. The Memoirs of Captain Stormont Gibbs, MC*, ed. Richard Devonald-Lewis (London: William Kimber, 1986) 87n19.

566 Clout, H., *After the Rains: Restoring the Countryside of Northern France After the Great War* (Exeter: Exeter University Press, 1996) 263.

567 *1916: The Somme* (Maidenhead: Commonwealth War Graves Commission, n.d.) 2–3, 14.

568 Schweder, 24/01/1917.

569 *MO3*, 70–1; *RE*, 90–1, 222.

570 *RE*, 142–3, 221–2, 241, 264–6.

571 *RE*, 90–1.

572 *RE*, 90–1, 138, 142, 247, 278.

573 *RE*, 53–4, 91, 223.

574 *BEFT* (12/02/1916, 20/03/1916); *RE*, 90.

575 Eachus, 23/02/1917.

576 Carrington, *Soldier*, 164; Orpen, *Onlooker*, 16–17.

577 Lewis, *Sagittarius*, 74–5.

578 Orpen, *Onlooker*, 82, 150.

579 Brophy & Partridge, *Dictionary*, 49–51.

580 Richards, *Old Soldiers*, 119.

581 Durham, 02/04/1915.

582 Williamson, *Patriot's Progress*, 142–4.

583 *BEFT* (12/02/1916, 06/03/1916, 17/04/1916, 01/05/1916).

584 Carrington, *Soldier*, 5.

585 Richards, *Old Soldiers*, 11–12.

586 Carrington, *Soldier*, 163–4.

587 Foot, 24–5.

588 Orpen, *Onlooker*, 16, 57.

589 Gibson, 'Sex & Soldiering', 543.

590 Stringer, 05/12/1916.

591 Eachus, 03/03/1917, 04/03/1917.

592 Schweder, 23/02/1917.

593 Schweder, 21/04/1916.

594 *VS*, 544.

595 Schweder, 06/01/1918.

596 Schweder, 30/03/1918, 03/04/1918, 19/04/1918, 22/04/1918, 08/07/1918, 03/08/1918.

597 Wheatley, 23/03/1918.

598 Luther, 43–4.

599 Cude, 23/03/1918, 25/03/1918.

600 Cude, 01/04/1918.

601 *MSS*, 227.

602 Cude, 01/04/1918.

603 Wheatley, 26/03/1918.

604 Capron, 10.

605 Stringer, 23/03/1917.

606 Stringer, 28/03/1917, 29/03/1917, 30/03/1917, 31/03/1917, 01/04/1917.

607 Hamilton, *Diary*, 396.

608 Carrington, *Soldier*, 149–50.

609 *TWF1*, xviii, 215, 217, 331–2.

610 *TWF1*, 158, 167, 215, 352–3.

611 Stringer, 13/03/1917.

612 Wilson, J. M., 70.

613 Carrington, *Soldier*, 259.

614 Foot, 119.

615 Cude, 1.

616 Schweder, foreword.

617 Lewis, *Sagittarius*, 2.

618 Stormont Gibbs, *Somme to Armistice*, 35–6.

619 Espley, R., '"How Much of an 'Experience' Do We Want the Public to Receive?": Trench Reconstructions and Popular Images of the Great War', in Meyer, ed., *British Popular Culture*, 342–3; Fussell, *Great War*, 203–4, 207.

620   Winter, J. M., *Remembering War: The Great War Between Memory and History in the Twentieth Century* (New Haven: Yale University Press, 2006) 66.

621   Schweder, 26/12/1915, 06/03/1916.

622   Hamilton, *Diary*, 157.

623   Espley, 'How Much of an Experience', 345.

624   Capron, 11.

625   Stringer, 12/03/1917, 18/04/1917.

626   *MO3*, 107; *VS*, 380–1.

627   Hamilton, *Diary*, 191.

628   Carrington, *Soldier*, 28; *VS*, 60–1, 63, 67, 514, 522–3, 380–1.

629   Eachus, 31/03/1917.

630   Gibson, 'Sex & Soldiering', 550–8.

631   Carrington, *Soldier*, 162.

632   Lewis, *Sagittarius*, 74–5.

633   Richards, *Old Soldiers*, 11.

634   Graves, R., *Good-Bye To All That: An Autobiography* (London: Penguin, 2000) 195.

635   Carrington, *Soldier*, 163.

636   Leed, *No Man's Land*, 184–5.

637   *MSG2*, 346.

638   Graves, *Good-Bye to All That*, 195.

639   Gibson, 'Sex & Soldiering', 558–9; *MSD2*, 130; *MSG2*, 76, 94.

640   Anon., box misc. 221(3180), 9.

641   *MO3*, 93; *MSC*, 73.

642   Gibson, 'Sex & Soldiering', 562–3; Harrison, M., 'The British Army and the Problem of Venereal Disease in France and Egypt during the First World War', *Medical History* (vol. 39, 1995) 142.

643   Moore, W., *The Thin Yellow Line* (London: Leo Cooper, 1974) 132; Harrison, 'Venereal Disease', 144.

644   Harrison, 'Venereal Disease', 145–6; Moore, *Yellow Line*, 134; *MSC*, 73; *MSD2*, 125.

645   *MSD2*, 125.

646   *MSD2*, 118–19, 121, 123.

647   Gibson, 'Sex & Soldiering', 548.

648   *MSD2*, 120–1, 127; *MSG1*, 201–2.

649   Burke, E. T., 'The Treatment of Gonorrhoea in a Field Ambulance', *Lancet* (vol. 1, May 1917) 756.

650   Luther, 38.

651   *MSG2*, 46.

652 Schweder, 07/12/1918.

653 Schweder, 06/04/1917, 30/05/1918.

654 Wilson, J. M., 49.

655 Gibson, 'British Army, French Farmers', 215.

656 Wheatley, 23/03/1918.

657 *SME*, 582–3.

658 Gibson, 'British Army, French Farmers', 225–6, 233–5.

659 Pegum, 'Old Front Line', 221.

660 *MSS*, 221.

661 Eachus, 02/12/1916.

662 van Bergen, L., *Before My Helpless Sight: Suffering, Dying and Military Medicine on the Western Front, 1914–1918*, trans. Liz Waters (Farnham: Ashgate, 2009) 94.

663 *MSD1*, 4; *MSP*, 79; *MSH1*, 319; *MSS*, 134–7, 140–1, 143–7.

664 *MO3*, 93, 153; *MSC*, 106; *MSD1*, 2–3; *MSG1*, 96–101, 106, 372–6; *MSG2*, 87–8; *SME*, 741.

665 *MO3*, 38–9, 91, 94; *MSG2*, 23–4, 38–9, 42, 69, 87–8; *MSG3*, 55.

666 *MSG3*, 34–5, 230–1, 233–4, 299–300.

667 *MO3*, 91; *MSG2*, 16–17, 19, 21–2, 24–32, 42–3, 46, 48–9, 51, 59; *MSG3*, 15, 301; *MSH1*, 278–9; *MSS*, 134, 208–13.

668 *MSG3*, 59–62.

669 *MO3*, 92; *MSC*, 106; *MSG2*, 52–6; *MSG3*, 40–1, 43–4, 50–1; *TWF1*, 175–6.

670 Wilson, J. M., 78.

671 Eachus, 14/04/1917.

672 Cude, 15/12/1915.

673 Goodliff, 22/03/1918, 27/03/1918.

674 Schweder, 27/05/1917.

675 Richards, *Old Soldiers*, 16–17.

676 Stringer, 125–6, 21/04/1917, 16/06/1917.

677 Stringer, 04/12/1916.

678 Leland, 12/12/1916.

679 Hamilton, *Diary*, 326.

680 *MO3*, 133, 134n.

681 Eachus, 31/03/1917.

682 Stringer, 12/04/1917.

683 Schweder, 29/04/1918.

684 Schweder, 18/04/1917.

685 *RASC*, xxv–xxvi.

686 *MO3*, 140.

687 Hamilton, *Diary*, 273.

688 Durham, 01/03/1915.

689 Carrington, *Soldier*, 163.

690 *SME*, 595; *TWF1*, xviii.

691 Richards, *Old Soldiers*, 136.

692 *MO3*, 283n; *TWF1*, 157–8.

693 *TWF1*, 156, 244–5.

694 *MO3*, 283.

695 *TWF1*, 50–1.

696 *SME*, table (i) 517–18, table (i) 606–10, table (ii) 611–12; *TWF1*, 252.

697 Schweder, 10/02/1916.

698 *TWF1*, 50–1.

699 Eachus, 31/03/1917.

700 Stringer, 27/01/1917; *TWF1*, 402–11, 418.

701 Eachus, 13/09/1916, 21/11/1916, 10/01/1917, 19/04/1917.

702 Gibson, 'Sex & Soldiering', 573–5.

703 *SME*, 867.

704 Schweder, 24/01/1916, 30/01/1916, 10/02/1916.

705 Eachus, 30/07/1916.

706 Stringer, 02/04/1917, 04/04/1917.

707 Cude, 24/04/1917.

708 Anon., box misc. 221(3180), 9.

709 Orpen, *Onlooker*, 16–17, 31–2, 91.

710 Orpen, *Onlooker*, 34–5.

711 Schweder, 20/04/1917, 08/05/1917.

712 Durham, 13/03/1916.

713 Carrington, *Soldier*, 145–6.

714 Luther, 18, 38.

715 Wilson, *Landscapes*, 148.

716 Southwold, S., 'Rumours at the Front', in O'Riordan, ed., *Martial Medley*, 105–22.

717 Schweder, 12/03/1916.

718 Stringer, 17/03/1917.

719 Gibson, 'My Chief Source of Worry', 431–3.

720 Stringer, 72–3.

721 Williams, J., 27/04/1917, ?/05/1917.

722 Capron, 11.

723 *MO2*, 87; *MSG2*, 343–4; *MSG3*, 55–6.

724 Carrington, *Soldier*, 165.

725 *MO3*, 140.

726 *MO3*, 143.

727 Naylor, 01/06/1917.

728 Luther, 14.

729 Bursey, 23/06/1916.

730 de Caux, 16.

731 Stringer, 22/03/1915.

732 Schweder, 03/03/1917.

733 Stormont Gibbs, *Somme to Armistice*, 43.

734 Durham, 04/05/1916, 02/01/1917.

735 Schweder, 04/06/1917.

736 Schweder, 19/09/1916, 01/10/1916.

737 de Caux, 3.

738 Schweder, 26/01/1916.

739 Cude, 20/03/1916, *c*.15/05/1916.

740 Leland, 04/11/1916.

741 de Caux, 21.

742 *MSS*, 230–1.

743 Schweder, 22/10/1918.

744 Cude, 24/10/1918.

745 Richards, *Old Soldiers*, 11–12, 55–6.

746 Hamilton, *Diary*, 111.

747 *MSH1*, 7.

748 Cude, 23/01/1919.

749 Schweder, 04/12/1915, 21/01/1916.

750 Cude, 31/01/1918.

751 Stringer, 15/07/1918.

752 Schweder, 11/06/1917.

753 Stringer, 142–52.

754 Duffett, R., 'A War Unimagined: Food and Rank and File Soldiers of the First World War', University of Essex: PhD, 2009, ch.5.

755 Schweder, 25/03/1917, 04/04/1917.

756 Leland, 13/06/1917.

757 Duffett, R., 'A War Imagined: Food and the Rank and File Soldier of the First World War', in Meyer, ed., *British Popular Culture*, 51.

758 Duffett, 'War Unimagined', 116–17, 183; *MO3*, 104–5; *MSH2*, 2–8, 45–52; *SME*, 586.

759 *MSH2*, 41–4.

760 Schweder, 16/03/1917.

761 Schweder, 09/12/1915, 07/10/1916.

762 *MSH2*, 298.

763 Naylor, 16/06/1917.

764 Peterson, 03/06/1915.

765 Brophy & Partridge, *Dictionary*, 15.

766 Foot, 71.

767 *MSG2*, 345; *TWF1*, 214.

768 Stringer, 26/03/1917.

769 Hamilton, *Diary*, 353–4.

770 Stringer, 17/06/1917, 18/06/1917.

771 *TWF1*, 257.

772 Schweder, 07/10/1916.

773 Wilson, *Landscapes*, 137.

774 Foot, 66–7.

775 Schweder, 04/04/1916, 25/04/1916, 19/03/1917, 09/07/1918.

776 Carrington, *Soldier*, 165.

777 Taylor, 03/06/1915.

778 Stringer, 23/04/1915.

779 de Caux, 35.

780 Capron, 16.

781 Anon., box misc. 221(3180), 21.

782 Anon., box misc. 221(3180), 12.

783 Campbell, 29/03/1918.

784 *MO3*, 98; *RASC*, 87–8, 94, 98–9; *TWF1*, 94, 103–6; *VS*, 102.

785 Anon., box misc. 221(3180), 22–3.

786 *RE*, 35.

787 *MSG3*, 301.

788 Durham, 01/03/1915.

789 Hamilton, *Diary*, 107.

790 Capron, 18.

791 Hamilton, *Diary*, 263.

792 Schweder, 25/05/1916.

793 Masefield, *Somme*, 85.

794 Capron, 18, 40.

795 *MO3*, 134n; *MSC*, table 1/2–3, table 2/4–5, table 1/157; *MSG2*, 46, 168–9; *SME*, 195, 197, 205–6.

796 *MSG2*, 91–3, 135, 137, 139, 147–8, 150, 153–4; *SME*, 160–1.

797 *MO3*, 65; *SME*, table (iv) 601–03; *TWF1*, 495.

798 *SME*, table (iii) (a) 65–6; *TWF1*, 222–3.

799 *MSG3*, 55; *SME*, 638; *TWF1*, 265, 271.

800 *MSC*, table 1/12, table 2/148; *SME*, 640–1.

801 Hamilton, *Diary*, 393–5.

802 Capron, 6, 43.

803 Schweder, 24/09/1917.

804 Eachus, 06/06/1916.

805 Carrington, *Soldier*, 29–30; Foot, 1–7.

806 *MSD2*, 17–18.

807 *MO3*, 491–3.

808 Campbell, 29/03/1918.

809 Schweder, 19/12/1916.

810 Naylor, 11/05/1917, 07/07/1917.

811 Petter, M., '"Temporary Gentlemen" in the Aftermath of the Great War: Rank, Status and the Ex-Officer Problem', *Historical Journal* (vol. 37, no. 1, 1994) 131, 133, 136–9.

812 Petter, 'Temporary Gentlemen', 139–42; Watson, *Fighting Different Wars*, 23–5.

813 Foot, 3–5.

814 Richards, *Old Soldiers*, 3.

815 Carrington, *Soldier*, 76.

816 Stringer, 21/01/1917, 01/02/1917.

817 Schweder, 06/10/1917.

818 Stringer, 19/02/1915, 29/07/1915.

819 Durham, 02/04/1915.

820 Schweder, 10/10/1918.

821 Hamilton, *Diary*, 163.

822 Schweder, 17/06/1918.

823 Stringer, 01/05/1915, 30/05/1915.

824 Stringer, 04/06/1915.

825 Appleyard, 17/06/1915.

826 Durham, 02/04/1916.

827 Leland, 09/11/1917.

828 *VS*, 494–5, 498–503, 533–7.

829 *VS*, 65–6, 85, 498–503, 540–1, 557, 668–9.

830 *VS*, 538–9, 513.

831 Luther, 28.

832 *VS*, 65–6, 498–503, 550–1.

833 Luther, 9, 14.

834 Luther, 21, 24; *MSD2*, 355–6; *VS*, 538–40, 674–5.

835 Schweder, 29/11/1917.

836 Newman, 23/02/1915.

837 Taylor, 01/06/1915.

838 Stringer, 04/06/1915.

839 Rogers, 22/10/1915.

840 Cude, 25/03/1916.

841 Durham, 04/05/1916.

842 Capron, 6 ('peregrinations').

843 Leland, 12/10/1916.

844 Bursey, 26/06/1916.

845 *MO3*, 122.

846 Naylor, 25/08/1918.

847 Schweder, 09/12/1915, 01/01/1916, 10/02/1916.

848 Leland, 17/08/1917.

849 Leed, *No Man's Land*, 119.

850 Carrington, *Soldier*, 90.

851 Schweder, 03/11/1917.

852 Capron, 14, postscript notes 1.

853 *VS*, 681.

854 *VS*, 476, 565, 570–3.

855 *VS*, 679.

856 *VS*, 681–2, 684–5.

857 *VS*, 560, 681–2, 685–7, 721 appendix B.

858 *SME*, 397; *VS*, 684, 686–8.

859 Capron, 21–2.

860 Schweder, 03/09/1918, 10/10/1918.

861 Goodliff, 22/01/1919.

862 *MSH1*, 185–209.

863 Foot, 73, 111.

864 Schweder, 25/12/1915.

865 Luther, 18.

866 Cude, 25/12/1915.

867 Wilson, J. M., 29.

868 Hamilton, *Diary*, 129.

869 Cude, 25/12/1917.

870 Capron, 35.

871 Richards, *Old Soldiers*, 49.

872 Schweder, 05/04/1916.

873 Downer, n.d./n.p.

874 Goodliff, 10/09/1918.

875 Schweder, 05/06/1916.

876 Eachus, 31/03/1917.

877 Cude, 30/01/1918.

878 Gill & Dallas, *Unknown Army*, 85–6.

879 Cude, 28/01/1919.

880 *AOS*, 90–1, 99n, 109; Gill & Dallas, *Unknown Army*, 89; *MO3*, 96–9, 106, 115–16, 128–31; *MSG2*, 65, 68–9; *RASC*, 87–8, 89n, 91, 94, 98–9, 104, 107, 109; *SME*, 580; *TWF1*, xii, 93, 103–06; *VS*, 19, 102.

881 *AOS*, 100–3; *MO3*, 103: *RASC*, 90.

882 Schweder, 16/06/1918.

883 *AOS*, 100–3; *MO3*,130; *MSG2*, 137, 158–9; *TWF1*, 166, 175–6.

884 Gill & Dallas, *Unknown Army*, 91–9; Rothstein, A., *The Soldiers' Strikes of 1919* (London: Macmillan, 1980) 71; Wintringham, T. H., *Mutiny. Being a Survey of Mutinies from Spartacus to Invergordon* (London: Stanley Nott, 1936) 311–26.

885 Cude, file summary.

886 Kenyon, 15/02/1918.

887 *MO3*, 96–9, 106, 139; Gill & Dallas, *Unknown Army*, 64; *MSG2*, 65, 68–9, 84–6; *MSG3*, 48–9; *SME*, 580; *VS*, 19.

888 Gill & Dallas, *Unknown Army*, 67–76.

889 Englander, D. & Osborne, J., 'Jack, Tommy, and Henry Dubb: The Armed Forces and the Working Class', *Historical Journal* (vol. 21, no. 3, 1978) 596.

890 Durst, 11/09/1917.

891 Cude, 15/07/1918.

892 Hamilton, *Diary*, 460.

893 Stringer, 16/02/1915.

894 Wilson, J. M., 14, 19.

895 Goodliff, 06/04/1918.

896 Schweder, 05/05/1916, 02/03/1917.

897 Goodliff, 29/06/1918.

898 *MSG2*, 44; Noakes, L., '"Playing at Being Soldiers"? British Women and Military Uniform in the First World War', in Meyer, ed., *British Popular Culture*, 141n61; Watson, *Fighting Different Wars*, 33.

899 *MO3*, 144; *MSG3*, 19–20; Wilson, J. M., 77.

900 Goodliff, 23/06/1918, 24/07/1918, 28/07/1918.

901 Durst, 25/11/1915, 14/07/1916.

902 Kenyon, 10/05/1918, 20/05/1918.

903 Anon., box misc. 61(947), ms essay 2.

904 Watson, *Fighting Different Wars*, 7, 61–86.

905 Goodliff, 15/07/1918.

906 Schweder, 22/04/1918.

907 Carrington, *Soldier*, 93–4.

908 Bursey, 26/06/1916.

909 Baker, T., 'In Trouble: Military Crimes', <http://www.1914–1918.net/crime. htm> (1996) n.p.; Englander & Osborne, 'Jack, Tommy, & Henry Dubb', 595.

910 *MO3*, 133.

911 Eachus, 01/08/1916.

912 Gibson, 'My Chief Source of Worry', 427.

913 Leland, 02/11/1916, 07/11/1916.

914 Bursey, 24/06/1916.

915 Carrington, *Soldier*, 93–4, 100–5; *MO3*, 133.

916 *BEFT* (06/03/1916).

917 Leland, 17/11/1916.

918 *BEFT* (12/02/1916, 01/12/1916, 05/03/1917).

919 Schweder, 03/07/1918.

920 *MSD2*, 123.

921 Kenyon, 25/05/1918.

922 Klein, D., *With the Chinks, by Daryl Klein, 2nd Lieutenant in the Chinese Labour Corps* (London: John Lane The Bodley Head, 1919) 249, 257–8.

923 Williams, J., 21/07/1917.

924 Naylor, 17/08/1917.

925 Campbell, n.d./n.p.

926 Downer, n.d./n.p.

927 Wilson, J. M., 40.

928 Richards, *Old Soldiers*, 38–9.

929 *MO3*, 104; *MSG2*, 142, 155; *MSH2*, 46–52; *RASC*, 95–6.

930 *AOS*, 22–34, 34n.

931 Eachus, 10/07/1917.

932 Kenyon, 07/07/1917.

933 D'Abernon, 29/07/1916, 24/08/1916, 15/09/1916.

934 Gill & Dallas, *Unknown Army*, 38–9.

935 Cude, 02/08/1917.

936 Schweder, 31/12/1918.

937 Cude, 21/12/1918, 22/12/1918.

938 Schweder, 07/06/1918.

939 Capron, 18.

940 Schweder, 02/04/1917.

941 Capron, 18.

942 Stringer, 19/04/1915.

943 Schweder, 11/04/1916.

944 Foot, 39.

945 Carrington, *Soldier*, 88.

946 *MO3*, 146.

947 *MO3*, 148; Naylor, 15/12/1914; Wilson, J. M., 45.

948 Schweder, 08/12/1915, 09/03/1916, 25/03/1917.

949 Stringer, 02/07/1917.

950 Schweder, 14/06/1918.

951 Capron, 'So much better? But was it? 9–10 (18–19).

952 Luther, foreword, 2–3, 6, 20.

953 *VS*, 59–60, 514.

954 *VS*, 701–2 appendix B.

955 *VS*, 655–6.

956 *VS*, 61, 68, 656.

957 *VS*, 63.

958 Schweder, 26/06/1918, 05/07/1918, 22/07/1918.

959 *MO3*, 95, 99, 106, 120; *MSG2*, 68–9, 71, 84–6, 136–8; *RASC*, 87–8.

960 Manning, 15/04/1919.

961 *AOS*, 167.

962 *MO3*, 99, 102; *RASC*, 91, 104, 107, 109.

963 *VS*, 684–8.

964 *MO3*, 116; *MSH1*, 317–21.

965 *AOS*, 103–4, 105n.

966 Orpen, *Onlooker*, 46–7.

967 Wilson, J. M., 55.

968 Schweder, 03/08/1918, 05/08/1918.

969 Orpen, *Onlooker*, 16.

970 *MSH1*, 13.

971 Richards, *Old Soldiers*, 26–7.

972 Stringer, 18/03/1917.

973 Foot, 38.

974 Carrington, *Soldier*, 90–3.

975 Appleyard, 17/06/1915.

976 Luther, 13.

977 *MSD1*, 66–7; *MSD2*, 297; *MSH1*, 2, 222–5, 237–45; *MSP*, 320, 340.

978 Jones, *In Parenthesis*, 207n37A.

979 Stringer, 28/09/1916.

980 *MO3*, 271–2, 276, 278; *MSH1*, 15, 99; *MSP*, 320, 340; *TWF1*, 122, 145n, 166.

981 Eachus, 16/08/1916.

982 *MSD1*, 66–7; *MSG2*, 61–2; *MSG3*, 49; Stringer, 18/03/1917.

983 Naylor, 30/08/1918; 13/12/1918.

984 Stormont Gibbs, *Somme to Armistice*, 43.

985 Cude, 11/11/1918.

986 Naylor, 12/01/1919.

987 Foot, 112–13; Naylor, 19/05/1919.

988 Schweder, 23/03/1916, 16/05/1916, 31/05/1916, 03/09/1916, 19/09/1916, 28/09/1916, 28/03/1917, 05/06/1917.

989 Appleyard, 22/11/1915.

990 Hamilton, *Diary*, 252–3.

991 Luther, 14, 34.

992 Naylor, 29/09/1918.

993 Eachus, 19/12/1916.

994 *MO3*, 128.

995 *MO3*, 128–9.

996 Richards, *Old Soldiers*, 2, 154.

997 Stringer, 17/02/1915.

998 Barnett, C., *The Collapse of British Power* (London: Eyre Methuen, 1972) 430.

999 *BEFT* (20/03/1916).

1000 *BEFT* (06/03/1916).

1001 Naylor, 26/01/1917.

1002 Schweder, 24/08/1916.

1003 Wilson, J. M., 24.

1004 Goodliff, 30/05/1918.

1005 *MO1*, 32; Naylor, 15/05/1915.

1006 *MO3*, 140n.

1007 *MO3*, 68; *RE*, 291.

1008 Eachus, 09/11/1916.

1009 *MO3*, 71–2.

1010 Schweder, 06/03/1916.

1011 Cude, 03/11/1918.

1012 Schweder, 04/04/1917.

1013 Williams, C., 08/08/1914.

1014 Gibson, 'Sex & Soldiering', 573–5.

1015 Gibson, 'British Army, French Farmers', 206.

1016 Schweder, 01/12/1918, 07/12/1918, 20/12/1918, 21/12/1918, 24/12/1918, 25/12/1918, 30/12/1918, 05/01/1919, 12/01/1919, 15/01/1919, 16/01/1919, 17/01/1919.

1017 Capron, 49–50.

1018 *SME*, table (i) (a) 91, 628.

1019 *MO3*, 99; *RASC*, 85; *SME*, table (i) 62.

1020 *MSC*, table 1/2–3, table 2/4–5.

1021 *RASC*, 93.

1022 *MO3*, 130, 137; *MSG2*, 138, 161; *SME*, 183, 190, 195, 197, 200–2, table (i) (a–b) 598–9, 642, 718; *TWF1*, 263, 255, 496.

1023 *MSG3*, 202, 208–11; *RE*, 291; *SME*, 639.

1024 *MSC*, table 1/12, table 2/148, table 2/166–67.

1025 Carrington, *Soldier*, 13.

1026 *MO3*, 99, 107; *RASC*, 85; *SME*, table (i) (a) 91; Stringer, 02/03/1917; *VS*, 43, 69, 498–503, 508, 510–11, 514, 537.

1027 *SME*, table (i) (b) 92, 396–7, table (i) (c–d) 402–3, 861; *VS*, 55, 92, 101, 508–9, 512, 643, 679–80.

1028 Schweder, 17/12/1918; 31/12/1918.

1029 *MO3*, 145.

1030 *MO3*, 129–30, 132; *SME*, 200–2.

1031 Lewis, *Sagittarius*, 97.

1032 Capron, 26.

1033 *MO3*, 132n; *SME*, 200–2.

1034 'The First World War Poetry Digital Archive.The Life of a WAAC', <http://www.oucs.ox.ac.uk/ww1lit/collections/item/5517?CISOBOX=1&REC=7> n.p.

1035 Malins, G., *How I Filmed the War* (London: Herbert Jenkins Ltd, 1920) part II ch. 1; 'The Battle of the Somme (1916). British Topical Committee for War Films', <http://www.cosmolearning.com/documentaries/the-battle-of-the-somme-827/> (2007) n.p.; *Somme – Viewing Guide*, 3.

1036 Schweder, 04/09/1916; 30/12/1918.

1037 Mayer, A., 'Internal Causes and Purposes of War in Europe, 1870–1956', *Journal of Modern History* (vol. 41, no. 3, September 1969); Loewenberg, P., 'A Critique of Arno Mayer's "Internal Causes and Purposes of War in Europe", an Inadequate Model of Human Behavior, National Conflict and Historical Change', *Journal of Modern History* (vol. 42, no. 4, September 1970); Sipes, R., 'War, Sports and Aggression: an Empirical Test of Two Rival Theories', *American Anthropologist* (vol. 75, no. 1, February 1973); Fornari, F., *The Psychoanalysis of War*, trans. Alenka Pfeifer (Bloomington: Indiana University Press, 1975).

1038 Leed, *No Man's Land*, 80–96, 105, 110–13, 181, 186–7.

1039 *MSD1*, 18, 44, 54.

1040 Brophy & Partridge, *Dictionary*, 17–23, 33, 55.

1041 Fussell, *Great War*, 64.

1042 Bourne, J., 'The British Working Man in Arms', in Hugh Cecil & Peter
      H. Liddle, eds., *Facing Armageddon: The First World War Experienced*
      (London: Leo Copper, 1996) 339.

1043 Schweder, 01/04/1917.

1044 Naylor, 12/11/1922.

1045 Petter, 'Temporary Gentlemen', 127–52.

1046 Naylor, 30/08/1918, 25/05/1919.

1047 Londonderry, 04/03/1919.

1048 *MSH2*, 328–9.

1049 Luther, 11.

1050 Leland, 28/09/1916.

1051 Foot, 49; Schweder, 27/02/1917.

1052 *MSH2*, 458–9.

1053 Stringer, 102, 11/08/1915.

1054 Schweder, 13/08/1916.

1055 Appleyard, 13/07/1915.

1056 Hamilton, *Diary*, 227.

1057 Orpen, *Onlooker*, 36.

1058 Leland, 15/03/1917, 29/04/1917, 10/05/1917.

1059 Schweder, 15/03/1916.

1060 Capron, 5.

1061 *MSG3*, 325; *SME*, 43, table (i) (b) 92, table (ii) 93, table (viii) (a,b) 106,
      table (x) 108, 195, 197.

1062 Taylor, *Good-Bye to the Battlefield*, 127–30.

1063 Spagnoly, *Salient Points*, 136–8.

1064 *The Guardian*, 14 April 2001, in 'Aftermath', <http://www.aftermathww1.
      com/mustard.asp.> n.p.

1065 *Toronto Globe and Mail*, 20 April 2001, in '54th Canadian Infantry
      Battalion 1915–1919', <http://www.54thbattalioncef.ca/WARPAGES/
      Opsorderly_room.htm> n.p.

1066 *SME*, table (i) 510, table (iii) 513, 739, 742.

1067 *SME*, 363.

1068 *MSC*, table 1/12, table 2/108, table 2/148.

1069 Moore, *Yellow Line*, 229.

1070 *SME*, table 1/480.

LIST OF WORKS CITED

Archival sources

Documents and Sound Section, Imperial War Museum, Lambeth:

Anon.	Catalogue 9373 / box misc. 61(947)
Anon.	Catalogue 11697 / box misc. 221(3180)
Appleyard, S. W.	Catalogue 7990 / box 82/1/1
Bursey, H. F.	Catalogue 5646 / box 96/48/1
Campbell, C. E.	Catalogue 3220 / box 95/14/1
Capron, J. T.	Catalogue 1483 / box 87/33/1
Cude, R. M .M.	Catalogue 129 / box PP/MCR/C48
D'Abernon, H.	Catalogue 1856 / box 92/22/1
de Caux, E. G.	Catalogue 564 / box 88/46/1
Downer, L.	Catalogue 6569 / box 79/15/1
Durham, G. W.	Catalogue 348 / box 90/7/1
Durst, R.	Catalogue 15039 / box 06/100/1
Eachus, S. T.	Catalogue 11667 / box 05/51/1
Foot, R.	Catalogue 3354 / box 86/57/1
Girling, T. W.	Catalogue 110 / box 89/7/1
Goodliff, P. E.	Catalogue 257 / box 88/51/1
Kenyon, K. M. R.	Catalogue 3949 / box 84/24/1
Leland, H. J. C.	Catalogue 6280 / box 95/51/1
Londonderry, Lady	Catalogue 15569 / box 06/128/1
Luther, R. M.	Catalogue 1325 / box 87/8/1
Manning, R. B.	Catalogue 4763 / box 80/21/1
Naylor, J. W.	Catalogue 2352 / box 86/21/1
Newman, W. J.	Catalogue 4067 / box 84/52/1
Peterson, J. N.	Catalogue 2058 / box 92/36/1
Rogers, W. A.	Catalogue 1704 / box 87/62/1
Schweder, R. P.	Catalogue 3387 / box 86/65/1
Stringer, G. E.	Catalogue 468 / box 87/66/1
Taylor, R. A. G.	Catalogue 15078 / box 06/57/1
Wheatley, D. Y.	Catalogue 4020 / box 84/43/1
Williams, C.	Catalogue 13193 / box 04/40/1
Williams, J.	Catalogue 4176 / box 83/14/1
Wilson, J. M.	Catalogue 11951 / box 02/26/1

Newspapers

BEF Times
Kemmel Times
New Church Times
Some-Times
Wipers Times or Salient News

Official histories

Beadon, R. H., *The Royal Army Service Corps. A History of Transport and Supply in the British Army.* (*Vol. 2*) (Cambridge: Cambridge University Press, 1931).

Blenkinsop, Sir L. J. & Rainey, J. W., *Veterinary Services. History of the Great War Based on Official Documents* (London: HMSO, 1925).

Edmonds, Sir J, E. & Wynne, G. C., *Military Operations. France and Belgium 1915. Winter 1914–1915: Battle of Neuve Chapelle: Battle of Ypres.* (*Vol. 1*). *History of the Great War Based on Official Documents* (London: Macmillan, 1927).

Edmonds, Sir J. E., *Military Operations. France and Belgium, 1915. Battles of Aubers Ridge, Festubert, and Loos.* (*Vol. 2*). *History of the Great War Based on Official Documents* (London: Macmillan, 1928).

—, *Military Operations. France and Belgium 1916. Sir Douglas Haig's Command to the 1st July: Battle of the Somme.* (*Vol. 1*). *History of the Great War Based on Official Documents* (London: Macmillan, 1932).

—, *Military Operations. France and Belgium 1916. Sir Douglas Haig's Command to the 1st July: Battle of the Somme.* (*Vol. 1. Appendices*). *History of the Great War Based on Official Documents* (London: Macmillan, 1932).

—, *Military Operations. France and Belgium, 1916. 2nd July to the end of the Battles of the Somme.* (*Vol. 2. Maps & Appendices*). *History of the Great War Based on Official Documents* (London: Macmillan, 1938).

Forbes, A., *A History of the Army Ordnance Services.* (*Vol. 3*). *The Great War* (London: The Medici Society, 1929).

Henniker, A. M., *Transportation on the Western Front 1914–1918. History of the Great War Based on Official Documents* (London: HMSO, 1937).

—, *Transportation on the Western Front 1914–1918.* (*Maps*). *History of the Great War Based on Official Documents* (London: HMSO, 1937).

Historical Section of the Committee of Imperial Defence, *History of the Great War Based on Official Documents. Principal Events 1914–1918* (London: HMSO, 1922).

MacPherson, Sir W. G., Bowlby, Sir A. A., Wallace, Sir C. & English, Sir C., *Medical Services. Surgery of the War.* (*Vol. 1*). *History of the Great War Based on Official Documents* (London: HMSO, 1922).

MacPherson, Sir W. G., Herringham, Sir W. P., Elliott, T. R. & Balfour, A., *Medical Services. Diseases of the War.* (*Vol. 1*). *History of the Great War Based on Official Documents* (London: HMSO, c.1922).

—, *Medical Services. Diseases of the War.* (*Vol. 2*). *History of the Great War Based on Official Documents* (London: HMSO, 1923).

MacPherson, Sir W. G., Horrocks, Sir W. H. & Beveridge, W. W. O., *Medical Services. Hygiene of the War.* (*Vol. 1*). *History of the Great War Based on Official Documents* (London: HMSO, 1923).

—, *Medical Services. Hygiene of the War.* (*Vol. 2*). *History of the Great War Based on Official Documents* (London: HMSO, 1923).

MacPherson, Sir W. G., Leishman, Sir W. B. & Cummins, S. L., *Medical Services Pathology. History of the Great War Based on Official Documents* (London: HMSO, 1923).

MacPherson, Sir W. G., *Medical Services. General History.* (*Vol. 1*). *Medical Services in the United Kingdom; in British Garrisons Overseas; and during Operations against Tsingtau, in Togoland, the Cameroons, and South-West Africa. History of the Great War Based on Official Documents* (London: HMSO, 1921).

—, *Medical Services. General History.* (*Vol. 2*). *The Medical Services on the Western Front, and during the Operations in France and Belgium in 1914 and 1915. History of the Great War Based on Official Documents* (London: HMSO, 1923).

—, *Medical Services. General History.* (*Vol. 3*). *Medical Services during the Operations on the Western Front in 1916, 1917 and 1918; in Italy; and in Egypt and Palestine. History of the Great War Based on Official Documents* (London: HMSO, 1924).

Mitchell, T. J. & Smith, G. M., *Medical Services. Casualties and Medical Statistics of the Great War. History of the Great War Based on Official Documents* (London: HMSO, 1931).

Priestley, R. E., *The Work of the Royal Engineers in the European War, 1914–1919. The Signal Service in the European War of 1914 to 1918 (France)* (Chatham: Mackay, 1921).

War Office, *Statistics of the Military Effort of the British Empire During the Great War 1914–1920* (London: HMSO, 1922).

Other published material

Alcock, L., *Arthur's Britain. History and Archaeology AD 367–634* (Harmondsworth: Penguin, 1985).

Ashworth, T., *Trench Warfare: The Live and Let Live System 1914–1918* (London: Macmillan, 1980).

Baker, J. A., *The Peregrine* (New York: The New York Review of Books, 2005).

Barnett, C., *The Collapse of British Power* (London: Eyre Methuen, 1972).

Benjamin, W., 'One-Way Street', in Hannah Arendt, ed., *One-Way Street and Other Writings* (London: NLB, 1979, first published 1936) 45–104.

—, 'The Storyteller: Reflections on the Works of Nikolai Leskov', in Hannah Arendt, ed., *Walter Benjamin. Illuminations: Essays and Reflections* (New York: Schocken Books, 1968, first published 1936) 83–109.

Berman, M., *All That Is Solid Melts Into Air: The Experience of Modernity* (London & New York: Verso, 1983).

Blunden, E., *Overtones of War: Poems of the First World War*, ed. Martin Taylor (London: Duckworth, 1996).

—, *Undertones of War* (London: Collins, 1965, first published 1928).

Blythe, R., *Akenfield: Portrait of an English Village* (London: Allen Lane The Penguin Press, 1969).

Bourke, J., *An Intimate History of Killing: Face-to-Face Killing in Twentieth-Century Warfare* (London: Granta Books, 1999).

Bourne, J., 'The British Working Man in Arms', in Hugh Cecil & Peter H. Liddle, eds., *Facing Armageddon: The First World War Experienced* (London: Leo Copper 1996).

Brophy, J., 'The Soldier's Nostrils', in Conal O'Riordan, ed., *A Martial Medley: Fact and Fiction* (London: Eric Partridge at The Scholartis Press, 1931) 123–6.

Brophy, J. & Partridge, E., *Dictionary of Tommies' Songs and Slang, 1914–1918* (London: Frontline Books, 2008, first published 1930).

Brown, M., *The Imperial War Museum Book of the Somme* (London: Sidgwick & Jackson in association with the Imperial War Museum, 1996).

Burke, E. T., 'The Treatment of Gonorrhoea in a Field Ambulance', *Lancet* (vol. 1, May 1917) 756–8.

Carrington, C. E., *Soldier From the Wars Returning* (Aldershot: Gregg Revivals in association with Department of War Studies, Kings College, London, 1965, revised edition of *A Subaltern's War*, published 1929).

—, *The War Record of the 1/5th Battalion the Royal Warwickshire Regiment* (Birmingham: Cornish Brothers Ltd., 1922).

Chasseaud, P., *Rats Alley. Trench Names on the Western Front, 1914–1918* (Stroud: Spellmount, 2006).

Clout, H., *After the Rains: Restoring the Countryside of Northern France After the Great War* (Exeter: Exeter University Press, 1996).

de Certeau, M., *The Practice of Everyday Life*, trans. Stephen F. Rendall (London: University of California Press, 2011).

Dorfman, E., *The Narreme in the Medieval Romance Epic: An Introduction to Narrative Structures* (Toronto: University of Toronto Press, 1969).

Duffett, R., 'A War Imagined: Food and the Rank and File Soldier of the First World War', in Jessica Meyer, ed., *British Popular Culture and the First World War* (Leiden and Boston: Brill, 2008) 47–70.

Dunn, J. C., *The War the Infantry Knew 1914–1919* (London: Jane's, 1987, first published 1938).

Engels, F., *Ludwig Feuerbach and the End of Classical German Philosophy* (London: Union Books, 2009).

Englander, D. & Osborne, J., 'Jack, Tommy, and Henry Dubb: The Armed Forces and the Working Class', *Historical Journal* (vol. 21, no. 3, 1978) 593–621.

Espley, R., '"How Much of an 'Experience' Do We Want the Public to Receive?": Trench Reconstructions and Popular Images of the Great War', in Jessica Meyer, ed., *British Popular Culture and the First World War* (Leiden and Boston: Brill, 2008) 325–50.

Fornari, F., *The Psychoanalysis of War*, trans. Alenka Pfeifer (Bloomington: Indiana University Press, 1975).

Frankau, G., *The Poetical Works of Gilbert Frankau* (*Vol. 2*) (London: Chatto & Windus, 1923).

Fussell, P., *The Great War and Modern Memory* (London: Oxford University Press, 1975).

Gibson, C. K., '"My Chief Source of Worry": an Assistant Provost Marshal's View of Relations between 2nd Canadian Division and Local Inhabitants on the Western Front, 1915–1917', *War in History* (vol. 7, no. 4, 2000) 413–41.

—, 'Sex and Soldiering in France and Flanders: the British Expeditionary Force along the Western Front, 1914–1919', *International History Review* (vol. xxiii, no. 3, September 2001) 535–79.

—, 'The British Army, French Farmers and the War on the Western Front 1914–1918', *Past & Present* (no. 180, August 2003) 175–239.

Gill, D. & Dallas, G., *The Unknown Army* (London: Verso, 1985).

Gliddon, G., *When the Barrage Lifts. A Topographical History of the Battle of the Somme 1916* (Stroud: Alan Sutton, 1994).

Goode, J., *Thomas Hardy. The Offensive Truth* (Oxford: Basil Blackwell, 1988).

Graves, R., *Good-bye To All That: An Autobiography* (London: Penguin, 2000, first published 1929).

Grieves, K., 'The Propinquity of Place: Home, Landscape and Soldier Poets of the First World War', in Jessica Meyer, ed., *British Popular Culture and the First World War* (Leiden and Boston, Brill, 2008) 19–46.

—, 'The Transport Mission to GHQ, 1916', in Brian Bond, et al., eds., *Look to Your Front: Studies in the First World War by the British Commission for Military History* (Staplehurst: Spellmount, 1999) 63–78.

Groom, W., *A Storm in Flanders: The Ypres Salient, 1914–1918; Tragedy and Triumph on the Western Front* (New York: Atlantic Monthly Press, 2002).

Hamilton, R. G. A., *The War Diary of the Master of Belhaven 1914–1918* (London: John Murray, 1924).

Hardy, T., *The Life and Work of Thomas Hardy*, ed. Michael Millgate (London & Basingstoke: Macmillan, 1984).

Harrison, M., 'The British Army and the Problem of Venereal Disease in France and Egypt during the First World War', *Medical History* (vol. 39, 1995) 133–58.

Higbee, D., 'Practical Memory: Organized Veterans and the Politics of Commemoration', in Jessica Meyer, ed., *British Popular Culture and the First World War* (Leiden and Boston: Brill, 2008) 195–216.

Hiscock, E., *The Bells of Hell Go Ting-a-Ling-a-Ling: An Autobiographical Fragment Without Maps* (London: Arlington Books, 1976).

Hynes, S., *The Soldier's Tale: Bearing Witness to Modern War* (London: Pimlico, 1998).

Illouz, E., *Consuming the Romantic Utopia: Love and the Cultural Contradictions of Capitalism* (Berkeley: University of California Press, 1997).

James, H., *The Sense of the Past* (London: W. Collins Sons & Co. Ltd., 1917).

Jones, D., *In Parenthesis: seinnyessit e gledyf ym penn mammeu* (London: Faber & Faber, 1978, first published 1937).

Jünger, E., *Copse 125. A Chronicle of the Trench Warfare of 1918*, trans. Basil Creighton (London: Chatto & Windus, 1930).

Keegan, J., *The Face of Battle* (London: Jonathan Cape, 1977).

Klein, D., *With the Chinks, by Daryl Klein, 2nd Lieutenant in the Chinese Labour Corps* (London: John Lane The Bodley Head, 1919).

Leed, E. J., *No Man's Land: Combat and Identity in World War I* (Cambridge: Cambridge University Press, 1979).

Lewis, C., *Sagittarius Rising* (London: Greenhill Books, 1993, first published 1936).

Lindqvist, S., *A History of Bombing*, trans. Linda Haverty Rugg (Granta Books: London, 2002).

Loewenberg, P., 'A Critique of Arno Mayer's "Internal Causes and Purposes of War in Europe", an Inadequate Model of Human Behavior, National Conflict and Historical Change', *Journal of Modern History* (vol. 42, no. 4, September 1970) 628–36.

Lowenthal, D., *The Heritage Crusade and the Spoils of History* (Cambridge: Cambridge University Press, 1998).

Malins, G., *How I Filmed the War* (London: Herbert Jenkins Ltd, 1920).

Marcuse, H., *Negations: Essays in Critical Theory*, trans. Jeremy J. Shapiro (Harmondsworth: Penguin University Books, 1972).

—, *One Dimensional Man: The Ideology of Industrial Society* (London: Sphere Books, 1968).

Marx, K., *Grundrisse*, trans. Martin Nicolaus (Harmondsworth: Penguin, 1973).

Masefield, J., *The Battle of the Somme* (London: Heinemann, 1919).

Mayer, A., 'Internal Causes and Purposes of War in Europe, 1870–1956', *Journal of Modern History* (vol. 41, no. 3, September 1969) 291–303.

Moore, W., *The Thin Yellow Line* (London: Leo Cooper, 1974).

Natter, W. G., *Literature at War, 1914–1940: Representing the 'Time of Greatness' in Germany* (New Haven and London: Yale University Press, 1999).

1916: The Somme (Maidenhead: Commonwealth War Graves Commission, n.d.).

Noakes, L., '"Playing at Being Soldiers"? British Women and Military Uniform in the First World War', in Jessica Meyer, ed., *British Popular Culture and the First World War* (Leiden and Boston: Brill, 2008) 123–46.

Orpen, Sir W., *An Onlooker in France, 1917–1919* (London: Williams & Norgate, 1921).

Partridge, E., 'Byways of Soldiers' Slang', in Conal O'Riordan, ed., *A Martial Medley: Fact and Fiction* (London: Eric Partridge at The Scholartis Press, 1931) 127–33.

Pegum, J., 'The Old Front Line: Returning to the Battlefields in the Writings of Ex-Servicemen', in Jessica Meyer, ed., *British Popular Culture and the First World War* (Leiden and Boston: Brill, 2008) 217–36.

Petter, M., '"Temporary Gentlemen" in the Aftermath of the Great War: Rank, Status and the Ex-Officer Problem', *Historical Journal* (vol. 37, no. 1, 1994) 127–52.

Pfungst, O., *Clever Hans. The Horse of Mr. von Osten,* ed. Robert Rosenthal (New York: Holt, Rinehart and Winston, 1965, first published 1911).

Richards, F. (Woodruff, F. P.), *Old Soldiers Never Die* (London: Faber & Faber, 1964, first published 1933).

Richardson, E. H., *British War Dogs. Their Training and Psychology* (London: Skeffington & Son, 1920).

Ricœur, P., *Memory, History, Forgetting*, trans. K. Blamey & D. Pellauer (Chicago: University of Chicago Press, 2004).

Rothstein, A., *The Soldiers' Strikes of 1919* (London: Macmillan, 1980).

Sassoon S., *Memoirs of a Fox-Hunting Man* (London: Faber & Faber, 1954, first published 1928).

Scott, J. W., 'The Evidence of Experience', *Critical Inquiry* (vol. 17, no. 4, 1991) 773–97.

Schama, S., *Dead Certainties (Unwarranted Speculations)* (New York: Alfred A. Knopf, 1991).

Sewell, W. H., *Logics of History: Social Theory and Social Transformation* (Chicago & London: University of Chicago Press, 2005).

Sipes, R., 'War, Sports and Aggression: an Empirical Test of Two Rival Theories', *American Anthropologist* (vol. 75, no. 1, February 1973) 64–86.

Southwold, S., 'Rumours at the Front', in Conal O'Riordan, ed., *A Martial Medley: Fact and Fiction* (London: Eric Partridge at The Scholartis Press, 1931) 105–22.

Spagnoly, Tony, *Salient Points: Cameos of the Western Front, Ypres Sector 1914–1918* (London: Leo Cooper, 1995).

Stormont Gibbs, C. C., *From the Somme to the Armistice. The Memoirs of Captain Stormont Gibbs, MC*, ed. Richard Devonald-Lewis (London: William Kimber, 1986).

Swinton, E. D., 'The Point of View', in *The Green Curve and Other Stories* (New York: Doubleday, Page & Co., 1914, first published 1909) 239–62.

The Battle of the Somme – Viewing Guide (Lambeth: Imperial War Museum Film & Video Archive, n.d.).

Taylor, H. A., *Good-Bye to the Battlefield: To-Day and Yesterday on the Western Front* (London: Stanley Paul & Co. Ltd., 1930, first published 1928).

Tynan, J., 'Tailoring in the Trenches: The Making of First World War British Army Uniform', in Jessica Meyer, ed., *British Popular Culture and the First World War* (Leiden and Boston: Brill, 2008) 71–94.

van Bergen, L., *Before My Helpless Sight: Suffering, Dying and Military Medicine on the Western Front, 1914–1918*, trans. Liz Waters (Farnham: Ashgate, 2009).

von Clausewitz, C., *On War*, trans. James John Graham (London: N. Trübner, 1873).

Watson, J. S. K., *Fighting Different Wars: Experience, Memory and the First World War in Britain* (Cambridge: Cambridge University Press, 2004).

Weinrich, H., *Lethe. The Art and Critique of Forgetting*, trans. Stephen F. Rendall (Ithaca & London: Cornell University Press, 2004).

White, H., *The Content of the Form. Narrative Discourse and Historical Representation* (Baltimore & London: The Johns Hopkins University Press, 1987).

Williamson, H., *A Patriot's Progress* (London: Geoffrey Bles, 1930).

Winter, J. M., *Remembering War: The Great War Between Memory and History in the Twentieth Century* (New Haven: Yale University Press, 2006).

Winter, J. M. & Prost, A., *The Great War in History: Debates and Controversies, 1914 to the Present* (Cambridge: Cambridge University Press, 2005).

Wintringham, T. H., *Mutiny. Being a Survey of Mutinies from Spartacus to Invergordon* (London: Stanley Nott, 1936).

Wilson, R. J., *Landscapes of the Western Front. Materiality During the Great War* (New York & Abingdon: Routledge, 2012).

Wynne, C. D. L., *Animal Cognition. The Mental Lives of Animals* (Houndmills: Palgrave, 2001).

Other material

'Aftermath', <http://www.aftermathww1.com/mustard.asp.> accessed October 2011.

Baker, C., 'In Trouble: Military Crimes', <http://www.1914–1918.net/crime.htm> accessed October 2010.

'The Battle of the Somme (1916). British Topical Committee for War Films', <http://www.cosmolearning.com/documentaries/the-battle-of-the-somme-827/> accessed November 2010.

Duffett, R., 'A War Unimagined: Food and Rank and File Soldiers of the First World War', University of Essex: PhD, 2009.

Evans, G., 'British War Dogs in the Great War', <http://freespace.virgin.net/sh.k/wardogs.html> accessed October 2010.

'54th Canadian Infantry Battalion 1915–1919', <http://www.54thbattalioncef.ca/WARPAGES/Opsorderly_room.htm> accessed November 2011.

The First World War Poetry Digital Archive. 'The Life of a WAAC', <http://www.oucs.ox.ac.uk/ww1lit/collections/item/5517?CISOBOX=1&REC=7> accessed November 2010.

Morgan, T., 'World War 1 Trench Dogs', <http://www.roll-of-honour.com/Bedfordshire/wardogs.html> accessed October 2010.

Schiller, F., 'On the Sublime', trans. William F. Wertz, Jr. (The Schiller Institute, 2001), <http://www.schillerinstitute.org/transl/trans_on_sublime.html> accessed July 2011.

Thierens, M., '7th Canadian Infantry Brigade. War Diaries 1915–1919. 3: 1917', <http://www.cefresearch.com/matrix/War%20Diaries/transcribed/.../bde7y1917.pdf> (2008) accessed November 2011.

Vanity Fair (September 1916), <http://www.oldmagazinearticles.com/WW1_dogs_pdf> accessed October 2011.

Living on the Western Front